Methods for the Social Sciences

Recent Titles in Contributions in Sociology
Series Editor: Don Martindale

Contemporary Entrepreneurs: The Sociology of Residential Real Estate Agents
J. D. House

The Handwriting on the Wall: Toward a Sociology and Psychology of Graffiti
Ernest L. Abel and Barbara E. Buckley

We, the People: American Character and Social Change
Gordon J. DiRenzo, editor

Buddhism in America: The Social Organization of an Ethnic Religious Institution
Tetsuden Kashima

Identities in the Lesbian World: The Social Construction of Self
Barbara Ponse

Zero Population Growth—for Whom?: Differential Fertility and Minority Group Survival
Milton Himmelfarb and Victor Baras, editors

Social Control for the 1980s—A Handbook for Order in a Democratic Society
Joseph S. Roucek, editor

Ethnics in a Borderland: An Inquiry into the Nature of Ethnicity and Reduction of Ethnic Tensions in a One-Time Genocide Area
Feliks Gross

Contemporary Issues in Theory and Research: A Metasociological Perspective
William E. Snizek, Ellsworth R. Fuhrman, and Michael K. Miller, editors

Nationalism and the Crises of Ethnic Minorities in Asia
Tai S. Kang, editor

History of Sociological Thought
Jerzy Szacki

Management and Complex Organizations in Comparative Perspective
Raj P. Mohan, editor

Methods for the Social Sciences

A HANDBOOK FOR STUDENTS AND NON-SPECIALISTS

John J. Hartman and
Jack H. Hedblom

Contributions in Sociology, Number 37

GREENWOOD PRESS
Westport, Connecticut • London, England

Library of Congress Cataloging in Publication Data

Hartman, John J
Methods for the social sciences.

(Contributions in sociology ; no. 37 ISSN 0084-9278)
Bibliography: p.
Includes index.
1. Social sciences—Methodology—Handbooks, manuals, etc. I. Hedblom, Jack H., joint author. II. Title.
H61.H294 300'.1'8 78-72796
ISBN 0-313-20894-8

Library of Congress Catalog Card Number: 78-72796
ISBN: 0-313-20894-8
ISSN: 0084-9278

First published in 1979

Greenwood Press, Inc.
51 Riverside Avenue, Westport, Connecticut 06880

Printed in the United States of America

10 9 8 7 6 5 4 3 2 1

Copyright Acknowledgments

Grateful acknowledgment is made to the following authors and publishers for permission to reprint material:

John W. Best, *Research in Education,* 2nd ed., © 1970. Reprinted by permission of Prentice-Hall, Inc., Englewood Cliffs, New Jersey.

Hans L. Zetterberg, *On Theory and Verification in Sociology,* 3rd ed., Copyright © 1965 by Bedminster Press, Inc. Reprinted by permission of the publisher.

Meredith Ponte, "Life in a Parking Lot: An Ethnography of a Homosexual Drive-In," in Jerry Jacobs, ed., *Deviance: Field Studies and Self Disclosures,* 1973. Reprinted by permission of National Press Books (now Mayfield Publishing Co.).

Scott G. McNall, *The Sociological Experience,* copyright © 1969 by Little, Brown and Company. Reprinted by permission of the publisher.

Robert K. Merton, *Social Theory and Social Structure,* copyright © 1968 by Macmillan Publishing Co. Reprinted by permission of Macmillan Publishing Co.

Gideon Sjoberg, *Ethics, Politics and Social Research,* 1968. Reprinted by permission of Schenkman Publishing Co.

William F. Whyte, *Street Corner Society,* 1955. Reprinted by permission of The University of Chicago Press.

Howard S. Becker, *Sociological Work,* 1970. Reprinted by permission of Aldine Publishing Co.

John T. and Jeanne E. Gullahorn, "Computer Simulation of Human Interaction in Small Group," *AFIPS Conference Proceeding,* vol. 25. Reprinted by permission of AFIPS Press.

Floyd Hunter, *Community Power Structure, A Study of Decision Makers* (Anchor Books, 1963, published by arrangement with The University of North Carolina Press). Reprinted by permission of The University of North Carolina Press.

Herbert Blumer, *Symbolic Interactionism: Perspective and Method,* © 1969, pp. 10, 15. Reprinted by permission of Prentice-Hall, Inc., Englewood Cliffs, New Jersey.

Dedications

I would like to acknowledge my debt to mentor, friend, and advisor Herbert F. Lionberger. Dr. Lionberger provided a role model characterized by concern for students and the courage to stand by one's convictions.

John J. Hartman

I would like to dedicate my portion of this work to John Sirjamaki, scholar, advisor, and friend. My debt is beyond measure.

Jack H. Hedblom

Contents

Tables

Illustrations

Introduction

This book can be used as a handbook or a text for classroom instruction. As a handbook, the work is intended to provide a ready reference addressing specific questions regarding the theory of methodology as a generic category or the evaluation of research already completed. This possible use is reflected in the fact that each chapter is a separate and distinct unit. Chapter 1 discusses research in general and its role in the development of various behavioral sciences as well as in the evaluation of existing social programs and the development of social policy in the private and public sectors. The chapter also discusses the basic steps involved in doing research and understanding the reporting of research. Specifically included are the categories of classification, hypothesis formulation, data collection, hypothesis testing, interpretation and generalization, and recasting or modification of theory. Chapters 2 and 3 expand upon this discussion, and in addition analyze two theoretical approaches basic to sociology—symbolic interactionism and structural functionalism. These two generic categories of theory were chosen because they include the widest possible range of theoretical approaches, cutting across sociology/anthropology as well as social psychology. However, our focus is on research or the act of research and not on a discipline.

Since various types of research are examined in this volume, individuals using this work as a handbook can find references to their specific needs, i.e., the evaluation of a particular social policy or program, the addressing of a given measurement of attitude or awareness, or the evaluation of a given report, purporting to support or deny support to a particular social program. Perhaps one of the most important uses of a handbook involves aiding in the estimate of the value of any given piece of research. Additionally, it should prove a useful guide in the preparation of funding applications for research projects or social programs proposed or already underway.

The importance of the integration of theory and research models cannot be overemphasized. Clearly, research cannot be understood if the assumptions underlying that research are not understood. Nor can an evaluation process be understood if the nature of that process is not understood. This work discusses this integration at some length, providing ready reference for general theoretical frameworks as well as delineating the importance of the assumptions with regard to both the planning of research and the interpretation of research. As aids to the users of this work, at the end of the book are a glossary, a section on further readings, arranged by chapter heading, and an index.

As mentioned earlier, the work can also be used as a classroom text. In fact, the thrust of this work combines "how to do," "how to evaluate," and a synoptic overview of various approaches to research. From the instructor's point of view, the review of theory found in Chapters 2 and 3 is sufficient for a basic understanding of the assumptions that pertain to most theoretical perspectives which provide the basis for research in the behavioral sciences (with the possible exception of psychology). As an aid in the instructional process, all chapters are independent units. The instructor can, therefore, arrange materials according to his own sense of logic or the interests of the class.

The work contains unique instructional possibilities. For example, it provides a logical frame of reference within which integration of theory and research can be understood. One chapter (Chapter 17) has a section that introduces the concept of probability, written for the undergraduate level, as well as a section dealing with basic elementary statistics. These sections are not geared to teaching the student statistics so much as to allowing the instructor to aid the student in understanding terms commonly used in research and in interpreting certain basic measures of difference and correlation.

The text presents separate chapters on survey research (12), evaluation research (16) and "participant" types of research, colloquially described as hard and soft research techniques (14). Both hard and soft approaches are discussed in terms of strengths and weaknesses; specific suggestions are given as to how such techniques can be implemented. The logic of each approach and the limitations that pertain thereto are likewise discussed in some detail.

Other special features include a chapter on computer simulation (15), geared to understanding the current process of computer simulation as well as developing models of other simulation. In addition, one chapter (20) contains sections on what research reports should contain and suggestions as to the logic of presentation.

In any book with joint authors, the contributions of both become fused.

In this work there is no senior author; the two names are simply listed alphabetically. Both are equally responsible for whatever errors or omissions have occurred. Special thanks should be given to Norma Hartman for her patience and understanding; to Janice E. Hedblom, for her willingness to forbear and believe, and to my father and mother, the authors of all my beginnings; and to Andrea Higgins whose abilities and sense of organization moved us along at an even pace.

John J. Hartman, Ph.D.
Wichita State University

Jack H. Hedblom, Ph.D.
University of Baltimore

Methods for the Social Sciences

1

Introduction to Science and Methods

The importance of research methods in any science cannot be overemphasized. In fact, concern with methods improves theory, measurement, and lends credence to research findings. This is not to say that the integrity of science is guaranteed simply by a focus on methodology. Rather, the development of scientific methodology in any substantive discipline reflects its sophistication. Methodologically, some disciplines are more developed than others, and although the social sciences are the least sophisticated of the sciences in this respect, they are growing in sophistication. Even so, within the social sciences, there are notable differences in the development of research designs and techniques. In addition, divergent opinions exist regarding theoretical postures and methodologies, each commanding allegiance with an almost religious zeal. Behavorial science has always attracted adherents interested principally in the development of mathematical and statistical techniques and others who approach the study from a more interpretative nonmathematical perspective. Both schools are well represented by individuals and institutions all over the world.

This text does not favor one perspective over another, but rather presents a number of different methods used in theoretical models in the social sciences. Hence, the focus of this work is on both "hard" and "soft" data collection methods.

No science can develop solely on the basis of its methods. Research requires a theoretical base. The advancement and development of a discipline, on the other hand, require research that questions, tests, and modifies its theoretical base. Research in the social sciences is an expedient—a structure to explore, or a means to generate or test assumptions about human behavior. Logically, theory precedes method. That is, any discipline must first develop its theoretical frame of reference before its phenomena are examined.

Characteristically, the social sciences do not exist on the basis of one theoretical orientation. Most have broad-ranging theories (*macro* or *grand* theories) which encompass larger elements of the sociocultural system with broad strokes. These are complemented by mid-range and lower level theories typically found in the "specialty" areas of the discipline. Whatever the scope of the theory, its validation or expansion depends upon the same general principles which pertain in the selection of a research design, data collection techniques, measurement techniques, and, when appropriate, statistical tests of significance. In turn, no matter how sophisticated the methodological techniques, the underlying theory must act to orient the design.

The tendency of social scientists to collect data without a thorough consideration of theory or a framework for analysis is well known. Many of them have found, to their chagrin, that they should have spent more time conceptualizing the entire project before collecting the data. No matter how carefully data are accumulated, they make sense only within the totality of the problem specification, theory, and analysis. The sense of data is a function of the theory that serves to organize it. Data are like the rocks of a conglomerate, cemented into form and order by theory. It is the theoretical framework that establishes the relationship between concepts and variables. Data with no theoretical base remain a limited collection of facts,[1] that may be related but not understood.[2] Moreover, the lack of a theoretical orientation and a poorly selected sample severely limit the possibility of generalizing beyond the sample to other populations.[3]

This work will argue that it is impossible to logically separate methods from their theoretical basis. While research techniques are at their best neutral and are, therefore, outside the substantive areas of sociology, the theoretical orientation of a researcher, or of the project by its very nature, often narrows the range of possible research designs.

BASIC STEPS IN SCIENTIFIC PROCESS

As mentioned above, research techniques are, at their best, neutral. They are not the private domain of any particular discipline, but rather are an abstract set of rules or contingencies that may be applied to both physical science and social science problems.[4] Certain principles are universal and pertain regardless of the field involved or the problem addressed. While differences do exist between disciplines with regard to the degree of measurement and exactness in specifying variables, all disciplines comply with definite principles aimed at assuring validity, reliability, and some relationship to existing theory.

What is in the scientific method that remains constant between and within various disciplines? Following a discussion of the relationship of theory to research, each step is discussed in turn:

1. Classification
2. Hypothesis formulation, or relationship specification
3. Data collection
4. Testing hypothesis or analyzing
5. Interpretation, generalization, or inference
6. Recasting or modifying theory when data do not support prediction or extend beyond present limitations

THEORY

No matter how carefully data are collected, they make sense only within the totality of the research problem's specification, theory, and analysis. Implicitly, all research has a theoretical base. Similarly, all research makes assumptions about the nature of human behavior, whether or not these assumptions are specifically noted.[5] The more clearly these theoretical underpinnings and assumptions are recognized and specified, the more precise data interpretation may become.

Theoreticians are seldom economical in their presentations, and they often venture into generalities that seriously weaken the viability of their research. Talcott Parsons' *The Social System*,[6] for example, is a voluminous discussion of an entire behavioral system, developed at a high level of generalization. As a result, Parsons has been criticized for being difficult to operationalize or to examine with available research techniques. Even the more frugal presentations, such as William Ogburn's theory of cultural lag,[7] which posits that technology tends to override or outstrip nontangibles (ideas, attitudes, and the like), may be as nebulous and difficult to measure as many of Parsons' specifications. Edwin H. Sutherland's theory of differential association,[8] specifying that those with whom you have most contact will be instrumental in influencing your behavior, has the same measurement difficulties. While many of these statements seem to be reasonable assumptions at the verbal level, fitting them to a research design, operationalizing relevant variables, subjecting them to statistical tests, and interpreting the results have proved to be exceedingly difficult.

Certain types of theoretical specification require research designs that do not involve hypothesis testing. Some researchers reject the hypothesis testing framework completely, charging that it ignores meaning in human interaction and is based on models of behavior that are deceptive. There is more to researching behavior than simply hypothesis testing and more than one way to add to theory. Loosely specified theoretical generalizations are difficult to test, but such research is mandatory if a science is to advance beyond its present boundaries.

A research design's theoretical base outlines the variables and relationships that may be examined within that design. Research methods are tools and, as such, they serve the research problem. The variables that may be included in a particular research design must logically be derived from its theoretical orientation; tools must never be allowed to structure research interests or problems. It is the process of logical deduction or induction that forms new propositions to be tested and used to expand theory and its predictive or explanatory power.

In the social sciences and sociology particularly, the following steps in the scientific process pertain. They form a composite of the process, but not all research studies will include all of the steps. Some research may be designed to address the first step or the classification stage, while others may move through all of the various stages, including recasting theory or even developing alternate hypotheses.

Classification

Once a research problem has been isolated and specified, the process of classification may be initiated, bringing order to the problem area. Often studies will be descriptive or exploratory wherein the objective is to study an area ignored or unnoticed by other researchers. The researcher must therefore measure, categorize, or define what he sees and in turn relate the problem addressed to existing theory. Measurement or description alone is an attempt to extend a present theory, while classification is a first step toward developing new theory or bringing new findings under the explanatory power of an existing theory. Both are necessary functions, but classification logically precedes all types of theoretical testing, development, and extension.

Hypothesis Formulation

After description and classification, it is possible to relate concepts to propositions at the abstract level.[9] A proposition consists of at least two concepts and a statement descriptive of the relationship between them. The statement may be relatively abstract and can be variously referred to as an abstract, conceptual, or theoretical hypothesis.[10] It may be a lower level abstraction and be called an operational or working hypothesis. The logical reduction process results in the test of a special kind of hypothesis, that is, the test of a hypothesis that states no association, difference, or relationship exists between variables.

Theory and Methods

It should be clear at this point that all research involves theoretical commitments. Consider the following examples presented by Hans Zetterberg. He demonstrates how variables (and concepts) are manipulated to arrive at logically derived propositions that were implicit, although not specified, in the original theoretical orientation.[11] Two types of reductionism are defined, the first being a reduction of a matrix of propositions from axiomatic theory, the second being "manipulation" of the definitions. Normally, both manipulations are done at the same time; however, here it may be more instructive to discuss each separately.

Definitional reduction may be demonstrated using the following list of propositions dealing with social aggregates:

1. Groups have less turnover than publics.
2. Publics show less emotion than crowds.
3. Groups show less emotion than masses.[12]

Zetterberg begins the reduction of these propositions by specification of the key terms:

A. Groups are *social aggregates* interacting in terms of *specified* roles and with a *common leader* (e.g., a voluntary association).
B. Masses are social aggregates interacting (if at all) in terms of unspecified roles but with a common leader (e.g., a radio audience).
C. Publics are social aggregates interacting in terms of unspecific roles and without a common leader (e.g., a market).
D. Crowds are social aggregates interacting in terms of unspecified roles and without a common leader (e.g., milling in Times Square).[13]

In examining the original propositions, Zetterberg first defines and then gives an example of the different classifications of relationships. That is, groups are characterized as having more stable social relationships and as being physically as well as psychologically closer than publics, which are characterized by physical separation and are held together only by a common focal point. A public could be the theater or radio-listening audience, or it might consist of city dwellers going their usual way.

Combining the definitions of these key terms, Zetterberg develops the following two theoretical propositions:

I. If a social aggregate has a common leader, then its turnover is low.
II. If a social aggregate interacts in terms of specified roles, then its level of emotion is low.

He concludes:

> The most interesting part of this procedure is that these two propositions do not merely imply the three that we had as our starting point but also a fourth. Proposition 1 and Definition B imply that masses have less turnover than crowds. This is a novel hypothesis which, to the best of my knowledge is presented here for the first time. Thus, we see how an axiomatic format not merely organizes existing propositions but generates new ones implicit in the existing ones.[14]

The possibility of adding a third theoretical proposition to the two generated by Zetterberg has recently been noted. Given Zetterberg's breakdown of social aggregates into four distinct categories—group, masses, publics, and crowds—a third proposition could be: If a social aggregate (mass) has a common leader calling for psychological commitment, then emotional action will result. Here the direction and degree of emotional level have been altered. An example of this proposition would be the case of some spiritual leaders (television evangelists) who are capable of raising the emotional levels of a large number of their viewers and listeners. The third proposition has been derived from the original propositions and definitions and an analysis of key terms, and by setting the interaction process into the contemporary situation of the television-viewing audience. This proposition was inherent in Zetterberg's original work, but the development of the original propositions occurred before the general availability of television. Thus, the contemporary setting resulted in new propositions such as the notion of emotionalism through primary type relationships made possible by television. This proposition characterizes social movements for civil rights, the Chicano movement, the efforts of the American Indian Movement (AIM), women's liberation, gay liberation, and affirmative action programs.

The reduction process derives from an existing theoretical orientation. In addition, some research efforts generate hypotheses rather than testing them. Such studies differ in orientation and purpose, but not in quality or importance. Both types of studies, derivative and exploratory, have a role in the development of any discipline.

Data Collection

The data collection process should be limited to providing data to test the problems stated in the research design. It might take the form of observation or attitude measurement, or it might combine any number of data collection techniques. Any amount of data may be collected to clarify or examine a given problem. These data may include primary as well as secondary sources, such as records, archives, and census materials. Observational techniques as well as the attitudinal data collection process are discussed in Chapter 5, 6, and 7, and the use of secondary sources of data is discussed in the chapter on analysis of secondary data (Chapter 18). Both techniques are valid when used in conjunction with an appropriate problem.

Testing the Hypothesis

After data are collected, they must be analyzed and reported. In most cases, the analysis and format of the research report have been anticipated and structured prior to the data collection process. Testing of hypotheses involves moving from higher levels of abstractions to identification and operationalization of concepts and variables. The process is finally resolved in the application of an appropriate measure of relevance or significance. These hypotheses are called the general, operational, and null hypotheses. A more detailed examination of hypothesis testing is presented in the chapter on hypothesis formulation and hypothesis testing (Chapter 5). The reader should be aware, however, that there are research traditions whose purpose is neither the testing nor the generation of hypotheses. Nonetheless, they are related to theory and contribute to the development of the theoretical elements in the discipline. In addition, the social action branches of various disciplines whose research purpose—the amelioration of conditions viewed as pernicious to the human condition—should not be ignored. These studies contribute to the growth of both methodology and theory. In fact, it is all too frequently forgotten that the early behavioral sciences were born as an attempt to reorganize the world and its social institutions along scientific lines. Little wonder that this principle was reaffirmed at the first meeting of the American Sociological Society in 1885, which defined sociology as the "science" with social work concerns and deliberately geared it to direct its findings to social service needs.

Interpretations and Generalizations

After hypothesis testing, the researcher must analyze the findings and arrive at some meaning of the results. The interpretations and conclusions drawn from the data must be contained within the data and analysis themselves. While research design structures define what data are relevant to the problem being addressed, they also allow for development of unanticipated results or consequences to be reported. The process may become relatively complex, as is shown in the chapter on evaluation (Chapter 16).

Generalizing to other populations is contingent on the sampling process. The sample type and size directly affect the researcher's ability to extend his findings to other populations. Generalizations must be tested in replication studies. An application of findings to other populations is usually stated in guarded terms. Nevertheless, the generalization process is important and relates to the origination and testing of theory.

Recasting and Modifying Theory

Theory is inferentially tested. In other words, it is possible to test portions of theory and not theory as a whole. The hypothesis testing process is usually, though not always, a test of the theory itself. A major consideration is that one understands the nature of the scientific process, which includes a willingness to recast, amend, or modify existing theory when research studies fail to substantiate or support predictions. A single nonsubstantiating study is not sufficient reason to modify theory. However, cumulative nonsupporting evidence gathered through replication studies should lead to a change in or expansion of existing theory. Of course, several areas of the process must be examined before this change or expansion can occur.

In evaluating a research project, which is a way of examining the validity of the result, the sampling procedure, resulting sample, measurement device, analysis techniques, and conclusions must be reviewed before an existing theory can be challenged or modified. Errors often exist in these areas or in the areas of validity or reliability, thereby distorting data or prohibiting accurate data interpretation. Evaluation and modification of research are discussed more fully in the chapters on theory, theory-design problems, and generating hypotheses.

Each of the steps in the scientific process has been presented here only briefly. The remainder of this work describes one or more of these steps in greater detail. The emphasis is on methods and not on the entire scientific process. The work that follows is therefore an introduction to methods and survey of selected research techniques and specialty areas.

INTERRELATIONSHIP OF THEORY AND METHODS

While the methods of data collection in the social sciences are available to all the sciences, certain designs are more amenable to the study of certain types of problems than are others. In all research, replication is necessary if theory is to develop predictive accuracy.

As data are collected and the number of substantiating studies increase, the researcher may become more confident that the results achieved are valid. However, the test of validity does demand that the replication include duplication of design, data collection instruments, samples, measurement, and interpretation techniques. Hence, the researcher must guarantee intra-subjective testability. That is, he or she must provide sufficient specification of the research design to enable the research project to be replicated. Among other things, he must formulate a careful definition of the sampling techniques and population sampled. If, for example, replication studies are not conducted on equivalent samples, serious questions concerning the validity of findings may be raised. The researcher's interpretation of results should not be entirely subjective, although certain types of research do rely almost exclusively on the creative decisions of a single researcher. Intuitive research is often more generative than other types and at times must rely on a less rigorous form of validity check, namely, "face validity."[15] Other types of validity checks do exist, however, such as triangulation, which will be discussed in the chapter on researchers' covert behavior. Rose[16] has noted this inextricable relationship between theory and methods, stating that the selection of a theoretical orientation limits the choice of relevant research designs. This is particularly true in sociology where different theoretical commitments characteristically make different assumptions about the nature of human behavior and, therefore, require different data collection techniques to examine the various dimensions of the human experience. One type of research usually consists of data collected through the use of questionnaires or scales. Individuals are asked to complete a questionnaire (often in a group setting), with each individual responding to his own questionnaire. These instruments are often referred to as "paper and pencil" tests and can be used in a wide range of studies ranging from the most simple to the most complex. Although the questionnaire data collection technique is not limited to any particular theory, it is most limited to those studies which focus on attitudes, opinions, and the like, and not observation of behavior.[17]

Another technique equally capable of generalization involves observational techniques. Traditionally, such techniques involve the counting and noting of frequencies of observed behavior relating them to the fabric of symbols and meanings existent in the culture. It is sometimes difficult to quantify data derived in such fashion. Despite this apparent limitation, many of the "classics" in sociology have utilized these techniques to great advantage.

Students of society should become familiar with methods of social research for a number of reasons. Research may be a necessary aspect of their roles as students, workers, or practicing sociologists. Research can be viewed from a number of perspectives, but for the moment, let us concern ourselves with problem-solving, short-range research.

Of course, research in any discipline is directed toward verification, further testing, and then expansion of theory. Behavioral science could not advance without the interest, testing probing, and expansion of present theory. The desire to add to the base of knowledge and to our ability to predict and explain social behavior underlies our reason to study methods.

NOTES

1. An obvious exception is lower level descriptive or exploratory research, often surveys, which are intended to ascertain what constitutes social relations at a given time and place. These studies are often descriptive and supplement rather than test theory.

2. Merton has labeled such findings "empirical generalizations" or statements of relationship that can be tested and supported but are devoid of theoretical explanation. One of these empirical generalizations is the positive correlation between the percentage of women in the population and the urbanization index. This statement may be tested and verified, but no existing theory underlies it. Hence, its use is limited.

3. Sampling inadequacies may lead to "data bound" studies, the definition of which is addressed in Chapter 10.

4. Note, however, that measurement techniques and the degree of problem specificity are relevant at the operational stage of the research problem.

5. For example, in many theories dealing with deviant behavior, authors frequently assume that behavior is problem-solving. In many cases, such assumptions explain the direction behavior takes. An example of such use might be "subcultures form to ameliorate stigmatization of members." Note that such behavior is problem-solving.

6. Talcott Parsons, *The Social System* (Glencoe, Ill.: Free Press; Tavistock Publications, 1951). In the major sociological journals today, Parsons is seldom cited as an authority, and in those in which his name appears, the reference is usually rather general.

7. W. F. Ogburn, *Social Change* (New York: Viking Press, 1959).

8. Edwin H. Sutherland, *Criminology* (Chicago: J. B. Lippincott Co., 1924).

9. Whether a statement or relationship between two concepts (or variables) is a proposition or hypothesis depends on the statement in context. One cannot actually tell whether a statement is a hypothesis or proposition merely by looking at the statement. Hence, whether a statement is a proposition or a hypothesis lies with the researcher, and the essence of each is not self-evident.

10. The term *general hypothesis* is used, but the reader is warned that there is no standardization of use and the other terms are found in other works.

11. Hans L. Zetterberg, *On Theory and Verification in Sociology*, 3d ed., (Totowa, N.J.; Bedminster Press, 1965), pp. 94-96.

12. Ibid., p. 95.

13. Ibid., pp. 95-96.

14. Ibid., p. 96.

15. Some say that these techniques are more an art than a science; nonetheless, they have a place in the behavioral sciences.

16. Arnold Rose, "The Relationship of Theory to Method," in Llewellyn Gross, ed., *Sociological Theory: Inquiries and Paradigms* (Evanston, Ill.; Harper and Row Publishers, 1967), pp. 207-219.

17. This particular approach is most often associated with "structural" approaches. It is often attacked by interactionist-oriented sociologists who claim that the method ignores the meanings of human interaction and imposes answers on the respondent in terms of the question asked.

2

The Research Act and Symbolic Interaction

It is axiomatic to say that there are differences both between and within the behavioral sciences with regard to how human behavior is viewed. Basically, these differences are reflected in the assumptions they make about human behavior. Such differences are important because these assumptions provide the organizational framework within which disciplines make sense of observed behavior or use in relating behaviors to one explanatory-predictive posture or another. Because of its cross-cultural origins and its remarkable diversity, sociology contains within it several "schools," each characterized by commitments apparently at odds with a number of others in the discipline.

Although these differences between the diverse approaches within sociology appear to be antithetical to one another and mutually exclusive, in fact, they are not, and it is exceedingly difficult to find representative examples of research that are "pure in type." Despite this, sociology is characterized by two principal assumptive bases, the first of which is characterized as structural functionalism and the second as *symbolic interactionism*, a term coined by Herbert Blumer. Of course, there are differing opinions as to which theories fit under each rubric; yet, the two positions are capable of dichotomous comparison. Here, the intent is not to advocate one position over the other, although both are delineated with regard to basic assumptions and the operational framework. Rather, the existing differences between the two postures are used to demonstrate that assumptions made about human behavior in terms of etiology provide the framework within which such behavior is investigated and that each posture carries with it impositions on the research act itself. This is not to say that both orientations are tautological when buttressed by empirical research.[1] However, the assumptions made about the nature of human behavior, i.e., the relationship of motivation to behavior or the way one defines motivation as a concept, structures the research act. Given this, an analysis of research must begin with careful delineation of the assumptions upon which that research is based. Too often this is not the case. Clearly, there are differences in the way in which a dramaturgist, who views personality as a presentation to an audience and dependent on that audience for content, perceives behavior when compared with a structuralist who views personality as a product of a culture imposed on the individual as a function of the socialization process. Do choices exist?

Just as the way in which one perceives and interprets interaction is affected by the sociocultural fabric of which the behavior is a part, so the assumptive base of one's theoretical orientation implicitly builds findings into research interpretations, as well as methodologies. Such impositions should not be defined as bias in the ordinary use of the word, for if such things are labeled bias, then no sociological research model can escape the charge. Each of these assumptive bases has its merits, and differences between them are far from resolved. Therefore, each can add to the growth of the discipline. It may well be that the various approaches are not as mutually exclusive as they are presently defined to be.

Given this, the following material will address the nature of symbolic interactionism and the assumptions it makes about behavior and enumerate some of the differences existing between its orientation and that of structural functionalism.[2]

The interactionist-oriented approach has been a dynamic part of sociology for a long time, and even its critics admit that it has provided insights into behavior occurring in natural settings. Its adherents, on the other hand, view it as a step away from the increasing quantification of sociology as a discipline and, in that sense, a step in the right direction. In general, its adherents tend to view symbolic interactionism as the least biased mechanism for coming to grips with the real world.

As its name implies, the basic focus of symbolic interactionism is on meanings in the human experience.

1. The first assumption made by symbolic interactionists is that human beings "act toward things on the basis of the meanings that the things have

for them."[3] Interactionists mean by this that the external world has meaning or coherence only with specific regard to individuals who interpret externalities and impose meaning upon them. This position is much like Jean Paul Sartre's position in defining fragility. He points out that form and things external to man exist only in being interpreted. In his definition of the term *destruction*, he suggests that what we as people define as destruction is, in fact, only a change in the ordering of forms as far as the objects themselves are concerned. Therefore, an apartment building being blown up does no violence to the essence of the matter of the building, other than to bring about a change in its form and, by implication, its function. The "destruction" of the building is therefore a man-made imposition of meaning on a particular ordering of form.

2. The second premise of symbolic interactionism is "that the meaning of such things is derived from or arises out of social interaction one has with one's fellows."[4] The point is that meaning constitutes an agreed-upon definition. Interaction, therefore, by its very nature is composed of sets of mutual agreements on designations of value and priority with regard to the external world of actors engaged in such interactions.

3. The third premise is that "meanings are handled in and modified through an interpretative process used by the person in dealing with the things he encounters."[5]

Blumer discusses the fact that meaning is very largely ignored in researching human behavior. He states that meaning is either taken for granted or is viewed as the neutral link between behavior and what supposedly causes it. Fundamentally, he suggests for many researchers that meaning is treated as if it has a life or an existence outside of the agreed-upon responses to it, manifested by actors in interaction. This posture is, of course, not ascribed to by the symbolic interactionists. In his focus upon meaning and its relationship to human behavior, the interactionist does not assume, as psychologists often do, that meanings are stimuli or conscious or unconscious motivations to behavior in the causal sense of those terms. The symbolic interactionist likewise does not interpret meanings to be merely antecedents to behavior occurring within a rigidly defined kind of structural matrix, characteristically referred to as a social system or a culture. As Blumer states:

> if one declares that the given kinds of behavior are the result of the particular factors regarded as producing them, there is no need to concern one's self with the meaning of the things toward which human beings act; one merely identifies the initiating factors and the resulting behavior. Or one may, if pressed, seek to accomodate [sic] the element of meaning by lodging it in the initiating factors and the behavior they are alleged to produce. In the first of these latter cases, the meaning disappears by

being merged into the initiating or causative factors; in the second case, meaning becomes a mere transmission link that can be ignored in favor of initiating factors.[6]

For the symbolic interactionist, meaning has a central value, and the meaning of things that people hold in common are central in their own right. Meanings cannot therefore be reduced to simple aspects of initiating or motivating elements in human behavior. The symbolic interactionist's position is that to ignore the meaning of things toward which people interact or respond is to falsify the behavior under study.

For the symbolic interactionist, the origin of meaning is firmly rooted in the ways in which persons act toward other persons with regard to specific objects or things. Meanings are therefore social products which are formed through the defining activities of people as they interact. Possession or ownership of particular objects—and, by implication, the value of said objects—is derived by the defining of interaction of other persons. Such defining interaction resolves itself in the establishment of agreement on the relative value of the object in question as well as the priority of ownership. Meaning, therefore, is a part of the physical dimensions or "setting" of interacting individuals.

As Blumer suggests, interaction occurs between actors and not between the factors that are imputed to them. It is illogical to make the "jump from . . . causative factors to . . . behavior they are supposed to produce."[7] Mead has also explored the concept of meaning and interaction, defining it as occurring on two levels: "the conversation of gestures and the use of significant symbols."[8] He distinguishes between symbolic behavior and nonsymbolic interaction, which he defines as reflexive responses to situations. He uses the boxer who raises his arm to parry a blow as an example of nonsymbolic behavior. The actions of the boxer become symbolic at the point where he begins to consider the meaning of the blows struck. Individuals therefore respond to other individuals on the basis of how they perceive the meanings presented by the other individual and what qualities he perceives the other individual as manifesting and how he responds to these qualities. Within this framework, the initial phase of interaction consists of a mutual kind of establishment of commonality of definition, meaning, symbol, and the like. As Blumer states, individuals take into account these symbols and actions of others:

> They do this by a dual process of indicating to others how to act and of interpreting the indications made by others. Human group life is a vast process of such defining to others what to do and of interpreting their definitions through this process. People come to fit their activities to one another, and to form their own individual conduct. Both such joint activity and individual conduct are formed in and through this ongoing process; they are not mere expressions or products of what people bring to their interaction or of conditions that are antecedent to their interaction.[9]

Within this framework the mind is defined as reflexive, and interaction can occur between the individual and himself in terms of how he symbolically perceives his fellow creatures. Mead describes how he differentiates the symbolic activity of animals from that of man. It is the ability to symbolically generalize from one situation to another and to interpret the individual's relationship to objects (which are defined as anything which can be pointed to or alluded to) that result in manifest continuities of behavior occurring outside the interactional framework. For the child, mother need not be physically present in order that he or she relate mother's prohibitions on certain activities to precluding these activities. Thus, as Blumer has stated, "the human being who is engaging his self-interaction is not a mere responding organism—an organism that has to mold a line of action on the basis of what it takes into account instead of merely releasing a response to the play of some factor on its organization.[10]

It is therefore in the nature of human action that the individual must form action with due regard to his setting as well as his organization, interpretation, and relative weighting of meanings and objects around him. In this way joint collective action can be explained just as continuities of culture or meaning present in a given culture can be explained in terms of the collective agreements of actors. (This point is expanded later.) According to the symbolic interactionist, joint action is made up of diverse components, each providing articulations or linkages for what might possibly be described as a system. The fallacy of functionalism lies in observing this apparent systematization of behavior and dealing with it as if it were the system that imposes behavioral mandates on individuals rather than the actions of individuals creating the system. In this regard,

> the preponderant portion of social action in a human society, particularly in a settled society, exists in the form of recurrent patterns of joint action. In most situations in which people act toward one another they have in advance a firm understanding of how to act and how other people will act. They share common pre-established meanings of what is expected in the action of the participants and accordingly, each participant is able to guide his own behavior by such meanings.[11]

Again, this does not imply the existence of a system of norms acting as antecedents to behavior since interaction by its very nature is more new than repetitive and as such must realize new meanings, new hierarchies of values and priorities, which in turn act as referents to actors constructing their behavior. Consequently, group interactions are always problematic and must consistently go beyond existing solutions to those problems. Meanings that are antecedents to behavior have their own setting in unique social interactions. However, such meanings do not arise out of a context of values and meanings, making up the complex reference whole of individual actors. Within this framework, new forms of joint action emerge out of the current interaction and are simultaneously related to previous joint actions. As Blumer states: "One cannot understand the new form without incorporating knowledge of this continuity into one's analysis of the new form. Joint action not only represents a horizontal linkage, so to speak, of the activities of the participants, but also a vertical linkage with previous joint action.[12]

This, then, briefly is symbolic interactionism, its focus and the assumptions it makes about human behavior. Next we explore how these assumptions structure research done within this particular framework. Following this section, we present yet another form of symbolic interactionism, namely, dramaturgical sociology, and delineate it in the same way.

In a sense, research in the symbolic interactionist mode can be defined as an attempt to analyze, isolate, measure the importance of, and understand meanings arising out of interactions, and in turn relate these meanings to the way in which people construct their behavior. Methodology within this framework can be described as "mere instruments designed to identify and analyze the obdurate character of the empirical world and as such their value exists only in their suitability in enabling this task to be done."[13] This methodology, however, differs from other methodologies in that it defines human action as being, at least in part,[14] volitional; in contrast, the structural functionalist mode tends to view man as a kind of cybernetic automaton responding computer-like to input and feedback. Such a posture assumes that behavior is predictable since behavior, arranged in one typological order or another, has antededents that allow the researcher, after isolation, to make probability statements about the occurrence or nonoccurrence of given behavior, granting certain conditions. This is probably the most classic form of research and is defined as hypothesis testing. Its antithesis is symbolic interactionist research, if for no other reason than its volitional content and its statement that individuals construct behavior with regard to meanings arising out of mutualities of agreement with other individuals.

As indicated previously, it is difficult to find research that is exclusively of one pure type or another, or examples that involve in vocabulary only those terms and concepts unique to any one particular theoretical stamp. There are, however, many examples of research done within a symbolic interactionist framework which are less stringently defined. Notable among them are Howard Becker's *The Outsiders*, Erving Goffman's *Asylums*, and, at least in part, William Foote Whyte's *Street Corner Society*. Such work and techniques are described in some detail in Chapter 14. It is important to note that Whyte's work focuses on meanings arising out of interaction and on the impact of interaction and how perception of significant others influences behavior. That there are functionalist overtones in the work is, however, undeniable. In this sense, his work provides a kind of interactionist model. The ethnography-plus quality of symbolic interactionist research is also captured quite effectively in *Hustlers, Beats and Others* by Ned Polsky, paticularly in his section entitled "The Village Beat Scene, Summer, 1960."[15]

DRAMATURGY

An important offshoot of the symbolic interactionist tradition, and one gaining increasing attention in sociology, is the dramaturgical approach which views presentation of self and interaction as a drama with all of the trappings and accoutrements attached thereto. In general, the dramaturgical approach is viewed as a kind of heuristic stance in the behavior setting of ongoing behavior. The dramaturgical analyst conceives of the individual as a performer whose activities function to create the self or character for an audience. The analyst focuses on the creation of the character on the part of the actor and the reception on the part of the audience. This success or lack of success (i.e., the audience's acceptance or rejection of the character) permits the individual to direct his behavior toward the most rewarding line of activity and to avoid unrewarding activity resulting in his being "discredited" (this means that his character is not being believed). Thus, the consequences of the activities of actors depend upon others' perceptions of the act and not the actor's consciousness or the way he views the world. It is the impressions that the actor makes on others that are of concern to others, and in this sense, they are the focus of the dramaturgical sociologist. Impressions created actually structure audience responses and determine the way audiences act toward actors.

The power of dramaturgical analysis lies in the discrepancy between the perspective of the actor and that of the analyst. The theatrical simile is utilized to analyze how actors and audiences manage to produce through their own activities realities which they assume are "out there" or have a reality external to themselves. The theatrical simile allows the analyst to stop taking for granted what his subjects do and to begin relating what impressions the actor is relating and, in that very act of creation, what the actor is communicating about himself.

One criticism of the dramaturgical model is that it analyzes conscious acts performed by people aware of watching a performance, the implication being that the actors involved are aware of the fact that they play roles. Receivers or audiences, therefore, accept in a kind of Shakespearean sense the reality of the play without seeking the reality behind the play. The thrust of this criticism, of course, is to the nature of "meaning": is meaning a reflective process as far as the individual himself is concerned, or does it relate specifically to others' perception of the actors' presentation? From the dramaturgist's point of view, meaning simply "is." Likewise, the dramaturgist states that the human being is an active animal. Meaning, therefore, becomes a matter of agreement. In this way, the dramaturgist avoids the seemingly endless philosophical debates about meaning, the individual's perception of meaning, and the like. He can instead relate perceptions of meaning to behavior and leave the absolute nature of meaning to those disciplines whose province it is to deal with obscurities. Actors understand the world in certain interactive terms. Thus, the analyst relates actions to the interactional complex wherein they occur with all their value-laden, culture-defined imperatives.

What does the dramaturgical analyst assume about the human animal which distinguishes his technique from that of other analysts? As indicated, the dramaturgical approach views social interaction as a theatrical production or a play-in-progress, consisting of individual and team performances in a complex patterning of interesting role and behavior settings. The emphasis is on interaction and not on the characteristics of the actors.[16] The behavior of actors is itself viewed as a social production. Assuming the individual's activity as a function of being and defining activity as directed toward meaning, the dramaturgical analyst does not speculate on the normative conditions antecedent to behavior, nor on isolated determinants of behavior itself, but relates to behavior as is. In this sense, the thrust is more toward understanding than toward prediction. Dramaturgists are interested in what motives individuals ascribe to their activities in terms of their ongoing interaction. In this light, imputations of motives are seen as having definite consequences for continuation or termination of social relationships in terms of maintenance or lack of it.[17] Meaning, therefore, relates more to the ongoing quality of behavior and depends in a sense on whether or not it will continue. Meaning and interaction, as well as those guideposts of behavior that all in the culture take for granted, are in reality a process rather than being as the functionalists would suggest, static guideposts existing in a relatively static structure within which all members operate. To make them a process is to make them flexible, capable of change through interpretation and, above all, an aspect of the collective agreements making up the understandable world.

Both dramaturgists and symbolic interactionists tend to view interaction and meaning as a function of consciousness and agreement. Since meaning is established only when a response is elicited by a symbol which is the same for the actor who produces the symbol as it is for the audience receiving it, meaning has within it an element of uncertainty emanating from the actor to the audience. His response is characterized by an unanticipatable quality. Complete agreement, therefore, never occurs between individuals in the sense of agreement being predictable from a statistical kind of framework. Perceptions by their nature exist uniquely and, within this framework, total agreement seldom occurs. Where total agreement between symbol and presentation and audience reception exists, this state is referred to as boredom by dramaturgists. Such a coincidence of lines of action is also defined as identification.[18] The following list of terms and short discussions constitute a research vocabulary of dramaturgy. When considered as a whole, they also tend to be descriptive of limitations and concepts of the dramaturgical approach.

Appearance

Appearance establishes the identification of the participants and is communicated by such symbols as gesture, grooming, clothing, and location. Personal appearance may arouse challenges or validations of self. For example, in the wearing of clothes, when *reviews* or *programs* coincide, the self of the one who appears is established or validated.[19] A person's dress, therefore, arouses another's anticipation. It can also conjure up typologies of preconceived personalities complete with action sets and already existent responses ready to be cued. This is the audience's writing a part of the script.

Identity

Identity establishes "what" and "where" the person is in social terms. By identity, actions or functions indicate situation and announce placement. Furthermore, by establishing "what he is in social terms," the individual assembles a set of *apparent symbols* (hairdo, makeup, clothing, contents of wallets, purses, and so on) which he carries from transaction to transaction. Such symbols are called *identity documents*, enabling others to validate announced identity. Identity is further qualified by value and mood. The moods of participants must be established prior to initiation of discourse, in order that certain consequences be taken into consideration. For example, Stone indicates that for most men value had the greatest saliency in their conceptions of self and others, while for most women, mood had a greater saliency. Identity also involves positions of attitude:

> The establishment of identity, value, and mood by appearances represents the person "as there" stratified "or assigned a particular distance and wrapped" or "engrossed". There remains the matter of his activation, the assessment of the path along which he has traveled, the path he is traveling and where he is about to go. These aspects of the person . . . that he has acted, is acting, and will act further . . . are established by appearance. We refer to them as attitudes. Attitudes are anticipated by the reviewers of an appearance, proposed by the one who appears.[20]

Therefore, responses are reflexive in character. They are returned in part to those from whom they emanate, that is, actors read audiences in terms of response to presentation. The identification of others is always complemented by identifications of self, i.e., responses to one's own appearance. Appearances become meaningful when the reviewer establishes or validates consensus by the supplied information of the wearer's appearance to which he, as a programmer, calls out similar identifications. Thus, the self is established reflexively and in terms of audience responses.

The key concepts of the dramaturgical model are role, audience, and character presentation. Character and role, however, must be differentiated. *Character* is a person with a distinctive organization of such personal characteristics as physical appearance, mannerisms, habits, traits, motives, and social status.[21] Within this framework *role* is defined as a plausible line of action expressive of the personality of the character. If the actor's performance is congruent with that role and the audience attributes the corresponding character to him, then the audience accepts the act. Audiences, as well as actors, differ in their ability to perceive plausible characters and roles playing what are essentially merely parts. Because audiences are willing to reach interactional agreement with actors, they must clothe what they perceive with dramatic reality. The actor, therefore, is a composite of self in three dimensions, that is, the self as performer, the self as audience to that performance, and the self as character or as presented. The individual as performer has the capacity to train for his part which encompasses projections, needs, and anxieties. These attributes, as Goffman has suggested, can be interpreted as psychobiological; they seem to arise out of intimate interaction, with the contingencies of staging performances.[22] To the extent that mind and body are one, it is interesting to toy with notions relating to biology and behavior. However, these present entirely different methodological problems.

Dramaturgical sociologists likewise use the language of the theater in describing and relating behavior. For example, they suggest that the self as a performed character is a product of the performed scene that leaves the audience which is taken in to impute a self to a performed character that is credited. Hence, the *scene* that gives rise to the performed character's self is set by the team members who engage in activity on stage in conjunction with available props in the front regions, which is where the process of ongoing activity is occurring. In such a setting with actors performing, the back region, or backstage, provides for an interesting analysis. First, a region may be defined as any place that is bounded to some degree by barriers to perception.[23] Regions vary in the degree to which they are bounded and are provided with a sense of time. The audience is located in a position to observe the performance and to be guided by the definition of the situation which the performance fosters.[24] In the back region, suppressed facts make an appearance. Goffman defines a back region, or backstage, as a place relative to a given performance, where the impression fostered by the performance is knowingly contradicted as a matter of course.[25] It is here that illusions and impressions are openly constructed. Stage props and items of personal front are stored here along with the ceremonial equipment, costumes, and the like. Actors can check for offending expressions with no audience present to confront them. This is the area of personal review. It is the place where the individual is most honest with himself, where he presents to himself that which he will present to others. He reviews it, he restructures it, he changes it. In modern vernacular, "he gets his act together."

The rhetoric of space is set up to accommodate the performer who may at times need assistance while the performance is in progress. The back region of a performance, therefore, is commonly located at one end of the place where the performance is presented, and the passageway from the front region to the back region is usually blocked off and hidden from members of the audience. The actor, having consciously prepared himself with a costume of identity and a psychological repertoire of self-knowledge, is ready to meet interactions that arise in everyday life on center stage. The social encounter provides for the individual such an opportunity for interaction. Goffman describes a social encounter in the following manner: "A social encounter is an occasion of face-to-face interaction, beginning when individuals recognize that they have moved into one another's immediate presence and ending by an appeciated withdrawal from mutual participation."[26]

In each encounter, individuals act out what has been defined as *"a line."* The line is defined as a pattern of verbal and/or nonverbal acts by which actors express their view of the situation and evaluations of participants and self. Whenever an actor intends to take a line, he finds that he has done so because other participants assume he has more or less willfully taken a stand. In this sense, he reveals his "face." The face is defined as a positive social value presented by actors and reinforced by others in the interaction process. Face is an image of self which is delineated in terms of approved social attributes and is confirmed by evidence conveyed in situations. "Face work" pertains to the actions taken by a person to make whatever he deems consistent with face. Face work serves to counteract incidents, that is, events whose effective symbolic implications threaten face or presentation. Involved in such presentations are things like poise and control of physical and psychological space, that is, the fixing of behavior within specific boundaries. Social groups, or more appropriately, stagings for particular interactions occurring within larger stage settings (i.e., small groupings occurring within large parties) may well have anterooms, foyers, halls, and the like, each demarking very clearly the individual's physical proximity to the central core of onstage interaction.[27]

In addition, self and situation are often defined in terms of props. Props are arranged around a setting in an orderly manner referred to as the decor. Ordinarily, props are not moved during transactions or interactions but are typically rearranged or replaced between major changes of scene, marking changes in life's situations. In a sense, the typical home might be viewed as a collection of props. Any scene that an actor deliberately contrives to enhance his presentation of what he views as a requisite self can be viewed as being made up of props. Props and equipment are moved, manipulated, and the like, as the result of social interaction. Equipment can range from words to physical objects. A loss of control over such equipment is a frequent source of embarassment, i.e., slips of the tongue, stalling cars in traffic, spilling food while trying to present a sophisticated appearance. Stone gives one example of these acts occurring at a formal dinner:

> A speaker was discovered with his fly undone. On being informed of this embarrassing oversight after he was seated, he proceeded to make the required adjustment, unknowingly catching the table cloth in his trousers. When obliged to rise again at the close of the proceedings he took the stage props with him and of course scattered the dinner tools about the setting in such a way that others were forced to doubt his control. His poise was lost in the situation.[28]

Clothing presents a dramaturgical front for actors. In a sense, clothing is as much a part of the body as the physical attachments. Clothing conveys the impression of body maintenance by paradoxically concealing body maintenance activities. Unexpected exposure of "privates" or underclothing is a frequent source of embarrassment for actors.

An individual plays many roles, but he is saved from confusion by his sense of appropriateness in terms of role presentation following *audience segregation* and *role segregation.* The individual plays out one role to one audience but does not confine his definition of self to that single role, rather tending to define what he is in terms of the audience that he is presenting to. Role segregation relates to the actor's unwillingness to present incompatible roles or roles with unsustained harmony. Such perceived disharmony does not make one role valid and another invalid. Rather, it suggests that a decision must be made between the two in terms of which role to present as appropriate in a given context.

Within this framework, there are many qualifying kinds of terminologies, all of which serve to clarify the relationship of the actor to the audience in terms of a particular interactional matrix. They include descriptions of such things as dramaturgical loyalty, discipline, circumspection, and so on, in terms of presentation itself as well as impression management. Such concepts refer not only to physical presentation itself with implied social-psychological cues of presence, but they likewise relate to use of language, including use of language to differentiate one group from another. Or as Lyman and Scott state: "Linguistic collusion involves a complex set of processes by which territorial integrity of the group is reaffirmed and the intruder is labeled as an outsider.[29]

Within this framework, ethnic groups may speak their own dialect, e.g., Jewish shopkeepers speak Yiddish and Chinese merchants speak Cantonese when discussing prices, bargaining rights, and product quality in the presence of alien customers. Mood and tone of voice are regulated to exaggerate a particular posture or to stage a particular kind of interactional presentation. Examples include professors who escalate their use of jargon and academic terms in conversations held in the presence of uninvited students or other outsiders. Homosexuals engaged in flirtations in a gay bar may exaggerate their femininity or masculinity when heterosexuals enter such establishments. These staged displays call attention to the exclusive culture of the interactants, suggesting that outsiders lack cards of identiy.

This, then, is the dramaturgical perspective. From a research point of view, it allows a careful ordering of presented behaviors without having that ordering include labeling devices or value intonations.

There are examples of dramaturgically oriented research in the literature of sociology. For present purposes, however, we first reach outside of sociology to Robert Brustein, *Revolution as Theatre.*[30] As Brustein suggests, "I am no longer simply an observer of theatrical events, but occasionally an unwilling performer as well, and like most actors, I can grow a little too preoccupied with my own role."[31] Throughout his work, he presents student reaction or overreaction to the condition of the American university: "The main thing . . . is that the rebellions start off by despising make-believe. . . . If we behave like the other side, then we are on the other side, instead of changing the world, all we'll achieve is a reflection of the one we want to destroy."[32] In a sense, Genet in *The Balcony* has presented the perfect dramaturgically oriented house of prostitution, wherein actors not only achieve the physical satisfactions they seek but also can achieve them within the dramaturgical setting appropriate to them.[33]

The dramaturgical perspective is also manifest in such works as *Asylums*[34] by Erving Goffman or *One Flew Over the Cuckoo's Nest* by Ken Keasey.[35] The approach makes few assumptions about the nature of the human being out of the interactional context but places the "humanness" of people within the interactional matrix itself. It does not begin with preconceived notions about motivation, but rather begins from a perspective that is at once observing of behavior and analytical of those meanings arising out of behavior.

CASE STUDY TECHNIQUE

The case study technique is yet another interactionist research technique. Every year brings new volumes to enrich this already rich literature. In this concluding section on symbolic interactionism, typical questions raised with regard to the assumptions and the validity problems that surround the technique are discussed. The technique of "data" generation is not described; the story is the data. Case stories ordinarily have a time sequence imposed on them and find focus with regard to the author's specifications. In the storytelling, the author interacts with himself. Meanings, not acts, are the thrust of this interaction.

It is axiomatic that we all have a story to tell. The concept of self-perceived motivations as a valid explanation of the etiology of human behavior is, however, often questioned. Who is to state as fact that the etiology of personal behavior is not recognizable to the actor and thereby not related to his or her story? Even so, this assumption is common to many theories in both psychology and sociology. According to a large segment of social scientists involved in explaining behavior, such behavior is intelligible not through awareness, cognition, and context, but through interpretation and predetermined constructs. That this often means force-fitting behavior to various models of explanation appears to be of little consequence.

Many studies have been based on assumed needs, assumed involuntary distortions, and hypothesized psychic mechanisms that preclude the individuals being able to answer the question "Why did you do that?" Conversely, few studies have focused on the assumptions surrounding the proposition that motivation is hidden from those motivated. In order to study such assumptions, the methodologist must focus on two levels of self-report material. The first, of course, is the self-report that describes life careers, life definitions, and processes. It may also discuss significant relationships and interactions. To the extent that it relates such factors to what it defines as resultant behavior, and, therefore, assumes an explanatory mode, it is theoretical. The second form of self-report material is more of a counting nature. This is the report that gives numerical sequences or time sequences to events under scrutiny. That such behavior reporting is generally viewed as more objective than straight self-report material. Why this is so is most confusing, since the intrusion of the psychological set of the researcher, as well as the bias of his structured interpretation of the derived "data," is quite evident here. The reason would appear to be that at the point an individual tells his story through the interposed medium of a questionnaire, his responses become mysteriously less self-reporting and concomitantly more objective, and the results, rather than being self-interpretation, magically become data. Responses derived through the use of one instrument or another are viewed as perhaps more objective since they are more removed from the subject. One might well question the assumption that as the distance from the subject increases so increases "the objectivity of the study."

In a way, all responses to questionnaires can be viewed as "self-report material" or data. The fact that questionnaire responses are more quantifiable and, therefore, more respectable in today's mainstream of sociology does not alter the fact that essentially an individual is reporting on his own life. Let us ignore the question of the individual interacting with the questionnaire for the present. Suffice it to say that the individual has a frustrated feeling when completing a questionnaire (often defined as "I couldn't find a response that expressed what I wanted to say"). Such an individual is really saying that interaction with the instrument was incomplete. To buttress this argument, consider the many people who write all over questionnaires. Such unsolicited (often forbidden) interactions are not satisfactorily dismissed by the researcher's smug assertion that he can "predict behavior from the question responses." Such reasoning is most often tautological. The researcher sets the parameters of behavior and then predicts responses that are generated by the nature of the questions asked.

It is not enough to know associated factors of behavior. Such factors can only be understood as actor perception, for it is the actor's perception that assigns priorities of impact on motivation. What motivates Actor A will not motivate Actor B. Motivation is itself a derived set of assumptions that create a set within which we attempt to make sense of behaviors. Such "sense" depends upon a number of factors, some of which are structural and some of which are derived of interaction or are interactional. Behavior occurs within many "sets" or forms or, if you prefer, levels of abstraction. As the actor interacts, he is at once actor, reflector of past interactions, integrator of past interaction, integrator of culture in a broad social system sense (i.e., imperatives-norms-prescriptions-shalls-shall nots), and interpreter of the immediate which has the dimension of presentation, reception, interpretation, and integration. He marks a place in a drama that has a set, a form, acts, and stage. He is a part of a Gestalt—a whole—and as such can relate only to explanations that include the fabric of self. He (the actor) can predict certain aspects of his life—body functions, appetite, sexual expressions, taxonomic responses such as bigotry. But these aspects are understandable to the actor and to his audience (defined as those with whom he is interacting) only with regard to the entire fabric of his existence.

In the abstract, then, we relate to the research effort as a search for meaning, or what Weber called Verstehen sociology. Implicit in this definition also is the notion that all behavior models are time and cultural bound. It is a lesson of history that questions are more important than answers. As the varieties and the context of behavior change, then so must explanations, and for that matter models of predictions of human behavior.

SUMMARY

This chapter shows the student that theory outlines, guides, limits, and directs the development of the research project. Within the theoretical orientation, decisions have already been made as to the type of research design to be implemented. For example, implicit in the interactionist approach is the idea that data will be collected entirely or in part through observation; because of the nature of the orientation data, collection will occur over a time dimension. On the other hand, many attitudinal studies have single data collection times where survey data are collected. By the very nature of the interactionist framework, the classical research design of an experimental and control group is not a possibility. While it is possible to observe one group and then make comparative evaluations of how the two groups are similar, dissimilar, or in any way comparable, it is almost impossible to induce the treatment or stimuli on the experimental group. This is particularly true when the observer attempts to operate in a covert manner. Hence, one finds that decisions on sample, analysis techniques, data collection techniques, time frames, and amount and degree of involvement with the research subjects are all governed by selection of the theoretical orientation.

NOTES

1. Here the authors mean that such research was not definitely structured in such a way that definition or research interests have been used to purposely develop tautologies. Rather, the meaning is that certain decisions or choices having been made, others are thus limited or restricted. What must evolve is a logical connected whole in terms of the research design to test the problem.
2. The authors are heavily indebted to Herbert Blumer, *Symbolic Interactionism: Perspective in Method* (Englewood Cliffs, N.J.: Prentice-Hall, 1969), for much of the following discussion of symbolic interactionism.
3. Blumer, op. cit., p. 2.
4. Ibid.
5. Ibid.
6. Ibid., p. 3.
7. Ibid., p. 7.
8. Ibid., p. 8.
9. Ibid., p. 10.
10. Ibid., p. 15.
11. Ibid., p. 17.
12. Ibid., p. 20.
13. Ibid., p. 27.
14. William Foote Whyte, *Street Corner Society* (Chicago: University of Chicago Press, 1955; paperback edition). See also Howard S. Becker, *The Outsiders* (Glencoe, Ill.: Free Press, 1963) and Erving Goffman, *Asylums* (New York: Anchor Books, Doubleday and Co., 1961).

15. Ned Polsky, *Hustlers, Beats and Others* (New York: Aldine Publishing Co., 1967).

16. Dennis Brissett, "Collective Behavior: The Sense of a Rubric," *American Journal of Sociology* 74 (July 1968): 72.

17. Kenneth Burke, *A Grammar of Motives* (New York: Prentice-Hall, 1945). See also Kenneth Burke, *A Rhetoric of Motives* (New York: Prentice Hall, 1950).

18. Nelson N. Foote, "Identification as a Basis for a Theory of Motivation," *American Sociological Review* 16 (February 1951): 14-21.

19. Reviews concern audience-making responses to the actor presenting appearance, while programs are responses made about the presenter made by the presenter.

20. Foote, op. cit., p. 100.

21. George J. McCall and John L. Simmons, *Identities and Interactions* (New York: Free Press, 1966), p. 58.

22. Goffman, op. cit., p. 15. Performances may be defined as all the activity of a given participant on a given occasion which in any way influences the other participants (audience, observer, and co-participant).

23. Ibid., p. 106.

24. The definition of the situation is the selected perspective used in defining a situation. Tamatsu Shibutani, "Reference Groups and Social Control," in A. M. Rose, ed. *Human Behavior and Social Process* (Boston: Houghton Mifflin, 1962). W. I. Thomas states that the "definition of the situation has a stage of examination and deliberation of a situation"; Lewis A. Coser and Bernard A. Rosenberg, *Sociological Theory* (London: Macmillan, 1969), pp. 245-47.

25. Goffman, op. cit., p. 112.

26. Erving Goffman, "Embarrassment and Social Organization," *American Journal of Sociology* 62 (1956): 265.

27. Edward Gross and Greg P. Stone, "Embarrassment and the Analysis of Role Referent," *American Journal of Sociology* 70, No. 1 (July 1964): 7.

28. Ibid., p. 10.

29. Stanford M. Lyman and Marian B. Scott, *A Sociology of the Absurd* (New York: Appleton, Century and Croft, 1970), p. 104.

30. Robert Brustein, *Revolution as Theatre* (New York: Liveright Press, 1971).

31. Ibid., p. 3.

32. Ibid., p. 4.

33. Jean Genet, *The Balcony*, translated by Bernard Frectman (New York: Grove Press, 1966).

34. Goffman, op. cit., p. 15.

35. Ken Keasey, *One Flew Over the Cuckoo's Nest* (New York: Viking Press, 1962).

3

Theoretical Base for Structural Functionalism

As stated in Chapter 2, the stance which the researcher assumes with regard to his theoretical model makes impositions on the research act itself. Not as new as symbolic interactionism, structural functionalism has its antecedents in the very roots of sociology. Of all approaches, structural functionalist explanations have probably played the greatest role in shaping the development of modern sociology. Witness the pervasive influence of organic models and system models in general.

There are many dimensions of theory and many theories diverse in their handling of the human equation. Like symbolic interactionism, structural functionalism is a generic category. All of the theories with this designation, however, commonly share broad-based assumptions about the nature of human action and of the social structure within which such interaction occurs.

The two most crucial aspects of structural functionalism are the concept of "system," or interrelatedness, and the mutual interdependence of parts of a given social system. By interdependence is meant that all parts of a social system are articulated one upon the other, so that change in one element of the system will bring about change in yet another element. In a sense, the social system is analogous to the workings of a watch. As one wheel turns, it acts on other wheels and causes movement in another part of the watch; each wheel is articulated one upon the other, with movement in one bringing about movement in the other. The same process occurs in the social system; however, rather than wheels, the elements of the social system are articulated upon one another. The elements in the social system are roles, status, institutions, social units, and so on. Just as each wheel has a function in the total working of the watch that contributes to its existence and to its entire function, so elements of the social system work in conjunction to aid in the total operation of the social system. This explanation of the working of any element in the social system must be understood in terms of its relationships to other elements and what it does (its function). Social systems tend to seek equilibrium, and disturbances or intrusions upon the system in one sector or another are responded to by tendency of the system as a whole to return to its previously balanced state.

> . . . functional analysis premises the operation of a "principle of functional reciprocity," a principle variously employed by Marx, by Mauss, by Malinowski, by Levi-Strauss, and by Homans in different empirical contexts. This underlying functionalist assumption might just as well be made explicit and could be stated in the following generalized form: 1. Any one structure is more likely to persist if it is engaged in reciprocally functional interchanges with some others; (1.1) the less reciprocal the functional interchange between structure, the less likely in either structure, or the pattern relation between them to persist, (1.2) unless compensatory mechanisms are present.[1]

Within this framework, the functionalist would typically argue that the persistence of A may be demonstrated by its functional relationship to B; therefore, A is both a necessary and sufficient condition for the existence of B, and B implies the existence of A.

Historically, functional analysis is a modification of teleological explanation, that is, explanations whose focus is on what brings about a given phenomenon or "causes it." As Hempel has suggested:

> The kind of phenomenon that a functional analysis evoked to explain is typically some recurrent activity or some behavior pattern in an individual or a group; it may be a physiological mechanism, a neurotic trait, a culture pattern, or a social institution, for example. And the principal objective of the analysis is to exhibit the contribution which the behavior pattern makes to the preservation or the development of the individual or the group in which it occurs. Thus, functional analysis seeks to understand the behavior pattern for a sociocultural institution in terms of the role it plays in keeping the given system in proper working order and thus maintaining it as a going concern.[2]

A crucial notion underlying structural functionalism is that human behavior is culturally structured, permitting labor divisions and relatively orderly consistencies and enduring interactions that make what we call the human existence possible. Culture as such is viewed as being composed of meanings and definitional agreements with regard to "preferred versus nonpreferred" behavior, as well as the static element or what we may refer to as the skeletal structure (institutionalized) of the culture.

In general, the structural functionalist tends toward macrotheoretical considerations. He or she tends to analyze social behavior by identifying structural antecedents to behavior and assessing these behaviors in terms of their functional or disfunctional aspects. The use of social systems models for analysis of description is also associated with functionalism. Meanings within this framework are antecedents to interaction rather than integral portions of interaction arising out of the very nature of interaction. Behavior is characteristically defined as the result of factors acting upon individuals "causing" them to act in a certain way. Behavior, then, can be predicted by isolating factors that are normally associated with the appearance of that behavior. Behavior is defined as related not to choice but to "cause."

Regardless of its historical antecedents, structural functionalism makes certain assumptions about the very nature of interaction and those who interact. As we have indicated, the model assumes that action in one segment of the system will result in reaction in another, and that action takes place in specific situations and includes relevant aspects of both the biological and social world. Second, the model assumes that action is conducted in terms of anticipated states of affairs, meaning that people relate their activities to goals or to resolutions that they perceive to be particularly important and cogent to the interaction at hand. Behavior is assumed to be motivated to the extent that there is an end to be achieved by behavior and that human beings expend energy toward that end. Finally, the model assumes that action is normatively regulated, that individuals are socialized to respond to and to accept the legitimacy of the rules of the game. These rules are institutionalized as a part of the normative order and are accepted as legitimate by actors on the screen. As Loomis and Loomis state:

> The more specialized frame of reference of sociology is limited to reciprocal action or interaction. Interaction as a special type of action (activity, terms which are here used as synonymous) loses none of the afoementioned attributes of activity, but is distinguished by additional attributes. The important characteristics include:
>
> 1. a plurality of actors
> 2. communication between the actors by means of a set of symbols
> 3. a duration of time dimension possessing a past, present, and future, which in part determines the character of the ongoing action and,
> 4. an objective, whether or not its specification from the view point of the actor coincides with that of an objective observer.[3]

Examples of structural functionalist theory are given in the following pages. From these examples, the operationalization of one type of functionalist approach and the resulting research model can be delineated. Here it is not possible to examine examples of all uses of functional theory, or even to mention all of the approaches included under this particular theoretical rubric. Initially, a highly abstract social systems model is presented, followed by a structurally oriented theory of mid-range abstractions. Lastly, research is presented which operationalizes key concepts in the structural functional model. The examples go from the most abstract to the concrete act of research.

PARSONS' SOCIAL SYSTEM MODEL

Let us begin by examining the highly abstract structural functional model given by Talcott Parsons. In many regards, Parsons' work is an attempt to integrate several structurally oriented models concerned with the basic nature of man. The first model, the utilitarian or classic economists' approach to understanding behavior, defines behavior as characteristically individualistic and rationalistic; the second, the positivistic approach, views human behavior within a framework of determinant scientific laws; and finally, the idealistic approach emphasizes the importance of cultural values as behavioral antecedents. Parsons explicitly states that the role of theory is to provide a posture from which we can make sense of the interrelationships defining institutions, cultural content, and the varied interrelationships of the social system. Theory, therefore, provides an interpretive frame of reference and not only gives the limitation of a particular empirical research but also offers a unified conceptual vocabulary. Parsons indicates his awareness of the limiting quality of theory. Although committed to economic theory, he notes that economic motivation could never explain the ongoing economy of the empirical world since economic interactions were never solely economic in content. Economic activities tend to organize themselves in ways that become part of the complex social setting. Economic theory can never attain the status of general theory since it does not take social order into account; it simply assumes that order occurs and that people automatically act in their own best interests. For Parsons, economic theory is simply an integrated part of the interconnected structure which, from a structural point of view, defines the social order.

For Parsons, theory must explain order in societies or systems. He suggests that order cannot be the result of individual rational self-interest or of externally imposed sanctions. Order must rest upon a core of institutionalized common values.[4]

Parsons' model of social action is essentially an attack on hard determinism.[5] He views behavior as being either rational or nonrational. Behavior that is motivated and intelligible is rational, while behavior that is devoid of goal orientation is irrational. Goals and values, therefore, become mechanisms whereby the future can be predicted. Parsons argues for an element of voluntarism in behavior, which he defines as the only way that action can be "meaningful." Without such a framework, morality and responsibility have no conceptual content, and without the element of freedom in human behavior, normative factors become epiphenomenon. In a further discussion of positivism, he suggests that the approach leads to a kind of reductionism in that groups are reduced to individuals or that groups may be defined in terms of the functions of individuals. Within this framework, Parsons argues that the group is a subsystem and as such is defined by those same patterns that define the larger system as well as those other systems upon which the group subsystem is related. This, of course, means that rather than defining the group as greater than the sum of its parts, the sum of the parts of the group relate to the function of the subsystem, which is more than the simple sum total of its parts. Groups therefore take on characteristics of the higher abstracted system and as such develop maintenance mechanisms as well as equilibrium directions.

Clearly, Parsons defines theory as a highly abstract, general set of conceptualizations incorporating broad enough generalizations to include all interchanges, and yet specific enough to allow for empirical reference within the structure of common modes of pattern relationships. In this sense, Parsons is suggesting that social systems at whatever level share common control mechanisms which in many regards curb the nature of voluntaristic human activity. Theory must be general as well as systematic and include all types of factors relevant to the operation of systems conceived of in an organic sense. Theory must also include an expletive of action which takes into account actors orienting themselves to situations, including relations to goals, values, and norms. Since sociological theory must likewise be a theory of action, it must be based on voluntaristic postulates. Therefore, ideas, ideals, goals, and norms are treated as causally relevant variables. They are parts of an interdependent system which comprises part of the motivational aspect of the general theory of actions. Theory, then, must include the concept of emergence which in many regards is the vehicle by which Parsons explains innovation and social change. Emergence is defined as a kind of situational emergency (or a kind of organizational complexity) which is met by an almost serendipitous system. This emerging system cannot be divided into component parts and could be interpreted as being related to exigencies of the existent systems. These emergent properties must be treated as causally relevant variables. At each emergent level certain new degrees of freedom are created.[6]

Within our structural model, action constitutes a central focus of attention. The social system as a concept has several meanings; as can be seen in Figure 1, these meanings appear to be different levels of abstractions. Initially, the social system can be interpreted to mean a plurality of individ-

Orientation

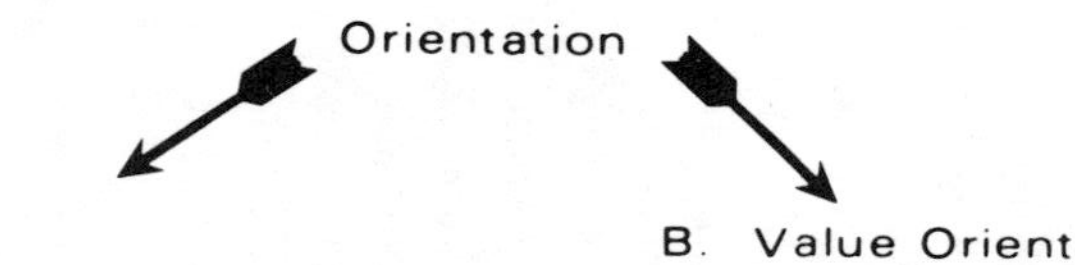

A. Motivational Orientation
1. Cognitive - situation perception
2. Cathetic - invest object with emotional qualities
3. Evaluative - Judgment with regard to choice

B. Value Orientation
1. Cognitive - situation perception
2. Appreciative - How perceived commitments are to value (once prescribed commitment)
3. Moral - (what is right and and wrong)

Analytic Systems

1. Social System	- link to culture for personality Plurality of individuals - seeking gratification Pattern relationships between actors Norms
2. Personality System	internalizations actor perceptions
3. Culture System	ideas and beliefs systems of expressive symbols value orientation - integrative systems

FIGURE 1 Action and Related Systems Plus Actor Perception

uals interacting one with another. In this regard, systems of mutual exchange define the relationship as being a system. The social system can also be defined as a network of relationships between actors; in this regard, it is possible to remove the actor from the situation and substitute a kind of pattern analogy. In this latter instance, the focus is on the quality of the relationship in a general sense rather than in a specific actor-oriented sense. One might ask whether the material points of the social system are the actor's or the relationships themselves; it is our feeling that the two terms are inseparable. The term *actor* is useful by virtue of its generality and is thus typical of structuralists in that all forms of analysis and all levels of abstraction relative to analysis are basically of the same format. Therefore all systems are analyzed along the same axis or dimension. It is the dimensions themselves that have a universal kind of quality, while the individual's systems are analyzed within this univeralistic frame of reference.

The social system may also be defined as a plurality of individuals who are motivated by a tendency to optimum attainment based on pre-prescribed goals. The relationships between these actors would be structured by the normative order, that is, by culturally defined structured and shared patterns. Here, "needs" may be defined in terms of types of motivation as an example, either cognitive or cathetic. Motivational patterns within this frame of reference can relate to a patterned interdependent relationship. (In a sense, this is a way of saying that people tend to react to and possess normatively derived expectations.) While values are not explicitly delineated in this description of relationships, they are implied. They are, after all, a dimension of motivation, a facet that is contingent upon the congitive aspect as well as the defined perception of a situation.

Social system is conceived of as the bridge to the cultural system. It is almost as if Parsons is suggesting that the cultural system is derived from the social system. The dynamics for social change, however, are missing in this specification, and its concepts seem to focus almost exclusively upon the stability of social systems.

CULTURE

Society is conceived of as a collectivity or a system of concrete interacting individuals as the primary bearer of the distinctive but well recognized institutionalized culture which is oriented to the functional necessities of the social system itself. Culture, on the other hand, is defined as a product as well as a determinant of the social system of human interaction. (Remember that systems of social action are the product of the sets of relationship between actors, and these relate to motivation with all of its facets which in turn relate to the personality system.) Culture has been defined as having three elements: (1) systems of ideas or beliefs (in terms of the pattern variables this represents cognitive priority involving situational perception);

(2) systems of expressive symbols (that is, in part, almost a definition of a cathetic symbol exemplified by art forms and implying acceptance or rejection); and (3) systems of value orientation which are integrative systems or patterns. The study of culture per se, Parsons leaves to anthropologists. The culture system is of interest only to the extent that it affects social systems and personality systems. Cultural patterns tend to become organized into systems on the basis of logical consistencies of the belief systems leading to the development of a body of moral rules which are compatible with the harmony characteristics of the particular cultural pattern.

SYSTEM FUNCTIONS

System functions can be both internal and external. External functions are primarily of two types: (1) the adaptive function, or the phase involving instrumental action, i.e., the production of a product or a service for export,[7] and (2) goal attainment, which is the second phase of the external dimensions of a functional imperative. This type of activity is consummatory in the sense that the activity itself is the goal. An example is the body politic or organizations which generate power, such as organs of government functions or banks. Adaptive functions lead to the attainment of particular goals and are not necessarily satisfying in and of themselves; such activities are therefore defined as instrumental. Consummatory activities, on the other hand, are self-satisfying in and of themselves.

Internal functions are likewise divided into two types: (1) The first is the function of pattern maintenance and tension management; this involves an instrumental activity and includes elements of structure or systems which tend toward the maintenance of equilibrium or stability. We find examples of government, family groups, kinship groups, and institutions such as marriage. (2) The second is the integrative function, which is viewed by Parsons as being a kind of consummatory activity once again. Examples of this kind of function are churches, hospitals, and charitable organizations. This type of activity always bears relation to institutionalized values and characteristics of the given culture, and so in this sense, could include schools or other conscious agents of socialization.

Since each category has a particular function, each offers a particular type of organization with unique kinds of problems. For example, concrete formal organizations exhibit different activity levels separated by observable boundary points. Each level is responsible to a system for a particular imperative, and each faces one of four functional imperatives or problems unique to that level. Given the adaptive process, formal organizations must provide a set of mechanisms by which resources can be brought to bear on actual processes of goal implementation in changing situations.

In addition, there are four basic categories of activity, and all relate to social systems or the problems of functional imperatives. Action is generated in a society and can be:

(1) in work or externally directed,
(2) horizontal patterns vs vertical patterns,
(3) defined as instrumental, and may be so defined if the activity is directed toward a goal,
(4) defined as consummatory if the activity is an end, in and of itself.[8]

SOCIALIZATION

The concept of socialization is also central to Parsons' theory and to functionalist theory in general. Parsons views it as occurring within the context of preestablished stages and to be the process whereby the individual learns the "rules of the game," wherein he learns the very core of what enables him to interact in the social system as a human being. Parsons classifies the process of socialization in terms of the pattern variables involved and states that it varies from the beginnings of awareness through to maturation, constantly structured by the content of the sociosystem. The socialization concept provides the key to understanding the continuities of shared beliefs and forms of interaction existing in the social system. It explains both the stability and similarities and cultural continuities, although it does not explain instability. Within this framework, action occurs in response to needs that are subject to both cathetic and cognitive interpretation. These interpretations are in turn dependent upon the transmission of cultural norms and values through socialization. Parsons suggests further that real balance among systems and subsystems never exists; relative system stability is sown with the seeds of its own disfunction. If social systems have equilibrium tendencies, they must likewise have tendencies toward disequilibrium.

AN OUTLINE OF THE SOCIAL SYSTEM

It is in the outline of the social system that the assumptions of the structural functionalist approach become most apparent. There are basically four functions or functional classifications which underlie the system's model of the social system:

(1) Pattern maintenance
(2) Integration (system integration)
(3) Goal attainment
(4) Adaptation

The structural analysis of these functions must include the following four categories:

(1) System values
(2) Institutionalized norms
(3) Collectivities
(4) Roles

The first four categories are essentially regulatory mechanisms in the interchanges between systems existent in the interrational mechanisms between all types of systems.

Analysis is of two types. It is (1) morphological, focusing on analysis of structure, or it is (2) dynamic, focusing on process. While both types have the same priority, at any particular level it is necessary to have stable points of structure allowing the analysis of process to go on. If one presupposes an equilibrium level, one can then safely assume a given structure. Dynamic analysis would focus then on the study of changes in structure or in process. In attempting to explain change in subsystems of the more general system, it is often necessary to assume surrounding structures. Thus, analysis of dynamic change is always rational and related to structure, whether assumed or observed.

In discussing the concept of "social systems," it is important to stress the logical interdependence of all propositions in sociological theory. In this regard, Parsons states that all major propositions in a given theoretical scheme must be capable of being derived from a set of basic postulates and definitions. This is an ideal, however, and he does not say that his grand theory meets this requirement. In fact, he suggests that the relationship of theory to empirical research is explicit in that it is impossible to study anything "at once" empirically. An empirical system is defined in terms of interrelationship, which in turn is defined by the relevant theory. Hence, it is the function of theory to make sense of the real world or to clarify observations about the real world. Theory precedes the generation of data and does not arise from it.

> The social system has its focus on the conditions involved in the interaction of actual human individuals who constitute concrete collectivities with determinant membership. The cultural system, on the other hand, focuses on patterns of meaning, e.g., of values, of norms, of organized knowledge, and beliefs of expressive form. The basic concept for the integration and interpretation of the true is institutionalization which will be a subject of much attention.[9]

This definition represents a blend of cultural and social systems and brings the study of culture under the umbrella of sociology. Although the two are inseparable, Parsons insists that they must be kept separate, and he identifies institutionalization as the bridge between the two.

A further distinction that must be made is the one between the organism and the personality. Social and cultural systems are difficult to differentiate, and it is equally difficult to differentiate the organism from the personality. One is, after all, part of the other, i.e., the individual is part of an interactive process and a group. He is both the affected and affector. In this same sense, the group as a system is affected by and an affector of the larger system. All systems, regardless of size, are integrated one with the other and share the derived symbols and structures of culture.

Parsons views social systems as being open and engaged in complicated processes of interchange with environmental systems, including cultural systems. He defines environmental systems as including cultural systems, personality systems, behavior systems, and the physical environment. All subsystems are likewise open. The larger the system and its modifiers, the larger the environmental system of subsystems. All of this implies boundaries and maintenance functions.

What are the essential differences between structural and functional modes of analysis? "Structural" refers to a stable, almost mechanical kind of superstructure or system of reference points that are constant over a period of time. Subsystems of structure may exist and change; yet, the larger structure remains constant. Moreover, both structural and functional systems may have subsystems.

The functional reference is always dynamic. It refers to both the working out and articulation of any system, but it also relates to the purpose of particular structures. And, too, it refers to process. For example, it can relate to the mediation between two existing systems of structure. In general, structural analysis refers to an examination of those institutionalized elements in the culture that exist as referents to action rather than as action themselves. Functional modes of analysis focus on relationships and define purposes as being identifiable with the reason for existence.

The focus of pattern maintenance in the social system is reflected in its structure of values. Values are pattern maintaining at the cultural level through the processes which articulate institutionalized values and the existing belief system. Both belief systems and value systems are subject to change. However, even when such changes occur, control exists in the system that makes such changes orderly and slow.

The fact that a social system survives in its environment, despite deviance and many changes, demonstrates that it has somehow managed to cope with its complex problem needs. The heart of the analysis lies in specifying the needs and the mechanism through which such needs are served and then attempting to arrive at some notion of the overall balance of forces coursing through the system. It has been previously noted that equilibrium is a tendency rather than a reality and that disfunction leads to disequilibrium. In many regards, equilibrium is a dynamic and can be defined as a tendency to return to a state of balance rather than as a continuing condition. In the case of the individual, the equilibrium function is called tension management. Although tension management as a process and as a variable can be applied to subsystems and to other systems, in the personality system, the motivational sentiment of the individual is defined as a tension management function. Even after the individual has been socialized, the internalized values and beliefs are always subject to strain and change. In some regards, rituals and similar mechanisms play a pattern maintenance function. Pattern maintenance is also reflected in social systems in that they demonstrate a tendency to maintain their structural patterns. This tendency provides a reference point for an entire range of variations arising from sources other than processes of structural changes in the system; and it puts the study of structural change in quite a different category from the study of equilibrium.

Although the models presented here comprise only a small sampling of Parsonian structural functional models—or for that matter, a small sampling of structurally oriented models available in the literature in sociology—they are representative of a category of reasoning. In all of the models and all of the concepts, it should be noted that original behavioral motivation tends to be located outside of the actor-individual. Meanings are those things which individuals are socialized to accept, and deviance that which is viewed as a disfunction. Relationships between individuals are largely patterned and exist in terms of roles, norms, values, cathetic imputations, and the like. Regarding motivation, there is a general assumption that in structural models, motivation is on the one hand external to individuals and on the other hand somehow rather magically necessary in order that behavior occurs. The next model to be presented more clearly demonstrates the extent to which the structural functionalist relates behavior to antecedents that exist outside the individual's interactive framework.

MIDDLE RANGE THEORY

Robert Merton is most frequently associated with his work on social structure and anomie,[10] in which he relates elements of what he defines as "The American Dream" to deviant behavior. Since his approach is decidedly structural and his writing style is clear, his theoretical model is easier to grasp than Parsons'. Consequently, it has been empirically tested by various research efforts.

Merton's structural functional commitment is most clear in the early section of his *Social Theory and Social Structure:*

There still remains the further question of why it is that the frequency of deviant behavior varies within different social structures and how it happens that the deviations have different shapes and patterns in different social structures. Today, as then, we have still much to learn about the processes through which social structures generate the circumstances in which infringements of social codes constitute a "normal" (that is to say an expectable) response.[11]

Even more explicitly,

Our primary aim is to discover how some social structures exert a definite pressure upon certain persons in the society to engage in non-conforming rather than conforming conduct.[12]

Summarizing Merton's argument, all societies are characterized as having goals that are institutionalized and accepted as positively sought after ends. Additionally, societies institutionalize means viewed as appropriate in seeking these goals. These goals are more or less integrated and ordered in a hierarchy of values which roughly expresses their difficulty or achievement but likewise reflects either prestige or relative status. By implication, some of these goals, highly valued in the American culture, provide a kind of common denominator by which the individual's worth is gauged. In the case of the United States, the ideological foundations of the culture differ from those norms prescribing the institutionalized means of goal achievement. The ideology maintains the existence of universal goals and a universal distribution of the means of goal achievement. Success opportunity structures thereby provide the culture with an open social class system. Consequently, the practice of certain virtues will result in success, which in all cases is deserved and is indicative of individual worth. Unfortunately, the reality differs from the ideology, a condition which in turn generates deviance.

Merton's definition of deviance has never been particularly clear. His best definition is that it "refers to conduct that departs significantly from the norms that are socially defined as appropriate and morally binding for people occupying various statuses."[13] He also notes that all cultures are characterized by regulatory norms which determine areas of activities that are specifically prohibited or heavily value laden. He states further that in all cases, striving toward these cultural goals is limited by institutionalized norms. Hence, one cannot assume that highly valued goals in the culture are necessarily accompanied by institutionalized means of goal attainment, one articulated upon the other. Indeed, quite the reverse is true: goal achievement is often related to factors extraneous (as is the case in the United States) to the ideology, giving high cathetic values to the goal itself. Therefore, as Merton affirms:

With such differential emphasis upon goals and institutional procedures, the latter may be so vitiated by the stress on goals as to have the behavior of many individuals limited only by considerations of technical expediency. In this context, the sole question becomes: WHICH OF THE AVAILABLE PROCEDURES IS MOST EFFICIENT IN NETTING THE CULTURALLY APPROVED VALUES? Technically, the most affective procedure, whether culturally legitimate or not, becomes typically preferred to institutionally prescribed conduct. As this process of attenuation continues, the society becomes unstable and there develops what Durkheim called "anomie" (or normlessness).[14]

Further describing the conditions under which anomie manifests itself, Merton posits two "ideal types" of society: (1) the integrated and (2) the malintegrated. In the case of the integrated, differential goals for differential social classes exist, making the relationship between institutionalized means of goal achievement and institutionalized goals perfectly articulated. Therefore, where a goal exists for a particular group or social class, the means of achieving that goal are available to that goup or social class. In the case of the malintegrated society, there is a universal distribution of goals, with full ideological support for these goals and a differential distribution of the institutionalized means of achieving these goals. By this definition, the American culture is malintegrated and manifests a high degree of anomie, as a result of the disfunctional relationship between its institutionalized means and institutionalized goals. This condition is complicated by an ideology which posits the universal distribution of goals coupled with the universal distribution of means to achieve these goals. To verify this perspective, one need only to point to the differential opportunity structuring many rewards made available to the various social classes of the United States, or the reduced opportunity characteristic of the various minorities in the culture.

The ideology supporting the conditions conducive to anomie is embodied in what Merton calls the American Dream. According to this ideology, all men are born equal in an open class society; all have equal opportunities to achieve; all will be treated equally and fairly and will be presented with the same opportunities by dominant institutions, i.e., schools and other socializing institutions; hard work, a certain moral commitment to the deferment of gratifications and the careful use of time, coupled with the martialing of one's particular energies, will result in success. Success in this culture is almost universally defined as pecuniary (materialistic) success, as reflected by the possession of automobiles, houses, clothing, and the like.

The dream, however, has some severe side effects. Initially, there is no end to the American Dream; therefore, ambition is never truly satisfied. At one point, Merton cites a study which attempted to measure what the typical American wanted and found the response to be "about 25 percent more."

> The anonymity of an urban society in conjunction with these peculiarities of money, permits wealth, the source of which may be unknown to the community in which the plutocrat lives, or if known, to become purified in the course of time to serve as a high status. Moreover, in the American dream, there is no final stopping point. . . . In this flux of shifting standards, there is no stable resting point, or rather it is the point which manages always to be "just ahead".[15]

From Merton's pont of view, the entire culture operates to socialize and to condition actors to believe in this particular ideology.

> As we shall see, parents serve as a transmission belt for the values and goals of the groups of which they are a part—above all, of their social class or the class with which they identify themselves. And the schools are, of course, the official agency for the passing on of the prevailing values, with a large proportion of the textbooks used at city schools implying or stating explicitly "that education leads to intelligence and consequently to job and money success." Central to this process, of disciplining people to maintain their unfulfilled aspirations are the cultural prototypes of success, the living documents testifying that the American dream can be realized, if one but has the requisite abilities.[16]

The culture, therefore, teaches that all its members should strive for the same high goals since they can be obtained by all. Failure is not a shame in and of itself; shame lies in an unwillingness to continue trying. The lowering of one's ambitions to levels of present achievement is the definition of true failure.

These axioms deflect the guilt for failure from the system to the individual—"Among those so situated in a society, that they do not have full and equal access to opportunities".[17] This ideology also tends to perpetuate the status quo in that it inhibits the development of class consciousness. In addition, it suggests that individuals identify with people above them in the status hierarchy, since this is where they aspire to be. The third axiom clearly indicates that failure is an individual responsibility and to achieve anything less than the highest of goals is less than success. Thus, the individual is defined as being unworthy of complete participation in this wonderful cultural system. Raising basic research questions, Merton asks,

> . . . in short, what are the consequences for the behavior of people variously situated in a social structure of the culture in which the emphasis on dominant success goals is becoming increasingly separated from an equivalent emphasis on institutionalized procedures for seeking these goals?[18]

Having defined the condition of anomie as a disfunctional relationship between institutionalized means and institutionalized means of goal achievement complemented by an ideology that provides for belief in the universal distribution of means and goals, Merton suggests that anomie manifests itself in terms of individual perceptions. This can be seen in certain kinds of behavior. With the exception of conformity, all of these patterns represent a type of deviance. He refers to these as modes of adaptation. They include:

(1) conformity, which implies an acceptance of both the cultural goals and the institutionalized means of achieving them;
(2) innovation, which includes acceptance of cultural goals but a rejection of institutionalized means of goal achievement;
(3) ritualism, which is a rejection of goals but a utilization of institutionalized means;
(4) retreatism, rejection of both means and goals; and
(5) rebellion, which means rejection of both cultural goals and the means of achieving these goals.[19]

As is typical of the structuralist approach to the explanation of behavior, individual adaptation modes are not the result of meanings that arise from individuals interacting in a changing social context. Rather, the explanation for behavior is to be found in pressures exerted by the "culture-system," which does not by definition even require the individual's perception. The individual has little or no awareness of his own motivation, and in fact, he is unable to do little more than, parrot-like, repeat the mandates of the culture that has socialized him so thoroughly. In this sense, it is rather like correlating certain types of criminal behavior, i.e., theft with poverty. One might logically assume that poverty is strongly related to a number of other cultural factors considered to be antecedents to theft behavior. The theory breaks down since it cannot explain why those individuals existing under exactly the same poverty conditions do not likewise commit theft. It is generally accepted that two explanations for a single behavior set do not exist (namely, one to explain conforming behavior and the other to explain nonconforming behavior) in the same circumstances. Typically theories address this problem by considering the individuals' perception of themselves and the conditions in which they exist. This is a decidedly symbolic interactionist approach, and it is for this reason that it is difficult to find explanations of the functional variety that are pure in type.

Since Merton's anomie paradigm is not being criticized here, it is not necessary to describe it further. The thrust of the theory is quite clear: the social structure produces a strain toward anomie and results in deviant behavior. The social order manifests pressure with regard to competition, the result of which is an ideology that equates pecuniary success with personal worth and failure with personal responsibility for the condition. The important aspect of the paradigm from a research point of view is the model which assumes antecedents to behavior operating uniformly throughout the system, as well as specifically delineating those conditions that would tend to produce particular types of behavior, most specifically deviant behavior. The system's model changes the entire nature of research as well as the methods appropriate to investigating things within this particular framework. If indeed people do respond to pressures that are external to their daily interaction and meaning sets, then it would be expected that crime would be statistically more prevalent among groups that perceive anomic strain, or among groups whose physical life characteristics correspond to those delineated in the model.

The very existence of anomie is assumed and as such constitutes a legitimate realm of investigation. Within this framework, all of the concepts and terms would require operationalization for research purposes, and any design would have to clarify the criteria for decision-making. In this regard, the research of Leo Srole, specifically his attempt to operationalize and empirically test the anomie model, should be considered. Srole's work (done in 1956), like Merton's, assumes that anomie exists as a condition that is perceived as well as an element in the social structure itself. Srole's attempt to measure anomie was based on the development of a scale involving five items, each purporting to measure individual perception of his social environment and his place in it. Does the individual feel that:

(1) Community leaders are indifferent to his needs.
(2) Little can be accomplished in a society whose social order is essentially unpredictable.
(3) Life goals are receding from him rather than being reached.
(4) No one can be counted on for support.
(5) Life is meaningless and futile.[20]

Ignoring the fact that the scale assumes the existence of anomie as a condition, note that positive responses to the scale would serve to reify the existence of anomie. Given the operationalized definition of anomie, the "condition" is given, and the research question addresses the question of how much anomie and not whether or not anomie exists. Subsequent research has shown that anomie is more prevalent among the lower classes than the upper classes. Bell and others have also discovered that the perception of anomie varies inversely with economic status. In their article "Anomia and Differential Access to the Achievement of Life's Goals,"[21] Meia and Bell found that respondents perceived fewer institutionalized means to goal achievement within their social strata as their measured anomia score increased.

Since our purpose is to demonstrate the relationship between theoretical assumptions and research design, we will not evaluate the research cited. Note, however, that assumptions re anomie, its existence, its perception by affected individuals, its relationship to social class and to cultural elements structured the nature and design of the research involved.

Exploring this subject further, Tumin and Collins, using the Srole scale, found that "In general, the higher the status, the lower the anomie; the lower the anomie, the higher the readiness for desegregation . . . 'it is position in the social structure of either type of community, rather than urban or rural residents, that is most likely to be associated with differences on anomia.'"[22]

From our research perspective, it is clear that the Merton model as well as other cited studies operationalize the definition of anomie in terms of perceptions of basic qualities of the human condition. They likewise assume that behavior is rational and that individual behavior can be best understood in terms of a means-end scheme. The research models examined assume that if anomie exists, it exists as a quality that can be perceived by actors in the culture and that these factors are structurally related. This assumption is most clear in studies that hypothesize that if a lack of institutionalized means to the achievement of institutionalized goals is a factor related to the perception of anomie, then a greater amount of anomie would be perceived by the lower classes or the working classes than in the upper or middle classes. Therefore, studies designed to test this hypothesis are based upon these previously delineated assumptions. Given the definition of anomie and the nature of the structural functionalist approach, the assumptions involved in the theoretical model underlying the concept of anomie have clearly made impositions on research models of this particular type.

Both symbolic interaction and structural functionalism provide research models or, perhaps more appropriately, impose themselves upon research models with specific regard to the assumptions they make about human behavior. Both, however, clearly focus on understanding why people behave (act) the way they do and, at least in some instances, on predicting certain kinds of behavior. In the case of research geared to the amelioration of a particular aspect of the human condition or to controlling behavior that is culturally defined as dangerous, destructive, or even inappropriate, the importance of prediction is clear. That these are value judgments and potentially dangerous is also clear. However, it must be discussed which types of research are most appropriate for the study of particular types of behavior. This should not be interpreted to mean that one can alter the assumptive base of research by changing research techniques and theoretical models without carefully noting the importance of these changes and recognizing that structural functionalism and symbolic interactionism are at opposite ends of the continuum. One must understand quite clearly where the locus of meaning is before it can be researched. It is either embedded in the very act of interaction itself and agreement between actors, or it is external to actors, related to them only with regard to the socialization process and the resultant programming of individuals with regard to requisites of the culture itself.

NOTES

1. Alvin W. Gouldner, "Reciprocity in Autonomy in Functional Theory," in Llewellyn Gross, ed., *Symposium on Sociological theory* (Evanston, Ill.: Harper and Row, 1959), p. 249.

2. Carl G. Hempel, "The Logic of Functional Analysis," in Gross, ed., op. cit., p. 278.

3. Charles P. Loomis and Zora K. Loomis, *Modern Social Theories* (Princeton, N.J.: D. Van Nostrand Co., 1961), p. xxxiii.

4. This is repetition of an idea that can be found in the "social consciousness" concept of both Comte and St. Simon. It has antecedents in Weberian theory in that Weber stressed the importance of the transmutation of power into authority which comes about as the result of the acceptance of the legitimacy of power.

5. This is the view that states that man has no choice in behavior and does not act of his own volition. His behavior is "determined" by the social system.

6. Max Black, et al, *Social Theories of Talcott Parsons, A Critical Examination* (Englewood Cliffs, N.J.: Prentice-Hall, 1961), p. 20.

7. Instrumental activities are directed toward the attainment of a specific goal, making a profit, or providing a service. Instrumental activities are contrasted to expressive activities, which are organized for the pleasurable or cathetic experience provided. This dichotomy is not mutually exclusive, either instrumental or expressive, but rather goals of system organization are usually structured around one or the other. A manufacturing corporation would be an example of instrumentally organized goals, and a dance club could be considered an example of the expressive. The distinction is analytical, and in the real world, most organizations have elements of each and are not "pure types" of one or the other.

8. Recently, Parsons has added another pattern variable: "long vs. short run focus on valuation." He has made no attempt to make use of this additional variable.

9. Talcott Parsons, Edward Shils, Kaspar D. Naegele, and Jesse R. Pitts, *Theories of Society: Foundations of Modern Sociological Theory*, (Glencoe, Ill.: Free Press, 1961), p. 34.

10. Robert K. Merton, *Social Theory and Social Structure* (Toronto: Collier-Macmillan, Canada Limited, 1968), pp. 185-214.

11. Ibid., p. 186.

12. Ibid.

13. Robert K. Merton, "Social Problems and Sociological Theory." In Robert K. Merton and Robert A. Nisbit, eds., *Contemporary Social Problems* (New York: Harcourt, Brace, Jovanovich, 1971), pp. 723-24.

14. Ibid., p. 189.

15. Ibid., p. 190.
16. Ibid., p. 191.
17. Ibid., p. 193.
18. Ibid.
19. Ibid., p. 138-39.
20. Leo Srole, "Social Integration and Certain Correlaries: An Exploratory Study," *American Sociological Review* 21 (December 1956): 709-16.
21. Doriby Meia and Wendel Bell, "Anomia and Differential Access to the Achievement of Life's Goals," *American Sociological Review* 24 (April 1959): 189-208.
22. Melvin M. Tumin and Ray C. Collins, Jr., "Status, Mobility, and Anomie: A Study in Readiness for Desegregation," *British Journal of Sociology* 10 (September 1959): 253-67.

4

Synthesis of Theory, Design, and Problem

One of the most difficult areas for the beginning researcher is the selection of the research problem. This is not true, however, in the case of the individual who must answer a particular question or evaluate a particular program. The difficulty in selecting the research problem is compounded by the lack of clearcut examples in the literature of research containing sufficient description and detail on problem formulation. Unfortunately, while some sources broach the subject, most fail to describe the process and steps whereby a problem is selected. This literature gives lists of steps to be followed in the problem selection process, but characteristically does not state the intellectual sorting out processes or define the steps that pertain. The following material addresses these problems.

RESEARCH, ORIENTATIONS, AND PURPOSES

The preceding chapters on the major assumptions and variables of symbolic interaction and structural functionalism were intended to delineate the basis for theoretically based research. Most research done in the academic community consists of testing or generating hypotheses under alternative conditions or samples, expanding theory by testing logically derived hypotheses or attempting to predict or explain social phenomena with alternative theories. Some settings and disciplines are more germane to research than others. In the behavioral sciences, sociology is probably more committed to research than its counterparts. It is also true that research in the university setting is ordinarily more theoretical than that found in the nonacademic setting. Research specifically designed to ameliorate a particular social problem is most frequently associated with private foundation support.[1] The focus of such research is pragmatic, geared to furthering specific ends, not to advancing the theory, methods, or techniques of any particular discipline. The type of research which business and industry typically refer to as "basic research" is frequently similar to that associated with the academic setting. Its purpose is to advance the theory and the state of the discipline.

In short, there are many reasons for engaging in research. Both applied and more theoretically oriented research have a place in the realm of social science for both can contribute to the development of the discipline. Of the two types of research, however, it is frequently easier to develop and specify problems that are institutionally defined as social issues or conditions. Theoretical studies frequently pose greater problems with regard to both generation and specification. Even so, some difficulties in initiating research studies are common to both. Choice of research area should not depend on the supposed ease of one method over another. The distinction commonly made between "hard methods-heavily statistical" and "soft methods-no statistics" is largely nonexistent with regard to difficulty of accomplishment. These titles are given on the basis of the collection techniques, not on the degree of difficulty encountered in bringing a research project to fruition. In fact, it can be argued that there are elements of each in most research studies and that the division exists in the misunderstanding of those who reify one technique or the other.

PROBLEM SELECTION

As stated, one of the most difficult areas for the beginning researcher to master is the "statement of the problem." Part of the difficulty arises out of the vocabulary that pertains. It might be more accurate to use phrases such as "area of study," "focus of research," "goals," or "objectives" which would be more descriptive of the process that actually occurs rather than what is currently used in the literature. For clarity, this text will continue to use the traditionalized phrase "statement of the problem" while recognizing its limitations. Occasionally the terms "objectives" or "purpose" are used to inquire into the basic thrust of a piece of research. Such terms are synonymous with the "statement of problem" and may help the researcher eliminate repetition in writing.

AREAS OF DIFFICULTY

One of the four following areas usually presents difficulties in developing a well-stated problem:

(1) *Difficulties in linking a problem to a theoretical orientation* or underpinning. At whatever level this problem exists, it frequently results from the individual researcher's ambiguity and uncertainty. It is a problem solved by both experience and the development of expertise. The researcher is faced with a variety of choices in selecting a fit between theoretical orientation and the problem statement. The following example addresses this difficulty. The author Scott McNall emphasizes that functionalism focuses on those mechanisms that integrate and hold society together. He specifies that conflict theorists are as their name implies—those who see conflict as the inevitable result of structured relationships between individuals and who define this conflict as necessary for change to occur. He adds that symbolic interactionists emphasize meaning and shared symbolic communication, and tend to focus on those elements bearing on the maintenance of self-image.

> An example of empirical behavior may make this clearer. Take the phenomenon of the urban neighborhood tavern. People come there to drink alcoholic beverages. Why? A functionalist would begin by asking: "What is the function of the neighborhood bar?" He would probably be interested in finding out why the people come and how the bar serves to integrate their lives. The bar might be a means for lonely people to meet; it could serve as an "extended primary group." This same person would also want to investigate the social function of alcohol, e.g., Does it have a therapeutic function? Does the act of drinking actually serve as a safety valve for potential psychotics? *etc.* A conflict theorist, on the other, can start with the question: "What conflict does this bar represent?" He can go on to ask questions such as: "Does the drinking pattern of specific individuals lead to a conflict with other roles, such as employment or marital life? Is the bar itself a source of conflict in the community because of loud music . . .? A symbolic interactionist would probably want to look at the act of drinking itself and the means by which the various drinkers identify themselves and make contact with one another, e.g., the symbol world of the tavern. His questions could be: "How do the regulars identify a newcomer? What is the etiquette of drinking in a neighborhood tavern as opposed to that in a night club? How do people meet one another in a bar? How are pickups made? What are the different kinds of drinkers?" Each of these perspectives, then, can lead to ask different questions, all of which may be equally important. This is the importance of perspective.[2]

In this example, each time a question was posed it constituted a problem presented within a particular theoretical framework. Therefore, substantive areas can change. Research questions, however, remain essentially the same. For example, an examination of religion within the functionalist framework would raise essentially the same questions while changing the focus; "What is the function of the neighborhood church?" "Why do people attend church?" "How does the church serve to integrate their lives?" "Is the church a place for lonely people to meet?" "Does the church serve as an extended primary group"? The same paraphrasing of research questions could be extended to the conflict orientations as well as to symbolic interactionism.

The examples demonstrate the way in which theory relates to the problem area, gives definition to it, and outlines the major variables and concepts relevant to that perspective. Other problems can evolve from pragmatic problem orientations where the research effort is not focused on testing theory. Perceiving and interpreting in sociological terms is a matter of interest, preference, and training. Commitment to a particular theoretical orientation tends to structure the way in which one sees the world and makes sense of the meanings and interactions that make up the fabric of the human experience.

(2) *Specific errors in the statement of the problem* frequently trouble researchers; as a result, the remaining development of the research process becomes difficult, if not impossible. Errors such as too broad or too narrow a problem specification are frequently encountered. Problem statements that are too broad in specification are almost impossible to test. For example: "This research will focus on the relationship of alcohol to crime." Such a broad specification (or lack of it) makes it almost impossible to bring the problem to test. The basic terms require definition and specification sufficient to allow for test as well as eventual replication. In this regard, the review of literature in the area is of particular importance. It not only serves to ground a research project in theory, but it also roots it in the time sequence of historical process and the development of the relevant discipline. Basic operational and "use" definitions find their justification in the relevant literature surrounding a research problem. Research that is so grounded is an element of incremental growth in a discipline. In addition, such grounding helps preclude research aimed at reinforcing a preconceived idea or relationship.

In the example, the problem of "too broad specification" was related to operationally measuring variables to bring the problem to test. How can alcohol be operationally defined? As is the case with "crime," alcohol defies definition and will continue to do so until the "statement of problem" is made in such a way that the variables can be operationally defined. The "statement of problem" (which defines and relates relevant selected variables) has implications for the sample and analysis alike.

In McNall's discussion of the neighborhood tavern, he asked, "What is the function of the neighborhood bar?" But he further specified it to include the patrons' perception of its importance. This focus was repeated in the example dealing with the function of the church. In both instances, the questions asked were capable of being refined and tested.

Similarly, research questions that are too narrow in specification generate a number of difficulties. Consider, for example, the problem statement "The problem will be to examine the characteristics and sources of information of 'secondary tellers' in the diffusion of information on a major urban university campus." After the topic was selected, the researchers found that there were so few "secondary tellers" as to make analysis impossible. At first glance the problem appeared to be reasonable. It proposed to examine the characteristics of "secondary tellers" in the diffusion of the information process on a college campus. On the surface it was a testable problem, logically set within the theoretical framework of communications, including such identifiable concepts as "secondary tellers" and information diffusion. In this case, however, a pilot study could have prevented one's attempting a project that by its very nature could not be done.

Problem specification should not be too broad or narrow so as to interfere with the research process.

(3) *Problems lacking testability* are often formulated on the assumption that they can be brought to test. There are a number of reasons why problems cannot be brought to test. Among the more important of these is the inability to operationalize or specify a real world measure of the relevant concepts. A list of typical problems in rendering proposals incapable of being tested would include the following:

(a) *Too abstract a statement of problem.* Classic among the works suggested as being too abstract to test is that of Parsons in his theory of social action.[3] Parsons' work on social stratification did not correspond closely with then contemporary views and conceptions of stratification. Therefore, many had difficulty incorporating his concepts and social action theory into then existing methods and theoretical models. Some of Parsons' theories have been operationalized and successfully tested, but the majority of his work remains outside of empirical verification.

(b) *Indeterminate statement of problem.* Problems should be linked to theory and be capable of being tested in the real world. Most theory, while seeming abstract, is in reality grounded in phenomena. When the deductive specifications of problems are considered, one should be able to specify relationships between concepts and the directions of relationships between the concepts.

In a theoretically grounded problem, one would not state that religiosity will be related to "selected" variables. The theory would help to specify which other concepts religiosity would be associated with and would give some indication of the direction (or it would have to be deduced) for the problem to be tested.

(c) *Inability to operationalize concepts into measurable variables.* Often one has difficulty measuring concepts either because they are not clear or because no valid and reliable measure has been developed. The first problem relates to difficulties in attempting to bring about innovative and radical change. These same difficulties exist in science in general and sociology specifically. If one is to state as a problem that A is positively related to B, it will be necessary first to convincingly argue that these two concepts actually exist. After demonstrating their existence, it may then be possible to find or devise some manner of measuring them. (Recall the problem of establishing the existence of "anomie" as defined by Merton.)

(d) *Accessibility of data to test the problem.* It is often possible to develop a problem statement, only to find that data to test the problem are not available. One may wish to test whether welfare recipients have more of a "now" orientation (i.e., are geared more toward immediate gratification than to deferment) than the working poor. Obviously, data are available to bring this problem to test, but are the data available within the bounds of a reasonable expenditure of time and money? Can these data be obtained from the welfare records? Are sources of data consistent in content over time? Are such sources reliable in content to the extent that scientific conclusions can be drawn from their comparisons? Such questions must be raised in the process of deciding whether or not a problem, once formulated, can be tested.

While these problems of specification do not exhaust all possibilities, they are among the most common experienced by researchers at all levels, but especially by students. One of the best ways to approach a research problem is to read the literature in the area and to try to relate current interests to existing theory or models of research. The behavioral scientist is fortunate in that he lives in his laboratory and both observes and experiences the very subject of research interests. In this sense, the subject of research is the very stuff of reality. Hence, the researcher's awareness and theoretical commitments structure not only the research act itself but his perception of reality and the possible research problems therein.

PROBLEM-SOLVING RESEARCH

Much of the previous discussion has focused on the testing of hypotheses and the resulting implications for the theory underpinning the research. In evaluation research, however, the kind of program involved or the problem approached defines the population to be sampled and the relationship to existent theory (defined in terms of research traditions). The theoretical framework is still a matter of choice or commitment, however. Such studies can and do employ various types of samples and research techniques. The common thread through these studies is that most are of limited value in testing theory or advancing scientific knowledge. Such research is done for a number of reasons.

Evaluation research is most often at a lower level of abstraction and has as its purpose limited goals. In addition, its level of interest is usually limited to individuals concerned with a highly specific area. The emphasis is on problem solution and not on scientific generalization. Such specific researches differ from research that approaches a social problem (defined normatively) from an evaluation perspective. Such studies frequently have interest for a wide audience as well as being capable of modifying theory or generating new research questions. In *Tally's Corner*, Elliot Liebow never formally states his problem, this is, labeling it as such. The reader must sort out his intentions from a number of statements in the introduction. His opening statement is: "Problems faced by and generated by low-income urban populations in general and low-income urban Negroes in particular have become one of the chief concerns of the nation."[4] Having defined his task as one of national concern, he states: "At the purely practical level, the lower class Negro man is neglected from a research point of view simply because he is more difficult to reach than women, youths, and children."[5] At this point, he has said nothing about theory. He discusses the dearth of literature available on the Negro male, particularly on the lower-class life-style of the Negro male, and defines his task as that of ethnographically describing basic elements in the life-style of this large segment of American society. He comes close to a statement of problem in the following: "The present study is an attempt to meet the need for recording and interpreting lower-class life of ordinary people, on their grounds and on their terms."[6]

The opening statement thus gives a generalized statement of relevance; a justification on a practical level; and a statement of *how* the study is to be done ("recording and interpreting") which imposes structure on the data to be collected. In addition, the author pinpoints the *who* (the focus of the study being the "lower class life of ordinary people"), which has implications for the sample, and the *where* ("on their grounds and in their terms"). A comment on analysis adds further to understanding: "Since the data do not have 'sense' built into them—that is, they were not collected to test specific hypotheses nor with any firm presumptions of relevance—the present analysis is an attempt to make sense of them after the fact."[7] The reader has now been informed as to the nature of the analysis. It is to be an after the fact attempt to make sense of the data after they have been collected. Further, the author informs us that he intends to impose some structure on the data so that his work can be cast into a comparative framework and be extended into existing theory, models, and present knowledge. He states: "Still another advantage derives from this kind of framework. By organizing the materials around roles and relationships commonly recognized elsewhere in our society, the product should lend itself to direct comparison with similar models drawn from middle-class behavior or from other segments of the lower class."[8]

Problem formulation can be descriptive and can cover a number of pages, but an excellent study will contain a clearcut statement. Liebow, it is to be noted, focuses on the very difficulties we have listed as common to early research efforts. There is no problem in linking with a theory to be tested since none has been specified. Liebow's theoretical assumptions are symbolic interactionist in character. His problem is neither too broadly nor too narrowly stated. It does not lack testability in that it is neither too abstract nor indeterminate. Liebow made clear his intention to use an ex post factum design to analyze the data after they were collected, and before his study began, that he had the ability to gain access to the data needed.

Liebow's study specification is presented here to illustrate that a sound research design can be developed without a concise one- or two-sentence statement of the problem. Such statements, however, are inevitably made at one point or the other in the presentation of the work. Liebow's study is a classic in contemporary sociological literature. It has been included because its data collection techniques were based on observation field techniques. What follows is the description of a research project approached from a structural functionalist perspective.

COMMUNITY POWER STRUCTURE

An older study, a classic in the area of community power studies, is Floyd Hunter's *Community Power Structure.*[9] Although it has a different focus, research design, and unit of analysis, and is fifteen years older than the Liebow study, they are comparable since both focus on a community. Liebow focuses on the community of relationships and affectual feelings of black men and uses Tally's Corner as a base of operations, as well as the source of a primary group and place in which to establish an identity. Hunter, on the other hand, studies community as an ecological variable tied to a governmental structure, called a city, of approximately 500,000. The following contrasts Hunter's problem specification with Liebow's.

Hunter recognizes that important community concerns frequently appear suddenly and are acted upon by officials without proper information or knowledge of the citizenry. He views such actions as foreign to the basic tenets of democracy as espoused in the United States. In his words;

> With these thoughts in mind, I have studied power leadership patterns in a city of half a million population, which I choose to call the Regional City. If this study of leadership and power relations can help to clarify the fact that one may find out who our leaders are and something of how they operate in relation to each other, the present task will have been accomplished.[10]

Hunter defines his study in terms of community power and leadership, and how leaders operate in relation to each other. In that sense, his work is similar to Liebow's. Both saw an area of need and set as their task a study to improve knowledge and understanding in the area. Hunter, however, goes on to establish his theoretical orientation prior to the study:

> The difference between the leaders and other men lies in the fact that social groupings have apparently given definite social functions over to certain persons and not to others. The functions suggested are those related to power.
>
> Throughout this discussion, I shall be using the concept of community as a frame of reference for an analysis of power relations.[11]

The study's frame of reference is clear, as is the relevant concept of community. The focus is on the functions of those to whom social groupings have allocated social power. Hunter tells us the *who* (leaders in the community), *how* (an analysis of power relations), *where* (Regional City), and, by dating his work, the *when* of his study. Implicitly, he alludes to the *why* in his early discussion of an elitist distribution of social power and its exercise within a community.

Both studies do pre-present their statement of the problem but do not do so in the precise terms of a one- or two-statement example found in many texts. In each case, the problem statement had to be isolated and then reduced for the purposes of illustration. This is often the case in research presentations.

Since his work is both descriptive and exploratory, Liebow states that his data do not have "sense built into them—that is, they were not collected to test specific hypothesis nor with any firm presumptions of relevance—the present analysis is an attempt to make sense of them after the fact."[12]

Here Hunter differs markedly from Liebow in that he discusses the several aspects of community power and concludes by stating his research plan, including analysis, before actually performing the research task and reporting results.

> One other set of abstractions must be given before arriving at a more concrete description of Regional City and its system of power relations. These abstractions relate to the postulates and hypotheses of the study, and they are comprehensive of the several aspects of power already suggested. Drawn from readings relating to power relationships and from observations of power personnel extending over several years, the postulates and hypotheses to follow are put forward to guide the study of community power structure. The postulates are these:
>
> *POSTULATES ON POWER STRUCTURE*
>
> 1. Power involves relationships between individuals and groups, both controlled and controlling.

Corollary 1. Because power involves such relationships, it can be described structurally.

2. Power is structured socially, in the United States, into a dual relationship between governmental and economic authorities on national, state, and local levels.

   Corollary 1. Both types of authorities may have functional, social, and institutional power units subsidiary to them.

3. Power is a relatively constant factor in social relationships with policies as variables.

   Corollary 1. Wealth, social status, and prestige are factors in the "power constant."

   Corollary 2. Variation in the strength between power units or a shift in policy within one of these units, affects the whole power structure.

4. Power of the individual must be structured into associational, clique or institutional patterns to be effective.

   Corollary 1. The community provides a microcosm of organized power relations in which individuals exercise the maximum effective influence.

   Corollary 2. Representative democracy offers the greatest possibility of assuring the individual a voice in policy determination and extension.[13]

The postulates are treated as if self-evident propositions. During the field investigation, they formed a mental backdrop, an abstract frame of reference. The second portion of this frame of reference is contained in the hypotheses[14] presented below. It can be seen that an elaborate set of postulates[15] and corollaries has been presented and is identified as being "drawn from readings and from observations of power personnel." The relationship between theory, design, and problem is therefore brought together in this example. There is, however, more to bring together before laying Hunter aside. As has been said, the second portion of Hunter's frame of reference is contained in his hypotheses. They are few and are stated as follows:

HYPOTHESES ON POWER STRUCTURE

1. Power is exercised as a necessary function in social relationships.

2. The exercise of power is limited and directed by the formulation and extension of social policy within a framework of socially sanctioned authority.

3. In a given power unit (organization), a smaller number of individuals will be found formulating and extending policy than those exercising power.

   Corollary 1. All policy makers are "men of power."

   Corollary 2. All "men of power" are not, per se, policy makers.[16]

Here at last is a full-blown integration of theory, problem, and design. To be sure, it is more elaborate than Liebow's, but that follows since they are studies of a different type and were chosen for inclusion because of these differences. However, Liebow's theory, problem, and design are equally well stated. He presents what he is going to do, how he is going to do it, and, by implication, the theoretical assumption underlying his design and approach. While not as wordy as Hunter (there wasn't as much to describe), Liebow presents an excellent problem statement, though of a different order.

Hunter's work differs from Liebow's in one important aspect. In his appendix, he reports doing a pilot study, prior to data collection in Regional City, in which he tested field questionnaires and methods. In that section, he describes his methods: "The methods utilized in studying community power structure fall into three categories: (1) theoretical analysis prior to field investigation; (2) field investigation; and (3) an integration of field findings and social theory."[17] Clearly, Hunter felt he had engaged in all three areas and had attempted to integrate them into one study.

Both works are excellent and both have their shortcomings, but both are worth reading for their methodology alone. It is all too easy to get caught up in the street life of Tally's Corner or the elites in Regional City and forget about the excellent methodological examples in both of these pioneering works.

THE ROLE OF THEORY

The role of theory in integrating research designs has been well specified by Robert K. Merton. His works on the bearing of theory on research and the bearing of research on theory are well known and often quoted.[18] Merton states that many efforts in the name of theory are not theory at all, but really constitute (1) methodology; (2) general sociological orientations; (3) analyses of sociological concepts; (4) post factum sociological interpretations; (5) empirical generalizations in sociology; and (6) sociological theory.[19] To be sure, theory is not devoid of these six aspects. The point is that sociological theory should rest on and pursue so-called scientific laws. Hence, theory goes beyond the mere analysis of concepts, although it may begin there.

Indeed, some believe that the statement of two concepts with a linking or relationship term is the smallest reducible unit constituting a theory. For example, the statement "social cohesion is positively related to group size" has two concepts: cohesion and group size. Such a statement can, in Merton's terms, be (1) an analysis of sociological concepts if it is not linked to theory; (2) an empirical generalization if it is devoid of theory or cannot be linked to theory; (3) the result of a post factum interpretation; or (4) a proposition in sociological theory. Theory serves to locate the place of the statement since the essence of the statement is not self-evident. The important thing is not the proposition but what use is made of it. Merton refers to this by stating that theoretical pertinence occurs when the generalization is raised to a higher order of abstraction and relationship in theory.

Empirical generalizations are propositions or statements of relationships between concepts for which no theoretical home has been established. The statement that "as urbanization and city size increases, the percentage female population increases" is an empirical generalization. It can be tested empirically, and all of the sophistication of scientific research can be utilized to develop the research design, but it will remain an empirical generalization until such time as we can establish the theoretical pertinence of such a proposition. Can this generalization be linked to others and form an interrelated set of propositions such as those presented in Chapter 1? At the present time, they cannot. Hence, the fact that there is a proposition from which can be derived hypotheses and that these hypotheses have been brought to test does not necessarily mean that any theory has been tested. Theory should help to:

1. integrate propositions into meaningful frameworks,
2. serve as the higher level abstraction from which propositions are logically derived,
3. set the limits of which concepts are relevant to theory,
4. specify sufficiently abstract propositions that are devoid of substantive necessity, and
5. assist the sociologist in making predictions based on logically derived hypotheses, at least on a probability basis.

To conclude, a researcher must be an "open individual" receptive to alternatives and prepared to change positions when the data indicate that reevaluation and change are in order.

SUMMARY

This chapter is devoted to the importance of theory in the development of any research project. All too frequently the literature suggests how to test hypotheses and develop research designs (as well as compute statistics) in the evaluation process, and yet does not relate to the essence of scientific inquiry.

Research problems can be so tied to a particular pragmatic purpose that they have little or no relevance to theory. Nonetheless, essentially the same process of developing designs, data collection techniques, analysis techniques, and reporting formats pertain. All studies have the theoretical base of the assumptions underlying the framework of the researcher.

For any level of research, theoretical relevance is sought. For this reason, it is always good practice to do a complete review of the literature examining the development of relevant theory, concepts, variables, and analysis of both past and present.

NOTES

1. This does not preclude its being done under the quasi-sponsorship of a university.
2. Scott G. McNall, *The Sociological Experience* (Boston: Little, Brown and Co., 1969), p. 10.
3. Talcott Parsons, *The Structure of Social Action* (New York: McGraw-Hill Book Co., 1937).
4. Elliot Liebow, *Tally's Corner* (Boston: Little, Brown and Co., 1967), p. 3.
5. Ibid., p. 7.
6. Ibid., p. 10.
7. Ibid., p. 12.
8. Ibid., p. 14.
9. Floyd Hunter, *Community Power Structure, A Study of Decision Makers* (Garden City, N.Y.: Anchor Books and Doubleday and Co., 1963).
10. Ibid., p. 1.
11. Ibid., p. 2.
12. Liebow, op. cit., p. 12.
13. Hunter, op. cit., pp. 5-6.
14. Ibid., p. 6.
15. A postulate is defined as a logical statement of how the units or subjects in a system will behave or act, while a corollary is defined as a deduction or something that follows sequentially.
16. Hunter, op. cit., pp. 6-7.
17. Ibid., p. 255.
18. Robert K. Merton, *Social Theory and Social Structure* (New York: Free Press, 1968, revised edition).
19. Ibid., p. 120.

5

Formulating Hypotheses

Formulating hypotheses is one of the major steps in the scientific process. The hypothesis is so important that some have called it the essential unit or building block from which more sophisticated and complicated analysis evolves.[1] Considering its importance, one would expect consensus on its definition. Unfortunately, that is not the case. The term may mean different things to different authors. For example, Stephens uses the following definition: "All attempts to describe reality in words we shall call 'hypotheses.' Thus, what others have termed in other context, 'descriptions,' 'facts,' 'laws,' 'propositions,' also 'guesses,' 'hunches,' and 'speculations:' all such statements will here bear the common rubric 'hypothesis'."[2] Others define the term even more broadly. In her work *Reasoning and Research*, Thelma F. Batten states: "I use the terms 'hypothesis,' 'theory,' 'explanation,' and 'as if model' (or just 'model') interchangeably."[3] Be aware, therefore, that the term *hypothesis* may mean different things when used by different authors or found in different contexts.

It should be obvious that defining the hypothesis as the building block or the essential unit in the scientific process is a more specific use of the term than defining it to include explanation, models, and theory. For the purposes of this work, a hypothesis is defined as a tentative statement of the relationship between two concepts expressed as a probable statement of supposed fact. It is capable of being tested and verified by the data gathered to test it. This definition allows for modification of the hypothesis when data consistently fail to support the specified relationship between concepts.

Goode and Hatt state that facts are empirically verifiable observations, while theories link facts into a logically related set of relationships.[4] The origin of these concepts and their linking theories is at this time unspecified. As the following action shows, however, there are several types of hypotheses stated at varying degrees of abstraction and evolved from radically different sources. Later in this chapter, the hypotheses are related to the level of abstraction.

TYPES OF HYPOTHESES AND LEVELS OF ABSTRACTION

The example presented begins at a high level of abstraction and in reductive technique moves to lower levels of abstraction. The first hypothesis to be examined is the general hypothesis. Hypotheses elsewhere referred to as analytical, theoretical, or abstract are called general hypotheses (GH) here. This is the highest level of abstraction or is a statement generalized to apply to the largest number of widest possible explanation schemes. The next level lower in abstraction is the operational hypothesis (OH). The operational hypothesis is a functional step in the process of moving from the general hypothesis or abstract concepts to what exists in the measurable world. For example, is social class a concept or an operational measure? It could be either depending on how it is used. Above all, social class is an abstraction or a designation based on previously determined characteristics. Perhaps social class can be described in terms of definitional statements. For example as indicators of social class we use one's occupation, educational attainment, source of income, dwelling area, and house type.[5] If such characteristics are going to constitute the measure of social class, however, it must be recognized that they measure social class only because they have been so designated. The description of how the concept is to be measured is called the operational measure. When specified and used to measure social class, it could be argued that it measures social class, not social status. However, the reader knows what operational measures have been used in the research. The step of operationally defining concepts and phrasing an operational hypothesis is discussed after an examination of the null hypothesis.

Null Hypothesis

Further reduction of the hypothesis leads us to the null hypothesis (symbolized as Ho), or more properly the test of an hypothesis under conditions that state that there is no relationship or association between operational variables. The following example illustrates the "null" concept.

The null principle is based on the premise that it is impossible to prove a case by examining every possible case in the universe, but where closed logical deductive systems are found (geometry, for example) finding exceptions to a stated proposition would invalidate that proposition. Forget for a moment the subjectiveness of beauty and imagine that someone has declared an object to be the most beautiful of its kind in the world. In addition, imagine that there are quite a number of these objects in existence, and therefore, the one in question is not unique. If the original statement was true, each time another of these objects was found and compared to the original object, it could be concluded that the original object, was, indeed, the most beautiful in existence. The key to understanding this somewhat simplified example is comparison. It is comparison that validates our statement and elevates it above the level of feeling.

If another object was found to be more beautiful by standards of comparison, then the original claim would have been invalidated. Because of the nature of the original statement, a single exception invalidates the claim. In theory, the same principle applies to the null test: if we find a single exception, we must reject the null hypothesis as not being valid.[6] Before discussing the null hypothesis further, let us compare the same concept and relationship expressed as a "general" or "operational" and a "null" hypothesis.

HYPOTHESIS REDUCTIONISM

As a statement of the general hypothesis, consider that there is a relationship between the concepts of role strain and organizational complexity.

GH Role strain will be related to the degree of organizational complexity.

OH Job-related tension (measured by the JRT index) will be related to the type of organizational characteristics.

Ho There will be no relationship between JRT and organizational structure.[7]

It appears that the null hypothesis is exactly the opposite of the general hypothesis. As discussed earlier, disproving a statement of no association between concepts or items is a stronger statement than the simple affirmation of the same relationship since it is not possible to sample every type of organization. Examining a sample of persons from various types of organizations with differing degrees of organizational complexity should allow the test of the general hypothesis. If no significant relationship between job-related tension and organization complexity is found, then the null hypothesis of no relationship should be accepted. A relationship was postulated, but none was found to exist.

If the general hypothesis had been derived from theory, the rejection of this hypothesis would call into question the theory from which the relationship and concepts were deduced. An outright refutation of the underpinning theory would not be justified since there has been only one test of it. Research must be carefully evaluated in terms of its sample, measurement, statistical tests, and the like before the theory is rejected outright.

THE WORKING HYPOTHESIS

It is generally agreed that a hypothesis can come from any number of sources. Theory testing is just one of those sources: "Regardless of the sources of a hypothesis, it performs an important function within a study: It serves as a guide to (1) the kind of data that must be collected in order to answer the research question and (2) the way in which they (data) can be organized most efficiently in the analysis."[8]

A working hypothesis is made to be modified or changed relative to findings when it is tested. It differs from the general hypothesis only in terms of the researcher's statement that it is a working hypothesis and as such stems from a hunch or a desire to bring previously unrelated concepts together to determine if relationships exist. It may also be derived from ideas drawn from other research studies. The working hypothesis, while not testing a specific element of theory, can still serve as a guide to the kind of data needed and as an orderly way of structuring and ordering data.

The working hypothesis has limitations. First, the researcher should be aware of the relative cost factor versus the possible payoffs involved in terms of contributions to theory and to the literature. Second, there is no assurance that the results will hold in another study. Even should they hold, the result would simply be another one of Merton's "empirical generalizations." A study based on a working hypothesis that stops at reporting results may prove to be interesting and provocative, and may lead to other research. Until these results are integrated into a body of theory, the results and working hypotheses will remain empirical generalizations and of limited or no use to the discipline.

THE SUBHYPOTHESIS

A general hypothesis will often require a number of subhypotheses to bring a stated relationship to test. The earlier cited general hypothesis on job-related tension may help illustrate the point.

GH Role strain will be related to the degree of organizational complexity.

OH Job-related tension (measured by the JRT index) will be related to the type of organizational characteristics.

Note that the measure (operationalized) of job-related tension has been given, but the organizational measure has not been so specified. In addition, the problem is too broadly defined. To reduce the problem to a measurable one and still test the relationship between role strain and job-related tension, it was necessary to specify an area of interest. Role strain or job-related tension among nurses was not the only area or work group, respectively, that could be tested. At the time of the study, the researchers had an interest in and access to a sample of nurses from a number of hospitals in the city. Given the interest and access to the data source, the problem was formulated and was to be tested in the local hospitals. The problem was therefore reduced to a test of job related tension among nurses based on the organizational complexity of the hospitals in which they worked. Since no single measure of organizational complexity existed, researchers had to use a number of operational measures of complexity such as size of the hospital based on the number of beds, type of ownership (whether the hospital was public or private, denominational or nondenominational), whether it was a teaching hospital with an intern program, a diploma or degree nursing program, or had no nurses' training at all.

All of these measures of organizational complexity were selected from the literature as factors related to job-related tension for nurses. Since all were part of the literature and all logically can be considered facets of organizational complexity, each could logically be tested by a subhypothesis (SH). At this point, logic demands the introduction of the concept of dependent and independent variables. In our example, the researchers were trying to explain and/or predict job-related tension based on a number of independent variables. The operationalization of organizational complexity based on availability of data resulted in the specification of a number of independent variables to test against the dependent variable. Prior to examining other independent variables, consider the logic of the following diagram:

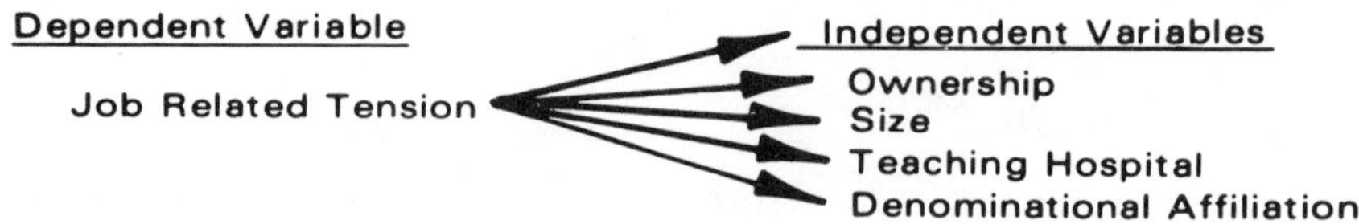

If the GH is a logical deduction from theory and if organizational complexity is (at least in part) measured by these variables, then each should be related in the same direction and significance test outcome. Hence, the hypothesis development would appear as follows. (The example skips the conceptual presentation of the subhypotheses and moves immediately to the operational subhypotheses.)

GH 1 JRT will be related to the degree of organizational complexity.
SH 1 JRT will be higher in private than in public hospitals.
SH 2 JRT will be higher in large (over 200-bed) hospitals than in smaller ones.
SH 3 JRT will be higher in teaching than in nonteaching hospitals.
SH 4 JRT will be higher in denominational than in nondenominational hospitals.

The problems of testing hypotheses using a number of subhypotheses are considered in Chapter 19. For the moment, the development of hypotheses in the single variable relationship is considered. Each of the four subhypotheses above would require a null hypothesis and a statistical measure. In the subhypotheses, the direction of the expected outcome has been predicted. It was predicted that JRT would be higher in private, large, teaching, and denominational hospitals. These specifications were not simply guesses but were based on relevant literature. A study by Snoek concludes that organizational complexity is related to job-related tension. His conclusions are based partly on the fact that larger, more complex organizations require daily associates to come from a wide range of complementary roles. Put another way, the more people the individual associates with in a work-a-day routine, the more likely he or she is to encounter individuals who hold conflicting or differing values and role expectations.[9] Snoek refers to this phenomenon as a problem of normative integration of the role set. Hence, role diversification would be expected to be higher in larger, more complex organizations. As a result, one could expect role strain and, subsequently, job-related tension to be higher in such circumstances.[10]

There are other dimensions of role strain and job-related tension; these are introduced into the study by additional hypotheses. Snoek's study also found that the degree of tension was not all explained by role diversification. He found that supervisors tended to reflect more job-related tension than nonsupervisors, regardless of the size of the organization.[11] A further finding indicates that role strain was more prevalent among the college educated, which may be a reflection of ambition or success motivation, but that the college educated also were more likely to have supervisory responsibility.[12]

Another study, one by Indik, Seashore, and Slesinger, examines the following demographic correlates of psychological strain: age, sex, and education. The job-related tension index was administered as part of a battery of tests. The authors concluded that job-related tension was higher among the young and males, but they discerned no relationship with educational attainment.[13] On the basis of these studies, two more subhypotheses can be developed to test in the study of nurses. The first is related to occupation:

GH 2 Role strain is related to occupational type.
SH 5 Supervisory nurses will report significantly higher role strain than will nonsupervisory nurses.
SH 6 Full-time nurses will report significantly higher role strain than will parttime nurses.

Both supervisory status and whether the nurse worked less than full time were operationally measured as reflecting occupational type associations. Snoek made the case for higher role strain among supervisors, and the less than full-time employment was deduced as a test based on the lesser amount of time the nurses would interact as a part of their total experience. Furthermore, parttime workers often work for specific purposes—a new car, furniture, children's college education, and the like. As a result, they may have lowered commitments to the profession, or they probably would be working full time if they did not have other commitments or demands on their time.

The last area to be examined was related to demographic characteristics and role strain. Hence, the third general hypothesis was stated as:

GH 3 Role strain is related to demographic characteristics.
SH 7 Younger nurses will report significantly higher role strain than will older nurses.
SH 8 College-educated nurses will report significantly higher role strain than will the hospital-educated (diploma) nurses.

The example has moved through the process of developing a set of hypotheses to be tested in a study. The logic of the study was displayed to show the grounds for each general hypothesis and how each was justified on the basis of higher level concepts such as organizational type, occupational type, and demographic characteristics. None of these concepts explicitly stated exactly what must constitute the operational variable measuring each of these concepts. The operational measures and variables were, in part, based on the fact that data were available to bring each to test. Obviously, each of the eight subhypotheses would have to go through the null hypothesis principle when subjected to statistical test.

As stated in the discussion of the null hypothesis, this process may be implicit and may not be formally written or expressed. Because of space limitations, null hypotheses are seldom presented in journal articles or research reports. The process of presenting general or conceptual, operational, and null hypotheses has been relegated to the thesis or dissertation and is rapidly disappearing from published works. An understanding of this process in turn aids an understanding of the entire process of hypothesis development and testing.

CRITERIA FOR JUDGING TESTABLE HYPOTHESES

Just as problem statements, designs, analysis modes, and samples must be examined for relevance and utility for the intended use, so must hypotheses be examined. A series of areas to be checked for hypothesis relevance was developed some years ago by Goode and Hatt. Their outline follows:

1. The hypotheses should be conceptually clear.
2. Hypotheses should have empirical referents.
3. The hypotheses must be specific.
4. Hypotheses should be related to available technique.
5. The hypothesis should be related to a body of theory.[14]

A sixth could be added:

6. Hypotheses should, when possible, relate behavioral concepts.

1. *Conceptually clear.* Because of the difference in existing concepts, definitions, and the like, it is best to operationally define concepts early in the research process and to determine which definitions are generally accepted in the literature. The beginning researcher may well be advised to use concept definitions commonly accepted in the literature of the discipline. In this way, the work can be compared with relevant work done in the field and related to existing theory. Obviously, this suggestion does not hold for those advanced in the field who are capable of developing new measures and tests of perceived relationships relevant to the advancement of theory.

2. *Empirical referents.* The need for empirical referents has been discussed elsewhere. Concepts remain sterile until they can be tested. Goode and Hatt[15] discuss the necessity of avoiding moral judgments in hypotheses such as good, bad, ought, no worse, and should. While these judgments cannot be operationalized since they are value judgments and are therefore incapable of verification, a concept can be impossible to measure operationally simply because it has not been defined properly. The existence of a concept also must pass the test of intrasubjective testability. Would a

number of disinterested observers see and agree that a concept exists in reality? It must exist in reality to be used as a concept in an hypothesis.

3. *Must be specific.* The researcher should be clear and specific in all phases of research, including hypothesis formulation. In the interest of being clear and specific, as well as making statements more amenable to test, it is best that single concepts be related to or contrasted with other single concepts. Stephens gives a good example of a sentence that is short but actually contains eight hypotheses: "Women, as compared to men, are more active in church, but less active in politics; mature earlier, live longer, drive fewer miles, and have fewer accidents; threaten suicide more often, but actually commit suicide less often."[16] It appears that it is much more meaningful to test all of the elements in the conglomerate as individual hypotheses than to test them all as stated in a single hypothesis.

4. *Available measurement techniques.* Early in the research process it is important to be certain that relevant hypotheses can be brought to test. If, for example, the researcher cannot find a measurement technique that is applicable to a particular problem, perhaps efforts should first be directed towards developing a measure before proceeding with the research project. The researcher must be knowledgeable in an area before engaging in research in it. For this reason, every research project should begin with a complete review of the literature, and it should be kept in mind that the most recent work in an area is probably not yet in print. Publication preparation, evaluation, delays in journal selection and acceptance, and finally delays in an issue being published make data obsolete or dated when they first appear in print. National and regional meetings provide one of the more productive sources of current data. Correspondence with those known to be active in the field of study may also prove helpful.

5. *Hypotheses related to theory.* Comments made by Goode and Hatt relate principally to research done in the hypothesis testing of theory as a contribution to a body of knowledge. The fact that the working hypothesis is often devoid of a specific theoretical orientation or statement to test has been discussed; in that case, the hypothesis serves as a structuring and limiting guide to relevant variables and the stated relationships between them. The working hypothesis has been made with the idea in mind that it will be changed when data mandates such changes. A hypothesis should be related to a specific body of theory when possible, but it should not be discarded for structuring a research project in either exploratory or descriptive studies. The general theoretical underpinnings of such studies may be clear in the specific relationship to exploratory theory. Theory test, however, must await the test of hypothesis so generated. If an hypothesis can be used to structure a research design and bring some degree of order to an otherwise unrelated set of sense impressions, it should be so employed—providing Merton's cautions about advances in the social sciences are

heeded: "The growing contributions of sociological theory to its sister-disciplines lie more in the realm of general sociological orientations than in that of specific confirmed hypotheses."[17]

6. *Relating behavioral concepts.* Hypotheses often specify expected differences based on a single behavior concept or on one or more socio-demographic characteristics. While this type of hypothesis should not be completely denigrated, it should be noted that it rests more in the realm of the subhypothesis than general hypothesis. An example is job-related tension for nurses:

GH 1 Role strain will be related to the degree of organizational complexity.
GH 2 Role strain is related to occupational type.
GH 3 Role strain is related to demographic characteristics.

GH 1 is the most generic hypothesis of the three and represents a much broader set of options to bring to test under a much broader set of conditions. For example, the third GH has theoretically a much more limited set of variables to use in testing the hypothesis, and in addition, it relates a behavioral concept (role strain) to a nonbehavioral one (demographic characteristics). Therefore, the third GH is a lower order of generality and from our point of view should be relegated to the status of secondary level analysis (which is discussed in Chapter 19). When theory indicates that demographic characteristics are relevant and related to the dependent variable, the decision to designate the level of abstraction rests with the researcher. Clearly, not all hypotheses designated as general hypotheses are of the same level of abstraction.

HYPOTHESIS-GENERATING STUDIES

In many ways, all studies can be said to generate hypotheses. In the case of the research project that returns negative results and fails to reject a null hypothesis or fails to substantiate a general hypothesis, an alternate hypothesis is indicated. In fact, frequently it can be as profitable to know what does not work as what does. In the case of positive results, implications for further cumulative research invariably exist. The focus in this short discussion, however, is more on studies which generate hypotheses than test them. This generation may take the form of implications of relationships derived from investigation and description of a particular "life form" or relationship. In methodology, such studies are referred to as ethnography; in sociology, they are frequently called exploratory or descriptive studies, or in some instances, ethnomethodology. Whatever the label, the basic rules of scientific research apply, and specific methodologies exist geared to maintain the integrity of such efforts. Research of this type is no less systematic and certainly no easier to accomplish than any other type.

Many of the specific research techniques and relevant theoretical frameworks are discussed in the chapter on researching covert behavior (Chapter 14). Following are a short discussion and an example. Exploratory research can and often does generate statements about phenomena or about relationships between variables that have many of the characteristics of theory statements or proven hypothesis. Such statements frequently have a predictive ability and are capable of organizing perceived data into patterns describing an element of the social fabric. In order, they are frequently of the general hypothesis level of abstraction and as such require further specification so that they can be related to the general body of theory in a discipline. This is the purpose of testing a specific hypothesis derived from exploratory studies.

In passing, note that exploratory studies can be of any type and can therefore include field research techniques as well as the more traditional survey methods. In this sense, they highlight the distinction between research tools (methodologies—analytic techniques) and research (theory building—testing and predicting) with regard to the human experience. All too frequently this distinction is blurred.

Despite the enormous body of literature that exists in the behavioral sciences, many issues in the human experience remain unexplored. As the social and physical conditions of mankind change, as they incrementally do, new areas and foci of research emerge. For example, the invention and increasing use of the transistor has opened new vistas of research for those concerned with social change viewed as a function of the impact of technology on human relationships.

In Chapter 14 we describe the development of an exploratory research project that focused on the social career of the lesbian. As the research progressed, it became evident that lesbians existed in a "society within a society." The parameters of this society appeared to be bounded by areas of service offered the lesbian which were not available in the general culture, which rejects lesbianism as a viable sexual alternative and stigmatizes the lesbian identity. Further investigation gave strong indications that lesbians perceived this stigmatization and were aware that their life-style was determined by their sexual preferences and their concomitant involvement in a lesbian subculture.

Other models of subculture exist in the literature, but they have typically pertained to a specific subculture such as juvenile delinquents. Prominent among such theories is one that describes the development of a delinquent subculture based on stigmatization (status deprivation) and "reaction formation." In the research on lesbians, a similar process of formation was found, however without reliance on the "reaction formation" concept;

rather, it focused on stigmatization as perceived, and it predicted the formation, existence, and perpetuation of the subculture by the subculture itself. As a corollary, it discussed commitment to the subculture, the degree to which that subculture served to focus the life-style of those involved, and the expected length of membership as being related to the normative strength of the stigmatization and its degree of institutionalization.

Although the model has been simplified for illustrative purposes, it remains untested. It serves to point out that a testable hypothesis empirically grounded arose from an exploratory study designed to delineate the social career of the lesbian. Its tentative relationship to the theory of deviance was established not only by drawing out the logical extensions of the derived general hypothesis but also by the theoretical underpinnings of the exploratory research itself.

SUMMARY

In judging whether hypotheses are testable, a number of different areas must be considered. Researchers often attempt to make their hypotheses more complex in the mistaken belief that complexity guarantees sophistication. Where both the simple and the complex are available as options, parsimony mandates choice of the simplest form. In reaching for sophistication, many designs and hypotheses produce little of value either to the immediate needs of the research project or to the discipline as a whole. Later chapters on testing and generating hypotheses show that accomplished researchers frequently overlook this synthesizing process.

NOTES

1. William N. Stephens, *Hypotheses and Evidence* (New York: Thomas Y. Crowell Co., 1968), p. 1.
2. Ibid.
3. Thelma F. Batten, *Reasoning and Research: A Guide for Social Science Methods* (Boston: Little, Brown, and Co., 1971), p. 9.
4. William J. Goode and Paul K. Hatt, *Methods in Social Research* (New York: McGraw-Hill Book Co., 1952), p. 8.
5. W. Lloyd Warner developed the Index of Status Characteristics (ICS) using these five items. W. Lloyd Warner, Marchia Meeker, and Kenneth Ells, *Social Class in America* (Chicago: Science Research Associates, 1949), pp. 121-59.
6. There are various levels of permissible error in any design. Rejection of the null hypothesis on the basis of a single example represents an ideal rather than a practical standard.
7. The hypotheses were developed and tested in a project resulting in a Master's thesis by Roger L. Goodwin, "An Examination of Role Strain Among Hospital Nurses," M.A. thesis, Wichita State University, 1970.

8. Claire Selltiz et al., *Research Methods in Social Relations* (New York: Holt, Rinehart and Winston, 1976).

9. Diedrick J. Snoek, ''Role Strain in Diversified Role Sets,'' *American Journal of Sociology* 71 (January 1966): 364.

10. Ibid.

11. Ibid., p. 370.

12. Ibid.

13. Bernard Indik, Stanley E. Seashore, and Jonathan Slesinger, ''Demographic Correlates of Psychological Strain,'' *Journal of Abnormal and Social Psychology* 69 (July 1964): 26-38.

14. Goode and Hatt, op. cit., pp. 68-73.

15. Ibid., p. 68.

16. Stephens, op. cit., p. 1.

17. Robert K. Merton, *Social Theory and Social Structure*, (Toronto, Ontario: Collier-Macmillan, Canada Limited, 1968), p. 142.

6

Research Designs

Research designs must be developed with regard for the nature of the problem to be studied. There are three generally recognized types of research designs: exploratory, descriptive, and analytical and/or comparative.[1] Regardless of the type of design chosen, the principles of proper methods and accepted research practices should pertain. Earlier, it was suggested that researchers frequently rush to collect data before they have completed the necessary preliminary stages of research. This is a poor practice for a number of reasons, some of which are listed below.

1. Research of this type is usually limited in hypothesis testing.[2]
2. Sampling procedures are frequently lost, forgotten, or nonexistent.
3. The practice leads to limited generalization or prevents it completely.
4. Data collected with no theoretical or specific intention in mind often defy interpretation.

5. Theoretical concerns have been completely neglected in collecting these data, and the resulting work has little or no relationship to the field as a whole.
6. Taking data (i.e., secondary data) and trying to force them into an appropriate framework often result in tautological reasoning. Often the tendency is to try to force the data into some framework to overcome difficulties of "now I have a lot of data, what do I do with it."

It is not suggested that the researcher ignore data that are already at hand. On the contrary, they should be used, but the researcher must be aware of their limitations and the process by which they were collected. If research is being done on responses to natural disasters, the researcher must be willing to go to the site of such disasters since they cannot be planned. The same can be said for research on prison riots and other events that occur spontaneously. The inability to control when and where an event will occur does not preclude researchers having a prestructured design allowing for the comparison of a number of these events.

Time spent in planning for anticipated difficulties, with alternate strategies to respond to unanticipated events, is time well spent prior to beginning the data collection process. Of course, few studies can be designed with total control and with no deviation from or adjustments to the original design. Unlike the laboratory researchers, the sociologist cannot control the total environment and all factors that may affect the project.

TYPE OF DESIGNS

Those considering a research project frequently ask which research design is best. Logically, the question should be, "Which is the most appropriate design for my particular problem?" The research design that will fulfill desired objectives is the best design. A number of alternatives are always available in terms of the total overall research design, and even more options become available as one evaluates the total research process and chooses appropriate samples, instruments, data collection methods, and mode of analysis. It is always preferable to have a well-designed, tightly knit project rather than an a priori preference for any one type design. Perhaps an example of the thought processes and choices going into design selection will aid in explanations.

Several years ago, researchers were asked to design a project which would evaluate a major nationally federated voluntary organization promoting increased use of milk and milk products. First, they were faced with the choice of theoretical orientation. (Actually, the problem already existed and the research was funded and commissioned by the organization studied.) Second, they wanted to address the problem in a way that would be of general sociological interest while at the same time serve the needs of the sponsoring organization. A number of options were available to them, and it was their responsibility to set the research problem logically within the interaction and behavior assessed by the chosen theory. They believed they had the following options:

1. structural functionalism
2. symbolic interaction
3. organizational theory (formal organizations)
4. collective behavior
5. role theory
6. systems analysis
7. theory of social action
8. voluntary associations
9. conflict theory
10. exchange theory
11. communications

Although the list appeared to be complete, it was not. Additional theories could have been considered. The orientation chosen was only one of many such theoretical choices available in selecting and developing the design. In the list above, numbers one and two are generic categories under which all of the other theoretical categories could have been subsumed. In committing themselves to a theoretical perspective, the researchers limited available options. In other words, theory defines the limits of what can be studied within a chosen research framework. If symbolic interaction had been selected, the researchers would have set limits on their unit of analysis[3] inasmuch as they would have collected information from individuals relative to symbolic meanings and would have attempted to see if others in the group understood and shared the meanings. In addition, they would have attempted to determine if these shared values were reflected in behavior. They would therefore have structured to a degree (1) the appropriate unit of analysis, which in turn would have been considered in (2) how the data were to be collected, i.e., through observation, interview, or both. (3) The sampling procedure would also have been structured, which in turn would have had implications for (4) the mode of analysis. All of these must have been consistent with testing the originally selected problem.

As the project discussed above shows, any project is developed within the framework of a number of alternatives. By choosing a communications framework to orient and implement the design, the areas of behavior mechanism were initiated and were clearly the focus of the research. Other areas of activity such as market research, new product development, and test marketing of new products were outside the scope of the project, but how the results of activities were brought to the attention of the membership was within the design consideration. The development of aerosol-powered cans of cheese spread was not within the major focus of the design, but how the national level of the organization brought the development of a new product to the membership and the general public obviously would be within the area of communications. Such distinctions are a part of all research projects. The theoretical orientation helps to specify which areas are relevant and which are not.

Exploratory Designs

Many researchers assign more importance to exploratory designs than to other types. An "aura" of glamor seems to surround the word "exploratory"; it smacks of excitement, pioneering, and delving into the unknown. Exploratory research is best employed in the investigation of problems where measurement techniques are not explicit or where no precedents exist, and where information that would ordinarily aid in the specification of a theoretical framework is not available. Lastrucci sums up the exploratory design:

> The main purpose of an exploratory study is an examination of a given field in order to ascertain the most fruitful avenues of research. The study may, for example, simply attempt to ascertain the kind (variety) and number (quantity) of elements present in the field of inquiry. It may, on the other hand seek tentative answers to general questions in order to suggest fruitful hypotheses for research. Or it may investigate the practicability of various techniques to be employed in a given set of study circumstances. In any event, its main emphasis is upon discovery of problems, of subjects, of techniques, or of areas for more intensive study; and its major attributes are adaptability and flexibility—i.e., it is designed purposely to permit examination of various alternative views of the phenomena under consideration.[4]

Within this framework, it can be seen that the term *exploratory research* is frequently used when the researcher is on a "fishing expedition." Consequently, with little or no structure, some research is undertaken and is forgiven its inadequacy by virtue of its being an "exploratory study." The exploratory study has its place in science, and its utilization is not an excuse to be lax relative to structure and design. "A good exploratory study should not, however, be designed as a sort of catch-all of research problems. The principles of parsimony should always be kept in mind. It is much more fruitful to limit the initial exploration to the major problems or research."[5]

An exploratory study, then, examines new areas of inquiry, including new or previously unintegrated social phenomena as well as techniques of data collection or measurement. The design should be employed in areas in which theory is lacking or disputed (mixed results), or when concepts, variables, measurement instruments, and techniques are poorly defined. The design should not be used when theory, methods, and procedures are well established in an area and available in the literature. A discipline develops through building on work already completed.

The working hypothesis is frequently used in exploratory designs. However, it is used as a guide to structure research designs, and it is intended to be modified as the research process unfolds, perhaps suggesting an alternative hypothesis.

In short, the exploratory design is typically undertaken when the problems approached are heretofore unstructured or poorly defined. Such a design assumes that concepts and relationships between variables have not been established or tied to existing theory. Its strengths lie in the fact that the design is free to follow the sense of the problem rather than being constricted by a rigid design. It should break ground and examine tools and techniques to be used in later, more extensive projects.

Descriptive Designs and Exploratory Research

A descriptive study logically contributes to the development of a scientific discipline at lower levels of analysis and abstraction. From a scientific point of view, an item must be described before it can be classified. Classification of concepts and variables begins measurement and later makes possible analytical and comparative studies.[6] Description, therefore, plays a large part in exploratory studies.

When engaged in exploratory studies, it is important to sufficiently describe relevant interactions, conditions of occurrence, and the units (persons, groups, etc.) involved in maintaining the integrity of all things described. Lastrucci, in describing the descriptive study, says: "The descriptive study basically tries to answer the question of who, what, when, where, or how much; and its essential function is largely reportorial."[7]

Hence, the emphasis in the descriptive study is on reporting the events examined as accurately as possible, without regard for how the units might be tied together or what relationship they might have to each other. For example, Malinowski observed and described Trobriand Islander fishing practices. It was only after he described the practices both in the open sea and in the lagoon that he became aware that magic and potions were used under conditions of uncertainty or in the open sea. When fishing in the lagoon or in waters known to them, they did not need to resort to other than their skill and knowledge of the area.[8] The lesson is that the description of the same activity, fishing, under two differing sets of circumstances led to a higher level analysis, namely, that lack of knowledge or uncertainty may result in seeking additional advantages through appeal to, or appeasement, of unknown forces. This last statement is analytical, which leads into the next section.

Descriptive studies are limited to the accurate description of the circumstances, situations, events, persons involved, interactions, and so forth, without necessarily trying to relate the events or interpret them. Babbie gives the following definition of a descriptive study:

> The United States Census is an excellent example of a descriptive social scientific research project. The goal of the census is to describe, accurately and precisely, a wide variety of characteristics of the United States population, as well as the populations of smaller areas such as states and counties. Other examples of descriptive studies are the computation of age-sex profiles of population done by demographers and computation of crime rates of different cities.[9]

Some researchers would not agree that the U.S. Census is an excellent example of a descriptive study, viewing it as demography and devoid of interaction. The Census simply presents characteristics of individuals based on geographical boundaries or sociodemographic characteristics such as age, sex, race, education, residence, and marital status. Babbie's comments are cited as an example of a descriptive study because the Census is well known and because in general it does not contain analytic or comparative associations.[10]

Descriptive studies are undertaken in the course of investigating a phenomenon, an event, or an interaction in which no known theory exists. Description, then, is the first logical step toward future studies of greater abstraction.

Finally, participant observation as a research technique should not be excluded as a descriptive study method. Many studies done in this mode have become important. Most early community studies such as Lynd's Middletown studies, Hollingshead's *Elmtown's Youth*, and more recently, Gan's *The Levittowners* and *The Urban Villagers* are all descriptive studies (discussed more completely in Chapter 14).

Assumptions underlying descriptive research are:

1. No definitive work exists in the area.
2. Further description and understanding in the area are needed.
3. Descriptions logically precede classification, relationships, prediction, and explanation in the scientific method; hence, description is a necessary and logical first step in any science.

Analytical Designs

The analytical design is based on the assumption that enough is presently known in an area of interest to designate theory, concepts, hypotheses, variables, and data collection techniques, and to begin addressing questions of association or causality. An analytical design ordinarily involves hypothesis testing (prediction) or attempts to establish causality by the use of probability statistics (explanation).

Analytical design does not usually involve new techniques of data collection or measurement. A common statement is, "We were able to explain 36 percent of the variance between the variables." This is really a way of saying that the investigators knew enough about a particular association of variables so as to be able to designate variables as dependent or independent and to analyze the degree of association between them. While most persons interested in research have learned not to assume that a causal relationship has been established by computing a statistically significant[11] correlation between two variables, the fact is that the correlation technique is based on establishing causal relationships between variables. This is so despite disclaimers by many social scientists![12]

The analytical design, then, is the most complex of the three major design types because it requires a priori designation of concepts and relationships, and because it usually posits direction in the form of a hypothesis which would specify the expected relationship between variables.

In summary, the well-designed project results from thinking through the research plan and anticipating alternate strategies in the event that unforeseen events require modification of the original research design. The research project development can be seen as a process of involving a number of specific tasks. Although there is no universal agreement as to exactly which tasks are required, most researchers would agree that all research requires some structure. The literature is replete with different lists of research designs; they may be subsumed under three types—the exploratory, descriptive, and analytical. Other techniques, often designated as research designs, are principally methods of data collection. The experimental, interview, case history, survey, historical, and comparative methods are just that: methods of data collection. There is no reason why any of these methods cannot be used within any of the three major design types, nor is there any reason why combinations should not be used (in fact they usually are) in the same design. For example, a later chapter (Chapter 14) examines surveys using the interview, questionnaire, and statistical methods, which are comparative in nature.

STUDY DESIGNS OR DATA COLLECTION FORMATS

At this point, it should be clear that it is best to use the best possible tools to improve research designs and studies in the social sciences. Disagreements exist, as evidenced by Lastrucci's statement about designs and methods. However, the student should be helped to understand methods.

The following presentation on study designs is intended for that purpose, not to continue the disagreement.

Lastrucci notes that:

> A study has as its purpose either a description or an analysis of phenomena, or both; but it may employ any number of techniques to achieve its ends: statistics, questionnaires, case histories, interviews, etc. . . . The use of any particular technique does not by itself determine whether the data derived there from will be either descriptive or analytical or both—only the employment of those data can determine their character.[13]

Methods of data collection must be presented and justified in light of the intentions and scope of the project. For example, a random sample for a project cannot be collected if the parameters of the research universe are not known. Sampling format and data collection techniques must match the total design and the purpose of the project. Thus, the essence of design is not in the data collection process. The following section helps elucidate the requisite time frames and the populations involved in various data collection models.[14]

The Experimental Model

Logically, exploratory and descriptive designs should precede the presentation of analytical designs. Analytical designs attempt to move toward either prediction or explanation, or both, and do so in a causal framework where possible. Moving toward causal analysis requires some form of control over the conditions under which data are collected. The best means of exerting some control over data collection in the social sciences is to use the "classical experimental model." The experimental design is based on both analytical and comparative analysis, a control, and on doing something to the experimental group that is not done to the control group. A graph may make this clearer. (See p. 85.)

1. Cell *A* subjects (respondents) should be similar (not significantly different) to cell *C* subjects on the criterion variable.
2. The assumption is made that because of an intervention, manipulation, or treatment, the experimental group will not score the same at T_2 as they did at T_1 if the intervention has had any effect.
3. Control group respondents (cell *B*) at T_2 will no longer be equal to experimental group respondents in cell *D* if there has been any effect as a result of the intervention.
4. There may or may not have been any change in the control group between T_1 and T_2. If any change is noted, it is because of extraneous factors, not the intervention, because the control group has not experienced it.

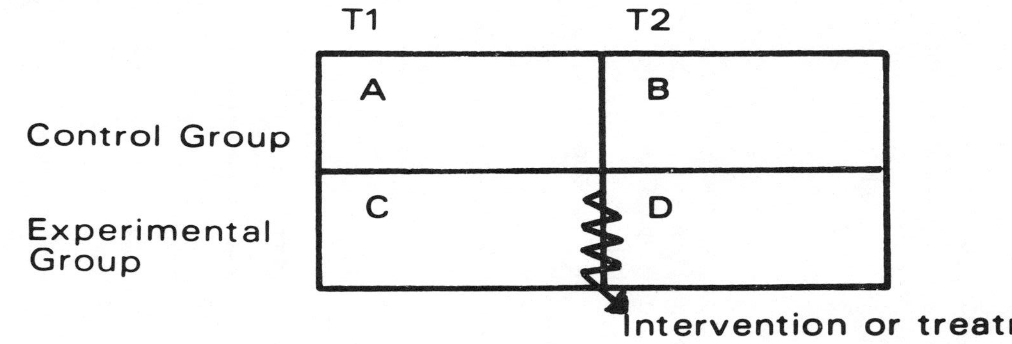

For ease of discussion, the blocks will be referred to as cells and give the assumptions:

1. $A = C$
2. $C \neq D$
3. $B \neq D$
4. $A \not\approx B$

T1 =time 1 (Pre)

T2 =time 2 (Post)

Experimental Design Model

The research design in which the experimental model is used could be exploratory, descriptive, or analytical, but it is most likely to be analytical. Any number of experimental groups would then be compared to the control group and to each other to determine which intervention has the greatest effect. Use of the experimental model has implications for the type sample to be used (usually random) and for the measurement (in this case, only one variable will be used to see if there are differences between the control group and the experimental group). This is called the "criterion variable" in sociological studies of this type. There are limitations on the data collection instrument. It would most likely not be a questionnaire, but it might be a scale. The important point is that the criterion variable is the only one used in this model. Other models to be presented are adaptations and/or the best possible attempts at collecting data with the highest degree of control possible. It will become evident that some models frequently lack controls completely.

The Longitudinal Model

For a number of reasons longitudinal studies are not commonly done in social sciences. This is perhaps explained by the problems that are unique to this particular approach. For example, it is difficult to keep track of respondents over long periods of time. In addition, little if any control can be exerted over the various experiences each original respondent has had between the T_1 and T_2 data collection periods. Moreover, circumstances that originally led to inclusion of a respondent at T_1 may have changed to the degree that he should no longer be included as a respondent at T_2.

The model is graphically shown as:

	T1	T2
Group 1		

Longitudinal Model

The major question addressed in this model is: has there been significant change in a criterion or designated variables between T_1 and T_2? Additional time periods (T_3, T_4, etc.) can be added to increase the number of times data are collected from the same original sample. Many variables are processual, but for the most part, it is difficult to measure process. Researchers typically measure a variable at one point in time and try to assume logically what has happened prior to the measure rather than empirically select those factors in the respondents' background related to their position at the present time. The longitudinal model attempts, in a small measure, to overcome these difficulties. It allows for some control or specification of events between T_1 and T_2, but it is not without problems of its own. Socialization, institutionalization, and boundary maintanence are all examples of processes in sociology. If socialization were to be measured today, again in five years, and a third time in ten years, could the understanding of the process be improved along a number of dimensions, i.e., increasing ability to handle complex materials or sensory data? Over a period of time the quality of the data could be improved. Consider a longitudinal study covering an eighteen-year period. Data were collected from all seniors graduating from an Iowa high school in 1948. The students were contacted and interviewed again in 1956 and for a third time in 1967. Without going into too much detail, their occupational, educational, and migration plans and aspirations were measured in 1948; by 1967, an excellent opportunity arose allowing the examination of the factors associated with those who had been successful in achieving their 1948 desires. In addition, it was possible to ascertain how their aspirations for their children compared with their own some eighteen or nineteen years earlier. Of 157 seniors interviewed in 1948, the investigators were able to locate and interview 150 in 1956 and 140 in 1967. This study demonstrates that it is possible to follow a sample and interview sufficiently large numbers of them, even over a long period of time.[15]

With regard to longitudinal design problems, a minimal time limit has been set between T_1 and T_2 because not all problems require the same amount of time between data collection periods. Studies in which less than one year elapses between data collection phases should not be considered longitudinal studies. Those with five years or less between T_1 and T_2 should also be seriously examined before being defined as longitudinal studies. Clearly, the time lapse required between data collection phases of a study is one of the major reasons that such studies are seldom undertaken.

Quasi-longitudinal Model

An alternative to the longitudinal model is the quasi-longitudinal model. It has special uses because it is not a true longitudinal model in that two different groups are employed: the longitudinal and cross-sectional models. It is often used in replication studies. The cells are graphically presented as follows:

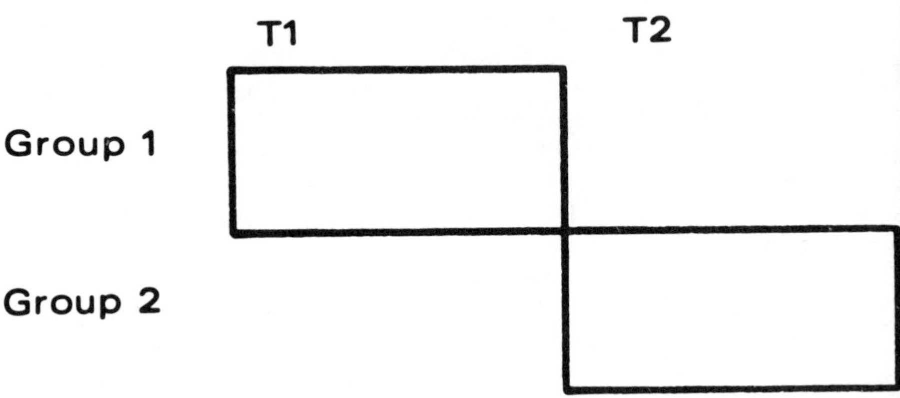

Quasi-Longitudinal Model

For example, consider a researcher who wishes to examine college female expectations from marriage for two generations. Obviously, those who have responded to questions about expectations in 1950 (T_1) cannot also respond in 1975 (T_2). Hence, two groups exist, assumed to be comparable in the sense that all were in college when they responded (some in 1950, Group 1, and others in 1975, Group 2) to questions about expectations in marriage, or age at marriage, desire to work, number of children, if any desired, and so forth. At the very least, the two groups should be equated on all demographic variables. The model is valid and has its use, but it is neither a true longitudinal model nor a true cross-sectional design. Its most serious fault is that it erroneously assumes that cultures and social-psychological milieus remain constant over time. In the example, the world in which the college women were socialized in 1950 was vastly different from that in 1975. However, the design does have the advantage of providing data that could not be obtained in any other design. It can be considered a special purpose design.

The Cross-sectional Model

Probably one of the most popular models for data collection is the cross-sectional one. It consists of two cells, one above the other as shown on p. 89.

Two groups deemed to be comparable are selected on the basis of some variable, and data are collected at essentially one point in time. Studies examining what differences, if any, exist between such groups as blacks and

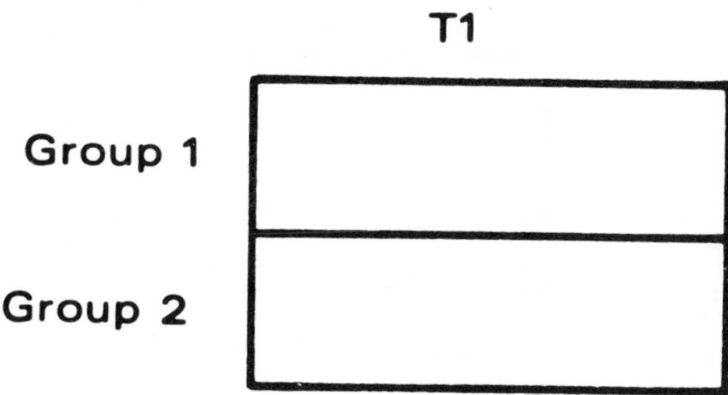

Cross Section Model

whites, males and females, the young and the aged, city dwellers and rural dwellers, are of this type. The variable(s) can be about anything a researcher wants to measure—significant differences between blacks and whites in their self-concepts, differences between males and females in grade point averages in college, attitudes toward increased social services between the young and the aged, or feelings about personal freedom between rural and urban residents.

While the model is essentially comparable, it can also be correlative within groups. For example, is the relationship between authoritarianism and income the same for blacks and whites? In this test, a statistic (correlation)[16] would be run between the two variables for each group and the resulting coefficients examined. Furthermore, the comparative nature of the examination can be reduced to sublevel analysis by comparing for differences in each variable between blacks and whites. In the first, the researcher wishes to see what relationship exists between two variables; in a second, he or she may want to test to determine if there are significant differences in income (one variable) between races.

Finally, the model can be enlarged by adding a third or fourth group, but the time frame would remain the same on T_1 only.

The Survey or Single Cell Model

Most survey researchers collect data from some type of randomly selected group or respondents (sample) at essentially a single point in time—not necessarily simultaneously, but at essentially the same time. It is not uncommon for a survey team to collect data in the field for three or four weeks or longer. This can still be regarded as T_1 in the cell illustrations. At the same time, care should be taken to avoid extended periods of time in data collection. In such cases, an implicit assumption exists that the social milieu has been the same for all persons responding to the survey. In fact, increased time frames extend the possibilities of extraneous influence affecting the results. Graphically, the model would be only one cell. (See p. 90.)

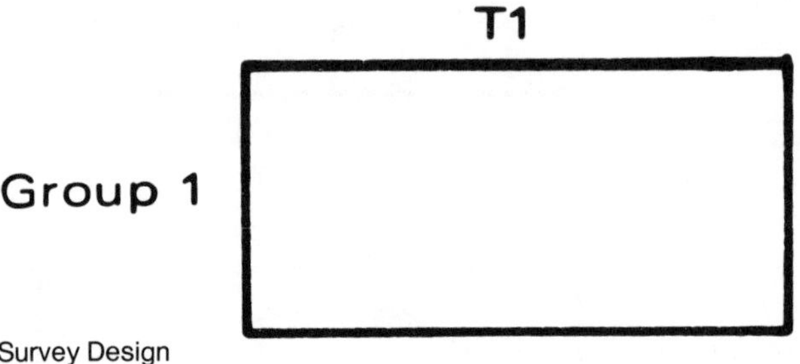

Survey Design

DISCUSSION OF DATA COLLECTION MODELS

None of the data collection models presented here is bound to any data collection technique. That is, the researcher can employ observation, questionnaires, or combinations of techniques to collect data for any of the models presented. The discussion above has not been exhaustive of all possible data collection models. Some researchers have attempted to develop quasi-experimental models where data were missing for a cell. Such a model would be graphically shown as follows:

	T1	T2
Control Group	A	B
Experimental Group 2	C	D

Quasi-Experimental Design

Data are collected for cells *A* and *B* for Group 1, and cell *D* for Group 2. The assumption is that if data were collected for cell *C* at T_1, there would have been no difference in the criterion variable between Groups 1 and 2. This model represents a "best attempt" to exert some control over the data rather than resort to the cross-sectional model.[17] Under normal conditions, data for cell *A* would of necessity already have been collected, recorded, and available since a researcher would not use this model when an experimental model might as easily be developed. The experimental model would be preferable, but in some ways the quasi-experimental model is superior to the cross-sectional model.

Research design, be it exploratory, descriptive, or analytical, is independent of the data collection method employed. Methods of data analysis likewise are independent of both research design and the data collection model. Parts of the research process must logically fit together into a meaningful whole consistent with the problem to be tested. Yet, each part has an integrity of its own. Utilization of one technique in one part does not necessarily mandate the use of other techniques for other elements in the total research process.

SECONDARY DATA ANALYSIS

The terms *dependent variable* and *criterion variable* have been used in the discussion of problem formulation, hypothesis derivation, and research designs, as well as data collection models. The research design is ordinarily set up with a number of hypotheses to test, all of which are independent of the design. There is no "best" number of hypotheses to be tested in any one research project. The number may vary from one to as many as the researcher wants to test. Again, a theoretical hypothesis may have any number of operational hypotheses. In addition, the researcher may want to determine whether there are any differences in the variables based on some other measure, such as on sociodemographic characteristics. For example, after reviewing the literature, the researcher decides to test the hypothesis that "social class is related to attitudes about social service (welfare) programs." In fact, it has been hypothesized that social class membership will influence attitudes about welfare programs. Social class as well as social service attitudes, could be operationally defined. If Warner's Index of Status Characteristics (ISC)[18] is used to develop a Likert scale of social service attitudes (SSA), then the principal task is to test the relationship between scores on the ISC and SSA. This would test the general hypothesis, but how could existing differences based on race, sex, or education be approached? It would be necessary to examine these relationships. The hypothesis would now be presented as:

General hypothesis:	Social class is related to attitudes about social service programs.
Subhypothesis:	The relationship between social class and social service programs will be contingent on sociodemographic factors.

The test for the general hypothesis would be respondent scores on the ISC correlated with SSA scores, or ISC>SSA[19] The subhypothesis test would appear as one option:

Race	Black Respondent Sample	ISC>SSA
	White Respondent Sample	ISC>SSA
Sex	Male Respondent Sample	ISC>SSA
	Female Respondent Sample	ISC>SSA

Education	High school or less Respondents	ISC>SSA
	More than high school Respondents	ISC>SSA

The decision to test the subhypothesis brings up a number of major questions. First, justification for testing for differences between race, sex, and education has been assumed, but what can be said after correlations have been run between the major variables, social class and attitudes toward social services?

If the results indicate a relationship between social class and attitudes toward service programs, the hypothesis has been suggested. If no relationship is found, the hypothesis that such a relationship exists must be rejected. There may well exist a negative but significant correlation between the two variables of social class and attitude, which in turn would indicate a significant relationship, although not in the predicted direction. What would have been added by a secondary analysis of the demographic variables? What about the subhypothesis? After running the same test used for the general hypothesis but dividing it into subsamples, a number of statements can be made about the problem based on results.

For example:

GH ISC SSA — Significantly related
SH ISC SSA — Sociodemographic characteristics

A. Race	Black not significantly related
	White significantly related
B. Sex	Males significantly related
	Females significantly related
C. Education	HS or less not significantly related
	HS or more significantly related

Thus, measures of the sociodemographic characteristics such as race, sex, and education existed. A difference was found between blacks and whites (one significant, one not), no difference was found based on sex (both significant), and some differences were found in education (one significant, one not). What would the conclusion be? No effect due to sociodemographic characteristics? Limited support for the subhypothesis? After all, four of the six statistical tests were significantly different. However, two of the three variables had mixed results—one subsample significant, one not. Which way would a researcher report the conclusions reached from these data? Some researchers would reject the subhypothesis based on mixed results for two of the three variables, race and education. Others would report limited support based on no difference in sex, limited support for race, and limited support for education. A conservative researcher would tend to reject or fail to support the subhypothesis based on these results.

Was the research example exploratory, descriptive, or analytical? It could have been any one of the three. The design included testing a hypothesis and required developing a Likert scale of social services attitudes. Therefore, the research could have been exploratory. Since this was also an attempt to examine and describe differences that may or may not have existed based on sociodemographic characteristics, the research could have been called descriptive as well. Since the design included analysis, both relational (association between variables) and comparative (differences based on race, sex, and education) dimensions, it could have been defined as analytical research.

What type of data collection model would have been required? In fact, it was a single cell model, a random sample with data collected at one point in time.

Consider Stouffer's words of twenty-five years ago:

> I do not intend to disparage all research not conforming to the canons of the controlled experiment. I think that we will see more of full experimental design in sociology and sociopsychology in the future than in the past. But I am well aware of the practical difficulties of its execution, and I know that there are numberless important situations in which it is not feasible at all. What I am arguing for is awareness of the limitations of a design in which crucial cells are missing . . . sometimes by forethought and patchwork we can get approximations that are useful if we are careful to avoid overinterpretation.[20]

SUMMARY

Any research effort requires thought and planning regarding choice of the research design, whether exploratory, descriptive, or analytical. After the design is selected, it is necessary to choose a data collection model consistent with the type of data needed to bring the problem to test. It is possible to involve the full range of analysis techniques available, as long as those selected are logically consistent with the type of data collected and with the test needed. The need is usually based on substantiation or rejection of the hypothesis.

Finally, extensive secondary data analysis is possible even in the simplest of research designs; the one-cell design is usually associated with survey research. The total research design, well developed and specified, can lead to advance in the field of sociology.

NOTES

1. Comparative designs are analytical, but not all analytical designs are comparative.
2. There are exceptions as evidenced in ex post factum research discussed by

Robert Merton in *Social Theory and Social Structure*, op. cit. (New York: Free Press, 1968).

3. The term *unit of analysis* denotes individuals, or groups, such as the family, friendship, and cliques, or larger groups such as organizations.

4. Carlo L. Lastrucci, *The Scientific Approach: Basic Principles of the Scientific Method* (Cambridge, Mass.: Schenkman Publishing Co., revised 1967), p. 105.

5. Ibid., p. 106.

6. The levels of measurement are nominal, ordinal, interval, and ratio. Early descriptive studies tend to rely on perception and description of behavior as a logical antecedent to later, more sophisticated and complex techniques of measurement. Hence, descriptive studies often contain nominal level measurement rather than ratio or interval measures.

7. Lastrucci, op. cit., p. 107.

8. B. Malinowski, *Coral Gardens and Their Magic* (New York: American Book Co., 1953).

9. Earl R. Babbie, *The Practice of Social Research* (Belmont, Calif.: Wadsworth Publishing Co., 1973), p. 51.

10. Although some of the census data are analyzed and comparisons made by the Bureau of the Census, Department of Commerce, none is made in the basic census PC Series.

11. See Chapter 17 for an explanation of "statistical significance."

12. However, correlative relationships do not establish a causal relationship between two variables.

13. Lastrucci, op. cit., p. 108.

14. Samuel A Stouffer, "Some Observations on Study Design," *American Journal of Sociology* 55 (January 1950): 345-59.

15. John J. Hartman, et al., "Relationship of Selected Socio-Demographic Characteristics and Parental Occupational Aspirations for Their Children." Journal Paper J. 5887, Iowa State University, Ames, Iowa, Project 1703, August 1968.

16. A correlative coefficient is a measure of existence, strength degree of, and direction of association and covariance. For example, if variable A is related-correlated with variable *B*, then when *A* goes up or increases so will *B*. If the correlational relationship is negative when *A* goes up, *B* will go down. The degree to which each variable rises or falls with regard to its counterpart is the strength of the correlation. Consider the correlation between *IQ* scores and school performance. They are positively correlated if school performance goes up when IQ scores go up. They are negatively correlated if IQ scores go up and school performance goes down. The relationship need not be perfect, however. Variables can be partially correlated.

17. If data had not been collected for cell C-T_1 and it was assumed that there would be no differences from A-T_1 and data were not collected for A-T_1, all that would remain would be T_2 and cells *B* and *D* which would be a straightforward cross-sectional model.

18. W. Lloyd Warner, Marchia Meeker, and Kenneth Ells, *Social Class in America* (Chicago: Science Research Associates, 1949).

19. The symbol $>$ most frequently used to designate "greater than" is used here to indicate a correlation relationship.

20. Stouffer, op. cit., p. 358.

7

Exploratory Research and Pilot Studies

In previous chapters, theory is defined as a set of interrelated propositions about human behavior having an explanatory power. Research is defined as being rooted in reality in the sense of being capable of being deduced from observation or verified empirically. In fact, the process of theory generation and verification is the subject of this book.

The propositions making up theory must be interrelated in the sense that the explanation of a particular relationship (i.e., crime to poverty) follows logically from the propositions. Theory may also be defined as an exploration of relationships existing between actors occurring in a time frame in a fabric of meanings, symbols, and interrelated interpretations. The more general the theory (the more abstract), the fewer such sets of interrelated propositions required to explain the greatest number of relationships.

These definitions of theory do not designate their origin, for they do not specifically state which theoretical base (assumption) has been used to derive a particular set of propositions about behavior. Theory can, therefore, be the result of deduction or induction. It can arise from what is essentially observation organized so that reporting guarantees the integrity of what has been observed. In addition, it can be derived from existing theory or highly generalized propositions such as "all men seek pleasure and avoid pain."

Regardless of how theory is defined, its elaboration and its final relevance depends upon verification. The first step in the process of this verification is the development of an organizational framework or a sequence of occurrences such as can be derived from exploratory research or pilot studies. The following examples consider exploratory research from the functionalist perspective.

AN INTERACTIONIST APPROACH

The study presented in this section focuses on the social career of the female homosexual. Although the study was ongoing over a long period of time, it was most instructive in its formulative stages. Not all exploratory or descriptive studies will include all the steps or problems encountered in the study below. All will, however, follow the same general logical pattern. The explicit delineation of the theoretical orientation and limitations is of particular interest.

The authors stated that the study was intended as primarily exploratory and descriptive. The exploratory aspect was mandated by the lack of realistic literature on the social and sexual career of the lesbian and by the fact that what literature existed disproportionately represented a psychiatric or medical view defining lesbianism as a perversion or a sickness. Considerable literature existed addressing male homosexuality, but it tended to approach homosexuality as a homogeneous phenomenon with both the male and female represented by the male example. It was felt that women in this culture were significantly different from men with regard to their unique and highly structured socialization, so as to call into question generalizations about women based on a male sample. The exploratory and descriptive nature of the study was also dictated by a purely technical consideration (discussed more completely in Chapter 14). It was not possible to estimate the parameters of the research universe; therefore, it was not possible to adequately define a population from which to draw a traditional type sample. Hence, it was not possible to satisfy any of the mathematical or methodological conditions that would allow the use of analytical techniques based upon parametric statistics.[1] Despite limitations on the powers of generalization inherent in the use of exploratory and descriptive research techniques, it was felt that the approach had strengths in that it allowed the combination of diverse data collection techniques such as field observation and questionnaires.

THEORETICAL FRAMEWORK

Even with the clear differences between interactionism and functionalism, the research literature of sociology contains few, if any, pure representatives of each type. This was true of this work as well. It is difficult to conceive of research that will not contain assumptions or references to concepts or elements properly associated with the structural functionalist terminology. And, too, it is often difficult to express anything about frames of interaction without lapsing into this terminology. It was also clear that the assumptions that the researcher makes about human behavior in terms of its etiology provide the framework within which such behavior is investigated and that therefore, the theoretical underpinnings of any research project carry with it impositions upon the research act itself. It is impossible to avoid a point of view as to the basic dimensions of human behavior in any research project. The researchers involved are in a better position to analyze data with minimal bias if they recognize biases inherent in the theoretical posture.

Given the exploratory nature of this study, it was decided that symbolic interactionism was the least biased or the least prejudiced mechanism for coming to grips with the real world of the lesbian. In addition, it has a history of use in sociology in the study of behavior as it occurs in natural settings. Finally, it suited our individual preferences in that it is a step away from the increasing quantification of sociology as a discipline. All too frequently, researchers in sociology today confuse tools with methodology and theory.

The interactionist perspective is discussed in a previous chapter, and so it will not be defined at length here. Recall, however, that it assumes that people act toward things, objects, or situations on the basis of meaning that they have for them.[2] Meanings, therefore, reside in the individual and are ascribed to things outside of that individual; they have coherence only with specific regard to individuals who interpret these things as having specific meaning based on learned and shared experiences. The interactionist further assumes that meaning that people impose upon that which is external to them, including other people, is derived from interaction with others which results in agreed-upon definitions. Interaction within this framework is defined as being composed of sets of mutual agreements on designations of value and priority with regard to the external world of actors engaged in interactions. The approach also assumes that there will be change with regard to interpretive process as an integral part of interaction on the part of each person engaged in interaction. Within this framework, symbolic interactionism allows for differences in motivation in a sense that it does not necessarily assume that factor *X* will mean the same things to

Actor *A* or *B*. Hence, the approach is unique in its conception of meaning. Meaning is not interpreted to be external to the individual resident in the culture or an antecedent to behavior occurring within a rigidly defined kind of structural matrix, which is characteristically referred to as a social system or as a culture. Meaning cannot be reduced to simple aspects in initiating or motivation elements in human behavior. In fact, to ignore the meaning of things toward which people interact or respond is to falsify the behavior under study. The origin of meaning is firmly rooted in the ways in which persons act toward other persons with regard to specific objects or things or conditions. Consequently, meanings are social products formed by the defining activities of interacting persons.

Social meanings can include perceptions of stigmatization of identity, involvement in particular culturally unresolved situations, and the like. What is important, however, is that meaning is defined as a part of the totality of behavior of all persons, including all of the experiences and the physical dimensions or the "setting" or interacting individuals. It is as Blumer suggests: behavior or interaction occurs between actors, and not between the factors that are imputed to them. Behavior is therefore symbolic, and individuals take into account the symbols and actions of others:

> They do this by a dual process of indicating to others how to act and of interpreting the indications made by others. Human group life is a vast process of such defining to others what to do and of interpreting their definitions through this process. People come to fit their activities to one another and to form their own individual conduct. Both such joint activities and individual conduct are formed in and through this ongoing process; they are not mere expressions or products of what people bring to their interaction or of conditions that are antecedent to their interaction.[3]

Given this, the lesbianism study was defined as examining the changing norms, values, and meanings toward sexual preference. The sexual relationships were viewed to have physical, psychological, and social dimensions. For example, sexual arousal, while a biological state, was initiated and structured by customs comprised of both psychological and social factors. In other words, the essence of meaning is not innate in the situation; rather, meaning has been superimposed by the actors over the relationship. This statement applies to both heterosexual and homosexual relationships.

Since certain behavior was viewed as "defining" and symbolic, these actions pinpointed specifics on which individuals form lines of behavior. Consequently, behavior could be viewed as problem-solving or ameliorative of intolerable conditions. This viewpoint, of course, formed the theoretical basis for perceiving subcultures (in this case the lesbian subculture) as arising out of individual perceptions of stigmatization or a problem uniquely created by the culture, yet unresolved by it. The interactional underpinnings of this resolution are obvious. It was also assumed that the individuals were capable of symbolic generalizing from one situation to another and of interpreting other individual's relationship to objects or norms that result in manifest continuities of behavior occurring outside of the interactional framework. In short, individuals can interact with themselves.

> The human being who is engaging in self interaction is not a mere responding organism but an acting organism—an organism that has to mold a line of action on the basis of what it takes into account instead of merely releasing a response to the play of some factor upon its organization.[4]

It is, therefore, in the nature of human action that the individual selects behaviors with due regard to the natural setting, the organization, the interpretation, and the relative weighting of meanings and objects around them. In this way also, joint collective action can be explained just as the continuity of culture and meaning present in a given culture can be explained in terms of a collective agreement of actors. In short, social systems do not form individuals; rather, individuals form social systems.

In a sense, research in the symbolic interactionist framework can be defined as an attempt to analyze, isolate, evaluate, and understand meanings arising out of interaction and in turn relate these meanings to how people construct their behavior. Methodology within this framework is at best comprised of instruments designed to identify and analyze the obdurate character of the empirical world. Their value exists only in their suitability to the task to be accomplished.[5]

MODIFICATION OF THEORY AND EXPLORATORY METHODOLOGY

Frequently, descriptive or exploratory studies can address theoretical assumptions about methodology because of the flexibility inherent in their design. In the case of the research being discussed here, an attempt was made to test the impact of various types of data collection techniques on the quality of data derived. Where studies have included use of the case history technique, field research, and questionnaires, it is a common assumption that each of these techniques develops a characteristically different type of data and that combinations of such data will result in the introduction of several types of bias. The case study technique was used in the early stages of the lesbianism study, since it seemed most useful in developing research instruments. The point of these instruments was to gather data about the social career and the fundamental interactive dimensions of the lesbian experience. The storytelling process itself was also defined as a subject of research. Since respondents were interacting with themselves, meaning and not acts was the central focus of this interaction, and such meanings were meant to relate acts (behavior) either as rationalizations or to "make sense" of behavior, but never as mere antecedents. Acts can therefore be understood only within a meaning framework created by individuals interacting with themselves and others as the story unfolds.

There appeared to be no reason to assume as fact that the origin of personal behavior is not recognizable to the actor and thus not related to his or her story. Given this, it was assumed that behavior is intelligible to individuals and that it was unnecessary to cloak questions or to hide our research intent from the research subjects. Even so, a review of the literature in the area indicated that many studies were based on assumed needs, assumed involuntary distortions of perception, and hypothesized psychic mechanisms that precluded individuals being able to answer the question "Why did you do that?" Conversely, few studies focused on the assumption involved in proposing that motivation is hidden from those being motivated.

In order to study such assumptions, the methodology had to focus on two levels of self-report material. (1) Self-report material that was descriptive of life careers and life definitions and processes, and that discussed significant relationships in interactions. (To the extent that this focus related such factors to what was defined as resultant behavior, it assumed an explanatory mode and was theoretical.) (2) Self-report material of a numerical nature. At this level, the researchers decided what events this self-report would focus on, as well as which areas would be described in terms of frequency of occurrence. After all, certain types of behavior, such as certain types of sexual behavior, lend themselves to numerical ordering. In this research numerical ordering was used to address such social process of the lesbian as "coming out." By arranging events in process, that is, in order of occurrence, it was possible to isolate commonalities of experience in the life career of the typical lesbian as she entered the homosexual subculture.

Within this framework, it was not enough to know associated factors of behavior. Such factors can only be understood as actor perceptions. It was felt that it was the actor's perception that assigns priorities of impact to motivation. What motivates one individual will not necessarily motivate another.

The perspective suggests that the actor interacts and he is at once actor, reflector of past interactions, integrator of past interactions, integrator of culture in a broad social system sense (i.e., imperatives—norms—perscriptions—proscriptions—shalls—shall-nots), and interpreter of the immediate. The immediate has the dimensions of presentation, reception, interpretation, and integration. The actor marks a place in a drama that has a set, a form, acts, and a stage. He is part of the Gestalt—a whole—and as such can only relate to explanations that include the fabric of self. The actor can predict certain aspects of his life (body functions, appetite, sexual expressions, taxonomic responses such as bigotry), but these are understandable to the actor and to his audience (defined as those with whom he is interacting) only with regard to the entire fabric of his existence. This process defines those meanings which provide the foundation for his self-perception and those things upon which he constructs lines of behavior.

In the abstract, therefore, it was intended that the research effort be a search for meaning, a numbering of behavioral sequences, and, above all, a description of lesbianism as perceived and defined by lesbians themselves.

At the beginning, the study was to cover a fairly long period of time to ascertain whether there was a manifest stability in numerical-ordered sequences of behavior or in attitudes as expressed by respondents. For this reason, the study spans the years 1964 to 1973. The study was ongoing throughout this period of time, as was the researchers' interaction in the gay community. It was felt that if sets of attitudes and sequences of behavior that were constant over a period of time could be isolated, this would lend support to the existence of a lesbian subculture. In further addressing this very question, researchers focused on the existence of a lesbian subculture—its perpetuity over time, its basic dimensions, as well as its universal qualities ties. The study included an essentially Eastern sample, an exclusively Midwestern sample, and a Metropolitan sample. Respondents were drawn from metropolitan areas of low population densities or relatively rural areas. Given regional differences, a finding of strong similarities in attitudes, numerical sequences of behavior, and other demographic factors among lesbians could lend credence to the existence of a lesbian subculture. The pervasiveness of such a subculture could perhaps best be explained through its cathetic import once to participating members and the fact that the problems of being a homosexual in this culture are universal and would appear to transcend specific regional differences. Similarly, it was felt that continuity in the homosexual subculture throughout regions and over time would be indicative of the pervasiveness of the stabilization of lesbians over time. This once again might well provide a measurement of the commitment of respondents to the ideological and ameliorative qualities of the subculture and, in general, the importance of the subculture of the average lesbian. In a sense, the researchers were assuming that individuals cannot tolerate stigmatization of self and continued reinforcement of negative definition throughout their life careers. They will seek to ameliorate this condition through one of two means. (1) They can attempt to change their psychosexual identity—a position which has had little success in the past but is currently being approached from the behavioral modification perspective. This approach finds greatest sympathy in the medical and psychiatric world, but probably presents the greatest amount of risk and stress for the lesbian. As research indicates, the lesbian will sometimes accept a heterosexual front that at one stage or another she will abandon, at which point she may have the additional complications of children, a heterosexual identity that must be shed, and a homosexual identity that must be assumed, accepted, and adjusted to. (2) They can identify with other lesbians and engage in the mutual hammering out of commonalities of ameliorative definitions, ideologies, and finally, services providing those points upon which lines of action are formed. In other words, the study was examining the formation of a lesbian subculture. While both alternatives offer amelioration, they are diametrically opposed in resultant behavior and with regard to the resultant strain upon the individual. It was felt, however, that in evaluating this behavior one or two alternatives would be chosen. A third alternative existed, but it was defined as either nonexistent or unresearchable. The alternative involved the lesbian in question leading a single, asexual, nonexpressive life-style wherein no aspect of her identity would be recognizable in her social career.

As an additional methodological dimension, it was planned to test the time-honored hypothesis that the homosexual bars are significantly different or at least atypical of homosexuals—lesbians in general. The most common argument supporting the difference between the typical bar population and the population in general goes something like this: Would you expect the population of a sampling of bars in a city to produce a population that is a microcosm of the population of that given urban area? It is often pointed out that this bar population would differ at least significantly in at least one dimension from some members of the urban population in that they drink and do so outside their home. This argument tended to assume that bars in an urban area were a homogeneous kind of phenomenon, and that all bars drew equally from all segments of the population and from all sectors of the city. In order for this idea to be true, bar populations would themselves have to be a homogeneous admixture constituting a sampling of the population of a city. It is known, however, that this is not the case. Certain bars attract certain types of people. There are specialties in saloons, just as there are specialties in all types of merchandising, and those specialties are geared to a specific segment of the population. The researchers did not intend to develop a typology of bars, but they did report on obvious differences between neighborhood bars and supper clubs that serve liquor, clubs that cater to persons with particular kinds of music, and bars that cater respectively to an after-work transient trade, and to persons passing through the city, after-hour bars, and so forth. There is a greater probability that homosexual bars represent a more homogeneous phenomenon than heterosexual bars. Gay bars certainly have one thing in common: they cater to homosexuals and as such have functions over and above those associated with normal sociability and the furnishing of alcoholic beverages.[6]

It was felt that the gay bar was comparable to the heterosexual bar only on the surface and that each serves a completely different function for its clientele and is meaningful to clientele in different degrees. Stressing the theoretical perspective once again, it was felt that the gay bar symbolically represents something to the lesbian that it could not represent to the heterosexual and that the heterosexual bar does not symbolically represent the same cathetic focus for the heterosexual as the homosexual bar serves the homosexual.

DATA COLLECTION TECHNIQUES

In addition to the other methodological questions addressed in the lesbianism study, a comparison of several data collection methods as to the quality of resulting data was planned. These methods were direct interviews, collection of case study techniques, in-depth interviews over a long period of time, structured questionnaires with interviewers present, and mailed questionnaires. In the pre-test, it was found that the presence of a male interviewer, particularly a "straight" (nonhomosexual) male interviewer, affected the data collection process itself: it appeared to generate hostility in potential respondents and precluded the cooperation of a number of women who might have cooperated had they been approached by a woman. For this reason, early on in the research process lesbian women were used as interviewers. In this early study, interviewers were paid $7.50 per completed interview and respondents were paid $5 as a way of thanking them for completing the questionnaire. The interviewers were instructed to tell respondents that they were paid not for their time but as a means of assuring them of the researchers' sincerity of purpose and commitment to generating honest responses from honest people. This process was repeated several years ago in the collection of the Midwestern sample. In the remainder of the data collection process, respondents were not paid. The collection process by interviewers included group situations as found in parties, social get-togethers, and invitation groups, individual administrations, administration to individuals in bars, in pairs, trios, and quadruplets, and finally, interviews in the respondent's home. In the case of mailed questionnaires, the mailing list was provided by a large Eastern lesbian organization. Until this time, the organization had never allowed use of their membership for research purposes. The list was never in the hands of the researchers, however; the mailing and addressing of envelopes and the collection of responses were all handled by a representative of the organization. The mailed questionnaires were accompanied by a letter written by an activist lesbian associated with this particular organization. While the letter did express some hostility toward the project, it recommended cooperation, which in the long run, was said to be preferable to noncooperation.

Over and above these methodological concerns, the study was initiated to provide the researchers with realistic self-report data on experiences that presumably defined the dimensions of the lesbian's social career. Obviously, many dimensions have not been included, and many would have been included at a later point in the research process had their inclusion not prevented shedding some light on the previously defined methodological concerns.

Despite the exploratory nature of the study, researchers were able to test a number of methodological issues as well as describe the social and, in part, the sexual career of the lesbian. Since the parameters of the research universe (the total number of lesbians in the United States) could not be estimated, it was not possible to draw a random sample. The only sample possible under these circumstances was a nonrandom purposive one. At a later point in the research process, some parametric statistics were used for analysis, but the justification was highly specified. Although findings cannot be reported here, a number of hypotheses and of other less specified areas for further study can be derived.

As indicated in Chapter 6, exploratory designs are usually undertaken when problems are ill defined, or when concepts and relationships have not been specified. An advantage of the design is that it can be loosely structured to follow the evolution and sense of the data. In the following section, an exploratory study is considered which is essentially functionalist.[7] As in the case of the interactionist study, the steps and logic of development are presented.

ANALYSIS OF FACTORS ASSOCIATED WITH SCHOOL BOND ELECTIONS

The study reported here focused on the attempts of school boards to instigate changes in their educational facilities by financing through school bond elections. This kind of community decision-making is different from that involving elected officials such as the mayor, school boards, mayor/council, or other similarly constituted authority. The decisions considered here require the involvement of the district electorate to change the school system and facilities.[8]

Even though many public school facilities are inadequate, those people interested in improvement must often struggle to convince the electorate of the need for additional facilities and to get a bond proposal passed. A review of relevant literature indicates that educators and the district electorate generally felt that education was "good" and that the "democratic process" (election) was the best way to resolve these issues. Issues are usually resolved on specifics, with opposition focusing on the selected site, increase in taxes, dissatisfaction with proposed plans, and so forth. Organized opposition seldom attacks the generalized need for educational facilities, although exceptions can be found.

The struggle to obtain funds is evident in the vast amount of literature available on the subject. Many of these articles recommend the use of communications techniques to inform and involve as many people as possible and to stimulate a large turnout at election time. There is no agreement, however, on which or how many communications techniques should be used. Some educators state that a well-informed electorate will recognize its duty and pass the bond issue. Others are equally sure that the less knowledge the electorate has and the lower the level of information about the issue, the more likely the issue will pass.

The thesis that school administrators desire to increase voter turnout seems to have been negated by evidence indicating that voter turnout was negatively correlated with percentage favorable vote.[9] Stone, however, believes that an extensive publicity campaign can offset the negative influence of high voter turnout.[10] At a generalized level, school administrators and board members feel that involving as many individuals in as many ways as possible will result in issue passage. Educators often describe this feeling as "talking it up" by members of the community.

Both education journals and educational administrative texts stress involving as many people in the community as possible, generally through the use of citizens' advisory committees.[11] The composition of such committees may vary from one member representative of the community[12] (representative carries a variety of interpretations) to several of the most "talented" community members.[13]

Educators generally stress the ideal of democracy and democratic procedures. Some writers state that any influence exerted by an informal power structure is suspect as representing selfish interests and is therefore denounced.[14] Kimbrough presents another viewpoint and urges educators to make themselves aware of their informal community power structure(s) and to use it to legitimize school bond elections.[15] Many studies, however, indicate that educators are not aware of the power structures in their districts. It seems that educators who do recognize the power structure do not manipulate it, are unable to interact at this social level, or tend to avoid involvement with community influentials.

The literature shows that a number of empirical researches addressing this phenomena have been completed. Researchers have examined the relationship of variables such as school size, school district population, bond issue total, and assessed valuation (total and per pupil) to passage of the bond issue and have found few of these variables to be significantly related.[16] One researcher, John Allan Smith, studied the characteristics of the voters, rather than those of the school district, in the Los Angeles School

District.[17] His findings indicate that demographic characteristics should be considered in selecting both the media and content of the message. He suggests that census tracts containing mainly young working-class families with school-age children should be "courted" with public relations campaigns and favorable newspaper publicity. He also suggests giving specific information to the voters, whereas others have stated that general descriptive information produces the most favorable results.

In summary, the available literature was found to be confusing on the best techniques and strategy for engineering the successful passage of a school bond issue. Few consistent relationships were found between independent variables and the dependent variable bond issue election results. Many of the studies consisted of impressionistic descriptive accounts of techniques that proved successful in a specific campaign but could provide no basis for generalization.

Recognizing the confusion in the literature and the assumed complexity of the bond election process, the researchers decided to follow Merton's suggestion, in the preface to *Sociology Today*, and to use a relatively simple research design in an area of theoretical uncertainty.[18] A simplified taxonomic social action model had been developed as a guide for the collection and analysis of the data. This model (shown in Figure 2) consists of classes of variables presented along a temporal dimension that is approximated in a school bond issue election at the school district level.

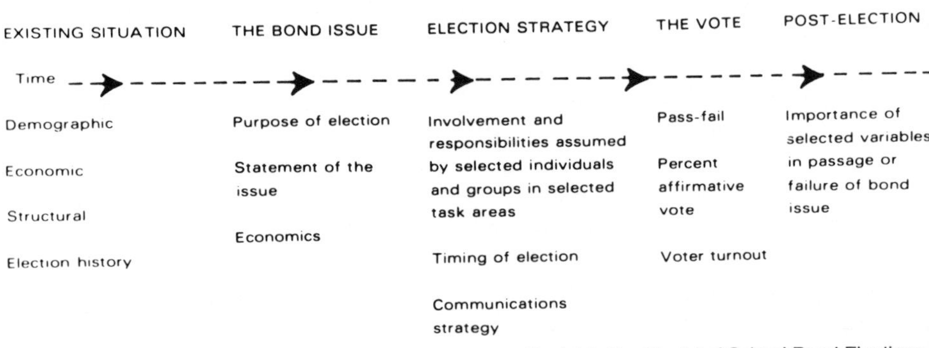

FIGURE 2 Summary Outline of Simplified Time Sequence, Social Action Model of School Bond Elections

As can be seen in Figure 2, the design of the study was mandated by the confusion reflected in the literature and the limited empirical investigation of the area. From relevant literature a time sequence table was developed which reflected movement through the school bond process. The research was therefore focused on exploration of the relationships specified in the chart. Below are some of the findings of the study and the logical process involved in the development of an alternative hypothesis.

The Findings

The major findings of this study indicate little relationship between election outcome and the traditional techniques presented by educators and reporters as essential in securing school bond passage.

1. There was no association between the demographic characteristics of the district and favorable vote.
2. There was little association between the economic variables and favorable vote. The significant variables were the 2½ mill school house tax ($r = +0.23$) and assessed valuation ($r = -0.17$).
3. Election history associations indicate that the norms of passage or rejection evidently exist in some districts. Passage was not related to amount of the issue or tax base or rate of tax increase. Some districts had passed five different issues during the five-year period. Others had defeated issues as many as nine times during the same period of time.
4. Communications variables and secondary service techniques were found to have little relation to percentage favorable vote in the district. In fact, any significant relationship was likely to be negative.
5. The percentage of the registered voters participating in these elections was not significantly correlated with the outcome of the issue.
6. The "closely contested" issues did not differ significantly from the remaining issues. They were quite similar to those that passed or failed by wider margins.
7. Simple research frameworks and methods based on impressionistic descriptive studies and data are not sufficient to analyze and make significant predictive statements about the outcome of school bond elections.

The data analyzed offer little encouragement in predicting outcomes of school bond elections when single variables are the basis for prediction. In some cases, aggregating these variables and correlating them with votes supporting passage of the bond issue did produce significant relationships with some categories, but they were very slight.

This particular work demonstrates that a relatively simple frame of reference should first be used when exploring an area in which sociological theory has not been developed to explain this complex community action.

An Alternative Hypothesis

When a general lack of association between the outcome of the election and the variables examined in this study was found, an alternative hypothesis was advanced: *"closely contested issues would differ from the remaining elections."* Closely contested issued were defined as those receiving from 50.1 to 69.9 percent favorable vote. This resulted in 89 of the 195 elections being classified as closely contested. The rationale was that if the outcome was predicted to be very much in doubt, different strategies might be used to attempt to secure a favorable vote on the bond issue. Subsequent data analysis resulted in the final rejection of this hypothesis as well.

SUMMARY

This chapter focuses on the development of two exploratory studies, each drawn from a different theoretical framework. Exploratory or pilot studies find their most frequent application when the literature in a given area reflects contradictory or confusing findings, or when it is clear, after a careful search, that the subject has not been investigated before.

In the case of the first study, the universe was not known, nor had all relevant concepts and variables been delimited. Much of the research effort was spent in generating means and designs, methods, and theory to examine this area of covert behavior. The development of the designs and the continuing involvement with the lesbian community through the process of research raised a number of methodological issues. These issues were in turn examined and provided insights leading to the generation of additional hypotheses. The thrust of this particular research was, therefore, twofold. It examined not only the social career of the lesbian but also a number of methodological issues relevant to this type of research, which were also capable of being generalized to other areas of research.

In the second study, there was uncertainty and lack of agreement on what constituted the relevant theory, concepts, and variables. Much was known about how school bond elections are held; however, relevant literature reports little beyond isolated impressionistic comments of superintendents and school board members. The purpose of this exploratory research was to bring comparative order to this process and to determine whether specific acts (functions) were related to the ultimate outcome (passage of the bond issue). An alternative hypothesis was also developed and tested and was finally rejected. The negative results were published, showing that situational factors did play a part in these elections and that no model existed to produce absolute results. The exploratory study is one of intent, not technique per se.

NOTES

1. At a later point in the research, it was decided that the sample size was sufficient to allow the use of some parametric analytical techniques. The different analytical levels and techniques are clearly indicated both in the text and in representative tables. It was necessary to make the reader aware of them.

2. Herbert Blumer, *Symbolic Interactionism: Perspective in Method* (Englewood Cliffs, N.J.: Prentice-Hall, 1969), p. 2.

3. Ibid., p. 10.
4. Ibid., p. 15.
5. Ibid., p. 27.
6. What is significant from a methodological point of view, however, is the fact it was found that an overwhelming percentage of the research samples attended gay bars frequently and that, in general, those respondents recruited in the gay bar situation itself did not differ significantly in any of their responses from those respondents recruited outside of the homosexual bar setting.
7. The school bond study was originally reported by George M. Beal, John J. Hartman, and Virgil Lagomarcino, "An Analysis of Factors Associated with School Bond Elections," *Rural Sociology* 33, No. 3 (September 1968): 313-27.
8. Ibid.
9. Richard F. Carter and William G. Savard, "Influence of Voter Turnout on School Bond and Tax Electins," *Cooperative Research Monograph*, No. 5, Washington, D.C., U.S. Government Printing Office, 1963.
10. Clarence N. Stone, "Local Referendums: An Alternative to the Alienated Voter Model," *Public Opinion Quarterly* (Summer 1965).
11. Dorothee Brown, "Criteria for Selecting a Citizens Committee," *American School Board Journal* 140 (April 1960); Robert R. Denny, "Selling Bonds," *American School Board Journal* 139 (November 1959); B. I. MacDonald, Jr., "How to Win Bond Issues and Influence Voters," *The School Executive* 74 (April 1955); S. P. Marland, Jr., "Stowage, Mr. Superintendent," *The School Executive* 70 (August 1951); E. J. O'Leary, "Garden City Reports Successful Bond and School Millage Elections," *American School Board Journal* 148 (March 1964); Joe B. Rushing, "Involving the Community in School Planning," *American School Board Journal* 141 (July 1960).
12. Ibid.
13. Ibid.
14. Ibid.
15. Ralph B. Kimbrough, *Political Power and Educational Decision Making* (Chicago: Rand McNally and Co., 1964); Edgar L. Morphet, et al., *Educational Administration: Concepts, Practices, and Issues* (Englewood Cliffs, N.J.: Prentice-Hall, 1959).
16. John E. Bregman, "A Study of the Ultimate Fate of Eighty-Six School Bond Elections in Sixty-Two Selected School Districts During the Period January 1, 1950 to April 1, 1955," M.A. thesis, State University of Iowa, August 1955; Lawrence Francis Kasperbauer, "School Bond Issues in Iowa," M.S. thesis, Iowa State University, 1959; Thomas N. Keating, "The Effectiveness of Procedures Used in School Building Programs in Nebraska," Ed.D. thesis, University of Nebraska, 1963; Robert N. Overson, "A Study of the Ultimate Fate of One Hundred Twenty-One School Bond Elections in Seventy-Eight Selected Iowa School Districts During the Period January 1, 1955," M.A. thesis, State University of Iowa, August 1955.
17. John Allan Smith, "An Appraisal of School Bond Campaign Techniques," *Southern California Educational Monographs*, no. 15, Los Angeles, University of Southern California Press, 1953.
18. Robert K. Merton, Leonard Broom, and Leonard S. Cottrell, Jr. (eds.), *Sociology Today: Problems and Prospects* (New York: Basic Books, 1959).

8

Scales and Data Collection Instruments

Although questionnaires are often referred to as instruments, schedules, scales, or opinionnaires, they are all basically cut from the same cloth. Only two such terms will be used: *questionnaires* and *scales*. The term *questionnaire* will be used to designate data collected by a standard set of questions (all respondents respond to the same questions). The term *scales* will be used to designate an instrument composed of a series of items (questions or statements) designed to measure some predetermined dimension such as job satisfaction, role strain, self-concept, or attitude toward the law. Each scaling technique is examined following a discussion of questionnaire construction.

The process involved in the development of a good questionnaire is more complicated than the simple gathering of a number of apparently relevant questions that appear to address a particular problem and then proceeding to collect data. Too many research surveys are of this type. A well-executed research design demands the careful evaluation of each question to be included in the instrument and a thorough pretesting of the entire instrument for validity and reliability.[1]

FIRST CONSIDERATIONS IN QUESTIONNAIRE CONSTRUCTION

Generally, the problem to be examined should be thoroughly specified prior to the selection of an existing questionnaire or the development of a new one. Occasionally, a previously used questionnaire might prove effective. In this case, the researcher has the advantage of having previous experience with it. Even when using an existing questionnaire, the problem to be addressed should first be stated and the questionnaire fitted to the problem rather than force-fitting the problem to the questionnaire. If the problem statement has been properly delineated, the dependent and independent variables should be contained within the concepts linked in the problem statement. Consider that frequently the only way of telling the difference between a concept and a variable is to consider them in the context in which they are presented. For example, the problem statement "an investigation will be made of the relationship between social class and drinking (alcohol) behavior" can be considered to be a statement relating the concepts social class and drinking behavior. Later in this chapter, social class is used as a variable in presenting the findings and discussing results. Social class might well be defined as the independent variable and alcohol the dependent variable. A decision would be made as to what constitutes a social class and what criteria are involved in assigning individual membership into one social class or another; hence, it is the dependent variable or what we are trying to explain. The process called "operationalization" designates what the "real world" measure (variable) will be. Operationalization is defined by assigning measures to concepts, and exact use of the measure is decided upon. For example, the particular problem delineation would likely include a statement defining social class. "For the purpose of this research, social class will be defined as A———, B———, C———, D———." Those wishing to replicate the research can do so without confusion or ambiguity about conceptual or variable definition. In this instance, the researcher could have defined what conditions had to be present to assign an individual to a specific social class. On the other hand, researchers could have used self-reporting and asked the individual to assign himself to a social class. Either measure is satisfactory as long as the operational measure is designated.

More importantly, this process of designating the operational measure results in a test to apply to questions considered for inclusion in the survey: Is this question really needed? What purpose does the question really serve? What will be made of it in the analysis? If such tests of relevance were applied to questionnaires early in their development, the resulting questionnaires would be less redundant, improved as research instruments, and usually shorter (fewer items). Hence, the *first key consideration* in questionnaire development is the function of the questions used in the survey.

A second major consideration pertains to choosing between "open-ended" questions or highly structured "closed" questions or a check-off format. This decision should be based on what data are to be collected and the number of respondents included in the survey (sample size). Can the individual researcher anticipate question responses and build a check-off code prior to the survey? It is time consuming and sometimes an impossible task to build similar codes from five hundred open-ended responses.

The research task is simple in terms of data analysis if it merely represents transferring coded numbers from structured responses onto data cards. On the other hand, some data can be collected only through the use of open-ended questions, and the technique should not be dismissed solely because it is difficult or time consuming. The data needed for problem testing mandate method and data collection techniques; techniques do not dictate what kind of problem will be examined.

The following is an example of an open-ended question: "We are interested in which problems you think are of most importance in our community; list those that concern you." This initial question could be followed with a request to explain one's answer. An alternative would have been to list several problems and ask the respondent to rank the three most important. If we left an "other" category at the end of the listed problems, we would in effect have asked for any additional problems of interest to the respondent.

A third consideration is the length of the questionnaire. In general, a respondent should be able to complete a questionnaire in one hour or less. More structured or specific responses (closed questions) can be asked in an hour than open-ended questions. Obviously, instruments that require a simple "yes-no" response can be answered more quickly than those that require the sorting out of multiple choice responses. Moreover, items in a scale that can be checked off or circled to indicate the desired response tend to move more rapidly. These scales are frequently used in the mailed questionnaire or in a questionnaire responded to in a group setting. Whatever method of administering the questionnaire, response time should be a consideration in developing the instrument.

A fourth consideration pertains to the reading level of questions. Generally, language level must be geared to the research population. Language that is beyond or below the respondents' level will not generate the desired data. In a previous example, it was found that dairy farmers preferred to be called "dairymen" in the upper Midwest, "ranchers" in California, and "dairy farmers" in the Southeast. Words have emotional content in addition to meaning. Given the impact of the women's liberation movement, it is not surprising that an increasing number of parenthetical comments appear on questionnaires regarding questions specifying sex of the respondent. Questions have also been raised about the use of sex-linked personal pronouns. Although the length and simplicity of a questionnaire are important, it may be worthwhile to include both terms. For example,

"If one receives conflicting suggestions, (he-she) should follow (his-her) own intuition."

Readability scales are available to estimate the reading competence of a questionnaire. If such considerations are ignored, the possibility exists of skewing or biasing the data. Such biases are difficult to detect. In instrument construction, therefore, there should be an awareness of the general educational level of respondents, the impact of certain emotionally laden terms, and the importance of communication.[2]

CONSIDERATIONS IN QUESTIONNAIRE CONSTRUCTION

The four considerations discussed above are rather general; the following material deals with the actual process of forming the questions or statements constituting the questionnaire.

Clarity. Questions should be phrased simply and clearly. A question with ambiguous meaning or interpretation leads to difficulty of response interpretation and questionable analysis. The question "What is your father's occupation?" may not provide the data actually sought. If the intent is to transfer responses to an occupational prestige score, the researcher might ask the respondents to check which of a number of categories most clearly approximates the father's occupation. If the question is open-ended, one might expect any number of responses, e.g., deceased, retired, don't know, semiretired, and unemployed. If the question is rephrased as "What is (or was) your father's principal occupation?" it clarifies the anticipated responses of those not presently employed and those deceased.

Single concept. It is best to avoid "double barreled" questions, that is, two ideas in a single question. Questions that form two distinct items which are not necessarily compatible can result in two responses or no response at all rather than the single response sought. Consider the following question: "Do you favor or oppose unemployment insurance and pension plans?"[3] A "yes" response would not tell the researcher whether the respondent favored one or both of the items. The single-thought or single-theme question can prevent this problem by separating the two elements or by moving to a higher level of generality. This question could be changed to:

Circle the response that best indicates your feeling about the following items:

1. Do you favor employee benefit packages? yes no
2. Do you favor unemployment insurance? yes no
3. Do you favor pension plans? yes no

This list could be expanded to a number of other benefits that could be part of a company program such as hospitalization insurance, income protection plans, and stock-sharing options. Most importantly, however, responses are no longer clouded and uncertain. This decision falls to the researcher and is structured by the objectives of the research program. If one wants to obtain a generalized response, Question 1, "Do you favor employee benefit packages," might be the only one to ask. If additional detail is sought, additional questions should be asked. The researcher should be certain that the question and the possible responses are clear to the respondents. This can best be accomplished through careful pretesting in an exploratory or pilot design.

Neutral nonleading questions. Questions should be as neutral as possible with no bias implied in the question. A question such as "What are your feelings about police enforcement in the community?" is relatively neutral. A similar question "Some persons feel police-community relations are strained in this community, what are your views?," may elicit a negative response because the respondent has been cued that he would not be alone if he agreed that police-community relations were strained. Cannell and Kahn provide examples of a neutral question, an obviously biased one, and a third somewhat subtle bias in question wording.

Neutral	"How do you feel about rent control?"
Biased	"You wouldn't say that you were in favor of rent control, would you?"
Subtle	"Would you say that you are in favor of rent control?"[4]

The biased question is so obvious that most individuals developing a questionnaire would not use it, although the subtle biased question is frequently seen in questionnaires. Bias should be avoided, but as Cannell and Kahn have pointed out, there is a place for the biased question if the researcher knowingly includes the question for a specific purpose. Their example was, "Would you favor sending food overseas to feed the starving people of India?"[5] Their purpose was to see how many people would reject the shipping of food out of the United States, even with the strongly emotional word "starving" used in the question.

Expectation of response. By asking individuals in a sample to respond to a questionnaire, the researcher assumes that they are able to respond, understand the question, possess the information requested, and are willing to respond. This may not be the case. Questions asked will frequently yield information which the respondent never considered. Not having thought about the requested information, however, may not prevent a respondent from answering. In fact, respondents need not know anything about a subject to discuss it at length or to express strong attitudes toward the object of the question.

Occasionally, items are included in questionnaires that are wrong or generally inaccurate in order to see if individual respondents would recognize these items and mark the correct response. A questionnaire administered to members of a voluntary membership product promotion organization asked them to rate how well the organization was performing in a number of areas. The example below illustrates the technique.

How well is the ——— organization doing in each of the following areas?

	Excellent	Good	Fair	Poor	Nothing	Don't Know
Promoting Dairy Products						
Research on Dairy Products						
Lobbying						
Raising Price of Milk						
Increasing Consumption						

ample Response Format

Lobbying was included because lobbying was expressly forbidden in the bylaws of the organization. It was used as a check on how knowledgeable the membership was about their organization. The correct response should have been "nothing" or "don't know." Most members rated the organization on this dimension, but researchers were not certain if the members actually didn't know about the restriction on lobbying and were responding because the question was asked, or if a "good" or "excellent" rating was based on their knowledge of activities of the state or local official engaging in an illegal activity. The other possibility is that these responses could be an example of the "halo effect," or the tendency to make positive comments or statements, or to make no statement at all. It is the psychological equivalent of the old adage "If you can't say something nice about someone, don't say anything at all." The point is twofold: (1) if you ask a question, you will probably get responses; (2) no interpretation of the absolute correctness of most responses can be made, and it is not possible to estimate the "halo effect" or relative correctness of the responses.

Socially desirable responses. Individuals responding to questionnaires usually do so in situations where no threat of action following responses exists. For example, if an individual responds to a call for volunteers, he can assume he will be requested to perform one duty or another. If a person volunteers to be the secretary of a group and is selected, he can expect to perform the duties of the secretary. When a respondent answers a question or marks a piece of paper (questionnaire), he does not expect to defend his responses or the validity of that response. In a survey, if the researcher asked "If you observed a street robbery in progress, what would you do?", respondents would be likely to give culturally approved responses and say that they would attempt to help or summon help. Does this response indicate what the respondent really would do or what he thinks others expect him to do? This question is crucial to data analysis. There are countless examples of persons witnessing crimes without being willing to help or get involved. The researcher can give no assurance that a respondent will necessarily behave in a manner consistent with his response. Where norms defining expected or approved behavior are well known, a pressure may be felt to give socially desirable responses. If researchers are aware of this pressure as they write the questions for questionnaires, it is possible to avoid questions that have a strong emotional content or will tend to elicit normatively prescribed responses. By so doing, the validity of derived data is increased. Questions should not have cues to answers built into them, regardless of whether or not the cues are socially desirable.

Tendency to acquiesce. Research in psychology indicates that at times individuals have a tendency to respond "yes" rather than "no" in a free choice situation.[6] This also seems to be true when people are asked to choose between positive or negative. In addition, this tendency is believed to pertain in situations where the individual respondent is not certain of his own response or where there is no strong feeling against the object of the question. In this regard, a twenty question true-false test was administered to a number of sociology classes. Correct responses on each test were all the same; "false" was the correct response to all questions in some tests, and in others all correct responses were "true." Results showed that students had lower scores and more difficulty responding to tests with twenty "false" responses than to tests with all positive responses for correct answers.

As a rule, it is best to avoid constructing instruments with a single direction of response. It is best to mix responses and make some items assertions (positive statements—assuming facts) and other items, questions. For example, the following statement could be reworded to change the correct response from true to false: (a) A small person will get drunk faster than a large person on the same number of drinks. The answer is true, but it assumes that a number of other factors are equal (having eaten, no previous drinks, and so forth). An alternate route to the same information is provided by the following wording: (b) A small person can drink as many drinks as a large person and not get drunk any quicker. The correct response is now false, but the same qualifications and assumptions apply. Which question is best? It really doesn't matter. It is best to mix up the possible responses to factual questions and to avoid any patterning of responses, such as one true, one false, or three true, two false, three true.

TECHNICAL CONSIDERATIONS IN QUESTIONNAIRE CONSTRUCTION

Each research study is unique, as is the population or universe from which the data are to be collected. There are no absolute steps or techniques to be followed in the development of a questionnaire relevant to every possible research design. Even so, there are a number of techniques that can be used in combination to build the best possible questionnaire for any particular study. It is not necessary to use all of the following techniques in every study that utilizes a questionnaire to collect data. The relevance of each point should be evaluated with regard to specific research needs. The listing is not exhaustive. A technique should not be dismissed if it is not included. Those that are listed have proven to be useful to researchers in a number of different situations.

Conversationalizing. Regardless of which of the three basic forms of data collection is used (interviews in group settings, individual interviews, or mailed questionnaires), bridges between topics addressed in the questionnaire should be used. In this way, the respondent is helped to switch gears and be aware of the change in information. If the questionnaire has been mailed, these bridges play the role of an interviewer and "explain" transitions. If the question is to be asked by an interviewer, these information bridges assure that the same transition has been presented to all respondents (with suggestions to inteviewers that they read these transitions and make no additional comments). Since the bridges being sought are meant to conversationalize the questionnaire and act as transitions from one section of the questionnaire to another, they require illustration. After asking respondents a series of technical questions about alcohol, laws about driving while under the influence of alcohol, and legal limits of presumptive intoxication, we wanted to obtain further information about their knowledge of folk beliefs about the use of alcohol. The following bridge was used: "Here is a list of statements about drinking and becoming intoxicated. I will read each statement and you tell me if you think it is true or false." The statements were read and responses recorded until the next bridge appeared. It was read: "How effective do you think each of the following methods would be in reducing the drinking driver problem?" A series of eight questions was read for response; then the next bridge was read: "Which of these actions would you as a citizen be willing to support if they were proposed by public officials?" The eight statements were read with responses now given for their willingness to support each.

There were other bridges in the research instrument. However, those presented will show the purpose of the "bridge." The transition between dimensions in a questionnaire serve a number of additional functions. they (1) alert the respondent that a change is being made, (2) give directions about a change in response format (you tell me if you think it is true or false), and (3) facilitate the change in dimension or response made without injecting a great deal of interviewer bias through each interviewer devising (his-her) own explanation. This has been proven to be a positive addition to most questionnaires unless the questionnaire consists only of items in a single scale.

Lead-in questions. Lead-in questions often serve the same function as the "bridges" already discussed. The lead-in question cues the respondent in the direction the interviewer wants to obtain information. The question can often be considered to be a "throw-away" question since it is used only to move the respondent to answer questions in a new area with a minimum of difficulty. As a result, many researchers believe it is better to start with more general questions and to move to more specific ones as they progress through the dimension being considered. For example: Assume you are interested in interviewing a sample of factory workers about any job-related tension they might experience. Would you approach each respondent with, "Hey, I'm interested in what bugs you about your job, tell me about it?" Probably not. Stilted language, on the other hand, presents similar difficulties: (Sir or Ms.) "I'm conducting a survey about job-related tension. Will you describe those situations or circumstances that tend to produce tension in your work role?"

When approaching a respondent, it might be more effective to state that a survey is being made of work conditions and employees are being asked to describe a typical work-a-day routine. If tension exists, the respondent should be allowed to bring it up and the researcher should not assume its existence. This type of research lends itself best to the open-ended probe technique of interviewing, utilizing a skilled interviewer. Data can be derived about job-related tension without a direct or disruptive question being put to the respondent.

Series questions. A researcher is frequently forced to ask a series of obviously related questions when the questionnaire includes the investigation of several dimensions. This technique has been referred to as the "funnel approach" by Cannel and Kahn.[7] Specifically, it consists of questions that go from the general to the more specific. Typically:

Question 1: How do you think this country is getting along in its relations with other countries?
Question 2: How do you think we are doing in our relations with Russia?
Question 3: Do you think we ought to be dealing with Russia differently than we are now?
Question 4: (If yes) What should we be doing differently?
Question 5: Some people say we should get tougher with Russia and others think we are too tough as it is; how do you feel about this.?[8]

The questions not only progress from the general to the specific, but also from the neutral to the more personal, frequently asking for personal feelings. This technique can be used in the construction of the entire questionnaire. It seems to lead individuals into being more cooperative than they often are at the beginning of the interview session.

Question placement-set-response. A number of points about question placement must be considered in developing the questionnaire. Among these are:

(a) Face sheet data, or the so-called sociodemographic data, can be asked for first or last, depending on the nature of the questions. Questions that are not too personal or threatening can be asked first; threatening questions should be moved to the end of the instrument. Questions on income, religious preference, race, sex, marital status, including previous status (divorced) or presently living with someone, may be considered invasion of privacy by some. The basic determinant here is what function does the question serve. If it has no function for a particular project, it should not be included.

(b) The researcher must be careful not to cue a response in a respondent. Research demands that a respondent respond as he or she thinks and not as the researcher wishes. In the example, questions were asked about general impressions of alcohol consumption. Respondents were then asked about penalties for alcohol abuse and about rating various alcohol educational programs. Those questions were placed at the end of the questionnaire because the researchers wanted open-ended questions that would elicit responses about treatment methods (or methods of dealing with the problem drinker) rather than simple responses to the definition of the "problem drinker."

(c) The term *set* is used to refer to a respondent's tendency to respond in a specific manner. "Acquiescence" can be an example of set, but of more importance is the tendency of some subjects responding to questionnaires, requiring responses on a continuum from "Strongly Agree" to "Strongly Disagree," to mark the extremes for each item. Others tend to mark toward the scale middle for each item. Yet another set is created by the respondent who tries to please the interviewer by giving the answer he thinks will please the interviewer. Respondents often ask, "Is that the answer you wanted?" In general, people want to please, but they often fail to understand that their honest response is sought rather than what they think will please.

Skip questions. "Skip questions" are often used to facilitate the data collection process. If a series of questions is asked using the funnel approach and the respondent does not know anything about the first question, it is more expedient to steer him to the next relevant question rather than have him or her go through each question and respond "not applicable." An example is presented:

Question 29: (If No to Question 28) Briefly, what are your reasons for not continuing your education? Go to Question 34 when finished with Question 29)

____

____

____

The skip technique is useful in both interviewer or self-administered questionnaires.

Traps or screens. Questions called "trap-screens" are used when there is a reluctance to skip or jump an individual to questions ahead because respondents are not aware of a very technical bit of information and cannot respond to a particular item. This technique usually requires two questions and is used in conjunction with the skip question. The purpose is to attempt to see how many know (or are aware of) the desired technical information, and also to give respondents a second chance to produce a more general response. An example should help to clarify this technique:

40. Have you heard of the Wichita Area Vocational-Technical School program?

    —Yes (If you checked yes, answer Question 42 next).
    —No (If you checked no, go to Question 41 next.)

41. Are you aware of postsecondary vocational and adult programs?

    —Yes (If you checked yes, go to Question 42 next.)
    —No (If you checked no, go to Question 47 next.)

Questions 42 through 46 were technical questions about postsecondary vocational-technical programs offered by the Wichita Area Vocational-Technical School (WAVTS) Program. The major consideration is whether or not those who do not recall the WAVTS program by its exact name should be excluded, or if this question should be used as a variable, to ascertain whether there are significant differences between those who recognize the technical name, those who have heard of the program, and those who have heard of neither.

Card assists. When the researcher wishes to assist the respondent within a structured framework in an interviewer-administered questionnaire, cards can help speed up the process. In the previous example of a "bridge," it was not stated that the last line of the bridge had instructions to the interviewer (Hand R [respondent] Card C). The interviewer was to hand the respondent Card C to indicate the desired responses to the following series of questions. Card C was a 5" x 7" with the following information:

CARD C

Very effective
Somewhat effective
Probably ineffective
No opinion

In our study, after Card C was handed to the respondent, the questions were read and one of the four possible responses on Card C was returned. This technique has the same effect as a rating scale and serves the same function as a multiple choice question in a test. While it does structure responses, it also is self-coded and minimizes discusssion or straying from the original question. The technique is also effective in obtaining information about yearly income. A card with the specified categories will at times work where a direct question fails:

CARD E

Less than $1,000
$1,000 — $2,499
$2,500 — $4,999
$5,000 — $7,499
$7,500 — $9,999
$10,000 —$14,999
$15,000 —$19,999
$20,000 —or more

As can be seen, categories are not separated by the same increment. Increments can be modified, but within categories some will respond who may take it as an affront to be directly asked the amount of their income. Cards serve a positive function in structuring responses and may well neutralize sensitive questions and obtain responses where they may otherwise have been refused.

It is believed that these technical procedures will improve the entire data collection process. This subject has not yet been exhausted.

SCALES AND SCALING TECHNIQUES

To this point, the questionnaire has been treated as a number of individual questions (some in a series) seeking data from a sample of respondents. A questionnaire often contains a scale as an integral part. In fact, it is possible to have a scale comprise the entire data collection instrument. There is a major difference between the scale and questionnaire as data collection instruments. The questionnaire attempts to obtain information relative to specific questions. Each question is analyzed independently of all other questions in the questionnaire. In the scale, the item (questions, assertions, statements)[9] are purportedly related in some way. Either the items can be added together, forming a scale score (a composite or total score) that has some meaning, or the items can be assumed to represent stages along a continuum. This statement will become clearer as different types of scales are examined, but first let us examine the questions of validity and reliability.

Validity. The study of validity in research methods need not presuppose sophistication in mathematics. Recall that a scale represents a number of related items on a single dimension. Respondents to the scale are in some manner assigned scores or rankings based on their responses to the scale items. These differences are examined here, as well as the three major types of scales used in the social sciences, i.e., Thurston, Guttman, and Likert scales. Questions about validity ask: does the scale score measure what it is intended to measure? If it does, it can be said to have validity or to produce a valid score. Unfortunately, most scales have no specific measure of validity.

The scale has been defined as a composite set of items resulting in a scale score that differentiates between respondents. The scale is designed to measure a single dimension as reflected in research literature. Most scales are constructed so that the magnitude of a score is indicative of a greater or lesser quantity of the dimension assigned to the respondent, i.e., a high score is indicative of more of the quality and a low score a lack of the quality. For example, if a researcher attempts to measure authoritarianism, the higher the scale score the more authoritarian the respondent is said to be. This generalization holds for the three major scale types—the higher the score, the more of the dimension measure.

Scales used in studies that report no technique for establishing validity usually have none except what has been termed "face validity." That is, the dimension measured is assumed to be valid because the questions obviously address the items to be measured by the scale, or only because the scale builders have said it was valid.

Validity is an easy concept to describe but a difficult one to guarantee or measure. In general, an instrument or measure is said to be valid if it measures what it purports to measure. For example, an IQ score is a measure of general learning ability. If the IQ score is indeed such a measure, persons with high IQ scores should perform certain learning tasks better than persons with low IQ scores. An examination or a formal study could determine this thesis. IQ scores would be a valid measure of general learning ability to the extent that they enable an individual to predict learning performance on the basis of the single score.

There are a number of ways to establish validity, but only one will be reviewed here: the *known groups* method which has been used with some success. If a researcher develops a scale measuring orientation to physical labor, it might be expected that those doing physical labor are doing so by their own choice. That is, if the scale does indeed measure positive orientation to physical labor, then a group of construction workers should have higher scores than a group of graduate students in sociology. A scale on student radicalism should produce higher scale scores and higher mean (average) scores from a sample of organized politically radical groups of students than scores resulting from a random sampling of college students. If for some reason results are mixed, construction workers score lower than sociology graduate students on the physical labor scale, and a student random sample scores higher than members of an organized group of radical students on a radicalism scale, then one must question the validity of the purported scale. If replications are undertaken and continued, and mixed results are produced, the scale can be assumed to have no validity. When the known groups method works under several test conditions, we have reason to assume and report a validity coefficient.

Reliability. This concept deals with whether a scale measures essentially the same thing each time it is administered. If an IQ scale is used as an example and an individual scores 120 plus or minus 10, it means that the "true IQ" is said to be between 110 and 130. If the individual is retested, it would be expected that the individual would score approximately 120 (not precisely) again, but certainly the score should fall within the 110-130 range. If this is the case for a large number of persons, the scale can be said to have test-retest reliability. The large number of cases helps establish standardized norms for the scale.[10] Few, if any, scales in sociology ever achieve the status of having standardized norms. However, establishing validity and reliability in a scale is a desirable goal. Reliability simply indicates that the same scale values are being obtained within expected deviations. It should also be noted that an instrument can be reliable and not be valid; on the other hand, instruments that are valid are always reliable.

Where no reliability or validity measures are reported, results should be examined closely.

LIKERT SCALES

In discussing scales, we will devote a disproportionate amount of space to the Likert scale since it is probably the most frequently used scaling technique in sociology. This popularity stems, at least in part, from the availability of the electronic computer. The technique is familiar to most students and usually has a five-response mode for each of the items in the scale, i.e.,

23. The study of research methods is necessary.
Strongly Agree ☐ Agree ☐ Undecided ☐ Disagree ☐ Strongly Disagree ☐

This scaling technique has the advantage of not requiring a number of judges to decide what value should be assigned to each item. It is developed by using a discriminatory device (item total correlations identifying the most valid questions), and the respondents (maybe from a pre-test) actually provide their own values for each item. It contains the following qualities:

(1) The scale is unidimensional; that is, it is assumed that only one dimension is measured by the scale.
(2) The scale is an attitude measurement scale.
(3) The items are additive; that is, the scores for each item are added together to form a single scale score wherein higher scale scores represent stronger attitude expressions than felt by those who score lower.
(4) No one item is more important than any other since all *can* contribute equally to the total scale score.

The Likert scale is easily constructed. For an illustration, let us take the orientation to physical labor previously discussed and the items used to measure it. Eight items were selected for the example since these items were originally administered in a questionnaire along with questions related to six other scale dimensions. Each dimension was scored separately, and each was considered to be a separate integral unit.

To build the scale of physical labor, twenty items addressing physical labor were written and administered to some fifty respondents in a pre-test to select the eight items most highly correlated with one another (that is, items that were closely related and tended to vary up or down together). In this way, from twenty items, the eight "best" items were selected and used in the scale. The items follow with a discussion of scoring and evaluative difficulties of the Likert scale.

Circle the response that best represents your attitudes (SA—Strongly Agree; A—Agree; U—Undecided; D—Disagree; SD—Strongly Disagree).

+ 1.	Working with my hands is satisfying.	SA	A	U	D	SD
+ 2.	Physical labor is more satisfying than thinking through a problem.	SA	A	U	D	SD
+ 3.	It is easier to tell if you have accomplished something with physical tasks.	SA	A	U	D	SD

− 4. I enjoy figuring things out more than actually doing them.	SA	A	U	D	SD
− 5. I prefer not to get dirty when working.	SA	A	U	D	SD
+ 6. Working with tools and machinery is more satisfying than working with people.	SA	A	U	D	SD
+ 7. If the money paid for a job was the same, I would rather work with my hands.	SA	A	U	D	SD
+ 8. It is difficult for me to say and write exactly what I think or feel.	SA	A	U	D	SD

These eight items now constitute a Likert-type scale. To score the scale, we assigned values from 5 to 1 to each item response. The range of possible scores, if all eight items are marked, was from a low score of eight to a high score of forty. The score of eight would result from a "one" score on each item; the score of forty would result from a five score on each item. Each item that had a + in front of it was scored 5, 4, 3, 2, 1 for Strongly Agree to Strongly Disagree (SA 5, A 4, U 3, D 2, SD 1). These items are positive in that it would have been expected that those who enjoyed physical labor would have a high positive orientation to physical labor score, or they should mark these + Strongly Agree or Agree. The scores were reversed for the − items. That is, SD = 5, D = 4, U = 3, A = 2, SD = 1. An individual with a positive physical labor orientation should disagree with these items; hence, the scale values were reversed. There were several combinations to arrive at each possible summated score except the extremes of eight and forty. It was assumed that a score of 24 was equal to a score of 24 even if individual score profiles produced radically different profiles. How this can occur is presented as an example.

	SA	*A*	*U*	*D*	*SD*
Item 1	5+	4	3#	2	1
2	5+	4	3#	2	1
3	5+	4	3#	2	1
*4	1+	2	3#	4	5
*5	1+	2	3#	4	5
6	5	4	3#	2	1+
7	5	4	3#	2	1+
8	5+	4	3#	2	1

*negative items reversed
individual 1# = 24
individual 2_{+} = 24

Each of the hypothetical respondents scored 24 on the orientation to physical labor scale, but they displayed quite different profiles. One individual had great difficulty making up his mind and so was undecided about all eight items. Individual number two was quite certain of himself with strong feelings about all eight, but four of his responses were not consistent with a positive orientation to physical labor. Although the individual attitudes reflected are quite different, from a scale point of view they are identical in that both were 24 scores on the scale. That is all one can say when using summated scores for statistical analysis.

This is one of shortcomings of the Likert scale; that is, no other interpretations can be given based on scale score alone. Despite this disadvantage, it has a relatively inexpensive computer scoring format and is quite popular. What about reliability and validity? No formal coefficients have been established on the illustrative scale, but among known groups, social science and education students tend to score lower than agricultural and engineering students.

Other means of establishing validity and reliability exist, and the following example describes one of them. In a study of prison personnel (we wished to see if what an individual did in the prison was related to how he felt about prisoners and their probable chances of rehabilitation), a one hundred-item scale was administered to two separate groups defined by experts (wardens) and by job categories as being committed to one ideology or the other (custody versus treatment). The first fifty items that most clearly discriminated between the two groups were then chosen to comprise the scale.[11] Given the pre-test, it was felt that the scale could differentiate between those who were committed to a custody ideology and tended to have a negative image of the inmate, and those who were treatment-oriented and had a positive image of inmate chances for rehabilitation. The study also found that treatment orientation was related to age, experience, education, and function in the prison. An example of some of our items follows. All items were scored on a Likert-type response format with a five-point scale from Strongly Agree to Strongly Disagree. Examples of both custodial orientation and treatment orientation follow.

Custodial Orientation Questions

1. Any reduction in security, no matter what the purposes might be, will jeopardize the internal order of the prison.

   SA A U D SD

2. Some people are always insisting that new treatment programs be experimented with; there are, however, enough at present.

   SA A U D SD

3. Any suggestions for reducing the amount of supervision inmates receive is destined to fail; changes of this nature are not needed.

SA A U D SD

Treatment Orientation Questions

1. Inmates are in prison to be rehabilitated and any changes based on this assumption should be implemented.

SA A U D SD

2. The warden should have an "open door hour" during which inmates could walk in and voice their complaints and grievances.

SA A U D SD

3. Opportunities for certain inmates to visit local communities frequently would be a satisfactory way of reducing the isolation of prisoners.[12]

SA A U D SD

Those with custodial orientations were expected to agree with custodial items, and those with treatment orientations were expected to agree with treatment-oriented statements.

THURSTON SCALES

This technique, developed by L. L. Thurston, enjoyed considerable popularity before computer facilities became generally available on the college campus. The major feature of this technique is the use of judges in assigning values to each schedule item. Procedurally, several hundred items are developed or collected representing positive and negative attitudes toward a class of persons (e.g., blacks, Jews) or objects (energy concerns, for example). After several hundred items are amassed, several hundred persons are chosen as judges (we have seen estimates of from fifty to three hundred judges needed) to rank the items.

Each of the items is ranked on an eleven-point continuum by each of the judges. The continuum represents attitude intensity from extremely favorable (11) through neutral to extremely unfavorable (1). Generally, values are generated for each item by judges giving each item a score of 1 to 11. Those with less deviation in score between judges are kept, and those with high variability are discarded. Variability is the focus, and not the magnitude of the score average on the continuum. Values for each item are obtained representing average judge scores along the eleven-point continuum. Each item, therefore, is represented by an average score that can range from 1 to 11. Any ten statements that span the eleven-point range can be used to form the scale. As a consequence, there are many scales in the items rated by the judges and found to have high agreement on the intensity value assigned among the judges. The major requirement is that the scale derived contain ten statements closely approximating the eleven points on the scale. Consider the following:

10.2 1. Criminals respect only strength.
9.1 2. The criminal is an enemy.
7.8 3. Criminal behavior is the result of mental degeneration.
6.9 4. Employees should attend a weekly class entitled "How to Handle Inmates" as part of an increased emphasis on guard training.
6.4 5. Inmates do not like to work because they are basically lazy.
6.0 6. Censorship of inmate mail is a necessary function and a precautionary measure which authorities cannot afford to give up.
5.4 7. Unrest in prisons is an outgrowth of the need for penal reform.
4.3 8. Prisons must become more geared to preparing men for parole through increased emphasis on post-release programs.
3.1 9. The home visitation program should be extended to include more inmates as long as there is little indication that the program will be abused.
1.9 10. One possible change in prisons would be to allow certain trustworthy inmates to be responsible for their own custody.

The items and their scale values form a scale of value intensity. The mean values beside the items do not appear on the scale as presented to the respondent. When the respondents select the items that are most consistent with their feelings or attitudes, they are unaware of their score of relative intensity. Instructions typically direct the respondents to choose the item most consistent with their position. That value becomes their individual score on the scale. The original format is preferable, that is, choosing the three items most consistent with their attitude. Their scale score becomes the medium value or the middle item chosen. For example, if items with 6.9, 7.8, and 9.1 values were chosen, the scale score for the individual would be 7.8.

The scale is an attempt to develop equal intervals between items and to overcome the difficulties noted in the Likert scale. Identical scores from different value positions cannot occur with the Thurston scale. Each individual must have come to the same score by essentially the same process. Since the technique requires a large number of items and judges, it is not as popular as it once was. Even so, it remains one of the major scale types.

GUTTMAN SCALES

The Guttman method of scale construction tests whether a series of items can be scaled along a single dimension continuum. A statistical procedure called the coefficient of reproducibility establishes the criteria to judge whether the items do indeed form a continuum. The scale is based on rank-ordering all items into a continuum of intensity. It is based on the premise that in endorsing an item all less intense items also would be endorsed. Perhaps an early example by Nunnally will help to clarify the scale. The response pattern found in the perfect Guttman scale is exactly what was obtained when people were rank-ordered on a physical height continuum. Suppose, for example, that persons are asked about their height, and researchers assume that they know how tall they are. The

> person who answers "yes" to the question, "Are you above 6½ feet tall?" will answer "yes" to "Are you above 6 feet tall?" and "yes" to all questions about heights down to zero. The person who answers "no" to the question, "Are you above 6½ feet tall?" but does answer "yes" to the question "Are you above 6 feet tall?" will answer "yes" to all questions about lower heights. Similarly with persons of all heights, by knowing the most extreme statement that a person endorses, his other responses can be predicted perfectly.[13]

Nunnally goes on to say that it is difficult to find a set of items that will scale perfectly.[14]

More recently, others have used the technique to develop a scale measuring things other than attitudes. Frank W. Young and Isao Fujimoto have used the technique to develop a scale of social differentiation for Latin American communities. Rather than focusing on attitudes, they used the provision of services to develop their scales. Instead of individuals, they rank-ordered communities on the basic services provided and developed their scales based on items such as the presence or absence of schools, a public square, branches of government, a bar, bakery, and butcher shop (see Tables 1 and 2).[15]

Fourteen steps are presented in Table 1. These items form the column headings in Table 2. Errors can be seen in the second table when a "one" appears after the series of zeros starts, or when a zero appears within a series of "ones" and the series of zeros has not started. For example, there is one error in column 13 (a theater where movies are regularly shown). The community Moche has a movie, but seven communities above it do not, which is an example of the first type of error. An example of the zero, or absence of services, can be seen in column 10 for Villa Reconcavo and Sayula. Neither of these communities had lodging accommodations, but several communities (8) below had such accommodations.

In essence, the Young-Fujimoto differentiation scale shows the relative complexity of Latin American communities based on the presence or absence of services. Indirectly, their scale would correlate highly with social structural complexity and the size of the community. The same type of scale can be applied to American cities, but the items would change. The Young and Fujimoto scale had a coefficient of reproducibility well above that required to state that the items and units (communities in this case) are scalable. It should be emphasized that these scales were developed from the data after collection and in that sense would probably be data bound (would not provide a basis for generalization to other populations). In other words, the items are limited to Latin American communities, and the scales would probably not be predictive or hold together if they were applied to the United States.

Table 1
Scale of Differentiation for Latin American Communities

STEP #	ITEM CONTENT	PROPORTION OF SAMPLE	SCALE ERROR FOR ITEMS
1	Community is autonomous and has a name that is publicly recognized.	100	0
2	There is an elementary school.	93	0
3	Village has a public square or plaza.	85	1
4	Village has at least one government organization such as a branch of agriculture, health, welfare, police, telegraph, post office, etc.	83	2
5	There is a bar or cantina.	78	5
6	There is a bakery.	72	5
7	There is a barber shop.	59	4
8	There is a butcher shop or butchering place where meat can be bought regularly.	44	2
9	A priest resides in the village.	41	6
10	There is a hotel, inn, or place known to provide accommodation.	37	2
11	There is a pool hall or place where similar commercial recreation is available.	24	3
12	There is a doctor resident in the community.	15	3
13	There is a theater where movies are regularly shown.	13	1
14	There is a gas station.	9	0
	Coefficient of scalability = .82		

Source: Frank W. Young and Isao Fujimoto, "Social Differentiation in Latin American Communities," *Economic Development and Cultural Change* 13 (April 1965): 347.

Table 2
Scalogram for General Differentiation Scale[1]

COMMUNITY	ITEMS (SEE TABLE 1 FOR CONTENT)													
	1	2	3	4	5	6	7	8	9	10	11	12	13	14
Bejucal	1	1	1	1	1	1	1	1	1	1	1	1	1	1
Turrialba	1	1	1	1	1	1	1	1	1	1	1	1	1	1
Quiroga	1	1	1	1	1	1	1	1	1	1	1	1	1	1
Bramon	1	1	0	1	1	1	1	1	0	1	1	1	1	1
Villa Reconcavo	1	1	1	1	1	1	1	1	0	0	1	1	1	0
Dzitas	1	1	1	1	1	1	1	1	0	1	1	1	1	0
Sayula	1	1	1	1	1	0	1	1	0	0	1	1	1	0
Chacaltianguis	1	1	1	1	1	1	1	1	1	1	1	1	1	0
Cunha	1	1	1	1	1	1	1	1	1	1	1	1	0	0
Cheran	1	1	1	1	1	1	1	1	1	1	1	2	0	0
Tepoztlan	1	1	1	1	1	1	1	1	1	1	1	2	0	0
Minas Velhas	1	1	1	1	1	1	0	1	1	1	1	2	0	0
Tobati	1	1	1	1	0	1	1	1	1	1	0	2	0	0
Huaylas	1	1	1	1	1	1	0	1	1	1	0	0	0	0
Mitla	1	1	1	1	1	1	1	1	1	1	0	0	0	0
Moche	1	1	1	1	1	1	1	1	1	0	0	2	1	0
Cantel	1	1	1	1	1	1	1	1	1	0	0	1	0	-
San Lorenzo de Quinti	1	1	1	1	1	1	1	1	1	0	0	2	0	0
El Palmar	1	1	1	1	1	1	-	1	1	-	0	2	0	0
Yalalag	1	1	1	1	1	1	1	1	1	0	0	2	0	0
Panchimalco	1	1	1	1	1	0	1	1	1	0	0	2	0	0
San Miguel Acatan	1	1	1	1	1	1	1	1	1	0	0	0	0	0
San Carlos	1	1	1	1	1	1	1	1	0	0	1	2	0	0
Oxchuc	1	1	1	1	1	0	1	1	0	0	-	0	0	0
Aguacatan	1	1	1	1	1	1	1	1	0	0	0	2	0	0
San Pedro La Laguna	1	1	1	1	1	1	1	1	0	0	0	0	0	
Cruz das Almas	1	1	1	1	1	1	0	1	0	0	0	0	0	0
Muquiyauyo	1	1	1	1	0	1	1	1	0	0	0	2	0	0
Teotitlan del Valle	1	1	1	1	1	1	1	1	0	0	0	2	0	0
Atzompa	1	1	1	-	1	0	1	1	0	0	0	0	0	0
Ita	1	1	1	1	1	1	1	0	0	0	0	1	0	0
Potam	1	1	1	1	0	1	1	0	0	0	1	1	0	0
Tzintzuntzan	1	1	1	1	1	1	0	0	1	0	0	2	0	0
San Juan Sur	1	1	1	1	1	1	0	0	0	0	0	0	0	0
Cancuc	1	1	1	1	1	0	0	1	0	0	0	0	0	0
Aritama	1	1	1	1	1	0	0	0	1	0	1	0	0	0
San Antonio Palopo	1	1	1	1	1	0	0	1	0	0	0	0	0	0
Chamula	1	1	1	1	1	0	0	0	0	0	0	0	0	0
Chinaulta	1	1	-	1	1	0	0	0	0	0	0	2	0	0

Table 2 (continued)
Scalogram for General Differentiation Scale[1]

COMMUNITY	ITEMS (SEE TABLE 1 FOR CONTENT)													
	1	2	3	4	5	6	7	8	9	10	11	12	13	14
Sta. Catarina Palopo	1	1	1	1	1	0	0	0	0	0	0	2	0	0
Peguche	1	1	1	0	1	0	0	0	0	0	0	2	0	0
Recuayhuanca	1	1	1	1	0	0	0	0	0	0	0	0	0	0
Amatenango del Valle	1	1	1	1	0	0	0	0	0	0	0	2	0	0
Santiago Chimaltenango	1	1	1	1	0	0	0	0	0	0	0	0	0	0
Chan Kom	1	1	1	1	0	0	1	0	0	0	0	2	0	0
Todos Santos Cuchumatan	1	1	1	1	0	0	0	0	0	0	0	0	0	0
Hualcan	1	1	1	0	0	0	0	0	0	0	0	0	0	0
Canas (del Tacuarembo)	1	1	0	0	1	0	0	0	0	0	0	2	0	0
Santa Cruz Etla	1	1	0	0	0	1	0	0	0	0	0	0	0	0
Soteapan	1	-	0	0	1	0	0	-	0	0	0	0	0	0
El Nacimiento	1	0	-	0	0	0	0	0	0	0	0	2	0	0
Punyaro	1	0	0	1	0	0	0	0	0	0	0	2	0	0
Buzios Island	1	0	0	0	0	0	0	0	0	0	0	2	0	0
Tusik	1	0	0	0	0	0	0	0	0	0	0	0	0	0

1. *Code:* 1—present within community; 2—not present in community, but service is readily accessible and regularly used; 0—absent.

Source: Frank W. Young and Isao Fujimoto, "Social Differentiation in Latin American Communities," *Economic Development and Cultural Change* 13 (April 1965): 348.

SUMMARY

This chapter introduces the reader to a number of concepts, rules, and techniques of data collection. Both the single question technique of questionnaire construction and the three major scale types are presented. In presenting material as suggestions for consideration in the data collection questionnaire construction, all possible material has not been exhausted.

Those interested in examining additional data collection and scaling techniques should consult the bibliography of general reference works at the end of this book.

NOTES

1. The obvious exception is the exploratory design wherein a new scale or measurement technique is being evaluated, and even under these conditions validation techniques are available.

2. Leon Festinger and Daniel Katz, *Research Methods in the Behavioral Sciences* (New York: Dryden Press, 1953), p. 336.

3. Ibid., pp. 347-48.

4. Ibid., p. 346.

5. Ibid., p. 347.

6. Jum C. Nunnally, Jr., *Tests and Measurement: Assessment and Prediction* (New York: McGraw-Hill Book Co., 1959), pp. 335-36.

7. Festinger and Katz, op. cit., pp. 348-49.

8. Ibid., p. 349.

9. Hereafter, the term *item* will be used to denote a single unit in a scale, while question will continue to refer to a unit in a questionnaire.

10. These standardized scores are familiar to students. With a large number (sometimes tens of thousands), norms are established that allow one to say that he scored in the top 10 percent on nationally standardized norms. Examples would be IQ tests, College Boards such as ACT Scores, and GRE or Graduate Examination Scores.

11. The study was pretested by the known groups method. That is, groups representative of each position involved in correction were chosen by a panel made up of wardens and custodial executives who were asked to respond to the questions. The entire instrument discriminated between these groups, but the terms that discriminated to the greatest degree were used in the actual test.

12. Jack H. Hedblom and George V. Brandmayr, *Program Change and Attitude in a Prison Setting*, Proceedings of the Canadian Congress of Criminology and Corrections, 1973, pp. 97-110.

13. Nunnally, op. cit., p. 309.

14. Ibid.

15. Frank W. Young and Isao Fujimoto, "Social Differentiation in Latin American Communities," *Economic Development and Cultural Change* 13 (April 1965): 347-48.

9

Preparation of Data for Analysis

The importance of careful thought and planning in the preparation of the research design before data collection actually begins cannot be overemphasized. As mentioned earlier, all too frequently, data are collected without sufficient time being invested in planning and developing the research process. Consequently, many research results are data bound or incapable of being generalized to other populations. This severely limits the value to the discipline and makes it more difficult to relate to other studies in the literature. A part of the planning process involves data handling and analysis. In fact, some have suggested that data handling, quality control, and thoroughness in preparation are the cornerstones of a good research project. Although the examples presented below are largely drawn from survey research, the principles and techniques that pertain are applicable to all research designs.[1]

DATA COLLECTION

The data collection stage is one of the most crucial steps in the research process. Data collection is occasionally mandated by the nature of the research problem addressed, but more commonly, an area of choice exists. The relative strengths and weaknesses of each choice must be carefully weighed with regard to the amount of time and money available for completion of the project. Although combinations of collection methods are equally possible in whatever data collection technique utilized, it is mandatory that some form of control[2] be employed in handling data. This is true whether one is engaged in library research or is handling data collected by questionnaires, observation, secondary data records, or any other source. Many of these control methods are very simple. For example, in researching literature the form presented below has proven useful in keeping track of material covered.

(JOURNAL-CHAPTER) ABSTRACT

Area

Scope

Major Variables, Concepts, and Relationships

Hypothesis (if any)

Sample Size, Type (if any)

Statistics

Major Results

Conclusions-Comments

These organizational categories are defined in the following way:

Area. General classification for filing for future use. Often used are broader classifications such as deviant behavior, juvenile delinquency, or social organization.

Scope. This term means the range within which an activity displays itself. For example, if the area designation was juvenile delinquency, perhaps the scope designation would be gang formation or leadership in juvenile gangs.[3]

Major Variables, Concepts, and Relationship. The dependent and independent variables under study are frequently designated in a reading; at other times, it will be necessary to deduce them from conclusions presented. Similarly, at times the relationship will be exactly specified; i.e., group solidarity (concept) decreases (relationship) as group size (concept) increases. In simple terms, group cohesion decreases as group size increases.

Hypothesis. At some level of abstraction, hypotheses will be apparent if used in the study. Because of space limitations, most journal articles will not show the derivation process and hypothesis at different abstract levels (if at all). Hence, at times it will be necessary to pull the hypothesis from the context of the article. The hypothesis (if only one has been tested) will often be the same as the variables, concepts, and relationships. For example, "group solidarity decreases as group size increases" is an hypothesis.

Sample Size, Type. If a sample has been used, the size and type of sample should be noted. This information may be needed in establishing the credibility of an article or in justifying the statistics (if any) used.[4]

Major Results. These usually can be taken from the summary and conclusions or discussion section of the material examined. At times, results may be displayed simply as a statement that the hypothesis in question was accepted or rejected. Negative results are seldom published, however.

Conclusions—Comments. Conclusions or items of interest in the article can be noted here. For example, one might read Nels Anderson's work, "The Hobo," and want to use the classification technique, with a completely different research subject.

This short form aids in avoiding duplication of effort caused by inconsistencies in notes. Where material to be organized is available only once, systematic notes can prevent serious error and loss of information.

Articles of interest should be cited exactly as they appear on the title page, including author, pages, journal number, and volume. It is not uncommon to borrow unpublished papers, journals, books, governmental reports, and the like, in the pursuit of a topic. As the literature search progresses, it becomes more difficult to remember exactly where all the information gathered originated. In the event the original sources must be consulted again for additional or missing data, it is a good habit to note the name of the library on the abstract records. Similar care should be taken with observation notes. In this case, the time of day, day, setting, and location of observations should be designated and the observation should be described completely. In all designs and in all data collection process, *it is better to overdocument than to underdocument.*

It is equally practical to make duplicate copies of all research materials, including notes, drafts, and data cards. Two copies of all research-related materials kept in two separate places provide inexpensive insurance when the cost of replacement is considered.

BUILDING A CODE BOOK

Just as it is difficult to remember all relevant journal citations, it is exceedingly difficult to remember exactly what decisions have been made in the ongoing process of a research project. Where a computer is to be used in the handling of data, certain organizational contingencies must be met. A code book must be built to provide information about the organization, identification, and location of data in IBM cards and to define what the punches in each column of each card mean relative to the identification code. In essence, a code book is a record of what data are contained in each column of the data card. It also provides information about how many cards (decks) are required to process the data contained in the questionnaire.

Perhaps it would be best to examine and understand what is contained on a single data card before considering multiple cards needed to record all of the data contained in a typical questionnaire. A typical data card is reproduced below.

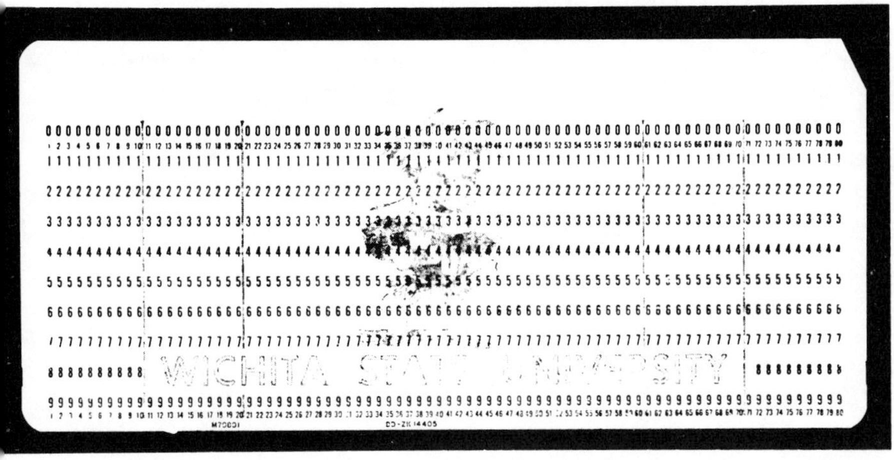

As can be seen, there are eighty columns in each card (vertical locations), and ten rows of digits (horizontal locations). Each column contains numbers from 0 to 9; however, there are two rows above the 0's in the vacant upper portion of the card. These rows do not show because their use is for alphabetical and special characters; therefore, there is no constant format such as is found in 0-9 rows. These two top rows are not generally used in statistical analysis because they represent the alpha portion of an alphanumeric digital computer system.[5] Most universities use such a system in registration and course card assignment. Typically, student name, course name and number, meeting time, and credit hours appear across the top of the data card. These letters are formed by punches either in the rows above the 0-9 rows, or in combination with the two upper rows and the ten numeric rows. These two upper rows are referred to by different names, but all designate the same data location. Although these two upper rows are frequently called *X* and *Y*, it is not uncommon to hear them referred to as the plus (+) and minus (−) designations, or sometimes used as the eleventh and twelfth codes for a question response.

In summary, there are eighty columns on the data card, and ten rows plus the *X* and *Y* rows which have limited analytical use. Each usually contains data for only one person or analytical unit. A combination of such cards for each person (unit) is called a "deck." For obvious reasons, it may take a number of cards to record the data from each respondent; it is possible to have a number of cards for each research project. Code books and data decks should be marked clearly so that continued use can be assured and guaranteed over a period of time.

In building a code for a project, it is often best to determine first what kind of data analysis is to be used. Is chi square (χ^2) to be involved? A means test (t)? Is it sufficient to know the number and percentage of cases in each coded classification? As an example, it may be sufficient to know how many and what percentage of respondents answered "yes" or "no" or "no response" or "don't know." In such a case, the following numerical values may be assigned to responses:

1 = yes
2 = no
3 = don't know
4 = no response

The 1-2-3-4 represent the number to be punched in the designated column of the data card. Whether the appropriate punch is a 1,2,3, or 4 will determine in which row the punch is made. In this case, the numbers used in the sense of gradation have no numerical value, and they serve only as identifiers of each of the coded categories "yes," "no," "don't know," and "no response." In other instances (codes), it can be seen that the numbers used actually have numerical meaning as discussed in the chapters on statistics and scaling. Meaning must be designated for each punch in each column prior to completing the code book for any project. Two items of information are vital to the completion of the code book:

1. What is to be done with the data? Is the analysis of a number of cases and percentage distributions for each question to be reported all that is required, or will it be necessary to compute additional statistics?
2. Do "canned programs" exist, that is, previously written and recorded tapes and decks of cards that "tell" the machine what information should be extracted from the data presented? What relationships are to be explored? Which of these programs are available at the digital computing service?

The first question is important because it has implications for how the code will be constructed. The second is even more important for data analysis and code building. In general, existing programs (canned programs) are easier and less expensive to use because they are "debugged."[6] This means that a manual of instructions is usually available, and the researchers need not worry about errors in the program affecting data interpretation. Special programs written for special projects are often plagued by technical problems. In the initial stages of research it is easier to plan to use an existing program known to be operating properly than it is to format data in such a manner that a specialized program has to be written for it.[7]

The same two questions raised earlier have implications for the assignment of variables to columns. In order to simplify this problem, we proceed in our discussion as if each column could handle each response to each question on the questionnaire. This is not ordinarily the case, and it is not unusual for data (answers) to require two or more columns to record. For example, if age is used as a continuous variable (raw scores for actual age), two columns are required to record the data. To record a respondent who is twenty years old where age is recorded in columns 11 and 12, a 2 punch is made in column 11 and a 0 is punched in column 12. Without a code, there would be no way of knowing that columns 11 and 12 together represent age as a variable.

The number of columns needed to record a variable on a data card is commonly called a "field" or "data field." By using existing or standard prewritten programs, there are great advantages to using a standard field size across each deck and preferably across all decks required for the study. For example, a researcher may be using a scale wherein it is necessary to analyze the responses to each item in the scale. However, it may also be necessary to analyze the summated score of all items in the scale. If there are ten items in the scale and the possible responses for each item are from 1 to 7, the summated score for each individual could range from a low of 10 (response of 1 to each of the ten items) to a high of 70 (response of 7 to each of the ten items). In either case, a two-column field would be needed to record the individual score between 10 and 70 for each response. Therefore, a two-column field would be necessary for the summated score, and it would be best to put each of the ten items into a two-column field rather than to have ten one-column fields then a two-column field for the summated score. For this reason it is best to go through the questionnaire to establish the widest field needed (in number of columns) and then to put all variables into the same size field (in our example, two-column fields).

This standardization will make it easier to write the work cards giving the computer directions to analyze the data. Standardization eliminates the need for the special program which analyzes nonstandard data fields.[8]

The single-column code shown in Figure 3 is included to illustrate how a simple code book would look. Many prefer to use the first ten columns of a card for information relevant to the project. These columns may be used as single-column fields, or they can be four- or more column fields. Since these first ten columns do not contain data to be tabulated, the field width (number of columns) is unimportant. Data may be contained in these columns, but if so, the data are used as "control" variables or to cross-tabulate other variables by these variables in columns 1-10 on the IBM card.

Figure 3
Code UYA Project
1974

Column	*Code Value*	*Question #*	*Variable #*
1	1 – 7	40 (residence)	Control
2	1 – 6	41 (race)	Control
3	0 – 9	42 (occupation)	Control
4	1 – 3	43 (employment status)	Control
5	1 – 9	44 (income)	Control
6	1 – 8	45 (education)	Control
7	1 – 6	46	
8-9-10	Schedule #		
11	1 – 7	1	1
12	"	2	2
13	"	3	3
14	"	4	4
15	"	5	5
↓	↓	↓	↓
49	1 – 7	39	39
50	1 – 4 Less than 25 = 1 25 – 44 = 2 45 – 64 = 3 65 + = 4	face sheet age	40
51	1 = female 2 = male 3 = not reported	face sheet	
52	6 = 1 18 = 3 7 = 2 25 = 4	face sheet tract number	42
53	1 = MNA	MNA = Model Neighborhood Area	43

The code sheet indicates that column 52 can have punches with values from 1 to 4, indicating census tract in which the respondent resides:

1 = Tract 6
2 = " 7
3 = " 18
4 = " 25

Further analysis was planned to see if there were differences between census tracts. For this reason residence is designated as a "control" variable. Column 2 indicates the self-designated race of the respondent and is coded:

1 = black
2 = white
3 = Mexican-American
4 = American Indian
5 = Oriental
6 = other

Because of the ethnic mix of the city, all categories were needed, including "other" as a residual category for nonresponses or those who indicated they did not choose to designate their race. It was also intended to use race as a control variable to ascertain if there were any differences in response that were related to it.

Similarly, all columns from 1 to 7 pertaining to occupation, employment, income, education, and race, were to be used as control variables to test for differences based on these responses. Columns 8, 9, and 10 were used to record the number assigned to the interview. Because the study required pooled data and not individual responses, numbers were assigned to each questionnaire in case a particular set of responses had to be checked for errors. As can be seen on the data pad, interview numbers are corrected from right to left. That is, if questionnaire one is recorded 1 in column 8, the computer would read the blanks in columns 9 and 10 as zeros, and the 1 in column 8 would be read as 100 instead of 001.

When we return to the UYA example, we note that possible responses to the interview questions ranged from (Strongly Agree) to (Strongly Disagree). This is noted in the code sheet column "Code Value." The question number is noted in the column to the right, in order to avoid confusing it with a response. In this study, it was planned that the data variables (right-most column) on the code sheet equal column number plus 10. For example, column 11 contains data for question 1, column 37 contains data for question 27, and so forth. Not all studies will work out in this manner because of the use of wider column fields, the existence of multiple response possibilities for one question, and for several other coding preference reasons.

The data statement pad contains all the data for each respondent contained in a single row. All data for respondent 1 are contained in row 1 marked 001 in columns 8, 9, and 10.

DATA QUALITY CONTROL

After data have been collected, some precautions should be exercised regardless of the mode of data collection.

Upon receiving data, particularly those derived from questionnaires, it is wise to look through the responses to check that all questions have been answered. If all questions have been answered on a given question, it should be marked indicating that it is complete. When questions have not been answered, a code mark on the face sheet should identify the incomplete question. All incomplete instruments should be examined as a group. By utilizing common criteria for all questionnaires, it should be possible to decide whether the nonresponses involve key questions making the questionnaire unusable. Although numbers of missing responses can be designated that absolutely render a questionnaire unusable, there are rules of thumb that can aid in decision-making. If a respondent has not provided a response to the question(s) being used for the dependent variable measure, probably that one missing response should eliminate the questionnaire from analysis. In questions where there are residual categories, such as "other" or "nonresponse," the missing data would not be of sufficient importance to exclude the questionnaire. In general, questionnaires that have 5 percent or more missing data should not be used. In the example cited, from the code, there were forty-six questions. By applying the formula of $46 \times .05 = 2.3$, questionnaires with three or more missing responses would be eliminated. There is no consensus on this cutoff figure, and there are techniques to supply these missing data (which will be discussed presently). Assigning a zero to a nonresponse is a form of filling in missing data that can have serious consequences in some statistical analysis. Moreover, the basic purpose of the research and the intended use of the data must be considered.

In making decisions, the following two points should be considered. (1) If at all possible, the same person should decide which questionnaires should be excluded. This approach will insure some consistency in decision-making. (2) The alternative is to establish objective criteria to be applied in all cases. Consistency of application of standards should result in systematic bias (if any bias at all) which is preferable to the introduction of random error. Allowing several individuals to apply their own standards for the inclusion or exclusion of questionnaires will result in random error since individuals differ in how they perceive things. The same reasoning pertains in the evaluation of open-ended responses. In short, a cursory examination should be made of the questionnaires, and exceptions to generally accepted practices in data analysis should be dealt with as exceptions but with consistent pre-prescribed, predetermined rules directing the inclusion or exclusion of questionnaires.

Finally, the practice of "full disclosure" should be considered. The researcher should be as clear and specific as possible in detailing and presenting data analysis techniques. When exceptions to stated procedures or criteria have been made, they should be explained with sufficient detail in order to let the reader determine whether exceptions have affected analysis or generalizations. Noting exceptions carefully can aid in replication which is essential to determinations of validity. Consider the following: "Questionnaires with insufficient data were excluded from analysis." For clarity and aid in replication the following would be preferable. "All questionnaires with three or more questions unanswered or nonresponse to question —(the dependent variable) were excluded from the analysis. Of the 501 questionnaires collected, 494 met the requirements for inclusion in our analysis." The second statement provides sufficient detail to allow replication of the study; the first merely mentions in passing that some questionnaires were excluded from the analysis. It does not state on what grounds the exclusion was made or the number excluded from the analysis.

After data have been collected and examined, the process of transferring them to card or tape storage to be used in analysis may be initiated. When questions are structured (see Chapter 8), there is little difficulty in transferring data from questionnaires to cards or tape. The totally structured instrument can frequently be used by the keypunch operator to punch cards directly from the questionnaire. Obviously, this direct punching cannot be used when open-ended questions are used or when numerical values must be assigned to verbal responses. When a study includes a large number of cases (usually survey research), it is both difficult and costly to have them contain open-ended questions. When keypunch operators are asked to punch from original schedules, a form of control is usually requested in the instructions to the computer center personnel. Requesting that cards be punched and verified assures a controlled measure of checking. The process requires that a second keypunch operator (preferably not the one making the original punches) use a machine to verify the original cards. This is done in the same manner as the original keypunch operator, but the holes are not punched. When the verification operator does not stroke the same key in the same column as the original punches, a red light comes on. This signal causes the verifier to recheck to see if either he or the original keypuncher has punched the wrong key. If the error is the verifier's, the card continues; if it is the

FORTRAN Coding Form

GX28-7327-6 U/M 050**
Printed in U.S.A.

PROGRAM

PROGRAMMER — DATE

PUNCHING INSTRUCTIONS — GRAPHIC — PUNCH

PAGE OF

CARD ELECTRO NUMBER*

COMM.	STATEMENT NUMBER	CONT.	FORTRAN STATEMENT	IDENTIFICATION SEQUENCE
1	2 3 4 5	6	7 8 9 10 11 12 13 14 15 16 17 18 19 20 21 22 23 24 25 26 27 28 29 30 31 32 33 34 35 36 37 38 39 40 41 42 43 44 45 46 47 48 49 50 51 52 53 54 55 56 57 58 59 60 61 62 63 64 65 66 67 68 69 70 71 72	73 74 75 76 77 78 79 80
1	2 3 4 5	6	7 8 9 10 11 12 13 14 15 16 17 18 19 20 21 22 23 24 25 26 27 28 29 30 31 32 33 34 35 36 37 38 39 40 41 42 43 44 45 46 47 48 49 50 51 52 53 54 55 56 57 58 59 60 61 62 63 64 65 66 67 68 69 70 71 72	73 74 75 76 77 78 79 80

*A standard card form, IBM electro 888157, is available for punching statements from this form

**Number of forms per pad may vary slightly

FIGURE 4 Data Analysis Statement Pad

original keypuncher's, a new card is made with the erroneous punch replaced by the correct one. When a deck of cards has been verified, a notch is cut in each card. In this way, the researcher can be certain that the data have been transferred from the questionnaire and verified before their release.

Many questionnaires are not totally structured with closed responses. In such cases, the data are often transferred from the questionnaire to a Fortran statement pad and the keypuncher punches cards from this pad. A copy of a sheet filled out for the 1-24 respondents in the code discussed earlier is shown in Figure 4.

While it is much easier to punch cards from these sheets, someone has to transfer the data from the questionnaire to the pads. In the first instance, additional time and money must be spent in keypunching because the actual questionnaire must be handled, pages turned, and so forth. In using a "statement pad," time and money are spent transferring the data to the pads. A cost-time decision must be made if both options are available. It should also be remembered that the more data are transferred or translated from one form to another, the greater the chance of error. Since data cards are usually verified, it is best to spot check the transfers from questionnaires to the data pads. This is accomplished by having someone, other than the person who made the original transfer, check each fifth, eight, or tenth questionnaire and record the number of errors discovered. If the errors are discovered in each questionnaire transfer, the whole transfer process will have to be checked and errors corrected. If there are comparatively few errors or, miraculously, none is discovered, the keypunch process may be initiated.

There are other techniques easily applied to facilitate sound data handling techniques. For example, a project involving five hundred questionnaires with four persons assisting with the data handling should not assign each of the four to do 125 questionnaires. The task should be divided by functions, and not by questionnaire number. The same person exercises the same judgments across all the questionnaires, not just the 125 questionnaires assigned to that individual. In the code example, there are forty-six questions in the questionnaire. Instead of assigning 125 schedules to each scorer, the following division would be preferable:

Person 1—Questions 1—12
Person 2—Questions 13—24
Person 3—Questions 25—35
Person 4—Questions 36—46

In this manner, each person will deal with the same questions on each of the five hundred questionnaires introducing a single bias of judgment (if any), not four different biases or perceptions on each question.

In addition, the persons involved in the questionnaire editing and transfer process should take staggered starts. For example, person 1 starts with number 1, person 2 with 126, and so forth. In this manner, the differing speeds of the workers will not slow the work.

All of the above presupposes that questionnaires were numbered from 1 to 500 and that a code book was made on column assignment and possible code responses. When a number of persons are involved in handling data, there is an increased need for checking and quality control. Each time a person uses a questionnaire for some purpose, it should be noted and initialed on the questionnaire. Clearly, data handling is a serious, time-consuming portion of the research process, but nonetheless an essential part of the total research process. The mundane day-to-day tasks of research cannot be relegated to untrained personnel or be done hastily. If the data base is not reliable and if it is not as free from errors as possible, the whole project has been built on a faulty foundation.

CHECKS ON DATA ADEQUACY

When data are collected and readied for analysis, a number of possible checks for adequacy are available but they are seldom employed. First, one should check to see if the data collected are representative of the population from which the sample was drawn. For example, it is possible to see, and even to run, tests to ascertain if the sample characteristics are similar to those in the general population.

It is important to check the sample with the universe when the universe statistics are known, in order to make generalizations from the sample to the universe. In fact, the quality of a sample can be measured by the degree to which it approximates the universe.

The second area of examination relates to the questionnaire and its validity and reliability. Tests of validity are checks to see if the instrument (questionnaire) is measuring what it purports to measure. Many books of scales give coefficients (computed statistics) of validity and reliability.[9] Since no statistical ability has been assumed on the part of the student of this text, two nonstatistical techniques are discussed. The first is "known groups." Consider that a scale purporting to measure student radicalism should have members of radical groups scoring higher on it than a random sample of students. If the questionnaire is administered to two randomly selected groups of radical students and nonradical students (perhaps defined by self-definition or lack of affiliation) and no significant differences in the scores of the two groups result, the validity of the scale can be questioned. The known groups technique can be used for any instrument where a known group can be designated or found to exist. This technique can also be used with statistical tests, but even a nonstatistical test is better than no test at all.

The "jury opinion" technique of scale validation is another method of ascertaining whether a scale measures what it is supposed to. It consists of using "experts" in an area to make judgments about the adequacy of the individual scale items. In fact, this technique is the same as the first step in item sorting and assigning scale values in the Thurston technique. Although expert opinions can be used in a nonstatistical manner, statistics can be used. Choosing the experts presumes some knowledge of the area on the part of the researchers.

Two methods of checking for the validity of the collected data are triangulation, or the use of individuals to validate data collected by questionnaires, and questionnaires, used to validate data collected by observational technique.

Although techniques exist to check the validity of what is being tested, in reality most studies report results obtained and reported on "face validity." Face validity is said to be a common sense claim of validity. That is, the scale has operationally been defined as measuring what it purports to measure without further validity checks. This technique is also sometimes referred to as the logical analysis method of scale validation.

Data may also be checked for reliability (defined as a measure capable of producing essentially the same results if used to test the same group at a point in time) by a method called test-retest reliability. Statistically, the results of the first test are correlated with the results of a second test, and the resulting statistic is called the coefficient of reliability. The method of testing for reliability applies more to scale construction and scales not previously used. Curiously, coefficients of reliability are seldom reported.

In short, techniques exist to test data reliability and validity, but, in most instances, they are not employed. The most serious shortcoming is in the area of validation. Many studies involve the development and use of a questionnaire (sometimes a scale) and rely on face validity alone. The reader must make his own assessment of the validity of the research and its generalization. If serious questions exist about the validity of the data and the extent to which the sample approximates the characteristics for the universe, the results and generalizations must also be seriously questioned. All too frequently, statements of caution are inserted in a research report after which the researcher proceeds to make dubious generalizations. For example, many community studies state: "No claim is made that the community is representative of all communities of this size, but it is believed that the community is sufficiently similar to other communities to warrant generalizations from the data." When such statements are made, the reader should be cautious about the generalizations made from the data.

SUMMARY

There are many techniques of data control that will assure the best possible data base for any given study. This includes care in handling, editing, and checking of data when they are collected. Care also results in better data to analyze and better storage of data in the interest of future use.

This chapter also suggests the use of certain data handling techniques to minimize errors in the data and presents techniques for dividing up tasks to keep the data preparation moving. Of course, these techniques apply principally to survey research of rather large sample size. When the research is a case study or participant observation study, the same degree of control and careful handling is required, but does not usually involve a division of tasks since one person generally does most of the work.

In studies using scales, further checks and tests are available to check for the validity and reliability of the instrument being used.[10] Checks can also be made on the characteristics of the sample against those of the universe when data are available for the universe. When the research is basically observation or participant observation, triangulation can be used as a validity check on what has been observed.

While many checks and tests are available, for the most part validity, reliability, and sample checks are seldom applied in research studies. It is imperative to develop the critical ability to question research results on a rational basis. All results should be analyzed, questioned, and examined for alternative hypothesis or explanations. The results of a particular study are only as good as the methods and data preparation used to derive them. Skepticism is a healthy attitude with which to approach the evaluation of a piece of research. In science there are no unimpeachable sources.

NOTES

1. See Chapter 7 and the description of the exploratory research on the social career of lesbians in Chapter 14.

2. By control we mean careful marking, handling, coding, storage, and so forth, of the data that have been collected. This is not to suggest the selection of cases favorable to some position and the elimination of those not supporting a preconceived position. Research integrity and credibility must start with the individual researcher.

3. The term *scope* is used in much the same manner as levels of abstraction or degrees of generalization are used.

4. See Chapter 17 for a short discussion of statistics.

5. The top two rows represent the alpha or alphabetical punches in this type of system.

6. "Debugged" indicates that the program has been run with an existing set of data, and that it has produced proper results and is known to be operating and free of errors.

7. Many institutions with data-computing facilities now have the Statistical Program for Social Science (SPSS) operating. This package contains nearly all the

program routines which most social scientists would use (except advanced or experimentals such as simulation). Certainly, it exceeds the needs of most students for whom this book has been written.

8. Other options are available, but they will not be discussed here.

9. See, for example, Charles M. Bonjean, et al., *Sociological Measurement: An Inventory of Scales and Indices* (San Francisco: Chandler Publishing Co. 1967), and Marvin E. Shaw and Jack M. Wright, *Scales for the Measurement of Attitudes* (New York: McGraw-Hill Book Co., 1967).

10. There are validity checks on observation-derived data as well. They are discussed in the chapter on researching covert behavior (Chapter 14).

10

Sampling

Learning to recognize and to use the proper sampling technique is one of the major components of research development and is essential to understanding research designs and results presented by others. The evaluation of research includes the suitability of designs and whether the results can be generalized to other populations and to the universe from which the sample was drawn. An understanding of design and sampling is therefore crucial to the research act and its evaluation.

The reason for sampling is clear; it allows the researcher to use a smaller size or reduced portion (sample) of an entire unit (universe) for ease of analysis. The reason for the use of the smaller portion usually relates to cost and time factors as well as ease in doing the research itself. This gives, in fact, a microcosm of a macrocosm. Indeed, the worth of a sample can be measured by the extent that its characteristics approximate those of the universe from which it is drawn. More details are presented on each of these points later in the chapter.

In some of its forms, sampling is familiar to all. For example, an individual engaged in cooking who tastes the dish being prepared is engaged in sampling. The spoonful of food tasted can be thought of as the sample, and the pan or bowl from which the spoonful was taken can be considered the universe. "Sample" and "universe" are major concepts in sampling. Again, in the example, it might be asked, "For what reason was the spoonful tasted?" It was tasted to ascertain if the dish in question was good or progressing satisfactorily. In essence, this tasting can be compared to the concept of "generalizing" from the sample to the universe. If the spoonful of food tasted good and all of the ingredients in the pot were included in the spoonful, it could be assumed that the entire pot of food would taste good. In essence, the researcher generalizes from spoon (sample) to pot (universe). This same process (and the same reasoning) is used when sampling is undertaken. The alternative to sampling in the example would defeat the purpose since it would require that the entire pot of food be eaten before the rush to judgment. Sampling does have its advantages.

When a number of persons are chosen for a sample, they are chosen in order to generalize to another population or universe. There is always concern about the representativeness of the sample: hence, in the example of food tasting, it is not uncommon to require that the food be stirred and tasted repeatedly. As expressed in yet another cooking example, a pie can be assumed to have been baked, sliced, tasted, and pronounced good. Can it be said that the entire pie is good? In most instances, such a judgment could be made. Assume, however, that part of the filling has not been stirred up in the sample, or a piece of topping missed, or that perhaps too much spice has been included in the sample piece. Assume further that this small portion has an offensive odor and taste. Recall that in the original example of cutting and tasting, pronouncing the pie "good" was based on the single piece sampled. What if the first piece cut had had the unstirred or overspiced portion in it? Would the sample then have pronounced the pie unpalatable? Would it if another slice had been cut and it too had bad places in it? In all probability, individual actions would differ. Some might have cut another piece, found it satisfactory, and eaten the rest of the pie. Others would have said the pie was "no good," thrown it out, and baked another. This example demonstrates two points. The first is called a *sampling error*. It is possible to select a sample of the universe that is not representative of the universe as a whole. Witness the bad slice in the pie. Therefore, the researcher must always be concerned with whether or not the sample is representative. Second, when the number (*N* size) of the sample is increased, the researcher may be more confident that the sample is indeed representative of the universe. When all of the pie has been found to have no bad places, one can be quite sure of being correct in saying "the pie is good" after eating one piece. Eating the entire pie to test its goodness, however, would violate the reason for sampling. A decision based on two pieces of pie (a greater sample) rather than one provides more confidence in the correctness of the decision. It follows then that confidence would increase with three pieces and four, until finally the sample size would equal the universe size—the whole pie. The representativeness of a sample can be said to increase as it approaches the size of the universe.

If one applies these principles to sampling a college class, it can be said that half of the class as a sample would eliminate some sampling error (not all) and would be a better (more representative) sample than one-fourth of the class, which in turn would be better than one-tenth of the class as a sample representative of the class as a whole.

In summary, the major concepts in sampling that have been examined are (in order):

1. sample
2. universe
3. generalizing to other populations or to the universe
4. sampling error
5. the relationship of *N* size to the confidence limits of the sample
6. the impact of sampling on research results and on cost and time limitations of research

All of these concepts are relevant to all types of samples. There are many kinds of sampling, each useful in its own unique way. Later in the chapter, a number of these special sampling techniques are examined in detail.

SAMPLES AND SAMPLING TECHNIQUES

One important initial problem in sampling is choosing the sampling technique that will best suit the research problem. This problem, discussed in part in Chapters 4 and 6, should be the researcher's first consideration. In developing the total research design, one of the first questions that must be asked, and soon answered (providing time and money are no concern), is, what kind of sample would be selected? The second question is, how many cases or individuals would constitute an ideal number (*N* size) guaranteeing the representativeness of the sample? Obviously, few researchers have unlimited time or funds, but limitations or deviations from the ideal must be made only as a last resort and with full knowledge of the effect that such deviations place on the sample, and, in turn, on the entire research effort.

Cochran and others have pointed out the following:

> Much effort has been applied in recent years, particularly in sampling human populations, to the development of sampling plans which simultaneously,
>
> (1) are economically feasible
> (2) give reasonably precise results, and
> (3) show within themselves an honest meaasure of fluctuation on their results.
>
> Any excuse for dangerous practice of treating nonrandom samples as random ones is now entirely tenuous.

This statement was made twenty years ago, but remains true and has became even more relevant today.

RANDOM SAMPLES

Although the term *random sample* commonly appears in the literature of research, few understand the mechanics of how a random sample is chosen. Few are aware of the underlying mathematical principles supporting the choices of individuals to be included in such a sample.

In most research efforts, it is assumed that generalizations can be made about a population, in detail and with predictable margins of error, if the sampling procedure has been correct. In some instances, it is even possible to make general statements about the attitude of millions of persons, based on the actions and attitudes of a few hundred. This is commonly done in the Harris, Roper, Gallup, and other opinion polls. It is less commonly known that much of the population data presented by the Census Bureau is based on one in twenty-five thousand sample with results generalized to the United States as a whole. As a result, when many persons are introduced to the concept of sampling, they come to feel that random sampling is the best of all possible samples. However, there are four different types of probability sampling:

1. Random sampling
2. Systematic sampling[2]
3. Stratified sampling
4. Cluster sampling

How do we define a probability sample? Its first distinguishing characteristic is that each person (unit) in a population has a known chance (probability) of being drawn in the sample. This presupposes that a list of names or identifying characteristics is available from which to select the sample. In fact, few such lists exist for very large units (cities) that do not build in bias or error into the sample. Where lists are available, they are often incomplete or represent specific reasons for existing, such as assessors' records, lists of social security recipients or welfare recipients, or telephone directories. Even when the lists exist, with the exception of the phone book, one cannot usually obtain them for use in drawing a sample. This is but one difficulty compounding the sampling process. Even so, it is on questions of sampling that most research projects stand or fall.

SIMPLE RANDOM SAMPLING

A simple random sample is a process of choosing individuals for study from a total population. The selection must be made so that each person has an equal chance of being drawn in the sample. It is at this point that a list of names is convenient. Such a list enables the researcher to assign a number for each member of the population. Assume that a researcher has a group of one hundred persons (population) from which a sample of ten is to be drawn. One technique would involve putting numbers on small squares of paper and then drawing ten numbers from the one hundred after they have been put in a box and shaken. These ten selections would constitute a random sample. On each of the draws, each of the one hundred would have the same chance of being drawn.[3]

The selection of a random sample is a precise, often difficult, task. For this reason, it must be assured that all individuals, including the typical and the hard to locate, do in fact have a chance of being drawn. In addition, each individual in the population must be listed once and only once.

In most practical research situations, obtaining the list will be the hardest task of all. Lists may exist, but often they are out of date—some individuals were not included, while others are no longer part of the population. As a cautionary statement, it must be remembered that no matter how accurate a list appears to be, its adequacy should always be investigated. A poor list can be worse than none if it leads to biased sampling.

What if the list is inadequate? If there are name duplications, they might be removed, if identified. Consider that a researcher wishes to draw a random sample of parents whose children attend a particular school. Some parents may have more than one child attending, so some means must be found to remove all but one of the children from the list, or include the parents only if their oldest child is chosen. The list is more likely to be incomplete and to have some omissions. It may be feasible to update it. If not, it may be possible to redefine the population. It is frequently possible to obtain a list of new additions to the population (such as new utilities users in a city) and a list of those removed from the population (such as utilities disconnected and service not resumed elsewhere in the city). These problems can in part be overcome by the use of other sampling techniques.

While choosing a sample by drawing numbered slips from a box has been illustrated, it is more practical to use a table of random numbers already constructed for this purpose. The details of its use will not be related here. Suffice it to say that the resource is readily available, and its use is not difficult to master.[4]

SYSTEMATIC SAMPLING

Systematic sampling is frequently confused with simple random sampling, and for many purposes may be used interchangeably with it. In systematic sampling, instead of using a table of random numbers, individuals are chosen from a list at specified intervals starting with a random selection of the first individual. For example, suppose a researcher wishes to draw a sample of one hundred from a list of one thousand persons. He or she would select each tenth name on the list, after choosing a random starting point in the first ten, chosen by the same process used to select each member of the random sample. If the seventh person was selected, then individuals numbered 17, 27, 37, 47, 57, and so forth, to the end of the list would be chosen.

For obvious reasons, systematic sampling is faster and easier than random sampling if a large sample is to be drawn or if the list defining the population is very long. Again, the technique requires the availability of the list of names, and it has the same difficulties (e.g., incompleteness and outdated information) as the random sample. The major caution in using this method is that the list should be so complied that it can be considered essentially random with respect to the variables being measured.

The systematic sample may cause serious biases in two types of situations. First, the individuals on the list may have been ordered so that a trend occurs. If persons have been listed according to office, prestige, or seniority, the position of the random start may affect the results. For example, if a one in ten sample is sought, a random start of nine would exclude the top eight officers—providing all the individuals on the list are ranked in order of importance (status) in the corporation. Hence, the nature of the list must be known before it can be used in the selection of a sample.

A second type of bias might occur if the list in question has some cyclical characteristics which correspond to the sample faction. For instance, suppose a survey is to be done of apartment house residents, with a one in ten sample sought. Every tenth apartment, however, is a corner unit, larger and more expensive than the other units. A sample might be drawn in which either all corner apartments were included or excluded. In either case, sample selection could be changed to one of several different random starts, e.g., so that after picking the first ten in the sample, a new random start would be used for the second ten, a new start for the third, and so forth.

Because systematic sampling is simple, it is used often. As with simple random sampling, the list must be both accurate and complete. If several cases were missing or unavailable, the ability to generalize to the population as a whole would be seriously compromised.

STRATIFIED SAMPLING

Differences between simple random and systematic sampling are minor in terms of cost saving or problems of analysis. The remaining two basic types of random sampling differ with regard to underlying assumptions. Under some circumstances, they may improve the efficiency of the sampling design, i.e., they may produce greater accuracy for the same cost or the same accuracy for less cost. In addition, the use of a different set of statistical tests becomes possible.

The definition of procedure for a stratified sample requires, first, that all individuals be stratified into groups based on some similarity and then that samples be selected within each group or stratum. It is important that the strata be defined in such a way that each individual appears in only one stratum. If the number of persons in each stratum are equal, we should select the same number from each stratum, then perhaps the proportional sampling technique should be used.

One reason for using a stratified sample can lie in the nature of the overall research design. We mean that the design may be a comparative one, testing whether there are differences between males and females in the dependent variable or theory. Field studies might indicate that race, age, education, or other variables might make a difference in the dependent variable. These proportions are expected to exist in the simple random sample, but for reasons mentioned previously, the inclusion of significant numbers of respondents from each stratum may be required. Another reason for taking this approach is to achieve a given degree of accuracy. To the degree that the strata are homogeneous with respect to the salient variables under study, the efficiency of the design can be improved.

PROPORTIONAL STRATIFIED SAMPLING

Proportional stratified sampling is most often used to assure a more representative sample than would be possible through other procedures. For example, assume a population of one thousand individuals exists, six hundred of them Protestants, three hundred Catholics, and one hundred Jews. If a simple random sample is drawn of one hundred, it would not be expected to contain exactly sixty Protestants, thirty Catholics, and ten Jews. The sampling error would most likely occur in the sample of Jews. Since there are only 10 percent Jews in the sample ($N-10$), even a 5 percent deviation ($N-5$) would result in a sample of either five or fifteen. In both cases, the stratum deviation is not 5 percent, but 50 percent, deviation from the needed proportional sample of ten. Such small number require special statistics.

In a random sample, there are two sources of variation: (1) errors *within* each stratum and (2) errors *between* stratum variation. If the criterion for stratification is highly related to the variable studied, the gain is probably considerable. Gaining some control over the variation insures more representativeness for a given size sample.

Before becoming overly enthusiastic about proportional stratified sampling, several cautions are in order. If the size of the sample is very large, chance factors alone (as in simple random samplings) will probably render a reasonably correct proportion for each stratum. In addition, it is possible to stratify only according to variables for which information is available at the time the sample is drawn. This means that researchers are most often restricted to stratifying on the basis of simple sociodemographic variables as age, sex, occupation, or area of residence. Since this procedure imposes some control on the sample, the possibilities of stratification should always be explored.

DISPROPORTIONAL STRATIFIED SAMPLING

Disproportional stratified sampling makes use of different sampling proportions within the strata to manipulate the number of cases drawn to improve the efficiency of the design. Consider three situations in which this type of sampling is desirable.

First, attention may center primarily on a separate subpopulation represented by the strata rather than the population as a whole. If the three major religious groups mentioned previously are to be compared with respect to their church attendance, simple random sampling and proportional stratified sampling might weigh the sample with too few Jews for meaningful comparisons unless the sample were extremely large. An option would be to select equal numbers from each stratum, i.e., fifty or one hundred respondents from the Protestant, Catholic, and Jewish subsample. If fifty were selected from each group in the original population of one thousand, the sampling fractions would be 1/12, 1/6, and 1/2. If generalizations were to be made to the entire population (one thousand) to estimate a mean attendance figure for the group as a whole, it would have to be adjusted or "weighted" by a statistical process which does not concern us at this time.[5]

Second, the use of disproportionate stratified sampling might be appropriate if there were considerable deviations within the separate strata. That is, if one particular stratum is unusually homogeneous with respect to the variable being studied, it would be unnecessary to select a vary large sample to obtain a given degree of accuracy. It is advisable to take a much larger sample from a heterogeneous stratum and fewer from the homogeneous ones. The resulting sample size may be smaller than that required in a random sample, but the inclusion of significant respondents from each stratum has been assured.[6] However, a particular stratum may be very homogeneous with respect to one variable and quite heterogeneous for another. Since more than one variable is usually being considered, it may prove difficult to ascertain disproportionate ratios which are optimal for more than one variable. In such cases, it is best to consult a sampling specialist before using disproportionate allocation. When in doubt, proportional sampling is the safest choice.

Finally, disproportional stratified sampling might be used when the cost of gathering data varies substantially from one stratum to another. The subject of cost has been neglected to this point since the selection of a sample has been considered under optimal conditions. Assume that this is not the case. Other factors being equal, it might well be less expensive to collect a larger sample from the most available strata. Since the use of disproportionate sampling tends to complicate problems of analysis, the cost factor may force its use. Such use should be undertaken with caution and due regard to its limitations.

CLUSTER SAMPLING

Cost and time factors are important in any research project. The time and difficulty involved in obtaining sample sources, lists of names, concerns about list accurcy as well as problems associated with sufficient information enabling the stratification of the sample into subpopulations can be avoided in some sampling techniques. Difficulties frequently arise in community surveys because of the geographical spread of randomly selected respondents in a given area. Moreover, it is sometimes difficult, if not impossible, to find the individual whose name has been drawn for the sample. Cluster sampling, nonprobability samples, and combination field procedures attempt to minimize field data collection cost without sacrificing representativeness of the sample.

In stratified sampling, the population is divided into groups called strata, and a sample is drawn from every stratum. It may be helpful to divide the population into a large number of groups, called clusters, and to sample from the clusters. For example, research emphasis may be amenable to measurement in census tract units. In a city with several hundred census tracts, forty might be decided on for a sample. The idea is to cut the cost of gathering data. The aim is to have clusters which are as heterogeneous as possible, yet small enough to cut down on the expenses involved in interviewing.

There are two types of cluster sampling. In the simplest, a *single-stage* cluster design, a random selection among clusters is used, and then every individual in the cluster is selected. In the other, *multi-stage* cluster design, a simple random sample of census tracts would be taken and then a simple random sample of blocks within these census tracts would be made (a smaller cluster). Finally, a systematic sample of every third dwelling unit within those blocks would be taken with interviews to be conducted with every second adult within those dwelling units.

In most cases, cluster sampling will be less efficient than any of the other three sampling procedures described. The probability for sampling errors is greater than with samples of the same size chosen by simple random sampling, systematic sampling, or stratified sampling. Since costs are usually less, the problem is one of balancing costs and efficiency.[7] The method that will yield the smallest error for the cost should generally be used (providing proper skill in applying appropriate analytic tests is available).

NONPROBABILITY SAMPLING

Research situations exist where it is impossible to satisfy the condition of a random or a random-like sample. This fact does not preclude research. Nonrandom sampling presents unique problems as well as unique advantages and disadvantages, not the least of which is that it is not possible to estimate sampling error.

The nonprobability-oriented sample is frequently exploratory (see the chapter on researching covert behavior). In an exploratory study, the main goal may be to obtain insights which may lead to testable hypotheses. It can also lead to viable generalizations. In such a case, probability sampling may be too expensive, or lead to fewer such insights, or simply be impossible, as is the case where one cannot estimate the parameters of the research universe. It may, therefore, be more helpful to interview persons who happen to be in a particularly good position to supply information. Perhaps interviewing extreme cases may provide more information than more traditional sampling designs can. In such cases, very helpful insights may be obtained and valid generalizations drawn, although only under very special conditions are they amenable to tests of statistical significance.[8]

In order to take advantage of the best features of the simple random, stratified, systematic, and cluster sampling techniques, the following multi-stage combination sampling technique is suggested. It is the result of a process geared to reduce sampling costs, minimize travel distances, and draw as small a representative sample as possible.

A COMBINATION FIELD PROCEDURE FOR DRAWING COMMUNITY SURVEY SAMPLES

The community survey researcher is constantly faced with difficulties of:

1. Selecting a sample from a universe that is not totally known.
2. Operating within time deadlines with regard to data collection and report requests.
3. Considering cost factors—time variables as well as personnel with cost factors of available time, personnel, and funds.

It is often impossible to draw a theoretically precise random sample because all units in the universe (community) are not known. Traditional examples of drawing numbered units from a box or casting an unbiased die (that is, one of a pair of dice) presuppose the ability to number all possible units in the universe. Further, textbook examples often assume that the unit can be returned to the population to be drawn again, thus not changing the probability as each additional sample unit is drawn.[9] These pure random sampling techniques cannot usually be utilized in the community survey. Certainly, various lists of the residents of a community are available, such as the telephone directory[10] and the criss-cross or (city directory) index which lists telephone numbers first and then provides the name and address of the individual who subscribes to the telephone service. Obviously, no sociodemographic data on social class, family size, sex, ethnic identity, marital status, income, and education are provided by these sources. Hence, any desired weighting or stratification in community sampling generally has to use the most recent U.S. Census data or more recent estimates or forecasts. These forecasts or projections provide sketchy detail, if any at all.

Fortunately, other records are available, such as credit bureau data, welfare rolls, tax records, and Dunn and Bradstreet listings. Most records, however, are not open or available to the survey researcher through legitimate channels. Even it these lists become available, none is complete because not everyone subscribes to the telephone service, pays taxes, is on welfare, or is listed in Dunn and Bradstreet. Each of the above lists could be considered a sample or even a universe of sorts, but the basic difficulty of not completely knowing parameters of the universe from which the sample is to be drawn remains.[11]

Selecting a sample from a list of individuals from any source and then tracking down these specific individuals is a costly and time-consuming process necessitating callbacks, appointments for convenient times for interview, and similar problems. If the sample is small, these obstacles can be overcome. However, cautions about using telephone directories, utility lists, voting registrations, school censuses, and the criss-cross index (city directories) still apply and are usually incorporated in presentations of these possible data sources. In essence, the problem centers on whether the sample is being drawn from a known or unknown universe. Most community surveys have to be drawn from a relatively unknown universe because of the mobility of many residents of a community at any given point in time. The amount of information that can be assumed about a universe is a function of recent trends in resident mobility: as mobility rates increase, the validity of assumptions of parameters decreases.

Stratified sampling techniques have been devised in order to overcome these difficulties and to assure some a priori weighting of criteria in the sample. Many variations have been developed, including area sampling systems from the U.S. Census, block sampling, cluster sampling, random selection of dwellings (systematic random sampling), selecting each *N*th dwelling, and various adaptations.[12]

The following attempts to overcome difficulties of sampling from a universe without a list of names of the individuals. At the same time, it allows for the control of selected sociodemographic characteristics of the respondents.

A SAMPLING MODEL—THE FIVE STAGES

A relatively simple but seemingly effective technique has been developed utilizing a five-stage random sampling process. It was developed to select respondents drawn in a survey sample of five hundred persons for Wichita, Kansas, a city of approximately 280,000 people. The process attempted to account for factors of age, sex, and geographical residential dispersion within the city.[13] This sampling technique has now been used annually for three years. It has been an excellent predictor of sociodemographic characteristics of age, sex, and race, considering the relatively small sample size in relation to the possible universe of 193,000, or those over sixteen years of age eligible for interview.

Sampling Procedure

A sample of approximately five hundred respondents was deemed the lower limit for sampling within time and cost factors of the project.[14] This provided a large enough sample for evaluation and was still within the constraints of time and money available. The sampling and subsequent interviewing produced usable samples of 493 respondents in 1971, 494 in 1972, and 497 in 1973.

Stage One—Office Selection

This sampling procedure requires that the first two stages be completed in the office and the other three in the field by interviewers. A map of the city was obtained that outlined the boundaries of all census tracts and also contained all streets marked within the city limits. The first stage consisted of randomly selecting approximately one-fourth of the census tracts in the city. This provided a spread across the city and at the same time provided clustering and reduced the geographic spread and cost of selecting respondents from all census tracts within the city. During each of the three years, a new set of census tracts was randomly selected. Hence, the same tracts were not used in each of the three yearly surveys. Some tracts were drawn only one year, some two years, and some randomly selected all three years.

Specifically, the technique was developed first by randomly selecting tracts from the eighty-two census tracts within the city limits. It was decided to sample approximately 25 percent of all possible census tracts using a table of random numbers and drawing randomly selected blocks within each census tract.

The number of interviews required from each census tract was obtained by adding the total number of residents in all selected census tracts. The population of each tract in turn was divided by this twenty tract summated figure to produce the percentage of the sample to be interviewed in each specific census tract. This percentage for each tract was multiplied by the five hundred sample size to produce the number of interviews from each tract. For example, if the twenty tracts contained approximately 70,000 persons, and one tract contained 6,300 or 9 percent, the tract would be used to select 45 or 9 percent of the desired five hundred sample.

Stage Two—Block Selection

After deciding how many respondents were to be obtained in each tract, the second stage was to choose randomly the blocks from which respondents would be selected. Each block in each selected tract was numbered on a city map, and blocks for each tract were randomly selected until the actual number of respondents from each tract was obtained. At this point, one respondent was selected for each block drawn. Each block was theoretically returned, and it was again possible to draw a previously selected block for a second, third, or even fourth time in some of the more densely populated census tracts. In actuality, some blocks were drawn three times in some of the larger tracts. The number of interviews needed per tract ranged from a high of forty-five to a low of six. A list of alternates was drawn in the same manner as the original list, and the procedure for selecting the house, age, and sex of the respondent was the same as the original block selection.

Stage Three—Field Selection

Selection of the household. The third stage was accomplished in the field by selecting the house from the designated block. For standardization, all interviewers were instructed to number the houses in a selected block, starting at the southwest corner of the block. They started with number 1 and then numbered consecutively north along the western edge of the block, east along the northern side of the block, south along the eastern side of the block, and west along the southernmost portion of the block. Hence, all of the houses on the block were numbered starting with 1 and going around the block, to the number of houses in the block. A set of numbers was provided in an envelope, and the interviewers were instructed to be sure that the corresponding numbers were included in the envelope. For example, if thirteen houses were situated around the block, numbers 1-13 were included in the envelope. After shaking up the envelope, the interviewer selected one of the numbers. This number designated the house from which a respondent was sought. Every effort was to be made to obtain an interview from that household. It should be recalled that in the larger tracts more than one respondent could be selected in a designated block. Many times two and, in some instances, three potential respondents were randomly selected from a single block. In this case, the interviewers were instructed to select the appropriate number of houses for that block. Hence, it was possible in census tracts to draw more than one respondent from the same block, but this was the exception and did not occur in all tracts.

Stages Four and Five—Respondent Selection

The fourth stage was relatively simple. After choosing the house from which to obtain an interview, interviewers were instructed to flip a coin to decide whether to interview a male or female at that house.[15] The house was then approached, and the purpose of the survey was explained to the individual who came to the door. Interviewees were then asked to provide the approximate ages of all individuals sixteen years of age and older, who permanently resided in the household. The researcher than selected which of the individuals residing in the household was to be interviewed. The fifth stage was to select the age of the individual by a random number that corresponded with the number beside the ages of the individuals entered on the face sheet of the schedule. (A copy of the front page of the questionnaire is presented in Figure 5.)

The block number was to be entered in the appropriate box in the top right-hand corner of the questionnaire. The interviewer also was instructed to enter the age of the respondent in the lower right-hand corner of the face sheet. All three of these items were necessary to analyze the data. For example, if there were three male residents of the household over sixteen

Sample No.

ASAP
Household Opinion and Attitude Survey
Wichita, Kansas
1971

Tract No.

Wichita State University

Block No.

This is a survey to obtain the opinions and attitudes of residents of Wichita, Kansas toward highway and traffic safety. It is being conducted by Wichita State University for the Department of Transportation.

To enable me to select the member of your household to be interviewed, I first need to know the approximate ages of all females over the age of 16 who are permanent residents at this address (oldest first, second oldest, etc.; list below). Now may I have the approximate ages of all males over the age of 16 who are permanent residents at this address (oldest first, second oldest, etc; continue list). (Check total household members and circle number indicating person interviewed.)

FEMALE		MALE	
1	______	1	______
2	______	2	______
3	______	3	______
4	______	4	______
5	______	5	______

	1	2	3	4
Date				
Time				
Results				

C - completed

RNH - respondent not home

APM - appointment made (state date and time)

CERTIFICATION

I hereby certify that the information listed on this form has been obtained by me from the respondents and is accurate and complete.

Age

Sex

____
Interviewer Signature Date

FIGURE 5 Questionnaire Front with Field Data Information

years of age and the coin flip determined that a male was to be interviewed at that household, numbers 1, 2, and 3 would be put in an envelope, shaken, and one selected. Interviewers were told to interview the individual whose age appeared opposite the number they selected. For example, the oldest person was listed first, and ages were ranked in decreasing order. If there were three males aged forty-two, nineteen, and sixteen and number two (2) was randomly selected, the nineteen-year-old male was interviewed.

Interviewers were told to be certain to interview the selected individual and not necessarily the person who answered the door. If the selected individual was not at home at that time, an attempt was to be made to make an appointment for a later time. If the selected individual was home, every reasonable effort was to be made to obtain the interview. After approaching a household, whether the interviewer was successful in finding someone at home, in interviewing an individual, or in making an appointment for a future time, the data, time, and disposition of the contact were reported in the appropriate boxes on the front page of the questionnaire (Figure 5). If no one was home at the time the call was made, the interviewer was to make three callbacks to that address during the time that they were in the field before moving to one of the alternates for selecting a replacement. Every effort was to be made to obtain the desired data from those originally selected by the five-stage selection procedure.

Results

This five-step random selection procedure produced a very close approximation of Wichita. Table 3 demonstrates the close approximations of the age, sex, and race factors and shows that the survey was not a survey of housewives more generally found at home during the daytime.

Table 3
Comparisons of Race, Sex, and Age for
Census Data and Household Surveys

RACE	WICHITA[1]	1971 SAMPLE	1972	1973
White	86.8%	86.8%	83.2%	82.8%
Black	9.7	10.4	13.9	10.8
"Chicano"	2.5	2.2	1.0	2.6
Other	1.0	.6	2.8	2.8
Sex				
Male	46.6%	45.0%	42.3%	46.9%
Female	53.4	55.0	57.8	53.1
Median Age	38.5 (yrs.)	38.8 (yrs.)	34.9 (yrs.)	39.5 (yrs.)

Total population 192,651 persons sixteen years of age or older in 1970, U.S. Census Reports.

The data presented in Table 3 indicate an oversampling of blacks in the 1972 sample and a slightly younger overall sample. In general, however, the age, sex, and race characteristics of the sample are excellent, considering the relatively small sample proportion, ease of selection, and the fact that it was not necessary to compile a list or directory and go to the expense of finding the actual individuals drawn in the sample.

While Wichita is generally a single-family-dwelling community, the five-step procedure could have been modified for use in multiple-family units, trailer courts, or apartment buildings. By using random selection in the field on age and sex, problems of interviewing those found at home during the day (mostly female) were averted. Interviewers simply selected individuals and called back to interview them if they were not at home when first contacted.

This particular model was used over a three-year period with ease, and the results from it were well within the expected diverse limits taken from the 1970 U.S. Census of Population. It proved to be a reliable and relatively inexpensive means of obtaining a random survey sample without the use of lists.

Technically, only age, sex, and residential dispersal were controlled for in this procedure. Race was controlled for indirectly in that it was highly correlated with specific residential areas of the city. This was contingent on the random selection of census tracts that were predominantly within the black and Mexican American residential areas of the city. Results of the distributions of these three sociodemographic variables are presented in Table 3. Three other variables used in the survey but not included in this sampling process are presented in Tables 4, 5, and 6.

Table 4[1]

Comparisons of Occupational Categories and Household Survey Results

	WICHITA %	1971 %	1972 %	1973 %
OCCUPATION	$N = 103{,}705$	$N = 360$[2]	$N = 342$[2]	$N = 377$[2]
Professional or management	18.1	18.3	21.9	15.4
Clerical or white collar	20.6	29.4	24.0	23.6
Craftsman or service	23.2	27.8	24.0	28.9
Labor	28.4	16.9	22.2	26.8
Sales	9.7	7.5	7.9	5.3
	100.0	99.9	100.0	100.0

1. Includes all those sixteen years and older.
2. Total listed as employed by occupation.

Table 5
Comparisons of Marital Status and Household Survey Results

MARITAL STATUS (14 + yrs.)	WICHITA % $N = 203{,}446$	SAMPLE YEAR 1971 % $N = 491$	1972 % $N = 494$	1973 % $N = 495$
Single	22.7	18.1	20.4	20.8
Married	63.5	65.2	67.4	66.1
Separated	1.5	1.8	1.2	3.2
Widowed	7.1	11.4	5.3	5.5
Divorced	5.2	3.5	5.7	4.4
	100.0	100.0	100.0	100.0

Table 6
Comparisons of Completed Education and Household Survey Results

YEARS OF SCHOOL COMPLETED (25 + yrs.)	WICHITA % $N = 146{,}379$	1971 % $N = 487$[1]	1972 % $N = 494$[1]	1973 % $N = 495$[1]
Under 8	7.8	2.1	0.4	4.0
8	11.2	7.2	5.3	5.7
9—11	17.7	15.2[2]	14.8[2]	22.0[2]
12	36.1	32.2	38.5	36.0
1—3 yrs. college	14.2	32.4[3]	27.0[3]	21.8[3]
4 yrs. college or more	13.0	10.9[4]	14.0[4]	10.5[4]
	100.0	100.0	100.0	100.0

1. Includes all those sixteen years and older for sample.
2. "Some high school."
3. "Some college."
4. "College completed" and "Graduate work."

Marital status, completed education of those twenty-five years of age and older, and occupation (excluding housewife, retired, and unemployed) were examined, and again the resulting distributions approximated the characteristics of the 1970 census data for the city. Admittedly, there are under- and overrepresentations in occupations and educational attainment, but again these variables were not used as a basis for selecting the respondents. Nonetheless, they support the representativeness of the sampling procedure in that the deviations from the 1970 data of this magnitude could occur in a pure random sampling process with an *N* of 500 from a possible universe size of 104,000 on the basis of chance. The procedures will be used in future research.

SUMMARY

It is important to know, recognize, and understand when and where to use various types of samples. Sampling is a crucial part of the research task. The process of generalizing from the sample to the population or universe is contingent upon it. Sampling is the very foundation of a research project and more than any other factor will determine a project's value and universality.

NOTES

1. William G. Cochran, et al., "Principles of Sampling," *Journal of the American Statistical Association* 49 (March 1954): 13-35.
2. Some methodologists argue that systematic sampling is not a bona fide random sampling procedure since after the selection of the interval, any case between two end points is automatically precluded from selection.
3. Strictly speaking, in order that the probability of choice be exactly the same for each ticket drawn, the squares of paper would have to be replaced after they were taken out of the box and their number noted.
4. Most statistics texts have a table of random numbers in the appendix with instructions for use presented in the text.
5. The concept of weighting requires that information be known about the universe that can be applied to the sample. For example, researchers could allow the answers from a subsample to represent only that part of the universe they represent. If the Catholic percentage of the universe was 8 percent, the researchers could allow their response to account for 8 percent of the summary statistics rather than one-third of the total.
6. This is occasionally referred to as a purposive sample. Frequently, however, use of this term confuses it with nonrandom sampling techniques whose validity is based on the researcher's ability to choose research subjects who are representative of a whole population.
7. The danger to type I or type II errors is referred to here. One must evaluate the cost of errors and then decide whether to take the risk. If one were to test the effi-

ciency of a cancer vaccine, one would want to be certain not to say that it worked when it did not. One would, therefore, try to avoid type I errors and set the highest standards for the evaluation of research findings. If only customer purchasing behavior were being predicted, error would be more permissible since the decision is not as crucial. The same reasoning would follow when considering the risks of saying you are wrong when in fact you are right (a type II error).

8. Things are said to be of statistical significance when they could not have been obtained by mere chance. Chance and probability are relatively simple concepts abstractly defined, mathematically expressed as the expansion of the binomial distributions, and depend upon a probability of 0.50 or 1/2. See Chapter 17.

9. Earl R. Babbie, *Survey Research Designs* (Belmont, Calif.: Wadsworth Publishing Co., 1973), pp. 73-74; Pauline V. Young, *Scientific Social Surveys and Research*, 4th ed. (Englewood Cliffs, N.J.: Prentice-Hall, 1966), p. 326.

10. Babbie, op. cit., p. 78; Young, op. cit., pp. 326-31.

11. Usually where list sources are cited, cautions are made to alert the researcher that telephone directories, criss-cross or city index material, vehicle registrations, and tax registrations are not complete listings, and most are ever changing and never totally accurate or up to date.

Joseph Perry, Jr., "A Note on the Use of Telephone Directories as a Sample Source," *Public Opinion Quarterly* 32 (Fall 1968): 691-95; David A. Leuthold and Raymond J. Scheele, "Patterns of Bias in Samples Based on Telephone Directories," *Public Opinion Quarterly* 35 (Summer 1971): 249-57. These two articles focus on bias produced by use of telephone directories and the effects of exclusion of those who do not subscribe to the telephone service and of those who have unlisted telephone numbers. Both circumstances would exclude the household or person from the survey. The same types of difficulties exist for each list available. However, because of time-cost factors, it may be necessary to use such a listing even with the known difficulties.

12. Any given number is designated as the *N*th. It is used in the same manner as *x* in algebra; hence, it can assume any given value.

13. Historical residential segregation into one quadrant of the city makes race a highly correlated factor with residence. The study was done by John J. Hartman, "Social Demographic Characteristics of Wichita, Sedwick County in *Metropolitan Wichita—Past, Present, and Future*, eds. Glenn Miller and Jimmy Skaggs (Lawrence, Kan.: Kansas Regents Press, 1978), pp. 32-37.

14. Only those sixteen years of age or older were eligible for interview in this survey.

15. An exception to this procedure was when only one sex resided at that house; if it was a single person (widowed, divorced, never married, separated), that person was to be interviewed. If more than one person of the same sex resided at the house, the respondent was randomly selected by age.

11

Interviewing

Interviewing is one of the major techniques for collecting social science data. Its successful use depends on personal awareness, experience, desire for improvement, and genuine enthusiasm. Many researchers do not like to interview and consequently avoid it; as a result, they also lose any opportunity to improve their skills in the area. Individuals are not "born interviewers"; rather they must learn interviewing as a skill. Hence, this chapter presents a number of recommendations and techniques that will help develop this skill.

The next chapter contains a discussion of the differences between the individual (one-to-one setting) and group data collection techniques (whereby a researcher is present, giving instruction, answering questions, and assisting respondents filling out a questionnaire). Some consider collecting data in a group setting interviewing while others do not. The question has yet to be resolved. (The group setting administration of questionnaires is discussed in the next chapter.)

DATA COLLECTION

Subjects are interviewed for a number of reasons. However, interviewing is particularly appropriate in two major areas with several subdivisions. In the first, the *data collection interview*, the social scientist interviews to collect data (information). There are many ways in which this interview is accomplished, but in each instance the major focus is on the data collection format. The second, the *clinical interview*, is for diagnostic or therapeutic purposes, and differs in both form and function from the data collection techniques of the social science researcher. The clinical interview is more likely to be the technique of the psychiatrist, psychologist, psychiatric social worker, or the social worker.

Data collection interviews as defined here have no motive other than the collection of information designated in a research design. Interim contacts may differ with regard to intensity or degree of contact as well as the number of times the interviewer actually interviews a respondent. In this setting, the interviewer structures the setting, tone, questions, and length of the interview before the interviewer has concluded. When a researcher wishes to collect data on the life history and experiences of a respondent, he or she is almost forced to interview them alone. It is impossible to obtain these data through observation, and it is exceedingly difficult to obtain them through other kinds of research.[1] Although values and attitudes can frequently be inferred through actions, they cannot be observed as such. Hence, they must be obtained through the interview. While behavior can be observed and causes or previous experiences imputed to it, the combination of observation and interviewing serves to generate richer data. Actually, the interview process adds the perspective of the respondent to that of the researcher, and in a unique way to the data derived from the interview schedule. Other points will become more salient as the discussion progresses.

CLINICAL INTERVIEWS

Although clinical interviews have some similarities to the data-generating interview, they differ in their most important aspect; intent. In the clinical interview, the interviewer seeks to have some effect on the person responding and not simply to obtain information for purposes of research. The objective of the interview is to isolate areas of concern to the respondent and to generate a plan of therapeutic measures. For example, when a medical doctor takes a patient's medical history, he is collecting information, but its use will be to diagnose the individual problem unique to the patient in front of him. Such an interview has no formal research intention and when this type of interview has been used for research purposes, the attempt is usually unsuccessful largely because of the motive and intent of the interview. The therapeutic setting, although similar to the data collection interview setting, differs from it dramatically in terms of intent and content.

Both the clinical and the data collection interview are legitimate methods of generating information. However, the clinical type is generally considered to be outside the realm of social science research, except possibly in some secondary data analysis research. There is another important difference between these two interview situations. In the case of the therapeutic interview, contact between the interviewer and the respondent is almost always initiated by the respondent. The roles of the participants are clearly defined with regard to who structures the situation and who is to benefit from the interview. Because of the nature of the contact and the roles and intent implicit in the setting, the cooperation of the respondent is virtually guaranteed. Service is provided by the interviewer, and the relative status of the interviewer and respondent is structured by that service. The clinical setting also provides other status cues and, more importantly, guarantees confidentiality. This encourages the respondent's cooperation and is augmented by norms supporting confiding in persons in the helping professions. In addition, the clinical interview often anticipates further contacts.

The data collection interview has none of these advantages. In this type of interview, contact is almost always initiated by the interviewer. He or she offers no service to the respondent; rather, it is the interviewer's needs and purposes that will be served, not the respondent's. The data collection interview can promise confidentiality, but no norms exist that invest it with the sanctity of the clinical setting. Similarly, there are no status cues to generate cooperation or respect for the intent of the research. The task of the social science interviewer is therefore a difficult one. He or she must develop the respondent's cooperation and willingness to respond in a contact originated by the interviewer. The accomplishment of these tasks constitutes successful interviewing. The behavioral scientist is therefore interested principally in the interview situation where the prospective respondent has been selected by some process by the researcher. The major points of departure between the two major interview types, then, are (1) purpose or intent and (2) method of selection.

TYPES OF INTERVIEWS

Interviews can be classified by criteria other than intent. One such classification is based on the structure of the interview. The three major types of structure are:

1. *Highly structured* with a standardized set of questions predetermined prior to the interview.
2. *Open-ended* (or uncontrolled, unstructured, or nonguided), a term which seems to have fewer negative connotations than the other terms. It is probably the most difficult of the three types to conduct well.
3. *The depth interview* which, as its name implies, involves an intimate, long-term conservation with a respondent in probing, expanding, and periodically summarizing his understanding of what the respondent has reported.

Perhaps an example of each type will make the distinctions more meaningful. At this point, the reader should be aware that interviewing as a process is directed solely for the purpose of clarification. Many of the techniques discussed are used without regard for the type of interview undertaken.

The structured interview is usually undertaken in survey research with a preselected group (sample) based on a common characteristic and usually involves use of a random sample. The questionnaire most often contains anticipated answers which are circled or checked by the interviewer. These questions or statements elicit rather specific information as a response. Long opinion responses are not characteristic of this type setting because they are difficult to code, and it is very difficult to handle open-ended questions from several hundred or even several thousand questionnaires. A sample question seeking information on sociodemographic characteristics might ask, "What is the present status of your driver's license?" The question should not generate a great deal of discussion, nor should it require many additional questions to find out whether they (1) have a valid license at present, (2) have never held one, (3) are presently suspended or under revocation, or (4) have a learners' permit. If all possible responses have been exhausted, a check or circle of the response is sufficient.

A large variety and number of questions can be asked in the structured interview. The technique is limited only in the sense that the interviewer is not free to explore areas as they arise that are not explicitly covered by the instrument. It does, however, allow the researcher to collect a large amount of data from a large number of respondents at a minimal cost per interview. A good interviewer will be able to keep the interview moving along without destroying rapport or jeopardizing the completion of the interview.

The open-ended interview is a good technique when coupled with an appropriate design and problem. In this type of interview, questions are designed to promote discussion and to encourage the interviewee to talk while concomitantly providing the center of attention. Respondents are encouraged to structure, dwell on, explain, rationalize, justify, or whatever they want to do within the framework of the subject of interest. The interviewer should maintain a low profile, offering additional questions or probes as needed to keep the conversational reporting flowing. This can be done by a nod, a nonword vocal response, or some show of attention. At the same time, the interviewer should be aware that facial expressions, impatience, or curtness can have a negative effect on continuing the interview.

While the open-ended interview is free flowing, it is not devoid of structure. The interviewer is free to raise additional questions to make sure the desired information has been obtained. Because of the obvious limitations of dealing with so much verbiage, the interviewer has to exercise some judgment as to exactly how much is written down. The interviewer frequently establishes a set of categories of response wherein he can record responses. He or she can also carefully keep field notes that will later help him reconstruct the more specific conditions of the interview. Exact duplication of conversation is not necessary for accuracy as a check on validity. It may be possible for an interviewer to check back with a respondent to check on the accuracy of his recording.

This type of interviewing is most often limited to a small sample, and usually the same person does most, if not all, of the interviewing. Depending on one's point of view, interviewer bias thereby increases or diminishes. Unfortunately, however, research design is limited to a small sample, and therefore its power of generalization is diminished.

The depth interview is similar to the open-ended type in that the interviewer is often seeking greater detail or intensity of feelings. In this regard, it is similar to the first part of the clinical or diagnostic interview. One will often find that some projective technique is used to elicit information from the respondent. As such, the depth interview technique has limited value for survey research, but it may be exactly the technique needed in a series of case histories or case studies. In fact, some works considered classics in the field have used this technique with great success.

The depth interview was originally intended to get at inner feelings or basic personality dynamics. It was used by Kinsey in his studies of sexual behavior and was considered unique at that time. In his discussion of his methods Kinsey stated: "In order to cover the maximum amount of material in a single interview, it is necessary to ask questions as rapidly as the subject can possibly comprehend and reply. This method has the further advantage of forcing the subject to answer spontaneously without too much premeditation."[2] Kinsey was seeking free expression of affectively loaded information that was not freely dispensed in the mid-1940s. At that time, the technique of rapid-fire questions to minimize rationalizations belonged more to the attorney than to the social scientist.

The depth interview has certain incidental effects of which the researcher should be aware. Some researchers who have used the technique in attempting to reconcile dissident factions in a group have found that it apparently broadens the respondent's awareness and perspective. The extension from individual concerns about self to the collective properties of a group is not a large or illogical step. Others have interviewed dissident factions of church groups to get beyond the affectual involvement level to the real issues. Often the individuals themselves were originally unable to move beyond the affectual level in emotionally charged issues. This use of the interview technique actually combines the open-ended and depth interview techniques. In this example, the problem did not relate to a theoretical question, but rather it was a pragmatic attempt to play the role of arbitrator and solve the problem.

PILOT STUDIES AND PRE-TEST INTERVIEWS

It has been recommended that researchers pre-test the questionnaire in the field before beginning the actual data collection phase of a project. During the pre-test period, the interview process is sometimes modified. One such modification is to inform the responding individual that data being collected are not part of a survey. The respondent is told that he or she is being asked to help check the questionnaire for clarity and understanding. Once this is established, the interviewer can interrupt the respondent and ask what came to mind when the question was asked. At this point, what was cued in the respondent's mind by the question is frequently more important than the response. Is the question evoking what it was intended to evoke? If not, now is the time to change the wording of the question. It is frequently profitable to tell the respondent what information is sought and then ask him or her to indicate which question would have prompted the most complete and accurate response. In this way, confusing words and phrases or questions can be avoided that might have been too personal or have evoked antagonism from the respondent.

Similarly, when a respondent is seen to hesitate to answer, it is best to stop the recording process and to ask additional questions to determine what caused the hesitancy.

At this point in the pre-test process, the purpose is to see if the questionnaire works, that is, if it provides a framework generating desired data, without contaminating it, and, further, if the respondents understand the questions. As such, any sample type or specific number of respondents are not considered. As a general rule, however, it is a good idea to pre-test on persons as similar to the intended sample as possible. It is also wise that the researchers who developed the interview schedule or questionnaire conduct some of the pre-test interviews since they are best equipped to evaluate responses and determine whether changes should be made.

The pre-test interview is a special-purpose interview intended to improve and/or check the questionnaire. It can also be used to familiarize interviewers with the schedule. Under no circumstances, however, should data collected in the pre-test be combined with actual survey results. The exact number of pre-tests to be done has not been specified. This is a function of time and money, but if the instrument is to be used for a survey of several hundred, twenty-five to fifty pre-test interviews should suffice. Moreover, the number of cases depends on whether the pre-test is also being used as an interviewer-training technique.

SUGGESTIONS FOR INTERVIEWING

Since there are a number of different types of interviews, not all of the following suggestions will apply to each interview situation. However, using as many as possible will enhance both the quality and quantity of the data collected for a research project, regardless of the type of interview used. The interview process can be seen as a serious social interaction in two areas. First, it is an intrusion into the life of the person being interviewed and may possibly have lasting effect. Second, it is becoming increasingly difficult to get individuals to participate in social surveys. The novelty of responding to survey requests of twenty to thirty years ago has long since passed. A number of factors, including increased crime rates, more single-person households, more aged females often living alone, and abuses of the social survey approach by photo studios, insurance salespersons, dance studios, magazine subscription offices, and, at times, home remodeling companies, have led to increased skepticism and refusals. The survey is a necessary tool of the social scientist, and these abuses have made our task more difficult, if not impossible.

The following subsections represent what may be considered a logical time sequencing of events in the interview process. Perhaps the order of some steps can be shifted, but all should be considered at one time or another in the project.

Background Knowledge

The interview process is in many ways analogous to communications processes. In the same sense that a communicator would not think of producing a message for the mass media without assessing the characteristics of the audience, neither should the interviewer. The researcher should be as familiar as possible with the characteristics of those to be interviewed. In some cases, the survey will span the full range of social strata, and it will not be possible to delve into the life-styles of all who might be part of the sample. On the other hand, in interviewing homosexuals one researcher found it best to be familiar with their word choices, areas of sensitivity, and whatever requirements were needed in collecting the needed data. For example, in an early form of the questionnaire dealing with certain dimensions of the social career of the lesbian the term *invert* was used as a synonym for lesbian. The word appeared frequently in the literature, and it was used for the sake of variety. In the pre-test, it was found that the word produced a violent reaction universally throughout the pre-test sample. Other words and phrases seemed to excite particular groups, such as feminists and black liberationists, within the pre-test sample. Hence, the final form of the questionnaire was written and structured by the experience of the pre-test. Parenthetically, it should be noted that one or two objections from individuals were not sufficient to justify change. The key to change was consensus in a given segment of the pre-test sample.

Other dimensions of interview-related difficulties uncovered by the pre-test are reported in Chapter 14. Suffice it to say here that where interviewers were male, potential respondents typically refused cooperation. When lesbian interviewers were used, cooperation among potential interviewees increased markedly. It may be that the background investigation will disclose that specific types of interviewers should be used, as, for example, a lesbian to interview lesbians, a black to interview blacks, and a Mexican American or Indian to interview their respective ethnic group. Research is an intrusion into the life of those who agree to participate in a survey, and investigators should endeavor to make the experience as pleasant as possible for those who choose to be cooperative.

Familiarity with Instrument

The interviewer should be totally familiar with the instrument or technique to be employed in data collection. Any card assists, letters of introduction, or any material needed should be readily at hand. The instrument should contain no words which the interviewer cannot pronounce or define and explain if asked to do so. The interview process is one the interviewer should control. He or she must appear nonthreatening, friendly, sincere, and committed to the purpose of the research.

Physical Setting

The physical setting of an interview can frequently influence the kind of data collected. Likewise, the interviewer by his very presence can influence both the respondent and the data. The nature of the interview and the information sought dictates, in part, the place where the interview is held. For example, interviewers have often experienced difficulty in interviewing a husband or a wife, only to have them both participate in the interview process when it occurs in their home. If information pertains to the household, discussions between spouses may promote useful additional information. In other cases, a researcher may wish to interview the husband and wife separately and thus would not want one to be physically present while the other is being interviewed—for example, discussing the frequency of sexual relations and the satisfactions derived by each. Will the attitudes of the husband affect those of the wife? Will they be open in the sense of risking elements of their relationships to be honest with the interviewer? Are individual and consensus attitudes being gathered? These are questions that must be resolved, and such decisions should have been made prior to the data collection process.

The presence of children, a television or radio playing in the room, or the conduct of the interview in a public place such as a shopping mall may affect the results, or even the chance of obtaining a completed interview. The researcher should try to anticipate these potential problems and avoid them when possible. In the case of interviewing individual members of a family, it is not difficult to move a member to a more neutral part of the house when seeking only their response. Most respondents understand the need for quiet and will cooperate if it is explained that their individual attention is required. It is important to stress the importance of their attitudes to the central purpose.

The timing of the interview is also important. The interview should not be conducted too early in the morning (9:00–9:30 A.M.), at meal time or during meal preparation, or too late in the evening, unless an appointment has been made with the person to be interviewed.

Opening Remarks

The first few words spoken by an interviewer may well determine whether an interview is obtained. If the interview is sought with no previous contact with potential respondents, a standardized opening or introduction may maximize cooperation among potential interviewees. In this opening, the interviewer should briefly state the purpose of the interview, under whose auspices it is being conducted, what is expected of respondents, and what purpose the research will ultimately serve. It is best to give respondents a chance to consider and ask questions. It is also a good practice to have a letter on official letterhead giving the name and telephone number of the project director or sponsor. This letter may be recognized as giving legitimacy to the research. An example of an opening statement is as follows:

This is a survey to obtain the opinions and attitudes of residents of Wichita, Kansas, toward highway and traffic safety. It is being conducted by Wichita State University for the Department of Transportation.

Purpose of the Interview

The purpose of the interview in a brief form should be included as part of the opening statement. This statement should also contain a description of the use of gathered information as well as guarantee anonymity to the respondent. The interviewer can explain that the data are to be pooled and that only group statistics will be used which do not identify the responses of individuals. The respondent should be assured that names do not appear on the interview form. If direct quotes from the interview are to be used, the respondent's permission should be obtained. This is called "full disclosure" and makes clear to the respondent exactly what will be done with obtained information. Although there is some controversy in this area, most feel that respondents should be promised anonymity and told the exact purpose of the research project. If they choose not to participate, so be it; the researcher has acted to guarantee his own integrity and that of the research. Growing concern for the human rights of participants in research on the part of university and major funding agencies is consistent with the need for full disclosure. It is often necessary to obtain university endorsement of these human rights in order to obtain funding from federal agencies. Although private funding or small grant sources do not have such requirements, it is still wise to adhere to the federal agency policy.

The following three statements demonstrate how particular characteristics of respondents can be described without identifying them as individuals.

(1) Mrs. Brown, mother of seven children in eight years, said that . . .
(2) A local mother of seven children in eight years said that . . .
(3) The mother of a large number of children in less than ten years of married life said . . .

Statement one obviously identifies Mrs. Brown. The second statement allows identification of Mrs. Brown if it is known that she has seven children and has been married eight years. The third statement contains most of the desired information that one would want to convey, but it does not point specifically to Mrs. Brown or a female who has borne seven children in eight years. Research findings can be related without identifying individuals. Even where the career of an individual is followed over a period of time as in Liebow's *Tally's Corner*, it is possible to cloak individual identity.

Finally, it is often possible to enlist participation in a study by offering a copy of the results when they are published.

Establishing Rapport

In establishing rapport with a respondent, a researcher must be sensitive to the prospective respondent's level of education and understanding. Establishing rapport is a process that begins when a potential respondent is approached. There is no known approach that can guarantee cooperation. Some people are simply not going to cooperate. There are many factors operating in establishing rapport with a potential respondent other than the personality of the interviewer. Frequently extraneous factors such as race, sexual preference, or even the sex of the interviewer can influence the data collection process. That is why earlier it was advocated that the interviewer be matched with the proposed sample, i.e., blacks with blacks, Chicanos with Chicanos, American Indians with Indians, or, as in the case cited previously, lesbians with lesbians. In addition, many researchers have found that professional interviewers provide the best possible combination of traits. However, it is the respondent, and not the interviewer, who defines the situation. Any effort to improve the probability of obtaining an interview should be undertaken so long as it does not violate the ethics or the integrity of the researcher, the research, or the respondent.

Neutrality and Opinions of Interviewers

The interviewers should be neutral in the interview process. They should say or do nothing to influence the responses of the interviewees. Voice shifts or changes of facial expressions can indicate approval or disapproval of response and contaminate the data. Some respondents are eager to please and try to give the response they feel the interviewer expects or wants. It is not uncommon for a respondent to say, "I really don't know what to say about that, just put down whatever you want to." We also have been asked, "what is your opinion about that?" Respondents should be told that there are no right or wrong answers and that their responses are the only correct ones. In short, there are enough extraneous factors that cannot be controlled without influencing the interview outcome by one's actions. These factors are summarized in a copy of instructions to interviewers issued to students collecting data in a number of research surveys, presented below.

INSTRUCTIONS TO INTERVIEWERS

I. *General Instructions*

The information that you are to collect on this project is to provide baseline information for a three-year study of drinking and driving behavior in the city of Wichita. We intend to collect a random sample of information, attitudes, and knowledge about the subject from a cross-section of the citizens of Wichita.

Hence, we want responses to the questionnaires from those who drive and those who do not. You should, therefore, not allow respondents to refuse cooperation simply because they do not drive or do not drink. His opinions as reflected in his response to the questions not relating to drinking will be of interest to us and to the Department of Transportation, the agency sponsoring this research. Both the census tracts and the blocks assigned to you have been carefully selected by a random process. It is our hope that you will be able to obtain the information from the house you select by your field procedure in each of the assigned blocks; however, when this is not possible, a list of alternatives has been provided. If for some reason you are unable to obtain an interview from the house chosen by your random process for the specified block, please go to the first alternative on the list provided for you. This list of alternatives is to be used only after you have exhausted the possibility of obtaining information from the household or if upon selection you find that a residence is vacant or the residents are on vacation and not available to you during the time you are in the field interviewing. It is essential to all concerned that you make every effort to obtain the interview from the first chosen household and that you view the alternative blocks as a last resort.

II. *Collecting Information*

In general, you are to regard yourself as an interviewer and as a neutral person. Your feelings about drinking or driving should not influence the information you receive on the questionnaire. Any comments you may wish to make should be reserved until your respondent has completed the questionnaire. If an individual makes comments requesting your attitude, please defer the individual politely to the end of the questionnaire. For example, you might choose to say, "Yes, of course, I have my own attitudes about the information, but we really prefer to have your opinion about the question, and I'll be happy to give you my opinion after the conclusion of the questionnaire." This is to avoid leading the respondent into giving socially desirable responses or responses that he believes that you as the interviewer are seeking. For most of the questions we are asking opinion-type questions that have no "right or wrong" answer. We seek a simple recording of the attitudes of the individuals who respond to our questionnaire. If for some reason respondents have difficulty in understanding or fail to respond to your request for information, please ask them if they do not understand the question or if it requires any explanation in terms of the words used in the questions. At this point, to the best of your ability, paraphrase or suggest in other words what the question means. Be certain to record that you have had to assist the individual by paraphrasing the question. It is essential to us that you collect information about all of the questions. Make an effort to have an individual give a response to all of the questions you ask them. Some individuals will say that they would like to skip a particular question and come back to it later. In some instances, you will not be able to avoid this and will have to go along with it, but in general, it is better to obtain the responses in the numerical order and to move straight through the questionnaire, because a number of cues are given in later questions. For example, after asking the individual to freely suggest some program areas that he thinks might be effective, the next series of questions might ask him how effective he believes a series of programs might be. If the individual asks you to skip that particular question and you then ask him the next four or five questions, you have in essence cued him to a number of programs that he might then come back to and give you in response to the question you asked earlier. When this occurs, the intent and purpose of the original question, asking him to freely suggest some programs, has been overcome by the next series of questions, destroying the validity of the first, open-ended, questions. Make every effort to have the individual respond to the questions in sequence. Also, it is important to us that you obtain an answer for every question. Please make effort to obtain a response for each of the questions. Mark the appropriate box for the individual's response immediately after he has responded. A most important point is that under no circumstances are you to leave the questionnaire for someone to fill out and return to you or for you to pick up at a later time. In all instances, you must be physically present and mark the individual's response on the questionnaire provided for that purpose. You will note that there are six questions in the questionnaire with which we attempt to structure the response of the individual by handing him a card. When this is the case, as in the first question which says "Hand *R* card *A*," after reading the question, hand the individual card *A* only and have him respond with whichever of the percentages on card *A* that he feels is appropriate. Then mark that particular number on the questionnaire. Do not give the individual any of the cards until they are called for in the questionnaire. Only when you have read the question which says "Hand *R* card *B*" is it appropriate to hand the individual the card. Do not hand him the packet of cards, and be sure to reclaim your set of cards from him before going to the next interview. It will be impossible for you to continue interviewing in other households without this set of cards.

III. *Questionnaire Disposition*

After you have collected a number of questionnaires and choose to no longer have responsibility for packing them around or having them at your house or on your person, turn them in to the office. Be certain that the secretary who receives the questionnaire marks the log for the number of questionnaires that you have provided and that she gives you a receipt for the correct number of completed questionnaires. Good luck in your interviewing, and if at any time during the study you have difficulty or need assistance, do not hesitate to call on me or one of the members of the staff. We will be most happy to assist you in any manner in collecting the information. This is a very important phase of our project and we very much need your full cooperation and your best effort in collecting these data for us.
Thank you.

ADDENDUM

Although it is not meant to reflect on the individual integrity of any of the interviewers selected for this project, each interviewer should be aware that provisions have been made to do a 10 percent callback on those households interviewed in order to ascertain the validity and reliability of the data collected.

Note-Taking Relative to the Interview

Field notes with regard to interviews are important not only to control for possible interviewer bias in the research process but also to note and later compare differing interviewee responses (e.g., belligerence, compliance). Field notes should be written as soon as the opportunity presents itself. As a rule, the longer the time after the interview the less accurate the notes. A tape recorder may prove useful at this point. There are a number of reasons why a researcher would wish to record the conditions of a given interview. For example, one might wish to compare the responses of those who were open and candid in the interview to those who seemed wary or skeptical.

It is useful to make notes on the questionnaire at the time the question is asked. Notes may also take the form of symbols that have some meaning or recall potential at a later time. There are no standard symbols. Researchers usually designate their own. It is a good practice for interviewers to use a slash (/) between comments when a probe has been used. A probe can be a simple statement of, "can you be more specific about that?", or "in what way do you mean?" In the study prefaced by the above "Instructions to Interviewers," when attempts to elicit more information were made and continued comments indicated to those editing and coding the questionnaire that the additional data were obtained as a result of asking for additional information, the data were not represented as a result of the first response to the question. How much probing, if any, is allowed should be the decision of the project director—a decision which all interviewers should carry out in the field.

Closing the Interview

How an interview is to be closed depends upon the sample and the type of interview that has been used. The type of sample has implications for the appropriate manner of closing an interview. A busy business executive or a housewife anxious to get on to other tasks will appreciate a brisk termination of the interaction. For example: "I know you are quite busy and we do appreciate the time and information you have given us. Are there any questions you would like to ask me before I leave?" The respondent has been given the opportunity to terminate the interaction or to continue it.

On the other hand, some researchers reported that respondents do not want to terminate the interview. This opportunity is particularly characteristic of older persons (sixty-five years and above) who reside in their own homes. Closing the interview is no problem when the researcher comes to the end of the instrument; however, leaving gracefully may prove difficult. Perhaps it is best simply to explain that research requires a schedule and work remains to be done.

Before leaving, the interviewer should answer specific questions put to him or her. In addition, the interviewer should insure that the interviewee is satisfied with the project and the respondent role.

Concluding Remarks

The following lists offer some helpful "do's and don't's" in interviewing.

Things to Do in Interviewing

1. Be familiar with the instrument and instruction.
2. Respect the integrity of the respondent and the interview.
3. Clearly explain the purpose of the interview.
4. Provide credentials without a show of annoyance if asked.
5. Be neutral in the interview process.
6. Control the physical setting to obtain the optimal possible setting in the circumstances.
7. Be courteous.
8. Establish and maintain rapport.
9. Thank the respondent for his or her cooperation.

Things to Avoid in Interviewing

1. Do not question or become argumentative over positions opposed to your own.
2. Do not regard information given as correct or incorrect; merely record it as information.
3. Do not waste the time of the respondent; close when appropriate.
4. Do not ask to use bathroom facilities or request something to drink unless invited.
5. Do not discuss other interviewees with the person being interviewed.
6. Avoid prolonged interruptions. If the person has too many distractions, ask for an appointment at a more suitable time.
7. Avoid skipping questions and missing data to the best of your ability.

SUMMARY

Interviewing is both an art and a science. While its basic principles can be mastered in a short time, its practice requires attention and experience. Interviewing will suit some better than others. For those who prefer not to interview themselves, knowledge of effective practices will enable them to supervise those hired for the interviewing process more efficiently.

NOTES

1. Some of this kind of information is available in private and public records.

2. A. C. Kinsey, et al., *Sexual Behavior of the Human Male* (Chicago: W. B. Saunders Co., 1948), p. 54.

12

Survey Research

Although the term *survey* has been widely used in the research literature, its definition seems to vary with usage. For the purpose of this discussion, it is defined as the systematic collection of data from a group (sample) of respondents utilizing a standardized (the same) questionnaire. A survey as such is not a research design; it is a data collection technique that can be used with all the three basic design types discussed in Chapter 4. Data collection techniques do not define the level of research to be approached. Instead, data collection techniques are dictated by the level or type of research chosen. While the manner in which questionnaires are administered may differ, i.e., individual interview versus group setting, or the use of mailed questionnaires, the basic method of data collection is the same.[1]

Research is an ongoing process, with most tasks either ongoing simultaneously or following closely one upon the other. It is not uncommon for the researcher to be involved in developing a data collection instrument, selecting a sample, and building a code book (or other interpretive framework) for data analysis all at approximately the same time.

The Gallup, Roper, and Harris opinion polls are well-known measures of public opinion. Not so well known is the fact that these major polls use a national probability sample of about fifteen hundred persons as a basis for their results. Hence, such polls reporting, for example, that 58 percent of the public approve of the way in which the president does his job as of a particular week are based on samples numbering approximately fifteen hundred. They are accurate to the extent that their characteristics as a sample approximate the population and, in turn, the universe from which they were drawn.

Most researchers (and institutions) do not have the prestige of the Gallup, Roper, and Harris opinion polls, and most are unable to pay respondents for their data collection surveys. Neither are most institutions able to analyze and present their results as rapidly as the nationally known research organizations.[2]

RELATIONSHIP TO THEORETICAL ORIENTATION

While the survey method of collecting data is not tied to any single theoretical orientation, it is more appropirate for some orientations than for others. It lends itself neatly to collection of data with individuals responding about themselves as the focus. Furthermore, it is best applied to those studies measuring or recording values, beliefs, attitudes, or propensity to act in a specified manner. Therefore, it is most frequently used with the structural functional orientation of the two theoretical/analytical postures presented in Chapters 2 and 3. That is not to say that survey collection techniques cannot be used to collect data from a symbolic interactionist perspective, which in this framework assumes the research instrument provides a vehicle, a kind of "self-report," i.e., perception of stigma, or expression of meanings. It is not the data collection technique that defines the type of research.

The theory to be tested and the relevant problem specification do not dictate the data collection technique absolutely; rather, they place limits on which techniques can most appropriately be used. The research process is ongoing and complex. Coordinating the entire effort is perhaps one of the researcher's most difficult tasks in a large-scale research effort. The integration of the various parts of a project can frequently be an elusive task. Even so, the clear delineation of the theoretical underpinning of the problem addressed, as well as the assumptions underlying the research design, are crucial to the development of a sound research effort.

EXAMPLE OF A SURVEY RESEARCH PROBLEM

Consider the following integration process. Among projects for term papers for education students, the following was assigned: Students were to make a comparative study of the "Self-Concepts of Two Groups of Negro Youth Attending a Segregated and an Integrated High School."[3] Without describing the design completely, examine the limiting factors and alternatives open in theory, the data collection technique, and finally, the analysis in the design.

Theoretical underpinning. As specified, the problem can be approached from the perspective of structural functionalism.[4] Certainly, it can also be approached from symbolic interactionism since self is one of the major concepts of this orientation. (This perspective would also address the situation of interaction and the concept of self, as well as perceived changes as a function of this interaction.)

Data collection model. The data collection design is relatively clear-cut. The problem states that we must have a cross-sectional design as discussed in Chapter 6.

Problem specification mandates that data must be collected from at least two high schools, one segregated, one integrated. These two groups are

ss-Sectional High School Study Design

shown in the figure. Is there anything in the nature of the problem that dictates the most appropriate means of collecting data? Participant observation might well require too much time, and in addition, it might well be difficult to assume the four requisite roles for any one researcher.[5]

Other observational techniques would be appropriate and would yield data descriptive of meanings and the interactional matrix unique in each situation. Given sufficient time, the use of survey methods and observational techniques simultaneously should result in both richer data and an excellent cross measure of validity. If, however, the researcher is caught in a time bind that requires the research task to be completed quickly, the survey technique will yield the largest amount of data in the shortest period of time. However, the quality of the data for analysis is independent of time requirements and time restrictions, in and of themselves, and should not be allowed to influence the sample type to the extent of weakening the entire research project.

Given the typical short-range research model, the following suggestions are offered. The first pertains to minimum sample size. Although there are no absolute correct sample sizes for any research project, the researcher should be aware that there are adjustments in statistical analysis for samples of thirty or smaller that compensate for small numbers.[6] There are no upper limits as to sample size. However, using the whole population is not consistent with the reasons for sampling. The law of large numbers indicates (and most methodologists would agree) that samples numbering a minimum of 100 to 125 cases usually assume normal distribution of the sample units.[7] That is, with samples of 100 or more, one tends to get a random-like distribution of the criterion variable (the criterion variable would be self-concept in our example).

In the example dealing with high school students' integration, no absolute figures exist which exactly define requisite sample size. A sample of approximately fifty randomly selected students from each of the high schools could suffice for the comparison. This is arbitrarily based in part on what is known about the data distributions and on how they are affected by increasing the number of cases or individuals included. It should also be considered that as sample size increases toward that of the population from which it is drawn, the greater the validity of generalization to the population. Population size therefore affects the sample size required for any research design. Absolute sample size is not so determined. Some populations can be approximated only by a large percentage of the whole constituency of the sample. For example, with a known population of fifty, the researcher would want more than a 10 percent sample to assure accuracy of generalization. On the other hand, when the known population is five hundred thousand, a carefully drawn sample constituting 1 percent or less might prove sufficient for research purposes. The researcher should recognize then that sample size relates to population size and to questions of validity. The purpose in sampling is to obtain a microcosm of the macrocosm, that is, the universe. In the sample, it remains to choose the operational measure of self-concept. For discussion purposes, the measurement scale is valid.

ANALYSIS OF THE DATA

Given the validity of the scale score measuring self-concept from each individual in the sample, a simple way of comparing these self-concepts could be the "Student's *t* test" which would measure the difference between means for the two school samples. If a significant difference existed (statistically) between the two samples, it would be possible to conclude that there was a difference in self-concept between the segregated and integrated high schools.[8] Conversely, if no differences were found, it would not be possible to assume that no difference existed. The validity of the instrument might be called into question, i.e., could it discriminate between two groups where differences of self-concept already are known to exist (the known groups teachnique). Granting the validity of the instrument, it would be necessary to assume that no real differences existed between the groups. There are many means of data analysis. In general, their use depends on the sampling technique used. It is the sampling procedure that determines what mathematical assumptions have been met, which in turn determine what techniques of analysis can be used.

SURVEY DATA COLLECTION TECHNIQUES

Interviewer-administered questionnaires. A number of data collection techniques are used in survey research, but certainly the most common is the questionnaire. The questionnaire has many variations and has proven to be highly adaptable to the requirements of data collection for any survey. For example, the questionnaire may be administered to a respondent by an interviewer who in turn records the answers to the questions asked. Although it is effective in that it generates responses from those chosen to respond, it is an expensive format. Even so, it has advantages. When an interviewer notes a respondent's refusal to answer a question, those involved in preparing data for analysis need not wonder if the question was omitted inadvertently. The individually administered questionnaire has the further advantage of obtaining better quality responses to open-ended questions. This follows since the interviewer can probe and insure complete responses. A predetermined number of probes should be specified, and then all interviews should follow the same routine in probing.[9]

By using a competent interviewer, it is possible to obtain a higher proportion of the designated interviews (through sampling). The quality and completeness of the data are better, and some control has been obtained by the interviewer reading the questions. Moreover, by using an interviewer it is often possible to obtain responses to longer questionnaires. When respondents have begun to reply to a questionnaire, most will continue to completion with a minimum of encouragement. The professionally trained interviewer who earns his or her living interviewing is the best interviewer to use. The use of female interviewers is also recommended because males generally respond better to female than to male interviewers and are less likely to refuse the interview at first request. Females, too, tend to respond better to female interviewers. The female interviewer is less threatening in the door-to-door interview situation when women are at home alone and less likely to talk to strangers. By the same token, the use of black or minority interviewers in black or minority neighborhoods will facilitate data collection. Using interviewers similar in background both improves the quality of data collected and minimizes refusals and resultant missing data.

Questionnaires administered in group settings. Having individuals respond to questionnaires in a group setting is a compromise between individual interviewing and the mailed questionnaire. This method has the advantage of having a researcher (or interviewer) physically present and able to give verbal instructions to the group before they start to respond to the questionnaire. It is, therefore, a much less expensive format than individual interviewing. In addition to the cost saving per interview, less time and travel cost are involved, and the quality of the interaction is not as intense as in the individual interview. Hence, the presence of the interviewer is less likely to result in biased data as a result of respondent interaction in group settings.

Despite its obvious advantages, the group format presents problems of a different order. For example, group sessions are often limited to those who can be assembled in a single place at the same time, and therefore it is difficult to fit into a sound sampling format.

This limitation is one of the reasons why so many studies use students, nursing home residents, prison populations, and members of churches and volunteer organizations as subjects. These populations are more readily available to the survey researcher whose work pertains to these relatively captive groups. A random sample of a population may never be present in the same location at any point in time. It is for this reason that group format surveys are limited to those populations that can be assembled in one place. From an analytic point of view, it is important to ask if the group intended to be interviewed would be representative of any larger universe. For example, it would not be possible to obtain valid information if the attitudes of factory workers with regard to urban renewal were measured, and then the data derived from this sample were generalized to the population in general. Clearly, there are attitudes indigeneous to the sample. The factory worker as a category would not span the full range of social statuses in most communities; consequently, as a sample factory workers are unrepresentative of the population to which we intend to generalize. Any conclusions drawn from such a sample would be erroneous for any category other than the sample itself or the category it represents.

One might ask, "Why not designate a time and place and ask individuals to come to to be interviewed?" This procedure would skew the sample since it would include only those people who wanted to be interviewed and could come to be interviewed at that time. Many contend that volunteer participapants similarly distort study results. Those who volunteer are apparently not typical of those who do not volunteer.[10] The universe being sampled contains both as should the sample.

Finally, in the group setting there is little or no interviewer interaction with the respondent. For various reasons, some responses collected in this group setting must be discarded as frivolous, unresponsive, or incomplete. Of the methods available, the individual interview technique is perhaps the best means for collecting data.

In a recent study of role theory focusing on the role of the juvenile probation officer, interviews were conducted on the following: judges and protems (four), juvenile probation officers (seventeen), and juvenile offenders (random sample, one hundred youths). The study was designed to show (1) how the court viewed the role of the probation officer; (2) how involved juveniles perceived the probation officer; and (3) how the probation officer himself viewed his role. In addition, second-order cognitions were sought dealing with how probation officers perceived others as seeing them. In order to minimize the interaction between the probation officers, researchers planned to assemble them quickly and have them respond to the same questionnaire all at the same time. This precaution was unnecessary for the offenders since they were randomly selected and the probability of interaction between these random sample respondents was small. It was equally unnecessary to interview the judges and judges protem all at the same time. Their position precluded such groups, and at any rate, their permission had been sought prior to beginning the study. In this design, a mixed mode of individual and group data collection was utilized. The group interview was chosen in order to reduce discussion of the project between respondents, and not as a time- and cost-reducing factor.

From any perspective, interviewing is an expensive data collection format. It is limited to the collection of specific kinds of information (mostly factual, perceptual, and attitudinal) and must be accomplished with the knowledge and consent of the respondent. This is a limitation not found in observational studies.

Mailed questionnaires. An attempt to collect large amounts of data with limited resources often results in a mailed questionnaire. The mailed questionnaire is a recognized data collection technique with considerably less cost involvement than the interviewing techniques. The data collection instrument or questionnaire may be the same one used in individual interviewing or in the group interview setting. Of course, the instrument must be free standing and self-explanatory (see Chapter 8). Since the mailed questionnaire lacks the advantage of the interviewer being physically present reading questions to the respondent, the paragraph bridges called "conversationalizing" in questionnaire construction are needed. In general, the mailed questionnaire has a place in the social sciences, but its shortcomings often outweigh its advantages.

First, the mailed questionnaire format requires a list of names and addresses of those to be included in the mailed survey. This problem is discussed in Chapter 10. The use of mailing lists presents problems of representativeness that are magnified by the typically low return of completed questionnaires.

In a mailed survey, it is best to keep the instrument short. An example of a simple but well-constructed questionnaire is that used prior to the 1971 White House conference on Aging (Figure 6). It is highly structured or it has what has previously been called a "closed" format (see Chapter 8). Each question is simply stated, each can be answered by a "yes" or "no" response, and question 18 has an "other" category in the event none of the anticipated responses fits the individual respondent.

Most recipients of this instrument were near or over sixty-five years of age, and educational levels were lower for this group than for the population as a whole. Many had not had as much experience with responding to scales and questionnaires as more recent generations. While the instrument might appear simplistic, it is a good example of a mailed questionnaire that is carefully tailored to the responding group. Since no interaction or research-respondent feedback is possible with a mailed instrument, it is best to design as simple an instrument as possible.

Some researchers have recommended the development of a simple technique for returning the questionnaire. Babbie suggests:

> The basic method for data collection through the mail has been the transmission of a questionnaire, accompanied by a letter of explanation and a return envelope. The respondent then completes the questionnaire and returns it to the research office through the mail, using the envelope provided for that purpose.[11]

While Babbie realizes that this is the most popular format, he advocates the use of self-mailing questionnaires:

> If the questionnaire is printed in the form of a booklet, it may be possible to obtain a three-panel, rather than two-panel cover. In this form, the back cover has a fold-out panel with an adhesive strip on it. —Upon completion of the questionnaire, the

WHITE HOUSE CONFERENCE ON AGING

OMB 83-S7008
Approval expires February 28, 1971

NCS USE ONLY				
0	0	0	0	0
1	1	1	1	1
2	2	2	2	2
3	3	3	3	3
4	4	4	4	4
5	5	5	5	5
6	6	6	6	6
7	7	7	7	7
8	8	8	8	8
9	9	9	9	9

President Nixon has called a White House Conference on Aging for November 1971. He has asked me, as his Special Assistant on the Aging, to direct it. In making plans for the conference, we want particularly to know what older Americans think their greatest needs are. Your answers to these questions will help us in our planning and in developing recommendations to the President. YOU NEED NOT SIGN YOUR NAME.

JOHN B. MARTIN
Special Assistant to the President for the Aging

INSTRUCTIONS: Please answer each question after the Chairman reads it. If your answer is "Yes", fill in the "O" in the Yes column. If your answer is "No", fill in the "O" in the No column - Like this: ●. Be sure to use a No. 2 or softer pencil. Ballpoint or any other pen may not be used. Do not make any stray marks on this sheet.

Yes No

1. O O Are you now retired?
O O — If not, would you like to be?

2. O O Are you working full-time?
O O — If not, would you like to be?

3. O O Are you working part-time?
O O If not, would you like to be?

4. O O Do you always have enough money to make ends meet?

5. O O Do you have enough money to buy the little extras you want?

6. O O Do you have a health problem you feel needs attention, but is not getting medical attention?

7. O O Are you usually able to see a doctor when you need one?

8. O O Are you usually able to see a dentist when you need one?

9. O O Did you get any drugs and prescriptions last month?
O O — Did you have enough money to pay for drugs and prescriptions?

10. O O Did you have any doctor expenses last month?
O O Did you have enough money to pay doctor bills last month?

11. O O Did you have any dental expenses last month?
O O Did you have enough money to pay dental bills last month?

12. Do older people need legal advice about:
O O making a will?
O O - probating a will?
O O — guardianship?

Yes No

13. O O Did you have any legal help in the past year?
O O — Did you have enough money to pay for legal help?

14. O O Do you have trouble paying for your housing costs -- including taxes, rent, electricity, etc.?

15. O O Do you live where you have to take care of repairs and maintenance?
O O If yes, would you like to live where you do not have to take care of repairs and maintenance?

16. O O Do you live where meals are available?
O O If not, would you like to have meals available?

17. O O Do you live where there is medical and nursing care available?
O O — If not, would you like to live where medical and nursing care is available?

18. O O Do you have trouble getting from home to places such as shopping, church or visiting friends? (if "No", mark "No" and go on to question 19; if "Yes", answer each of the following questions.)

O O - Is this because there is no public transportation (buses) near you?
O O - Is this because you do not have the money to pay the fare?
O O — Is this because it is hard to get on or off buses and subways?
O O — Is this because you find it physically difficult or tiring to get out and about?
O O — Is this because you do not have a car or are not able to drive a car?
O O — Is it for some other reason?

FIGURE 6 White House Conference on Aging

Figure 6 (cont.)

Yes No

19. O O Do you have enough money to buy the food you like?

20. O O Do you cook for yourself?
O O If yes, do you find it too much trouble to cook for yourself?

21. O O Do you eat alone?
O O If yes, would you like someone to eat with?

22. O O Is food packaged in too large amounts for your use?

23. O O Do you go to a senior citizen center?
O O If no, would you like to go to a senior citizen center?

24. O O Do you sometimes feel that you are just not wanted?

25. O O Do you sometimes feel that you have nothing to live for?

26. O O Do you belong to an organization for retired persons?
O O If not, do you want to belong to an organization for retired persons?

27. O O Do you live by yourself?
O O If not, do you live with your spouse only?
O O If not, do you live with one or more related persons such as children, other relatives or non-relatives?

28. O O Do you live in a retirement or nursing home?

29. Do you --
O O own the place where you live?
O O rent the place where you live?

30. O O Are you happy in the neighborhood where you live?

31. O O Have you been the victim of a consumer fraud in the past year?
O O Did you report this to anyone?
O O If you did not report this, was it because you did not know who could help you?
O O Were they able to help you?

Please mark only one answer for each of the following:

32. Do you live in --
O the country?
O a small town?
O a suburb?
O a city?

33. How far did you go in school?

O None
O Some Grammar School
O Finish Grammar School
O Some High School
O High School Graduate
O Some College
O College Graduate

34. Generally, how much income do you have each month?

O Less than $100
O $100 to $199
O $200 to $299
O $300 to $399
O $400 or more

35. Where does your money come from? (Mark more than one, if applicable)
O Earnings
O Social Security
O Employee pension
O Annuity
O Old Age Assistance
O Savings or investments
O Relatives

36. Generally, how much money do you spend each month?

O Less than $100
O $100 to $199
O $200 to $299
O $300 to $399
O $400 or more

37. Please mark how old you are:

O under 55
O 55 - 60
O 61 - 65
O 66 - 70
O 71 - 75
O 76 - 80
O 81 - 85
O 86 or older

38. Are you a --

O Man
O Woman

NCS P 332A (.16?

respondent may unfold the extra panel, lick the adhesive, and fold the panel around the questionnaire booklet. If the research officers' return address and postage is already printed on the extra panel, it can be placed directly in the mail for return.[12]

Any technique that helps maximize the response rate of a mailed questionnaire is good. Babbie goes into considerable detail about postage options (bulk mailing rates), techniques of followup mailings, and how to keep track of the returns in the event an outside event occurs while questionnaires are being returned. As an example he cites a researcher studying attitudes toward a political figure who during the data collection period is discovered to be supporting a mistress. As he states: "By knowing the date of that disclosure and the dates when questionnaires were received, the researcher would be in a position to determine the effects of the disclosure."[13]

Generally, return rates have been the area of most concern in mail surveys. The fact that all questionnaires are not returned may well introduce a bias. The researcher must ask, "are those who respond characteristic of all those to whom the questionnaire was sent?" The higher percentage of responses returned, the more confident one can be that the sample is truly representative of the universe.

What constitutes a satisfactory response in a mailed survey? Babbie has said, "Fifty percent is adequate, 60 percent is good, and 70 percent or more is very good."[14] Although Babbie is correct in seeking high returns, randomly mailed questionnaires, followup letters, and other reminders do not usually produce the desired returns. Many surveys have returns in the 30 to 40 percent range, and there are those that produce less than 20 percent responses. Obviously, low response rates must be examined carefully and one should be quite cautious in interpreting and generalizing from such results.

Generally, the mailed survey is a special technique to be employed in special circumstances. In some cases, money for data collection is minimal, and neither the individual nor self-administered group data collection methods can be employed. For example, if a researcher wanted to learn which concepts or text were most used by college teachers of family sociology, it would not be possible for him or her to interview a large number of teachers at the resident institution. National or regional meetings would constitute a biased sample (are sociologists who attend meetings representative of all sociologists who teach family sociology?) Hence, there are special uses for mailed questionnaires. They should be viewed as a highly specialized method because of the type of data they produce and because of the difficulties in getting returns.

Efforts to personalize mail questionnaire responses have resulted in increasing response rates. Dillman and Frey twice received 75 percent returns to a twelve-page (109 to 150 item) questionnaire mailed to the general public.[15] Their personalization efforts included individually typed names, inside addresses and personal salutations, individually signed letters (versus preprinted salutations and signatures), and prior contact by telephone.[16] In the Dillman-Frey survey, there was individual contact by telephone; the normal situation for the general mailed questionnaire did not hold, then, because the name, address, and telephone number had to be obtained, and time was required to make the telephone contacts. Hence, an added cost is incurred in this method. A comparison group returned a high (64.5 percent) but significantly lower percentage than those who received the telephone call.[17]

COMMUNITY SURVEY TECHNIQUES

Many social scientists are interested in surveying a community for either theoretical or pragmatic reasons. Whatever the reasons, there are procedures that will increase the probability of successfully obtaining the required data. From a pragmatic point of view, a survey can be used for satisfying contract obligations (as is the case with evaluation research), for making policy recommendations, or for any legitimate purpose defined by involved social scientists. The following outline and steps were developed by Baumel, Hobbs, and Powers;[18] the plan is presented with comments on each of the proposed steps:

1. *Identify the survey area.* The identification should include both the geographical area (i.e., all of the city within the city limits) and the substantive area. The substantive area is the more important of the two since it will define the nature of the questionnaire to be developed. For example, what is the community attitude toward revenue sharing?
2. *Engage a sponsoring group or organization who will agree to take major responsibility for organizing, planning, and executing the community survey.* Any time a researcher can involve a relevant group in the community, there is greater probability of obtaining the desired data. At times just sponsorship and association with a salient and respected group will insure obtaining results.
3. *Identify the groups or organizations relevant to the survey.* Who should the researcher be concerned with in the community? The researcher must be concerned with those private and public companies and agencies that relate to the interests of the survey. Coordinating agencies, such as chambers of commerce and fraternal or professional oranizations, are frequently of help.
4. *Contact key persons in the relevant groups.* The researcher should ascertain who can be most helpful to him in his project and make that person aware of the intent and benefit of the research. If actual cooperation cannot be obtained, an attempt should be made to secure the use of the name of the organization as a sponsor.
5. *Meet with representatives of relevant groups to discuss the survey.* Involving members of groups who have agreed to help with the survey is a good practice. Many interlinking relationships with other members of the community will

exist, and additional persons or organizations can be enlisted. The researcher should discuss the plans and mechanics of the survey process in order to enlist the aid of significant persons in deciding on the inclusion of any additional topics or subject areas that might be relevant to the survey.

6. *Develop the questionnaire.* After the areas of focus have been decided, develop questions and pay particular attention to the following points:
   a. Have representatives submit their ideas for questions and ask them which questions they feel are most important.
   b. Be certain that ideas are transferred into questions that elicit the data you require and at the same time are capable of being understood by potential respondents.
   c. Pre-test the resultant questionnaire with a small group to see if the desired data are obtained or if any of the questions should be reworded or deleted.
   d. Modify the questionnaire if necessitated by the pre-test. A good pre-test will determine any areas that are "sticky" and the reasons why (as discussed in Chapter 8). Prepare the number of questionnaires needed and make a considerable number of extra copies. (It is good practice to make about 30 percent more than the intended sample size as it is much easier to have them on hand than to have to run additional copies). These extra questionnaires are often used in preparing reports and tables, or for future reference.
7. *Define the geographic area in which persons are to be interviewed.* Some form of random selection of census tracts, blocks, or households may be made prior to actually determining the number of respondents desired. Obviously, steps 7, 8, and 9 can be changed in order of completion, but it is best to know something about the community prior to determining the actual number in the sample. One should know how many residents, households, and relevant organizations are in the community before determining sample size.
8. *Determine the number of households within the area.* Depending on the nature of the survey, the researcher may be involved in a neighborhood or only part of the community. If the community of interest is a large metropolitan area, U.S. Census block statistics are available. If the community is small, it may be necessary to compile your own information. One possible source of information that should not be overlooked is the county courthouse. Plat maps exist for most incorporated communities showing blocks and in many cases occupied dwellings. These records are open to the public in most states. A survey of a small community may also include rural residents in the nearby area. A decision must be made whether to include these rural residents in the survey.
9. *Draw the sample.* Any number of sampling techniques are available. (Most major ones are discussed in Chapter 10.) Some clustering procedures may be needed, depending on the community size and the number of respondents desired.
10. *Enlist volunteers to distribute and collect questionnaires.* This step is simplified or eliminated if most of the interviewing is to be done by professional interviewers. This step is precluded if the aid of the volunteer group has been obtained.
11. *Have training sessions for volunteer interviewers.* Explain the purpose of the survey, specifying what kind of information is being sought in the survey, and explain how to conduct an interview. In this regard, role-playing sessions have

proven helpful in familiarizing interviewers with the questionnaire. The amount of training required depends on whether these persons will actually interview prospective respondents or will simply make initial contact and leave the questionnaire to be mailed or picked up at a later time. Before attempting to interview a respondent, the researcher must be certain the interviewers become familiar with the questionnaire.

12. *Release publicity when interviewing starts.* In many communities, it will be possible to have news releases or newspaper mentions of the pending survey. The purpose of the survey and sponsoring agencies can be included in the release. Obviously, this will not be possible in many major cities, and even if it were possible, few people would become aware of the survey through these releases. Interviewers should be provided with credentials such as a letter. The credentials document should also state the purpose of the interview, promise anonymity to the respondent, and give a telephone number that the individual can call to check on the authenticity of the person. The letter should be signed by a well-known individual in one of the sponsoring agencies.
13. *Edit completed questionnaires.* This step is discussed in Chapter 9. As a reminder here, the step includes a check for missing data, nonresponses, multiple responses, and any parenthetical comments by the interviewer or respondent.
14. *Sort the questionnaires as they are returned.* If the researcher is involved in a large survey, it is better to keep questionnaires sorted by census tract or some geographic subdivision until the total number of questionnaires has been received. Decisions must be made whether to have interviewers turn in their questionnaires on a daily basis or whether the interviewers should be asked to keep all questionnaires for a tract or section. If the survey is large and interviewers assemble at a central meeting place, it is best to have interviewers turn in complete questionnaires on a daily or relatively frequent basis.
15. *Number questionnaires.* When all questionnaires have been returned, each should be assigned a number and filed. It is much easier to keep data in their proper folder than allow them to stack up and become difficult to find when needed.
16. *Develop a code for each question.* Many questionnaires (most survey instruments) are highly structured with check-off responses; however, residual categories such as "other" are often included. When a considerable number of "other" responses occur, a specific code should be built to include these new categories. Directions for building a code were presented earlier in the discussion of data handling.
17. *Code questionnaire responses.* In a structured check-off response instrument, this step usually consists of nothing more than circling the response with an "odd" colored ballpoint pen. Red, violet, green, or some color not normally used by the interviewers is easier to pick up on the page when transferring data either to data pads or to hand-tabulated tables. When open-ended questions are used, a coded response must be developed if computer tabulation is to be employed.
18. *Tabulate the coded response.* In small studies, categories and tables can be built by hand, but in most surveys the sample size would necessitate computer analysis of the data. (Preparation of the data is discussed in Chapter 9.) In general,

these categories and any cross-tabulations[19] should be planned prior to data collection.

10. *Analyze tabulated data.* This step would include examining percentage responses and reporting what these percentages and differences are. If statistics other than percentages are used, they should be computed at this time, more often than not by use of a computer routine. No matter what form of data analysis is planned, the planning should be completed prior to data collection and setting up table formats. Evaluations, table formats, any graphs, charts, or figures should be ongoing while data are being collected.
20. *Develop the survey report plan and a plan to distribute the results.*[20] If the survey has been sponsored and/or funded by an agency, this step must be in conjunction with any guidelines provided by the agency. If no guidelines have been provided, the responsibility falls to the researcher. It is recommended that the following outline be included in some manner. This does not mean the exact format must be used by the areas presented, but in some manner all points should be included. The report should be complete in its own right.

Introduction. Include the statement of the problem, theoretical orientation (if any), relevant literature, hypotheses to be tested (if any), and the plan of the following sections of the report.

Methods. Be thorough in presenting what you have done. It is better to overdocument than to be too skimpy in presenting methodology. The section should include:

(a) *sample:* size, type of selection.
(b) *data collection:* how data were collected, a comment on the questionnaire, any unusual occurrences in the timing, and the like.
(c) *analysis:* test or form of examination of the results.
(d) *results:* present results obtained without drawing conclusions, are hypotheses substantiated?
(e) *summary conclusions:* now it is appropriate to summarize the results and draw any conclusions.
(f) *appendix:* in most instances, the data collection questionnaire and any supporting tables not presented in the results section should be included in the appendix.

SUMMARY

This chapter covers the major considerations and techniques in survey research. It should be viewed as an introduction to survey techniques since survey research is probably the most used technique of data collection in the social sciences. As a departure, a step-by-step method of completing a community survey is presented which, if followed, should result in a well-ordered and structured survey.

The survey collection of data should be regarded as only one of the researcher's tools. Survey data are also collected by individual interviews, group setting interviews, and mailed questionnaires or opinionnaires. Each can be considered a special-purpose tool to be used in appropriate circumstances.

NOTES

1. Survey research is, for better or worse, always associated with the use of a research instrument, a questionnaire.

2. This statement does not apply to some large survey research centers at major educational institutions.

3. John W. Best, *Research in Education* (Englewood Cliffs, N.J.: Prentice-Hall), p. 31.

4. Other theories could be used; however, the examples are restricted to two major approaches used in the text.

5. (1) White in a segregated school; (2) white in an integrated school; (3) black in a segregated school; and (4) black in an integrated school.

6. Such techniques adjust distributions in that they allow methods of analysis to be used that presume an approximation of the "bell shaped curve."

7. Graphically, we mean that these tend to distribute themselves with regard to variation into what we know as the "bell shaped curve," which at the fiftieth percentile exactly splits the distribution.

8. The "Student's *t* test" is computed by the following formula:

$$t = \frac{\overline{X}_1 - \overline{X}_2}{S\bar{x}_1 - \bar{x}_2}$$

where

$\overline{X}_1$ is the arithmetic mean of sample number one.

$\overline{X}_2$ is the arithmetic mean of sample number two.

$S\bar{x}_1$ is the standard error of the mean of sample one.

$S\bar{x}_2$ is the standard error of the mean of sample two.

Standard error of the difference between means is symbolized by:

$$S\bar{x}_1 - \bar{x}_2 = t = \frac{\overline{X}_1 - \overline{X}_2}{\sqrt{\frac{S\overline{x}_1}{N_1} + \frac{S\overline{x}_2}{N_2}}} \quad \text{or} \quad t = \frac{\text{Mean}_1 - \text{Mean}_2}{\sqrt{\text{Standard error of difference between means}}}$$

Therefore, "*t*" is defined as the ratio of the difference between means to the standard means difference.

9. A drawback of this technique is interviewer bias. It is possible for an interviewer, through the inadvertent use of gesture or voice tone, to structure the response of research subjects. In order to minimize this effect, interviewers say the same thing to each research subject.

10. The problem of nonresponse and unavailability of some part of the universe is thoroughly discussed in Julian L. Simon, *Basic Research Methods in Social Science* (New York: Random House, 1969), pp. 117-19.

11. Earl R. Babbie, *Survey Research Methods* (Belmont, Calif.: Wadsworth Publishing Co., 1973), p. 160.

12. Ibid.
13. Ibid., p. 163.
14. Ibid., p. 165.
15. Don A. Dillman and James H. Frey, "The Contribution of Presentation to Mail Questionnaire Response as an Element in Previously Tested Method," *Journal of Applied Psychology* 59, No. 3 (1974): 297.
16. Ibid.
17. Ibid., p. 300.
18. C. Phillip Baumel, Daryl J. Hobbs, and Ronald C. Powers, *The Community Survey, Its Use in Development and Action Programs* (Ames: Iowa State University, 1964), Sociology Report 15, pp. 33-34.
19. Cross-tabulations refer to separation of data (a variable) from another variable. For example, a response to how well the president is doing in his job, by sex (difference in response by male and female) or by geographical residence (North or South), and so forth.
20. Baumel, Hobbs, and Powers, op. cit., pp. 33-34.

13

Population and Demography

Sources of Demographic Data
Measurement Rates
Ecological Variables
Migration
Population Pyramids
Population Projections
Simulations of Population Growth
Summary

Many social science students are interested in the sociodemographic characteristics of a sample or a group of individuals. The literature will frequently suggest that differences exist between groups based on sex, race, education, income, type or place of dwelling, and age. Sociology, psychology, education, political science, anthropology, and urban studies will all, at one time or another, be interested in these sociodemographic characteristics. One reason for including a special section on population analysis in this book is that the research methods used in this area are somewhat different from those used in any other area considered here. Most techniques in the formal study of demography are based on mathematics and standardization of rates to make possible comparisons of different size units of analysis. For example, stating that the birth rate for a county is 26.4 and for the state 15.4 allows direct comparison of a unit as small as a county to one as large as the state. A second reason for developing a separate chapter is that these demographic characteristics are not behavioral characteristics. Hence, for the most part any manipulation of figures represents simple nominal manipulations of sample characteristics. Nothing behavioral beyond the simple recording of the event (number of events) is included in this single manipulation. A chapter in *Sociology Today* is devoted to the consideration of "The Sociology of Demographic Behavior."[1] There Kingsley Davis concludes that simple demographic computations are devoid of theoretical underpinning; therefore, demography can be equally well practiced by individuals in mathematics, business, education, engineering, or any discipline where the individual has simple mathematical skills and interest in the area. Conversely, Davis points out that the demographic methods can and should be combined with sociological concerns and theory. He specifically points to studies in fertility, population change related to social and economic change, the labor force, and the family as fruitful areas of study by combining social theory with demographic techniques and skills. Finally, some knowledge of demography will assist the researcher in drawing samples, particularly where social stratification is a consideration.

Many studies and, in some cases, lower level theoretical propositions indicate there may be differences between groups or samples based on demographic characteristics. These characteristics include age, sex, race, educational attainment, income occupation, marital status, place of birth, and mother tongue. Where possible, researchers should use standard reporting categories (definitions) to facilitate comparisons with other research results. Such reporting categories not only make different studies more directly comparable, but they also make it possible to generalize from one group to another sharing similar demographic characteristics. In addition, demography should make the researcher more aware of sampling options available as well as what data are available, and where these data may be obtained.

SOURCES OF DEMOGRAPHIC DATA[2]

The U.S. Census has been taken at ten-year intervals in years ending in zero since 1790. A considerable amount of data are collected in these ten-year studies; the most recent data available are for 1970.[3] One of the difficulties of this ten-year census is that it is not sensitive to volatile shifts in an area resulting from economic changes. Even so, it would be impossible to keep a running inventory, such as the Census Clock at the Bureau of Census in Washington, D.C., for each community or county in the United States. The cost factor would not be worth the increase in precision of measurement of the population of a given city, county, or state. Statistics on the United States as a whole are presented in the United States Summary Series.[4] This series contains the data summated for each of the reporting units (states) and the District of Columbia, including characteristics such as total number, age, cohorts, sex, educational attainment, marital status, migration data, percentage voting in the last presidential election, civilian labor force, birth rates, death rates, and percentage who travel to work outside the county of residence. All data available at the state level are also available in the United States Summary Series.

Each ten years, four main volumes are compiled for each state. These are:

1. PC (1) 18 (A) Number of Inhabitants[5]
2. PC (1) 18 (B) General Population Characteristics[6]
3. PC (1) 18 (C) General Social and Economic Characteristics.[7]
4. PC (1) 18 (D) Detailed Characteristics[8]

Vital statistics are compiled and available for each state, each county in the state, and, usually, each city of ten thousand or more. These data (catalogued in most college libraries) are collected and reported on a yearly basis. The most recent statistics available can be obtained by writing the State Department of Vital Statistics at the appropriate state capital. These records provide the number of births (both by residence of the mother and place of occurrence), number of deaths, morbidity rates for selected illnesses, marriages, divorces, illegitimate births recorded, accidental deaths, and causes of death. A note of caution should be inserted here. Rates for each unit (state, county, or city) are computed on the basis of estimated populations for each of these units. Here it should be remembered that the U.S. Census occurs every ten years, and these rates have to use the 1970 population until 1981, or estimates have to be made for each of the political subunits unless a yearly census is taken by the state, as is the case in Kansas. With this method, the accuracy of some rates is questionable.

A second point to consider is that vital statistics data for most states are not very reliable prior to World War II because a number of births, deaths, and causes of death were not reported or recorded before this period. In addition, a number of states were involved in gerrymandering in the first two to three decades of the twentieth century, and not all county lines were stable in 1900.

Two additional sources of data for county and city are *The County and City Data Book*,[9] and *Statistical Abstracts of the United States*,[10] both of which are published every year. Both are limited since they also use the last U.S. Census data as a base until the next census, or until adjustments are made on population shifts or increases.

The student interested in local demographic data should not overlook two possible sources. In most of the larger cities, a center for urban studies may be part of a college or university. A second local source to be explored is within the local government structure. Ordinarily, an individual can locate an office, or a division of planning, sometimes known as the Metropolitan Area Planning Department. Any of these agencies will catalogue and compile data for the local city, county, and/or Standard Metropolitan Statistical Area (SMSA).[11]

The Census of Agriculture is taken every five years in the year preceding the U.S. Census. For example, the agriculture census was taken in 1969, again in 1974 and will be taken in 1979. In addition to the number of people living and farming in each county and state, information on land use, livestock, farm size, mechanization, and other characteristics are available in this source.[12]

The *United Nations Demographic Yearbook* is published annually and provides data on each country in the world for which data are available.[13] One must be careful because different definitions are used in some countries and not all data are compatible for comparisons with standard U.S. Census definitions. For example, for some countries any person who can sign his name is reported as literate. Time periods also differ considerably from country to country, with some countries not reporting data since 1939 and others reporting results of their most recent data collection period.[14]

MEASUREMENT RATES

Let us now examine the computation of the various rates reported in many of these demographic sources. Crude rates make no distinction or refinement of the units used to compute the rate. For example, the birth rate of 15.4 mentioned earlier would be computed in the following manner (as would all crude rates):

$$\frac{\text{number of events (births, deaths, etc.)}}{\text{TOTAL POPULATION FOR THE AREA}} \times 100$$

In a county with 6,800 residents, 105 births occur during the year. The crude birth rate would be:

$$\frac{105}{6{,}800} \times 1{,}000 = 15.4$$

Hence, crude rates include every man, woman, and child in the computation but standardize the rate for comparative purposes. A more meaningful rate would be one refined by being computed on the number of women in the country. A still more specific rate would be the number of births divided by the number of females in the fifteen to forty-four year cohort of females. Quite a number of different refined rates are computed on fertility; each is meaningful in its own context when compared with the same data from another unit. Most crude rates are computed and standardized on the basis of rates per one thousand; however, there are two notable exceptions. Sex ratios are expressed as the number of males per one hundred females. In our hypothetical county with 6,800 persons, let's assume that there are 3,550 females and 3,250 males. The sex ratio would be $\frac{3250}{3550}$ or 91.5 males per one hundred females in the country.[15] Numbers above one hundred indicate a surplus of males and are more likely to be found in rural areas, newly settled areas where men arrive first to prepare for their families, or where the presence of a military establishment distorts normal distribution of demographic data.

The second exception is that most morbidity rates are reported in rates per one hundred thousand, with some being reported in rates per ten thousand persons. Morbidity (illness, disease) statistics reported in the vital statistics for the state include rates for cancer, cardiovascular and upper respiratory diseases, heart attacks, and so forth. These events tend to be standardized on the one hundred thousand figure. The major consideration is that like units are being compared when comparisons are made. Whether a rate is crude or refined is not based on the number of events selected for computation. The number of births is the same, 105, whether for the crude birth rate or for one of the refined rates of fecundity, children ever born, replacement rates, fertility rates, and so forth. Only the denominator changes (usually becoming smaller), which has the effect of increasing the rate, but it becomes more meaningful when births are related only to females in the fifteen to forty-four year age cohort rather than to the overall population. The same comment can be made about death rates, aged percentage, educational attainment, income, and housing. Either crude or refined rates can be calculated for each of these variables. It depends on what is to be compared with another demographic area.

ECOLOGICAL VARIABLES

Differences in the distribution of individuals by geographic units give comparative information because of the ratio developed by using standard land units. In the United States, population density is usually expressed in the number of persons per square mile for a city, county, state, or the nation as a whole. Those nations on the metric system (and a large number of them are) generally use the hectare (1 hectare = 2.471 acres), or kilometers (1 square kilometer = 0.3861 square mile). The researcher must be certain he is comparing the same base when comparing density figures. Either the kilometer or mile can be used as a base. The base is divided into the number of persons per county, state, or nation to produce the density figure. Density figures range from less than one person per square mile to more than fifty thousand per square mile in some parts of the United States. The density figure gives some notion of the complexity of social organization possible and needed, but it is not a direct measure of social organization complexity. This figure can be misleading, however, in that again it is a crude rate and includes all land whether it is inhabited or not.

The student interested in techniques of analysis attempting to include more sophisticated analysis of city classifications should examine selected articles in *City Classification Handbook: Methods and Applications* edited by Brian J. L. Berry.[16] Although most of these articles are mathematical, they attempt to go beyond single variable relationships or descriptive rates and ratios of citizen characteristics. The second chapter by David R. Meyer has as its purpose:

1. To set forth a multi-dimensional analysis of standard metropolitan statistical areas (SMSA's) based on the characteristics of the nonwhite inhabitants.
2. To support some implications of the dimensions for understanding the intermetropolitan differentiation of nonwhites.
3. To propose a classification of SMSA's based on the characteristics of nonwhites.[17]

Meyer attempts to utilize a seven-factor matrix to develop his classification:

1. Socioeconomic status
2. Variations among nonwhite groups in socioeconomic status levels
3. Stage in life cycle
4. Size of housing and unemployment
5. Housing type
6. Position in urban hierarchy
7. Service workers[18]

These variables go well beyond the mere computation of rates and ratios, and attempt to get at the combination of demographic data and social interaction variables which Davis calls for. While Meyer's work represents a pioneering effort of this combination, it was not totally successful. As he concludes:

> In terms of classification of SMSA's according to the characteristics of nonwhites (mainly black Americans) we see that there is in fact a great deal of complexity, and it is difficult to interpret with our present knowledge because of the traditional interpretive bias. A variety of possible interpretations of the groups has been suggested but more research is needed before a definitive classification can be developed.[19]

It should be stressed that demographic data and those data termed ecological can be developed beyond the mere computation of rates and ratios; yet, much work remains to be accomplished in this area. The examination of ecological variables is more closely allied with sociological or behavioral research than the mere manipulation of the number of events recorded for any given group, births, deaths, percent married, and the like.

Much of the early work in this area evolved from the ecological approach employed by Park and Burgess in their studies of Chicago. Many concepts readily recognized today originated in their efforts at the University of Chicago. Their early studies centered on "natural areas" and the influence of geographical areas on social behavior as seen in Park and Burgess's "Concentric Zone Theory," with specified functions for each circle extending outward from the center and a description (ideal-type) of behavior of the residents of each of the zones as they extend outward from the downtown core area. Attempts were made to relate crime rates, mental illness, vice, and other forms of deviance to areas of the city based on the residents' characteristics. Concepts such as invasion, succession, integration, centralization, differential association, accommodation, acculturation, competition, conflict, and symbiosis have evolved from studies of the ecology of the urban areas.[20] Most of these concepts relate to process and are therefore rather difficult to measure in the statistical-empirical format. With notable exceptions, early writing in the area was descriptive rather than statistical, but it is a particularly rich tradition and should not be overlooked.

Rural-urban differences have changed so dramatically that it is almost meaningless to make a distinction between them in attempting to explain differences based on place of residence. The U.S. Census defines all population in communities of 2,500 or more as urban. Small communities of less than 2,500 and open farmland are classified as rural whether individuals living in the open country are engaged in farming, are retired, are working in a nearby community, or are totally involved in off-farm employment. Census data are available which indicate the number of persons classified as rural for each county, each state, and the nation as a whole. In addition, changes in the social structure and organization of communities are documented in the literature of rural sociologists published as Agriculture Experiment Station Bulletins through the land grant university in many states.

MIGRATION

The literature contains many theories and empirical generalizations about migration as a social phenomenon. In the nineteenth century, an Englishman, E. G. Ravenstein, observed and predicted differences in migration based on the sex of the migrant.[21] In his studies of England, he observed that females were likely to move shorter distances in search of work and were much more likely to move to a city or town as opposed to an outstate rural area, even though the surplus of males was to be found in the rural areas at that time.[22]

A relatively simple but useful measure of migration is called the residual method of computing migration rates. It is a crude measure which makes no attempt to redefine or sharpen the rate for age-specific cohorts. The rate is computed by recording the base-year population, adding all births for the time period examined, and subtracting the number of deaths; what remains is the "expected" population for the area. This figure is in turn subtracted from the actual observed population for that area and time. Differences between these two figures are assumed to be in-migration if the observed is larger than the expected figure. For example:

County A 1960 population	200,000
Births 1960-1970	30,000
Deaths 1960-1970	20,000
Expected 1970 population	210,000
Observed 1970 population	230,000
Difference	+ 20,000

Migration rate $\frac{20{,}000}{200{,}000} = 10$ percent

In this example, the migration rate is 20,000 ÷ 200,000 x 100 = 10 percent in-migration during the decade. The technique is considered to be a residual method since it takes into account only those who were present for the base-year count (1960) and those who were there for the 1970 census. It is not sensitive to factors such as a family being present in 1960, moving away for nine and a half years, and returning before the 1970 count. Nor does it take into account characteristics of the population at the base period compared to those in the 1970 observed count. As an example, the 1960 figure 200,000 could have been made up of 90 percent white population (180,000) and 10 percent black population (20,000). The 1970 examination could show that 40,000 blacks had migrated into the area during the decade. If we forget differential birthrates for the moment, this could mean that the 200,000 population had increased 40,000 or 20 percent. Perhaps 15 of the 20 percent would be attributed to in-migration (30,000), with the other 5 percent (10,000) attributed to natural increase or the surplus of births over deaths. In reality, the black population may have increased 200 percent from 20,000 (10 percent) to 60,000 (26 percent) in 1970. The net result would be that at least 20,000 whites had migrated from the area, or the 1970 population would be 160,000 whites and 60,000 blacks. This indeed has been the case in most of the central cities of the United States during the 1960 decade, but the point to be made is that these vast differences would not be revealed in the "crude" residual method of figuring migration in an area. The residual migration method allows no comments about the structure and composition of the population. The statistic is therefore only a crude rate examining the population at the base year and again at the last observed count. Returning to the example, one must turn to other techniques to explain differences in black population; hence, additional information beyond this simple technique would be needed. More sophisticated techniques for computing migration are available for those who require age-sex detail in their computations.

POPULATION PYRAMIDS

Population pyramids can be considered visual aids which serve demographers and the lay public alike in making comparisons between two or more populations at the same time, or of a time series of change by decades for the same county, state, or nation. Data on age and sex are necessary to compile population pyramids. Pyramids are usually made based on five-year cohorts for each sex. While census data are available for single years in the U.S. Census, single-year detail usually stops at age twenty-one and switches to five-year aggregates or cohorts throughout the remainder of the population. Table 7 below is useful in computing population pyramids since a percentage figure has to be computed for each five-year sex cohort. Rounding the upper limits of the pyramid at seventy-five years and over produces sixteen five-year cohorts for males and sixteen five-year cohorts for females. When a small number of pyramids are to be made, it is usually easier to compute the percentages with a small calculator. When a large number of pyramids are to be made, the percentages should be computed on the electronic computer, or better still on a plotting computer if available.

Data obtained and computed for Table 7 indicate that thirty-two calculations are necessary to build each pyramid. The number of persons for each five-year cohort must be divided by the total population for the unit under analysis. For example, the 12,425 males from 0 – 4 years in 1970 must be divided by 276,494, the 1970 census count, and then multiplied by 100. The resulting percentage (4.49 percent) is marked on graph paper to indicate where the line is drawn for the male 0 – 4 cohort in 1970. This process is continued until all thirty-two cohorts have a computed percentage figure. A check for accuracy may be run by dividing the number of males by the total population. This percentage figure should be the same as the total of the sixteen male cohort percentages, or those on the left-hand side of the pyramid. The same process is repeated for the female side of the pyramid. When all thirty-two percentages have been computed, the lines can be drawn on graph paper and the lines filled in to produce the completed pyramid.

By simply looking at a series of population pyramids (two or more) a competent demographer can say something about trends in the birth rate, migration direction and intensity, and aging of the population (see Figure 7). Of course, the discussion will be general, and exact rates cannot be specified merely by looking at the pyramids. The pyramids for 1950, 1960, and 1970

Table 7
Population Number and Percentage by Five-Year Cohorts,
Wichita, Kansas, 1970
Unit Wichita #

	MALE		FEMALE	
Cohort	Number	Percentage	Number	Percentage
0 – 4	12,425	4.49	12,001	4.34
5 – 9	13,411	4.85	12,968	4.69
10 – 14	13,996	5.06	13,723	4.96
15 – 19	12,070	4.37	13,256	4.79
20 – 24	12,380	4.48	14,108	5.10
25 – 29	9.060	3.28	9,004	3.26
30 – 34	8,363	3.02	8,311	3.01
35 – 39	7,749	2.80	8,225	2.98
40 – 44	7,152	2.59	7,593	2.75
45 – 49	7,936	2.87	8,771	3.17
50 – 54	7,326	2.65	8,096	2.93
55 – 59	6,196	2.24	7,002	2.53
60 – 64	5,118	1.85	5,916	2.14
65 – 69	3,083	1.11	4,570	1.65
70 – 74	2,846	1.03	4,218	1.53
75 +	3,250	1.18	6,371	2.30
Totals	132,361	47.9	144,133	52.1
		276,491		

for Wichita, Kansas, show a high birth rate immediately following World War II (or 1946 — 1950) in the wide extended base (0 — 4 cohort) of the 1950 pyramid. In general, the high birth rate continued through the 1950s and was still very high in 1960. However, the 1970 pyramid shows the drop in the birth rate in the 5 – 9 cohort which would have been born between 1960 and 1965, and an even further decline between 1965 and 1970. The 1970 pyramid shows the results of some in-migration in the 30 – 34 and 35 – 39 age cohorts, which were shown as the 10 – 14 and 15 – 19 year age cohorts in 1950. The most obvious change is in the increased life expectancy of females as the percentage of females seventy-five years and older in 1950 had increased by 1960 and almost doubled by 1970. Hence, without any knowledge about the size of population, a demographer can look at a series of population pyramids and obtain a feel for what has been happening to the population over a particular time span.

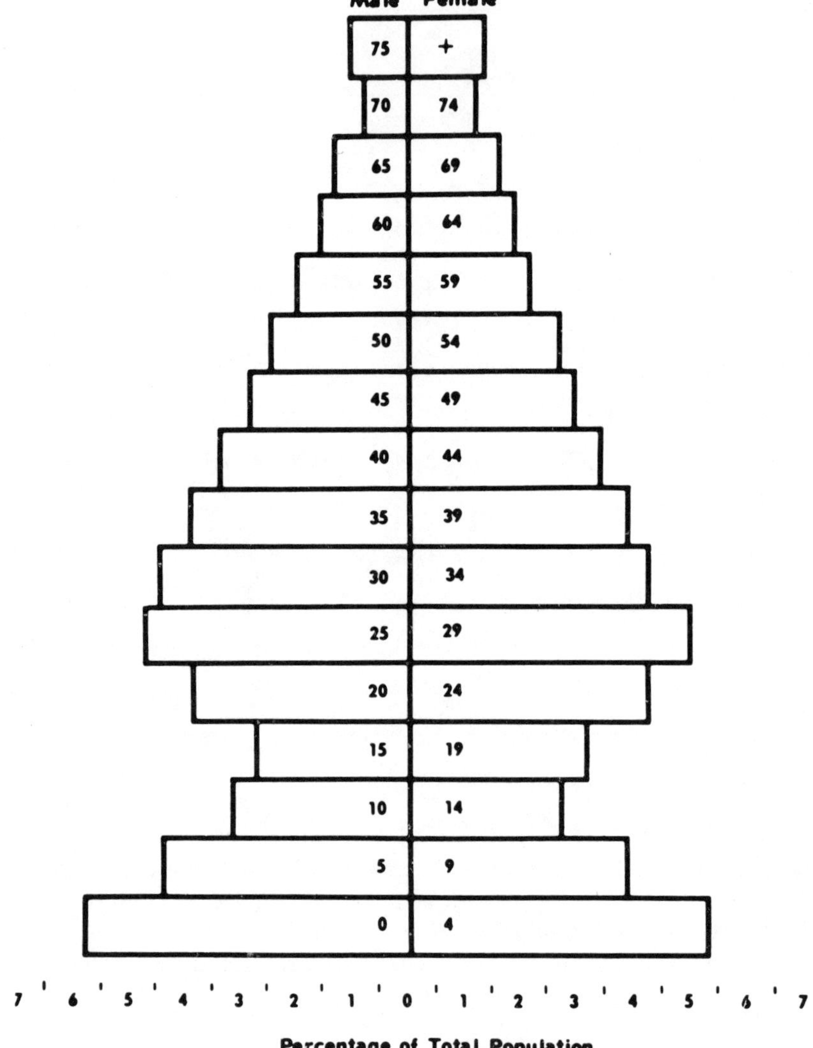

FIGURE 7 Three Population Pyramids, Wichita, 1950, 1960, and 1970. Population Distribution by Age and Sex.

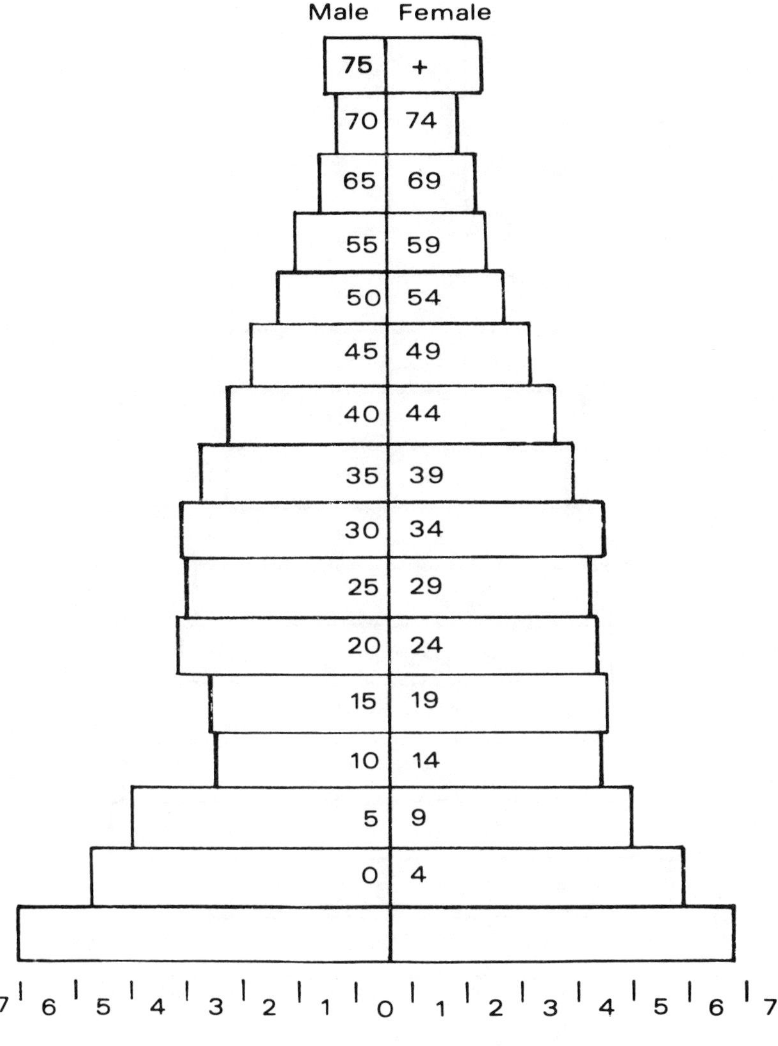

Male
Female
75
+
70
74
65
69
55
59
50
54
45
49
40
44
35
39
30
34
25
29
20
24
15
19
10
14
5
9
0
4
7 6 5 4 3 2 1 0 1 2 3 4 5 6 7
Percentage of Total Population

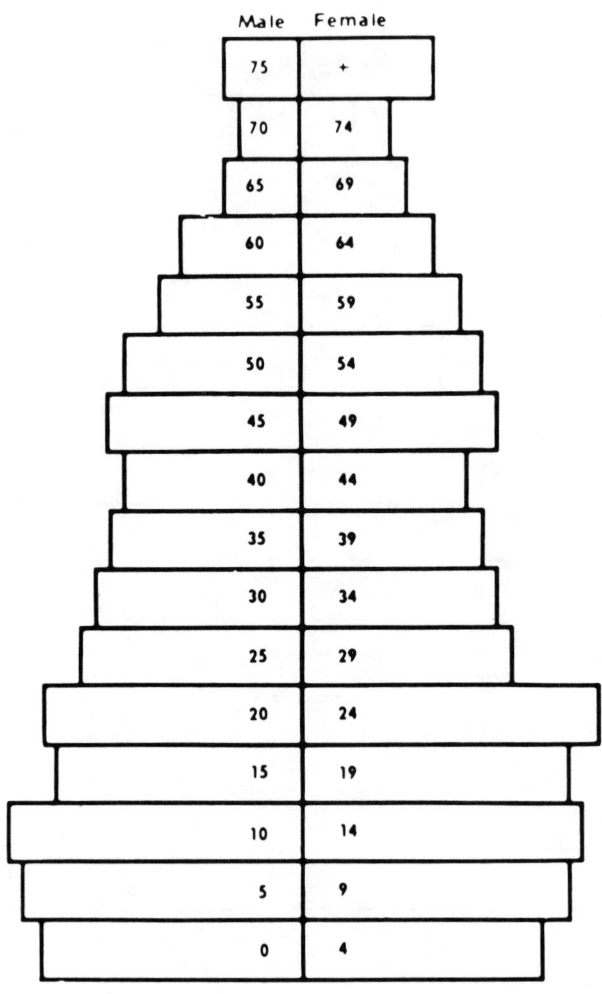
Male Female
75 +
70 74
65 69
60 64
55 59
50 54
45 49
40 44
35 39
30 34
25 29
20 24
15 19
10 14
5 9
0 4
7 6 5 4 3 2 1 0 1 2 3 4 5 6 7
Percentage of Total Population

POPULATION PROJECTIONS

In contemporary American culture, individuals tend to be defensive about the size of their home community in general and tend to exaggerate it. Growth has traditionally been equated with progress and "bigger equated with better." Much of this fallacy has been brought into focus recently with the nationwide emphasis on environmentalism and the crunch of the "energy crisis." With greater emphasis on community planning, it has become increasingly necessary to make population projections that help to evaluate today's decision on the basis of tomorrow's need. Several states with governor's committees or offices of programming and planning have made projections, or have had projections made, for their state as well as for each county in the state and, in some instances, for all cities over ten thousand population. These projections have then been used by various agencies in these states in planning to meet needs in areas such as education, parks and recreation, highways, economic development, and selected other consumer needs. These agencies at least had the advantage of operating on the same data base instead of each agency generating its own set of figures or projections.

A population projection can be defined as an extension of the most recent trends into the near future. To be accurate, it must take into account rates and direction of change for the three major components of population manipulations: births, deaths, and migration. These three rates can be computed from the recent past on births and deaths for each county or city above ten thousand. Since these vital statistics are available on a yearly basis, rates can be adjusted for an average of the last three years, the last five years, or the last decade. An option is available for mortality or death rates. Life tables are printed for each state by the Public Health Service.[23] Hence, an actuarial table for the appropriate state can be used to apply to the number of individuals in any given cohort rather than going back and computing a rate for each five-year cohort (thirty-two cohorts for each county or city). Since many states in the Midwest have one hundred or more counties, the researcher must consider 3,200 computations in applying the survival rate from the life table, 3,200 computations in applying the migration rate, and two hundred entries for the number of births to be entered over the usual five-year periods between projections—that is, if the state is the unit of analysis and if age and sex details are desired for each of the one hundred counties. For example, in computing projections for the state of Iowa and each of its ninety-nine counties, the technique described in the following section was used.

Assumptions Used in the Iowa Projection Model

Any population estimate or projection contains certain assumptions about the three major components of population structure: birth, death, and migration rates. Different methods employ different techniques for arriving at rates for the three components. Years of recordkeeping have shown that the birth and death statistics are somewhat more stable than the rates of population change because of migration. The three components and the assumptions included in this projection are discussed below.[24]

Births

Demographers often assume that the best predictor of the near future is the most recent past. Hence, most population projections utilize the most recent data available in their projections. The same is true in these projections. The birth figure and rate for the 1965 projection was not an estimation for the 0 – 4 cohort in 1965. Since the actual number of births (by residence) for each unit of analysis (county or city) was available, the actual number of births was used instead of an interpolation based on a rate for the past. However, the number of births had to be estimated for each five-year projection period after 1965. On the basis of known data or the actual number of births per unit of analysis for the five-year period 1960 – 1965, a crude birth rate per one thousand population was computed. This rate was then applied to the projected population for the last period (i.e., 1965) to obtain the total number of births in the 0 – 4 cohort for the next projection period (i.e., 1970). The rate obtained was an annual rate, which must be multiplied by five (5) years to obtain the total number of births for the five-year projection period. The assumption was made that the birth rate (obtained from 1960 – 1965 data from the Iowa Department of Records and Vital Statistics) would remain constant over all years in the projected period. For example, the crude birth rate for Iowa was 18.4 in 1965. However, inasmuch as it is precarious to make projections based on one-year data, the six-year averages were used. The average birth rate (1960 – 1965) for this decade was considerably lower than that experienced in the 1950s. Using the 1960 – 1965 experience produces a somewhat more conservative projection than that obtained using the higher 1950 – 1960 birth rates.

A sex adjustment was also made in the birth rates. Traditionally, more males than females are born. This ratio has been found to be about 106 males per 100 female babies born. This adjustment was made in the total number of births projected in the four five-year periods of time.

Death Rates

Mortality rates for the most recent period of time were used in this projection. The Iowa state life tables, 1959 – 1961 (published in 1966) were the most recent available.[25] These tables have served as the basis for utilizing abridged (five-year) survival rates by sex and age-specific cohorts. For example, survival rates indicate the number of a population expected to remain alive at the end of the projected period. Mortality rates are relatively high for the first year of life, decrease for both sexes until the 10 – 14 age cohort, and then increase throughout the remaining life expectancy of an individual. For at all cohorts, females have lower mortality rates than males in the same age cohort.

An arbitrary decision had to be made relative to the highest age (open-ended) cohort manipulated in the model. Seventy-five years of age and above was the highest age category manipulated in this projection, which resulted in a projected category eighty years of age and older in the five-year projection. A survival rate of approximately 50 percent of the individuals seventy-five years of age and above was used for each five-year projection period. For example, about one-half of the cohort seventy-five years or older will have failed to survive to the next projected period five years later. There is a sex difference favoring higher survival of the female cohort.

Migration Rates

Migration is obviously the most volatile and difficult segment to manipulate in any population estimate or projection. This statement proved to be true for the example projection. The most recent data available were used to obtain migration rates for each five-year cohort for each sex. Sixteen migration rates were computed for each sex for each county. Hence, a total of thirty-two migration rates were computed for each of the ninety-nine counties, for the state as a whole, and for the twenty-six cities in the ten thousand and over category between 1950 and 1960.

Iowa's general picture was one of out-migration which had been hidden by the natural increase (gain of births over deaths). It is not uncommon to see a county with a unit rate (total migration) in one direction with several of the thirty-two migration rates in the opposite direction. The point here is that the cohort rate is for a single five-year group alone, and the county or state rate is a picture of the accumulated results from the sixteen cohorts for both sexes. Hence, a county (or state) rate can hide rather severe deviations in either cohort or sex migration from the summated picture for the unit (county, region, or state).

The formula is straightforward:

$$M = \frac{Z}{X - X \cdot D} J/L$$

where M = migration

X = 1950 population

Z = 1960 population

D = 10-year death rate

J = number of years migration rate covers (5 years)

L = number of years between census periods used to obtain migration rates (i.e., 1950 – 1960)

The basic population projection utilizes the three components elaborated above. The formula for all cohorts in the base year is:

Let B = base population D = death rate or survival residual
M = migration rate P = projected cohort

Hence: $P = B - (B \bullet D) + M(B - B \bullet D)$

or projected cohort (P) equals the base-year population minus deaths plus its base-year population times migration rate. The projected cohort "ages" five years in the projection, or cohort 0–4 in 1965 becomes cohort 5–9 in 1970.

The above formulation applies to all cohorts alive at the base projection year. The 0–4 cohort for the projected year or those born during this time is entered by the following formula:

Let B = base population, both sexes
BR = birth rate (crude per 1,000) annual
MBR = male birth rate ratio
FBR = female birth rate ratio
Y = 0–4 cohort born during projection period
M = migration rate for 0–4 cohort, by sex, base year
SR = survival rate by sex for 0–4 cohort in base year
Ym = 0–4 male cohort projected year
Yf = 0–4 female cohort projected year

Hence: $Y = B \bullet BR \bullet 5$ (for 5-year projection period)
$Ym = Y \bullet MBR \bullet SR + M(Y \bullet MBR \bullet SR)$
MBR = 51.4 (male birth ratio)
FBR = 48.6 (female birth ratio)
$Yf = Y \bullet FBR \bullet SR + M(Y \bullet FBR \bullet SR)$

Projections were made in 1966 for 1970, 1975, and 1980. The base year was the 1960 U.S. Census data. Actual births and deaths through 1965 had occurred and were available. The rates were used and extended through 1980. This assumes that birth, death, and migration rates would remain constant over the period of the projection. Obviously, the researcher can make adjustments upward or downward in his or her rates of migration, births, and deaths. The problem is not the mathematics or programming; rather, it is the justification of why one would expect the death, birth, and migration rates to rise, drop, or remain the same. The Bureau of the Census usually makes three projections based on high, low, and average assumptions; the expectation is that the rates will fall between the high- and low-range projections. In making projections, a sophisticated technique does not insure accuracy. Indeed, the projection may not be as accurate as someone's guess of what the population will be in 1980 or 1985. It differs in that the "guess" or "forecast" is based on intuitive knowledge or feeling, focuses on the total number of persons, and is devoid of detail. The projection provides information on age and sex as well as other specific details, rather than just an overall figure as is the case with the Census Clock at the U.S. Department of Commerce. Detail is needed by the State Department of Education to a greater degree than, for example, by the Highway Department. Therefore, the projection is a better planning device, even if it should prove to be less accurate than someone's intuitive forecast.

SIMULATIONS OF POPULATION GROWTH

Recently, computer simulation has found its way into the social sciences from operations research and systems analysis. It has been used for a number of years in business-oriented disciplines, but because of the various difficulties of measurement and specification of relationships between variables, computer simulation has not often been used in sociology.

In general, a computer simulation differs from a projection in that the projection isolates population from all other factors and assumes that factors associated with migration are implicit within the migration rates developed for the projection because no further detail is sought or utilized in the projection. Unlike the projection which is deterministic to the degree that a survival rate, migration rate, or birth rate is applied with no option for variance from the pre-prescribed specification of relationships, most computer simulations provide interaction between the variables. That is, predetermined values of certain variables will bring about assignment of different values to other variables. For example, Orcutt combined population characteristics in some simulations done over ten years ago.[26] He manipulated the sociodemographic characteristics to include marriage, divorce, death, birth, age change, migration, and so forth, along with the economic variables being considered and manipulated. Different mixes of parameters produce different outcomes based on these interrelationships.

Among the best known and most significant of the simulations is the work of the Massachusetts Institute of Technology group, first under the guidance of Jay W. Forrester[27] and more recently under Dennis L. Meadows.[28] Both Forrester and Meadows, along with others in the "Club of Rome," have expressed concern over the increase in population, its relationship to natural resources, the birth rate, food, per capita income, and the material standard of living.[29] All three of these works are excellent reading for the student of society, even though they were not intended to instruct the student in the techniques of simulations.

SUMMARY

This chapter attempts to show that demographic methods differ from other social science research methods because in and of themselves they are devoid of theoretical underpinnings. Social behavior is not generally taken into account in these manipulations of secondary data. Hence, demography is not the domain of the sociologist except by tradition and is open to anyone with some mathematic skill and interest. Demography is of interest to sociologists because census data are often employed in their work; a further working knowledge of basic demography methods and sources of information can thus be of value to any sociologist. The formulas and ratios presented in this chapter are relatively simple. Those seeking more sophisticated techniques can find them in the sources in the bibliography for this chapter listed at the end of this book.

NOTES

1. Kingsley Davis, "The Sociology of Demographic Behavior," in Robert K. Merton, et al., eds., *Sociology Today* (New York: Basic Books, 1959).
2. The discussion on the availability of data will be limited to the United States for the most part, but some sources of world data will be included to assist the student in obtaining cross-cultural comparative statistics and rates.
3. U.S. Bureau of the Census, Census of Population: 1970, General Population Characteristics, Final Report, PC (1) -B1, United States Summary. Washington, D.C., U.S. Government Printing Office, 1972.
4. See note 3.
5. States an assigned number corresponding to their alphabetical order; for example, 18 designates Kansas, 17 Iowa, and 1 Alabama. 1970 Census of Population, U.S. Department of Commerce/Bureau of Census Report, PC (1) 18A, Revised, Kansas, Number of Inhabitants. Washington, D.C., U.S. Government Printing Office.
6. 1970 Census of Population, U.S. Department of Commerce/Bureau of Census Report, PC (1) 18B, Revised, Kansas, *General Population Characteristics.* Washington, D.C., U.S. Government Printing Office.
7. 1970 Census of Population, U.S. Department of Commerce/Bureau of Census Report, PC (1) 18C, Revised, Kansas, *General Social and Economic Characteristics.* Washington, D.C., U.S. Government Printing Office.
8. 1970 Census of Population, U.S. Department of Commerce/Bureau of Census Report, PC (1) 18D, Revised, Kansas, *Detailed Characteristics.* Washington, D.C., U.S. Government Printing Office.
9. U.S. Bureau of the Census, *The County and City Data Book, 1973*, Washington, D.C., U.S. Government Printing Office, 1973.
10. U.S. Bureau of the Census, *Statistical Abstracts of the United States, 1972*, Washington, D.C., 1972.

11. An SMSA is defined as one or more central cities of fifty thousand or more residents and the remaining contiguous county or counties socially and economically dependent on the central city.

12. U.S. Census of Agriculture taken every five years in years ending in 4 and 9.

13. *United Nations Demographic Yearbook*, New York, UNESCO, 1973.

14. Donald J. Bogue, *Principles of Demography* (New York: John Wiley and Sons, 1968).

A more general expression of this formula would be:

$$\frac{\text{frequency of criterion variable}}{\text{frequency of norming variable}} \times \begin{array}{c}\text{Numerical}\\ \text{base}\end{array}$$

In this formula, the criterion variable is the characteristic for which the researcher intends to establish a rate. The norming variable is defined as the base plane. Variance from this plane when multiplied by the numerical base gives the rate. The numerical base is simply the constant that provides the numerical expression of rates; for example, the number of births per one thousand (numerical base) as per ten thousand or per one hundred thousand.

15. By dividing the number of events (births) by the total population, i.e., 105/6,800 and then multiplying by 1,000, the resulting figure 15.4 means that there were 15.4 births per one thousand population. Since different reporting bases are used, the researcher should be aware of the basis on which the rate has been standardized. Births and deaths are usually expressed per one thousand population, sex ratios are expressed in terms of the number of males per one hundred females, and most morbidity statistics (e.g., sickness, causes of death) are expressed per one hundred thousand persons. Hence, the researcher should observe the general rule of knowing the basis of standardization before quoting or using demographic statistics.

16. Brian J.L. Berry, ed., with Katherine B. Smith, *City Classification Handbook: Methods and Application* (New York: Wiley-Interscience, A Division of John Wiley and Sons, 1972).

17. Ibid., p. 61.

18. Ibid., p. 62.

19. Ibid., p. 93.

20. Robert E. Park and Ernest W. Burgess, *Introduction to the Science of Sociology* (Chicago: University of Chicago Press, 1921).

21. E.G. Ravenstein, "The Laws of Migration," *Journal of the Royal Statistical Society* 48 (1885): 167-235; 52 (1889): 241-305.

22. Ibid. (1885), pp. 167-235.

23. *Iowa State Life Tables: 1959–1961*, U.S. Department of Health, Education and Welfare, Washington, D.C., June 1966. These survival rates are computed for the five-year cohorts commonly used in demographic analysis; hence, there are thirty-two cohort rates for each unit being projected, i.e., city, county, and state.

24. Thanks are extended to Rex R. Campbell for providing basic elements of the model and discussion of the final program and results.

25. *Iowa Life Tables*, op. cit., 1961.

26. Guy H. Orcutt, et al., *Microanalysis of Socioeconomic Systems* (New York: Harper & Row, 1961).

27. Jay W. Forrester, *World Dynamics* (Cambridge, Mass.: Wright-Allen Press, 1971).

28. Dennis L. Meadows, et al., *The Limits to Growth* (New York: A Signet Book, the American Library, 1971).

29. H.S.D. Cole et al., *Models of Doom: A Critique of the Limits to Growth* (New York: Universe Books, 1973). The interested student should also read the Sussex, England, Research Group's criticism of Meadows et al., *Limits to Growth*, in Cole op. cit.

The Club of Rome consists of a number of international scholars who meet to consider problems of world consequences. Their emphasis has been on such topics as population, environment, technological production, and transportation problems. They have been criticized for simulation projections predicting dire consequences based on present trends. Some authorities, such as Cole, have referred to this group as prophets of doom.

14

Covert Behavior—Field Studies

FIELD TECHNIQUES—PARTICIPANT OBSERVATION AND EXPLORATORY RESEARCH

The study of covert or deviant behavior has always presented unique challenges not encountered in traditional sociological research. Not the least of these problems involves the covert nature of deviant activity and the unwillingness of those defined as deviant to be the subjects of scientific inquiry. These problems are, of course, compounded when the researcher attempts to explore areas that are heavily imbued with emotional content or defined as of crucial importance by the membership of the culture at large: "Successful field research depends upon the investigators' trained ability to look at people, listen to them, think and feel with them. It does not depend fundamentally on some recorder or a questionnaire that is imposed between the investigator or the investigated . . . ."[1]

The thrust of Polsky's reference is obviously toward techniques that lend themselves to the less obvious forms of research methodology, that is, those not necessarily requiring confronting those defined as research subjects with their status as such. Such techniques, often referred to in the literature of sociology as field techniques or observational techniques, have organizational problems with regard to data gathering that are not found in other methodological approaches. These problems are not insurmountable, however, and it should not be implied that data derived from such techniques are less informative or less useful than those derived from the more formal or more appropriate questionnaire or survey-oriented research. In many instances, field research leads to the development of instruments, which in turn are utilized in a more traditional survey framework. In other instances, field researches are final in and of themselves, leading to additional insights into behavior, not capable of being approached from any other perspective. It is evident that observational techniques do not have the sense of data built into them. In fact, such research is ordinarily done outside of the traditional framework of hypothesis testing. The ordering of data collection is either sequentially dictated by the limited observation period or by the very nature of the behavior being observed, i.e., in the case of deviance, which is ordered by the nature of the phenomenon and the place where it occurs. Questions of validity and reliability are compounded by the lack of structure such as is the case of field research. Research instruments, such as questionnaires, impose structures. All interactions are unique and occur within a process that is, at least in part, created by them and is unique in the passage of time. It is, therefore, impossible to "replicate" an observational or a participant observation type of study in the traditional sense of the word. Its reliability must relate to continued observations of behavior as occurring within a generic category rather than to specific behaviors which having occurred can occur no more, and to the theoretical assumptions of the original study. Further, such replications must be related to clear directions with regard to notation but cannot contain the rigors of replications occurring within methodologies adhering more to "laboratory like specifications."

PARTICIPANT OBSERVATION

Of all of the means available to sociologists in the study of deviant behavior, none has a richer tradition, is used more frequently, or is more misunderstood than participant observation. As a technique, it is particularly suitable to the study of covert behavior and most frequently lends itself to the generative-exploratory posture. While the method is time consuming, it provides insights based on both interviews and observation, and more than any other technique, it locates the etiology of behavior in the very stuff of the human experience. Participant observation has been defined as:

> conscious and systematic sharing insofar as circumstances permit, in the life activities and on occasions in the interests in effects of a group of persons. Its purpose is to obtain data about behavior through direct contact and in terms of specific situations in which the distortion that results from the investigators being an outside agent is reduced to a minimum . . . a quest for the roles in the playing of which one can be

regarded by the members of the community as a participant in their activities and interests is the key to the use of this technique.[2]

Such a definition is clearly in keeping with the authors' feeling that research is very often an offshoot of life-style and that particular researchers are best equipped for particular types of research. By ignoring his own life-style and those positive elements that he brings to a research situation, the researcher is in the position of judging himself with regard to the broader culture and, in so doing, of influencing whatever research he undertakes. Certain research styles are more natural to individuals than others and as such should be encouraged as a natural inclination. One need only cite the work of Polsky or Becker or William Foote Whyte to buttress this point. The definition of participant observation also includes dimensions cited by Becker and Greer:

A participant observation would mean that method in which the observer participates in the daily life of the people under study, either openly in the role of researcher or covertly in the same disguised role, observing things that happen, listening to what is said, and questioning people over some length of time.[3]

By this definition, the technique itself provides a means of organizing behaviors into categories that are amenable to the development of survey instruments. Becker and Greer suggest:

The participant observer . . . gathers data into a social context which includes information of all kinds . . . sees and hears the people he studies in many situations of the kind that normally occur for them rather than in an adjusted and isolated and formal interview. He builds an ever-growing fund of impressions, many of them at the subliminal level, which gives him an extensive base for the interpretation and analytical use of any particular datum. This wealth of information and impression sensitizes him to subtleties that may go unnoticed in an interview and forces him to raise continually new and different questions which he brings to and tries to answer in succeeding observation.[4]

A note of caution should perhaps be extended to the beginning participant observer. Although immersion in the research milieu is often a criterion of the validity of observation, it is basic to the participant observation technique that the researcher submerge himself as "researcher" into the milieu of the community being studied without seriously disturbing that milieu. That is, the researcher does not necessarily blend the milieu as a member; the researcher avoids violating what others perceive to be the expectations of his or her role. In attempting to fit into the research setting, the researcher must not assume mannerisms that are unexpected in his or her own community. Such postures emphasize the role distance between researcher and those being studied, thus distorting observations.

At first I concentrated upon fitting into Cornerville, but a little later I had to face the question of how far I was to immerse myself in the life of the district. I bumped into that problem one evening when I was walking down the street with the Nortons. Trying to enter into the spirit of the small talk, I cut loose with a string of obscenities and profanity. The walk came to a momentary halt as they all stopped to look at me in surprise. Doc shook his head and said: "Bill, you are not supposed to talk like that. That doesn't sound like you." I tried to explain that I was using terms that were common to the street corner. Doc insisted, however, that I was different, and wanted me to be that way. This lesson went far beyond the use of obscenity and profanity. I learned that they were just interested and pleased to find me different just so long as I took a friendly interest in them. Therefore, I abandoned my efforts at complete immersion.[5]

Whyte's discussion is of particular significance to field research and participant observation since it emphasizes that one need not be of a particular type or a particular sex in order to be a participant observer studying such phenomena. In research on lesbianism, it is evident that a male researcher cannot immerse himself in a completely female society of lesbians without someone in the milieu taking notice of the obvious differences. The perceived validity of the researcher's role in this context (and in a sense, the validity of his research as a participant observer) is dependent upon his being perceived by the community as nonjudgmental, nonprofit-oriented, nonexploitative, understanding, and, above all, aware of the integrity required by virtue of the trusts given to him. By implication, therefore, the integrity of the participant observer's role is contingent, at least in part, upon how others perceive the role of his integrity as interactor.

Certain types of observation do not require actual interaction, but nonetheless qualify as field observations. An example is the work involved in Laud Humphreys' *Tea Room Trade.*[6] In many respects, Humphrey's work stands as a landmark with regard to observational techniques and the extent to which they are capable of generating more than exploratory information and a model of research design. Humphreys is particularly clear in stating that his is not a study of homosexuals but rather one that focuses on people who engage in homosexual acts. As he describes it, his research began with the isolation of certain areas in the city where males gather for homosexual purposes. He refers to these as "tea rooms." They are of necessity public places, open to all, yet sufficiently removed from the main stream of traffic as to attract a minimum number of people not interested in homosexual acts. Humphreys defines such "tea rooms" as public bathrooms in large parks accessible by automobile. Other tea rooms exist in such diverse places as court buildings and department stores. For illustrated purposes, Humphreys decided to focus on the tea rooms located in public parks since they provided easiest accessibility to social scientists, and at the same time, afford the least amount of supervision in the form of store detectives or security forces in one public building or another.

Humphreys' research purpose was clearly established before the process of data collection began. As he states:

> My concern in this study has been with the description of a specific style of deviant behavior and of the population who engage in that activity. Beyond such systematic descriptive analysis, I have tried to offer in the light of deviance theory, some explanations as to why and how these people participate in the particular form of behavior described. I have not attempted to test any prestated hypothesis. Such an approach tends to limit sociological research to the imagery of the physical sciences . . . hypothesis should develop out of such ethno-graphic work rather than provide restrictions and distortions from its inception.[7]

In these declarations, it is clear that Humphreys' theoretical framework had been decided upon. His decision on type of approach was made with regard to his theoretical orientations. What was unique to Humphreys' research was his willingness to engage in various types of observation as well as to interview as a cross-check on validity. Likewise, he had good fortune in connecting with a survey research ongoing concomitantly with his own which allowed him to interview, under the guise of the covering project, subjects he had observed in various homosexual acts in the "tea rooms." His method of isolating those engaged in tea room activity was unique. He took the license numbers of automobiles entering or leaving the tea rooms. By using this technique, he was able to gather significant amounts of background materials and attitudes without any threat of identification to individuals frequenting the tea rooms. Equally unique to his research was his ability to be a participant observer by adopting the role of "watch queen." (The watch queen is the individual who watches at the door or window in a tea room and warns when danger approaches.)

> Before being alerted to the role of look-out by a cooperating respondent, I tried first the role of the straight, and then that of the waiter. As the former, I disrupted the action and frustrated my research. As the latter—glancing at my watch and pacing from window to door to peer out—I could not stay long without being invited to enter the action and I could only make furtive observations of the encounters. As it was, the waiter and the voyeur roles are subject to blurring and I was often mistaken for the former.[8]

Humphreys' concern for his interview respondents is indicated in the following:

> . . . none of the respondents were threatened by the interviews. My master list was kept in a safe deposit box. Each interview card, kept under lock and key, was destroyed with completion of the schedule. No names or other identifying marks or code were allowed to appear on the questionnaire. Although I recognized each of the men interviewed from observation of them in the tea room, there was no indication that they remembered me. I was careful to change my appearance, dress, and automobile from the days when I had passed as deviant. I also allowed at least a year's time to lapse between the original sampling procedure and the interviews.[9]

The importance of Humphreys' work for the purpose of illustration lies not in the unique features of his research design but rather in the fact that his work bridges the gap between observation and the development of typologies of behavior and statements of behavior that are both theoretical and testable. (We mean theoretical in the sense of assuming an explanatory posture.) Humphreys' work, using observation and simple description, demonstrates that observation and field techniques need not be assigned a lower generative research level than other techniques which rely on larger samples and mechanisms or instruments imposed between actors and researcher. Such observations do not require interactional involvement with the milieu of those persons studied or the phenomenon studied. Instead, they require a systematic and detailed notation of the social and physical activities of the actors, organized in such a way so as to have those activities outline and structure the content occurring within them. Yet another example of this type of research is Ponte's description of male homosexual behavior occurring in a parking lot, adjacent to a public park. Ponte prefaces his work by stating that certain types of activity require observational techniques and that to approach such activities with more direct methods would preclude truthful responses. Citing the work of others, he relates this specifically to deviant behavior and more appropriately discusses the manifestation of stigmatized behavior and stigmatization of self reflected in certain types of deviant presentation.[10]

Previously discussed research has noted that as the stigmatization of identity on the basis of behaviors increases, so decreases the likelihood of obtaining cooperation with research subjects. It is, therefore, necessary to guarantee the anonymity of those being researched, either in terms of those with whom interaction occurs or in terms of those observed from "positions." Where interaction occurs, the impact of the researcher cannot be underestimated since he is by definition nondeviant. From the actor's perspective, the deviant might well define the nondeviant as "the other," or perhaps "the enemy." In the author's experience studying the lesbian, it was found that in gathering both survey data and field data note taking was severely hampered and finally precluded by the researcher's identification as a "straight male." When field researchers, who were themselves lesbians, were employed, data gathering proceeded unaffected by the presence of an outsider. Only in this way could the integrity and continuity of the area being researched be maintained. Ponte's work did not include direct contact with those being observed; consequently, his own sexual predilections or, for that matter, his impact on the setting being observed were negligible. Ponte nonetheless did encounter difficulties with regard to establishing the validity of his observations. He was unwilling to impose a taxonomic approach on the delineation of the behavior being observed:

> Often I was able to listen to conversations, especially those of one group concerning their own activities, as well as expressions of disapproval which indicated a pattern of socially approved behavior. For example, the behavior of one person suggested that he was engaged in male prostitution. My suspicions were partially confirmed when someone identified him to friends as "that whore."[11]

Whether or not this conversation was sufficient to justify the labeling of Ponte's observed individual as a "whore," given the variety of, and the variation within, the homosexual argot, it is clear that Ponte sought validity checks on his own observation. Conversations and other actors' definitions of the situations being observed offer a kind of triangulation or a validity check. As descriptions of activities in physical surroundings become more detailed and less interpretive, the validity depends more upon the accuracy of notation than upon guarding against the intrusion of the researcher's value or presence. In essence, Ponte defined himself as a passive observer. He indicated that by use of this posture, he would avoid having those persons observed performing for him, and thereby, validity would be increased. He cites Schwartz's work "Problems and Participant Observation" as relevant to this area.[12]

Schwartz's[13] work deals with problems involving those observed specifically creating performances for sociologists or other observers of behavior. She states that the presence of an audience often seems to demand specific responses by virtue of what they are (i.e., doctors or researchers or therapists) and that actors in fact tend to respond in a self-seeking way to these identities. This is, of course, an attack on the validity of observed behavior, suggesting that those observed play a definite role in what is observed, not only in the interpretive sense, but in the sense that audiences command specific responses from those they are observing. Schwartz's work specifically relates to the existing differences between observed behavior and actual behavior. Many would question the existence of "real observed behavior" and behavior as performed. Within an interactionist's perspective, behavior is behavior and includes all of the elements of the setting surrounding that behavior. Regardless of this type of contamination, Ponte's work was most certainly an attempt to organize, or at least explore, the relationship between behavior and audience. Methodologically, it was an attempt to explore clandestine activities occurring within the milieu conducive to it without having the researcher disturb that milieu. Addressing this point in a later article, Ponte has stated:

> The unique perspective of social phenomenon which is apprehended through ethnographic methodology, its interior in contrast to the external view yielded by a more objective perspective. The social system is seen from the inside. Consequently, many of the categories having their origin in evaluation made from the outside become difficult to maintain since they achieve little prominence in the interpretations and definitions of persons in every day life. And, it is these subjects, definition of the situation, the elimination and the comprehension of this view and the interpretation of the world as it appears to him, that is the aim of the researcher using an ethnomethod.[14]

VALIDITY AND RELIABILITY

Although Ponte suggests that problems of validity and reliability in such research rest on the researcher's ability to adopt this inner perspective, from our point of view, external verification of validity is imperative. Reliability, defined as replication, can be established through multiple observations by one observer over a period of time, or by a variety of observers viewing identical settings and having them report on those settings. The field researcher is committed, therefore, to the principle of rendering the world of phenomenon with fidelity and without violating its integrity. It is the trust of the field research and, for that matter, the principal observer to describe the structural, the physical as well as the interactional matrices making up the reality of those being observed. Even so, there is no reason to assume the superiority of one technique over another.

There is yet another validity check on observed interactions obtained through the use of more traditionally oriented survey instruments. Providing there is access to representative individuals of the community being observed, and providing the content of the instrument being used is based on observations, we would expect a very high correlative relationship to exist between observed or reported behavior and the same behavior delineated through the use of survey instruments. Although this is on the surface tautological, note that both techniques are essentially observing the same data, each acting as a check on the other. Survey instruments based on observations are consequently not self-fulfilling. It could be argued that since the instrument (i.e., the questionnaire utilized) is based on observation, the verification of the observation is built into the instrument; i.e., the questionnaire utilized is based on observation, the verification of the observation is built into the instrument. Note, that, however, all research instruments are based in one way or another on observations of the world which they intend to explore; consequently, the biases of those persons structuring the research instruments themselves are reflected. These instruments derived from field research perspectives are perhaps less likely to suffer from such contamination (given the descriptive, nonvalue-oriented notation characteristics of field research) than are other methodologies. In a sense, then, research instruments based upon carefully performed field researches and observations would, in Ponte's words, "interpret the world as it appeared . . . and maintain (ed.) the integrity of that world."[15]

Much of the literature dealing with field research and observational techniques seems to exclude research that occurs as an extension of life-style where noninvolvement is precluded by its very definition. Such orientations often escape the fact that the sociologist, unlike other behavioral scientists, lives in his own laboratory. It is not his value judgment or his commitments that structure his observations or his research, but rather the concerns reflected in his professional commitments and in the methodologies unique to his discipline. Within this framework, then, field techniques and participant observation fit neatly under the rubric of Verstehen sociology as defined by Max Weber. Within Weber's frame of reference, it was unnecessary to do detailed studies on the reasons why individuals stopped automobiles for red lights. The sense of the action was built into the action itself and was specifically located in the norms of the culture which made the stopping sensible and related it to the real world. Weber's point (and, indeed, the thrust of this chapter) is that, in many instances, activities make themselves sensible within the framework of the culture, and often it is the culture that makes activities sensible and relates motivation to action. Behavior therefore relates to the exigencies of the given social order and is understandable only within its framework of presentation. However, the task of the field researcher is very often twofold in that he or she must not only denote or make sense of behavior occurring within a particular structure of presentation but also must infer the nature of that sphere of presentation from the action itself.[16] In essence, Bruyn contrasts this role with that of the more traditional empiricist who "sets up many pre-conceptions of his subject through his study of background materials, his definition of variables, his hypotheses, and the cause of order he expects to find among his variables."[17] Field research, on the other hand, "puts stress on the fact that in field work, the formulation and testing of hypotheses begins early in research; there is a continuance and cumulative interweaving of observations and inference. The inference becomes expressed *[sic]* in field notes."[18] For Ponte, as with others, coding and data organization begin at a point where patterns, interactions, and structures begin to emerge from observed data. This very process is discussed by Whyte in *Street Corner Society* and has been an accepted tradition in sociology since the influence of the "Chicago School" research made itself felt upon the discipline.

The awareness of contexts as a framework for the presentation and the analysis of data helps to avoid pitfalls of ethnomethodology. The data is organized meaningfully for its reader and there is also a natural "fit" of the data which falls easily, almost naturally into such a framework. This "fit" grows out of the fact that using an awareness context to look at the subject is irrelevant as social dramas in the DMV office, we look at them in much the same way that they look at themselves.[19]

It is frequently difficult to ascertain where research begins and life-style ends. Perhaps it is most appropriate to suggest that association peaks interest in specific areas of interaction and that the research process begins at a point where an organizational framework begins to impose itself, within which one begins to interpret the actions of the actors he is observing. Typical of this type of research is Ned Polsky's work with the pool hustler reported in *Hustler, Beats and Others.*[20] One researcher related that his involvement in the study of female homosexuality began when he and his wife moved to an apartment building in a large eastern metropolitan area. Although the building was characteristically anonymous with regard to tenants, he and his wife became friendly with three girls living above them on the third floor. After several months of association and various types of interaction, including dinners, parties, and the sharing of other social institutions, the wife remarked on how discreet the girls were in that she never saw a man leaving the apartment or staying after ten o'clock and yet she knew the girls were entertaining. (The implication was sexual). She mentioned that she could hear "bedroom" sounds, often late into the night, and upon early morning visits saw cigars and pipes in ashtrays. She once again remarked upon their discretion, and then the subject was dropped. After a short period of time, the husband broke the news that the girls were homosexual. He reported that two of the three girls living upstairs had been "lovers" for some time and that the absence of men was a function not so much of their discretion as of their sexual preferences.

In this case, the research process was to await several years. In this instance, however, as in many other situations, research was an extension of the normal life process of the researcher and grew out of his awareness of the similarities and differences between himself and those with whom he interacted. At the point where this particular individual identified his interests as decidedly sociological, he declared his intentions to make a formal study of the phenomenon of homosexuality as perceived by friends and associates. His interactions in the milieu that he intended to study were not viewed as an intrusion, although clearly his identification as a researcher added a degree of complication and caused others in the milieu to view him as a dual personality; on the one hand, as friend and on the other hand, as researcher.

Just as the milieu was affected by the researcher, so the researcher was affected by his immersion in the milieu itself. The researcher is therefore affected by the role he plays in his chosen milieu, and those being researched are affected by their perception of the researcher, their interpretation of research, but above all, with regard to the social and political context surounding the position they occupy or identify with in the culture. Individuals being researched may well define the purposes of research in terms of a context unique to the period of time current with the research, reflecting dominant cultural themes unique in that particular time. For example, research on the female homosexual has been definitely affected by all of the liberation "struggles" since the very early 1960s. Indeed, it is difficult to conceive of studying female homosexuality out of context of the role women play in this culture. Just as radicalism has affected the consciousness of nonhomosexual women, so it has affected the consciousness of lesbians who may well be in a position of defining research as being hostile both to lesbianism and to women in general. The general rules derived from these examples, of course, apply regardless of what subject is being pursued or researched.

Most of this chapter has thus far concentrated on the role of the researcher. Some consideration should now be given to the role of the research subjects and the impact of research upon them. Very serious ethical considerations can be raised with regard to distinctions drawn between covert and overt participant observation research that touch upon the fundamental rights of the researchee. From our point of view, research that hides the identity of the researcher from those being researched has severe limitations and problems. In this extent, role playing is basically dishonest, and its very nature raises ethical questions as to how to deal with the data and results obtained. One might very well ask who has the right to do such research? Some contend that the covert posture seriously damages the possibility of valid data collection in that it precludes valid interaction and makes observed responses to the researcher's behavioral cues uncertain of interpretation. Since the researcher can never be certain that the individual being researched is unaware of the basic dishonesty involved in his role, behavioral cues are even more confused. Serious questions can also be raised pertaining to the ethics involved in presenting such data to the scholarly community. Such a presentation would appear to violate the implied social contract within which the initial interaction occurred while imposing a kind of hierarchical status differential in distinguishing between those researched and those doing the research.

William Foote Whyte, in the appendix to *Street Corner Society*, discusses a visit with one of his principal subjects of research after the publication of his research findings. He cites the involved nature of those being researched and the impact of that research upon them, both in terms of the way they perceive themselves and the way in which they see others as perceiving them. Much of Whyte's concern with regard to revisiting Cornerville had to do with following up on the life histories of some of the principal subjects of research. After recounting their histories, some with surprise and others with real enjoyment, Whyte discusses his encounter with Chick Morelli. Whyte felt that of all the people he had described, Chick was the individual who was most likely to have been hurt by the publication of *Street Corner Society.*

Upon visiting Cornerville, he found that Chick had moved out of the neighborhood but still lived in the same ward of the city. Doc, on the other hand, who was in many regards Whyte's entree into the society of Cornerville, had moved to the suburbs. Whyte found that Chick had married an attractive, pleasant woman who was neither from the neighborhood nor of Italian extraction. After passing some pleasantries, Whyte inquired as to Chick's feelings about the book. Indicating some displeasure, Chick suggested that Whyte had made him sound like a gangster and had not depicted his speech accurately, having failed to distinguish him sufficiently from the other Cornerville boys. Whyte states:

> I expressed surprise at this, and here his wife joined in with the comment that she thought I had made Chick look like a snob. Chick agreed that he had got that picture too. His wife pulled the book down from the shelf and reread the passage where I quote Doc on the occasion of a political meeting in which Chick is on and off the stage in order to take the tickets that he is going to sell for the candidate. . . . Chick commented that he would never do a thing like that anymore. She said that Chick told her before they got married that he had once had a book written about him, but she added that he didn't give her the book to read until after they had been married.[21]

Chick agreed that everything Whyte had reported in the book was accurate but criticized him for not stating that the boys on the corner were young and were bound to change. He also criticized him for not adequately protecting identities, in particular Doc's role in the research. He quotes Doc as saying,

> Can you imagine that! After all I did for Bill Whyte, the things he put in the book about me. You know that thing about when I said you would step on the neck of your best friend just to get ahead. Well now, maybe I said that, but I didn't really mean it. I was just sore at the time.[22]

Chick expressed considerable concern over the impact of the book on the relationships that had developed during Whyte's research time. Whyte did not tell Chick that Doc had read every page of the original manuscript prior to publication, but Whyte did acknowledge that after publication, Doc spent a long time going around the neighborhood repairing fences.

Chick criticized Whyte on other grounds, although the basis of his criticism seemed to be his personal interpretation of the book rather than Whyte's accuracy as a researcher or a reporter. This was, after all, Whyte's concern revisiting Cornerville. Too often researchers tend to forget that the subjects of inquiry are people, with feelings and careers existing over and above the researchers' interest in them. As Chick remarked: "The trouble is, Bill, you caught the people with their hair down. It's a true picture, yes; but people feel it's a little too personal.[23]

Whyte stated that Chick left him with a good deal to think over with regard to the impact of his work on the people he had studied. Doc had suggested that the book had helped Chick, making him a more mature and perhaps a less opportunistic individual. Doc certainly did not perceive the book as being harmful to him. Whyte also suggested that he felt a sense of relief after seeing Chick since he worried that reading the book must have hurt him. His sense of relief came as a result of seeing that Chick had taken the hurt in stride. Whyte nonetheless found himself becoming somewhat defensive in suggesting justification for the book in the appendix. This, at least in part, accounts for Whyte's description of a career developing out of this research for one of the people who helped him get a foothold in Cornerville. This individual became interested in field research, finally finding himself after considerable difficulty connected with the armed services and doing research for them. Whyte notes also that the book had considerable impact on professional social workers he met in the course of this study. He suggested that they tended to view him as a kind of Judas who had turned against his own people. Regardless of the impact of the book or Whyte's concern with it, the implications of the field research on research subjects are very clear. Foote Whyte's work stands as a monument to the kind of sensitivity that leads to both responsible research and responsible use of research findings.

Both overt and covert research have been discussed frequently in the literature of research. Each has strengths and weaknesses. Warren discusses overt research from a field perspective in the following way:

> The chief advantage of overt research is that it enables the researcher to ask for interviews and tape sessions; the chief advantage of sociological folklore, that the researcher . . . role alters the environment of what is being observed to such an extent that the setting is no longer natural.[24]

Further, quoting Becker:

> . . . the people the field worker observes are ordinarily constrained to act as they would have in his absence by the very social constraints whose effect interests him; he, therefore, has little chance compared to practitioners of other methods to influence what they do for more potent factors are operating.
>
> The people studied by the field worker are enmeshed in all the social relationships important to them, whether at work, in community life, or whatever. The events they participate in matter to them. [These are the] people whose opinions and actions must be taken into account, because they affect these events. All these constraints which affect them in their ordinary life continue to operate while the observer observes.[25]

Many authorities have cautioned that the researcher may become an important person to the individual being researched and so may evoke responses that are directly related to the research interaction itself rather than reflecting the ordinary life of the individual being researched. It would appear that this ignores the interaction that occurs between the researcher and the researched, and those meanings that would of necessity arise out of that interaction. Within this framework, critics of the position violate the very canons of symbolic interaction when they ignore the importance of the expectations of both the researcher and the individual being researched. It may well be that the researcher's intrusion into the milieu he is researching is a necessary evil, the consequences of which are difficult to predict. It follows, however, that the researchers would be in a better position analytically if they were to give credence to this intrusion and its possible consequences, rather than rationalize it or dismiss it cavalierly. The nature of the subject being researched is of crucial importance in defining the importance of the researcher's intrusion on the milieu he is researching. Certain subjects are less threatening than others, and needless to say, there are differential sanctions for different identities in the culture. The researcher's impact on an individual being researched might be considerably less if that individual had a highly praised identity in the culture. Quite the reverse would be true if the individual being researched had a stigmatized identity or was engaged in covert behavior where exposure was an ever-present danger, as in the case of the homosexual. This problem is not insurmountable, nor are the data derived from such research interactions incapable of generalizations: quite to the contrary. Simply stated, because of the researcher's intrusion, validation of data is of crucial importance. Validation techniques in such a situation include (1) multiple interviews over a period of time with the same sets of individuals comparing responses along several dimensions, (2) the use of several researchers' interviews conducted on the same population, or (3) interview sampling of several population groups over a period of time and comparison of these groups for similarities and differences. It is not sufficient to affirm simply that the sample interviewed was a purposive sample and representative of a larger group, and thereby dismiss the role of the researcher completely.

In discussing the advantages of the covert research posture, Warren points out that the way in which the researcher is perceived by the researched proves to be as important as was the attitude toward the research itself. "Because I was a sociologist, frequently the reaction of a contact who was a complete stranger to me was something like this, 'It's about time someone did a paper on us', or 'It's about time somebody told the truth about us.'"[26]

This quote shows that the researcher's expectations are of crucial importance to the research act itself. Many researchers of the gay community have found that gays will often express interest in research and indicate a positive need for such scientific inquiry. This opinion should not be taken at face value, however, since investigative research is by nature threatening and places the individuals being researched in a very special light and in very special relationships to the researcher. An interest group's perceived need for research and its willingness to involve itself in the research process may be two quite separate things. For example, at a homosexual conference held in San Francisco in 1970, an organization known as the Lesbian Mother's League made a plea from the speaker's podium for research. The organization complained bitterly that it did not have sufficient funds to conduct research or to attract persons to perform research. It cited specifically the need for solid scientific investigation, the validity of which would withstand courtroom appearances. It hoped to derive studies supporting the fitness of the lesbian to raise children without biasing their psychosexual development, and at the same time, it hoped to find research that would define the typical lesbian household (if such a case exists) as an appropriate place to rear children. It cited, quite accurately, the tendency of the court to take children away from homosexual parents and to award children in contention to the heterosexual parent.

A sociologist from the audience, who at the time was a participant in the conference, volunteered his services, and a strong possibility arose for funding such research, predicated upon the cooperation of the Lesbian Mother's League in the research effort. Conferences held after the meeting made it clear that the Lesbian Mother's League did not in fact want research done—at least not the type of research it had indicated a willingness to cooperate with. The group stated that, first of all, the sex of the researcher was wrong, since he was male and no male could possibly develop research on females, let alone on lesbians. It insisted that this was true despite many citations to existing literature and appeals to logic. It went further in stating that the research needs were unique and that as such could be structured only by another lesbian. The researcher then should fund the research but leave the actual operation of the research and resultant implications to lesbians. One particularly vocal member of the group stated that she felt that the psychosexual identity of her children would be a matter of choice rather than a function of "built-in" commitments fostered by a particular family structure. She stated that therefore, she would oppose any research that would in any way etiologically relate the sexual preference of family members to the psychosexual identity of the children. The group readily agreed with this idea. As a result, the possibility of research, of any type, was precluded. In its commitment to its ideology, the group was unable to relate to the exigencies or the implications of research. Rather than research, the group wanted some official certification of its own particular interpretation of the world.

This example is cited not so much to criticize the somewhat quixotic posture of the Lesbian Mother's League with regard to research, as to point out the differences between the distant objective commitment to do "one sort of research or another" and a willingness to participate in research with no attempt to structure findings. This problem is not an uncommon one. Those who seek research must be prepared to accept findings that do not reinforce their own vision of the world. There is a difference between verification and investigation, and the possibility exists that an established, creditable researcher will turn up findings contrary to those sought. An unwillingness to accept this possibility often precludes the research act itself. It is also clear from this example that research itself generates apprehensions in the group being researched which are not satisfied by the "good intentions" of the researcher or, for that matter, the positive thrust of the research itself. To the extent that the researcher requires the cooperation of those researched, he must learn to "sell the product."

Despite the difficulties encountered in enlisting the cooperation of research subjects, Warren suggests that overt research is less complex both philosophically and pragmatically and just as valuable as covert research. She notes, as have others, that the possibility of discovery when masquerading as something you are not poses serious problems. In this regard, she cites Polsky in his criticism of Sutherland and Cressy for stating that the participant observation orientation with regard to researchers and the study of criminal behavior requires association with criminals.

> Where Sutherland and Cressy got this alleged fact, they don't say and I can't imagine. It is just not true. On the contrary, doing field research on criminals, you damned well better not pretend to be one of them, because they will test this claim out and one of two things will happen; either you will, as Sutherland and Cressy indicate, get sucked into participant observations of the sort you would rather not undertake, or you will be exposed with still greater negative consequences. You must let the criminal know who you are and if it is done properly . . . it does not sabotage the research.[27]

While discussing their field work among deviants with regard to the role of the researchers, Weinberg and Williams note:

It is impossible to provide the student with a detailed set of rules whereby he may profitably structure his relationships while researching deviants. To do so, implies the knowledge of certain facets of relationships with which the researcher ostensively seeks. At the same time, however, we feel that some general rules can be presented with regard to the researcher's social relations with both subjects and other superior stages of research covered. . . .[28]

Just as his role in the milieu to be researched affects that milieu, and the very nature of the research involvement and involved interactions must affect the researcher, this raises the possibility of researcher corruptibility as he performs his research work. We do not mean this in a "moral corruptible" kind of framework of data interpretation. As Weinberg and Williams have stated: "It is difficult to cease relationships begun in a research situation and it is likewise difficult in the case of researching deviancy to avoid a kind of advocacy posture which will affect the data interpretation."[29]

Given the nature of the research process, the distinction between personal advocacy as a function of ideology differs significantly from the process of data interpretation and, in fact, need not affect it. In a sense, one's ideological commitments are reflected in the choice of research subject matter. It does not follow, however, that if one is in an advocacy position ideologically this commitment will necessarily affect data interpretation. No matter how remote this possibility, it does exist when data are being interpreted. It is necessary to separate the data collection process from the analysis of data which may be subject to several interpretations. The researcher must be constantly aware of his own feelings in interpretation and must understand that he has undergone a socialization process whereby he becomes socialized into the culture that is being researched.

Descriptions also may be affected by the successfulness of the socialization that occurred in a previous phase. There being no more opportunity for perception made at that stage could be modified . . . the researcher being pressured into the roles of experts by other people also has affect on the descriptions produced. For example, field notes are returned to and one's observations reinterpreted to fit the symposium or reflect on theories that they were not designed for.[30]

They suggest also that:

It is easy to forget that you are not simply dealing with "subjects" and others but with people. It is easy and natural to dehumanize people in reacting to problems they provide for research. This ignores the essential humanness from which these conflicts spring, an important factor in creating those stages we have outlined.[31]

Although interaction with the community or group is bound to have an impact on the researcher, the impact is mitigated by the researcher's self-perception. To the extent that the researcher's role is identified with and defined as one detached from the interaction observed, a buffer exists between the scientist and group influence. Conversely, the greater the identification with the ideology of the group being researched or with friendships that develop during the research process, the more likely the researcher will be socialized by the research milieu.

Let us return now to the example of the influence of extraneous variables on the research process. It is difficult to isolate particular research clusters from the social system within which they exist. Therefore, the dominant social themes of a given period of time, as well as the political flavor of that time, would affect not only data collection on any given phenomenon but also the willingness of certain persons to cooperate with the research effort. This obtains whether the individuals in the study are the subject of study or are acting as field researchers themselves. In many regards, a kind of stigma is involved in being studied that cannot be resolved by having a researcher state that he is simply interested in a phenomenon or a form of behavior and does not view that behavior as particularly strange or esoteric. Consider the current conditions surrounding the entire women's liberation phenomenon or, for that matter, areas with regard to women's roles, commitments, sexual activities, and the like. Although the social and political biases surrounding the subject do not preclude research, they must certainly complicate the effort. Given the flavor of the times, it would seem extremely unlikely that a male researcher would be able to interact freely in a researched milieu and obtain nonbiased results. Even so, it is only in field research, and participant observation in particular, that the researcher may be sensitive to such sweeps of opinion in the researched population.

Denzin has commented on this relationship of conceptualization and empirical observation and on the differences between observational techniques and traditional survey methods:

> . . . participant observation may be most profitably treated as a method of qualitative analysis that requires observer immersion in the data and the use of analytic induction and theoretical sampling as the main strategies of analysis and discovery. As such the method when appropriately employed entails continuous movement between emerging conceptualizations of reality and empirical observations . . . participant observation is one of the few methods currently available to the sociologist that is well suited to an analysis of complex forms of symbolic interaction. In contrast to the survey, which may be best suited to the analysis of stable forms of interaction, participant observation can better handle forms of interaction that are in change.[32]

Although the material quoted seems to indicate a clear and distinct separation of the two methodologies of survey research and field research, suffice it to say that nothing precludes the combination of the two. In the lesbianism research, for example, survey research was preceded by approximately four years of participant observation. Later, the instrument itself and responses to it were continually checked by ongoing participant observation. Hence, it would be unfair to suggest that the work represents anything other than a continuity of research experience, including survey techniques, interview techniques, a combination of interview techniques and participant observation, and field techniques.

It is generally agreed that there are four types of participant observers.[33] They are:

(1) The complete participant—This posture involves the complete anonymous immersion of the researcher into the milieu being researched. Researchers may fear that access to the community will be denied them if they reveal themselves for what they are, or they have decided that the disclosure of their identity as researchers would so seriously damage the chances of gathering information as to make the research effort a waste of time. Such was the case in *The Talk in Vandalia.*[34] This particular approach is replete with difficulties. Researchers may well find themselves in dangerous situations or situations where behavioral demands are made upon them that they, by virtue of their own moral standards, cannot perform. Likewise, they may well find themselves in insoluble difficulties with regard to disclosure and data presentation.

(2) Participant as observer—Within this framework, the identity of the researcher is disclosed, but the researcher must cultivate relationships with representatives of the milieu being researched. This particular approach, of course, alleviates role contradictions and strains as well as clarifying issues with regard to disclosure and the appropriateness of sharing data with the rest of the scientific community. In a sense, the relationships established by the researcher represent a kind of purposive sampling. The researcher in this situation is particularly vulnerable to pointed questions with regard to the direction the research is taking, the purpose of that research, and the extent to which the respondents' integrity will be maintained. This once again points up the value of doing research that is an extension of lifestyle rather than having the researcher adopt postures that are uncomfortable and less than authentic to the researched milieu—the audience.

(3) The third category is really an extension of the second and can be defined as the "categorical member" of the community. The presentation of this role depends upon relationships that already exist in the community. Such a position likewise includes at least the partial recognition of mutual responsibilities with regard to the research outcome. The researcher has an implied obligation to those researched to maintain the integrity of the relationship.

(4) The observer as participant—This particular role can be defined as involving only one or perhaps two contexts where the role of the researcher is clearly defined as that of participant (even participant as the role of observer) in the milieu he is researching. The researcher makes no attempt to establish relationships to those being studied.

In observational analysis, the emphasis is on not the strict analysis of variables, but on the nature of meaning and the life process.

The participant observer must be careful not to be compromised by his own ideological commitments as well as those resulting from socialization into the milieu being observed. The researcher must guard against being influenced by friendships and by involvement in the community itself in terms of mutually perceived obligations.

Denzin has outlined the following steps in participant observation:

(1) Definition of the problem formulated and recognition of theoretical perspective including review of relevant literature and an initial statement of research objectives.
(2) Selection of a field setting which is largely determined by the nature of the problem to be investigated.
(3) Initial field contacts and entrance into the community.
(4) Crystallization of working definitions of key concepts established. Frequencies of behavior are noted at this stage, and the historical context of the setting is documented.
(5) Informants selected, approached, instructed, and interviewed.
(6) Where appropriate taxonomic division of recordings and indicators of key concepts developed and isolated.
(7) Propositions tested against observed behaviors.
(8) Study conclusion, role disengagement, and final structuring of research reports.[35]

The reader will note that the last stages and their content depend upon the level of research he is attempting and the very nature of the research itself. As mentioned earlier, it is not necessary that research test hypotheses in order to have value. The value of research lies in the understanding of behavioral processes, not necessarily in the prediction of those processes.

Field research lends itself to exploratory research generating nominal data. However, it can be used as a means of hypothesis testing and hypothesis refinement. The process of logical induction from data is no different from survey research to field research, with the exception that most data derived from survey research are analyzed in terms of probability statistics. Probability statistics are not the only means of establishing the validity of a hypothesis, and, in fact, reliance upon probability statistics has probably done more to skew the attitudes of behavioral scientists with regard to what is and is not scientific than any other single factor. Such prejudice with regard to method does not make one approach better than another. In many ways, the model can be said to be independent of the theoretical posture of the researcher. Assumptions and attitudes toward theory make themselves appear at the point where data are interpreted. Hence, research models are more flexible than is commonly assumed.

A final reminder as to the researcher's responsibility to the individual being researched is in order, and it extends to others as well as to social scientists. In a recent case, two individuals who engaged in stigmatized behavior became the focus of extensive newspaper interview articles. One was female, one male. One was a lesbian, and the other a self-proclaimed "good" witch. Both were trying to enlighten the general public about the plight of people of "their type." Both were well educated, one being an illustrator and commercial artist, and the other a practicing clinical psychologist. Both were willing participants in the newspaper articles; both were named in the articles. Both are dead! Both committed suicide within approximately one year after the articles appeared.

The researcher must have a concern for himself, his co-workers and their safety, and the integrity of the data being collected. He must also be aware of his weighty responsibility to the subjects of research.

NOTES

1. Ned Polsky, *Hustlers, Beats and Others* (New York: Aldine Publishing Co., 1967), pp. 127-28.
2. Florence R. Kluckholn, "The Participant Observer Techniques in Small Communities," *American Journal of Sociology* 45 (November 1940): 331.
3. Howard S. Becker and Blanche Greer, "Participant Observation and Interviewing, A Comparison," *Human Organization* 6, No. 3 (Fall 1967): 28-32.
4. Ibid., p. 31.
5. William Foote Whyte, *Street Corner Society* (Chicago: University of Chicago Press, 1955), p. 304.
6. Laud Humphreys, *Tea Room Trade* (New York: Aldine-Atherton, 1970).
7. Ibid., p. 22.
8. Ibid., p. 28.
9. Ibid., p. 42.
10. Meredith Ponte, "Life in a Parking Lot: An Ethnography of a Homosexual Drive-In," in Jerry Jacobs, ed., *Deviance: Field Studies and Self Disclosure* (Palo Alto, Calif.: National Press Books, 1973), p. 9.
11. Ibid.
12. Barbara Schwartz, "Problems and Participant Observation," *American Journal of Sociology* 60 (January 1955): 343-353.
13. Barbara Schwartz, "Driving as a Privilege: License upon License," in Jacobs, ed., op. cit., p. 104.

14. Ponte, op. cit., p. 117.

15. Ibid., p. 119.

16. Severyn T. Bruyn, "The New Empiricist," *Sociology and Sociological Research* 51, no. 3 (April 1967): 317-22.

17. Ibid., p. 321.

18. Ponte, op. cit., p. 108.

19. Ibid., p. 109.

20. Polsky, op. cit.

21. Whyte, op. cit., p. 346.

22. Ibid.

23. Ibid., p. 347.

24. Carroll B. Warren, "Observing the Gay Community," in Jack C. Douglas, ed., *Research on Deviants* (New York: Random House, 1972) p. 141.

25. Reprinted by permission from Howard S. Becker, *Sociological Work*, Chicago: Aldine Publishing Co., copyright © 1970 by Aldine Publishing Company.

26. Warren, op. cit., p. 155.

27. Polsky, op. cit., p. 124.

28. Martin S. Weinberg and Colin J. Williams, "Field Work Among Deviants: Social Relations with Subjects and Others," Douglas, ed., op. cit., p. 182.

29. Ibid., p. 183.

30. Ibid., p. 182.

31. Ibid., p. 183.

32. Norman K. Denzin, *The Research Act: A Theoretical Introduction to Sociological Methods* (Chicago: Aldine Publishing Co., 1970), p. 186.

33. Raymond L. Gold, "Roles in Sociological Field Observations," *Social Forces* 36 (March 1958): 217-23.

34. Joseph P. Lyford, *The Talk in Vandalia* (New York: Harper Colophon Books, Harper & Row Publishers, 1965).

35. Denzin, op. cit., pp. 206-15.

15

The New Empiricists: The Participant Observer and Phenomenologist*

Recently, some social scientists have become interested in increasing mathematical sophistication in the analysis of the diffusion of information. The specimen simulation attempts to go beyond the formidable works of Lazarsfeld, Dodd, Churchman, and others,[1] who some years ago attempted to apply mathematical formulas to problems in communication and other related areas. More recently, computer simulation has been refined somewhat and calls for respecification of gross level theory and methods into dynamic or processual relationships. Early research in simulation was directed to the examination of a static (one slice of time examination) social phenomenon. At that time, limitations existed that do not presently exist, and much of what has been defined as progress is based on those early steps.

The use of computer simulation techniques calls for theoretical specifications that contain antecedent-consequential relationships within a structured framework. The antecedent-consequential relationship, not the causal framework, is stressed because a causal model can suffer the same difficulty as the one-time research design. It is not suggested that contemporary designs do not have implicit notions of process or that examinations of

*Thanks are due John T. Gullahorn for reading an earlier draft of this chapter and making helpful suggestions.

groups or systems are all theoretical and relative only to a specific time and place. One should be aware, however, that most specifications of this type have tended to be verbal models or theories with a low degree of specification. Hence, the discipline has had need for those concerned with macro theory as well as those who focus on more specific theories with limited scope. Highly structured models lose much of their generalization potential when specification of relationships must be made to manipulate the model. A researcher using simulation techniques cannot tolerate gross level generalizations or statements about the relationship between variables. He must be reasonably precise in establishing individual variable parameters, conditions under which his model is operative, as well as in the specifications of the previously defined relationship between variables.

In this chapter, the Dawson definition of simulation is followed:

> Simulation, as a social science research technique, refers to the construction and manipulation of an operating model, that model being a physical or symbolic representation of all or some aspects of a social or psychological process. Simulation, for the social scientist, is the building of an operating model of an individual or group process and experimenting on this replication by manipulating its variables and their interrelationships.[2]

The portion of this definition which deals with the replication of group or individual process by manipulating the variables under alternative conditions and under alternative operating assumptions will become clear as we proceed.

The second section of this chapter treats the work of John T. and Jeanne E. Gullahorn and demonstrates that, while rather high levels of specification are required to use simulation as a technique, lower levels of measurement (even nominal data) can be used to develop a computer simulation. Problems of measurement are not reduced in computer simulation, but in fact may become more acute in this type of research. At the same time, in order for a simulation to be run, difficulties relating to theory, the theoretical justification for variable change in direction and intensity, must be resolved. The problem is not in assigning values to specific variables as limits (called parameters) but in assigning exact increments of change for one variable given a known value of another variable. For example, the social sciences are riddled with loosely stated relationships often referred to as "the more the more" relationship. An example from communications would be, "as education increases, probability of exposure to certain media and messages increase," or the more education, the more exposure. The implicit idea is that certain values, education among them, would be related to exposure to an article in *Playboy* or *Playgirl* and, further, that on some dimension (education) these individuals might differ from those who read *Vogue*, *The Saturday Review*, or *Readers Digest*. A straight linear statement that increased levels of education result in higher probabilities of exposure does not give the researcher much help in establishing parameters. However, this simple problem has one easily measured variable, educational attainment, and is not as difficult to operationalize as the classic statement relating group size and social cohesion; or as "group size increases, social cohesion decreases." Questions immediately arise as to where (in number) this inverse process starts. When the group reaches twelve members? twenty-one members? fifty members? two hundred members? Does it matter whether the group is a voluntary organization or a profit-oriented organization or whether the group was organized for instrumental or expressive purposes? Indeed, few clues can be found to these questions in the available literature except more generalized comments without suggestions for parameters or amount of change to be expected for each known value. These questions are maximized in simulation and are a latent aspect of simulation in that in order to develop the simulation one may become so familiar with the problem that for this person simulation of the problem may not be necessary! These problems will be again addressed in the examination of the Gullahorns' simulation of interaction between individuals.

SIMULATION OF NEWSPAPER READERSHIP: A MIXED MODEL

In this chapter, the development of a research mixed model[3] is illustrated and defined as a model with both deterministic and stochastic (random occurrences) elements within its basic specification. The model provides that the degree of stochasticism is reduced in subsequent runs of the simulation completed under alternative sets of operating assumptions. In addition, predictability is increased as the model becomes more deterministic with regard to operating assumptions and with the inclusion of additional socio-demographic variables.

The content area examined in this chapter is that of newspaper readership, or "inoculation" of an individual through reading a "locally" oriented newspaper. Additional points of simulation techniques relate to the development of an "attrition" model and the establishment of parameter estimates from the best available sources. In the social sciences a simulation effort may encounter difficulties when the attempt is made to reduce the problem to a manageable number of variables or to specify the relationship of any one variable to the problem. The task is further confounded by the need to specify the nature of the relationship between variables as well as the relationship of each independent variable to the total problem.

The example that follows details the computation of a relatively complex simulation from inception to examination of the simulation under alternative sets of operating conditions.

For illustrative purposes, consider how information pertaining to a pending event of community importance is dispersed into a small community through a locally oriented newspaper.

The message is a notification of a pending community-wide civil defense exhibit. Any message content area could be included in the general attrition model developed in this chapter. However, the saliency variables and relationships would have to be adjusted to the contents being examined. The techniques under discussion are applicable to many contents and saliency variables, and relevant relationships are always defined by the "content" being examined. For example, the message content could be about any topic, sports, fashion, news, etc.; however, the relevant audience would change with the message content. The basic three-step attrition model (Figure 8) would not change. This again demonstrates the flexibility of computer simulation in that parameter estimates were used from theory to examine comprehensive data collected in a real world community.

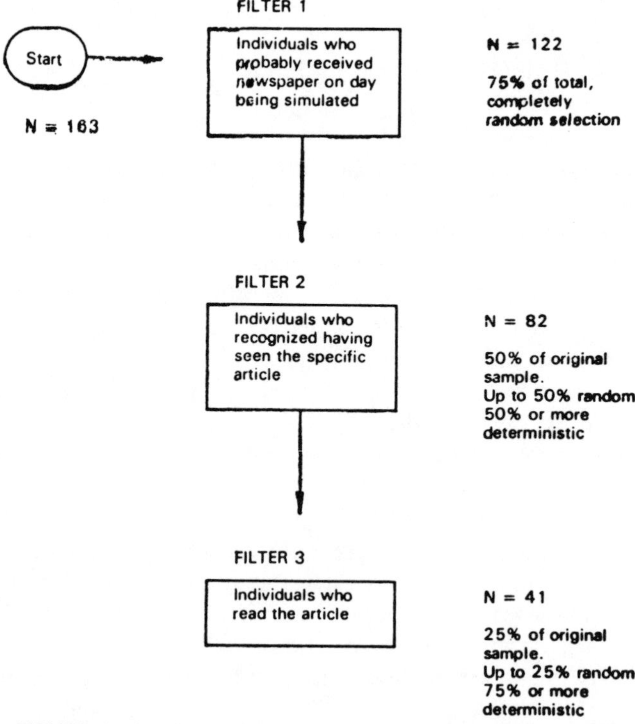

FIGURE 8 Attrition of Potential Newspaper Readership Audience Utilized in Simulation

In this specimen, simulation data from two different studies collected and reported elsewhere have been utilized to develop an attrition model and basic parameter estimates. Although the focus is on a portion of an overall simulation effort that is relatively complex, the portion reported herein is simple. Even so, reducing variables to statements of relationships is troublesome in the first stage of the simulation attempt. Although similar problems must be solved in any simulation attempt, these problems become more troublesome as simulation efforts become increasingly complex.

The basic variables manipulated in the model used are demographic and communications variables. Since a good deal of information was available about each of these content areas, it was felt that the simulation model could be worked out on theoretical grounds without having to collect additional data. The test model was located in a real world setting in order to enable a check on results generated in the simulation. A general dissatisfaction has been expressed with the heuristically oriented population studies often found in simulation efforts. Hence, the data used in this study actually represent the sociodemographic characteristics of a random sample drawn from a small Iowa community.[4]

Newspaper, radio, television, and secondary interpersonal (two-step flow) sources all contribute to the spread of information through a community. The initial portion of this simulation effort deals only with making individuals in the community aware of an event through reading a newspaper. Such awareness does not require overt action on the part of the "inoculated" individuals, but in a processual manner, it considers whether the individual is likely (1) to have seen the newspaper, (2) to have seen the particular article, or (3) to have read the article. Further simulation efforts will take into account the degree of reading and comprehension of the article, as well as overt action resulting from this information.

Social behaviors such as newspaper reading have been examined from various perspectives. Such examinations often remain descriptive and amount to little more than reporting. As such, they provide little of value for the individual interested in computer simulation of social processes. Statements of relationships are frequently expressed only in verbal form such as the exposure to mass media increases with the amount of formal education. Clearly, no exact relationship can be ascertained from this specification, but herein lies a clue and a beginning for the simulator. While the expressed relationship gives no clues as to whether the relationship is linear, curvilinear, or exponential, the mere statement of association between a dependent and an independent variable is more than can be found in many descriptive statements.

The following includes the general model shown in Figure 8 and the procedure used in combining deterministic and stochastic elements in the model. Hence, this is a mixed model that includes a large deterministic element and a limited stochastic one. Social scientists must be willing to specify which variables are operative in the simulation, to state how these variables are related, and whether the relationship remains constant over time. This has been accomplished in the model presented. Implicitly, it is assumed that not assigning weights to the variables designates that each has the same weight.

The General Model

Figure 8 presents the general level model and what have been termed *filter points* in this simulation. Several attitudinal dimensions have been utilized as parameter estimates at each filter. Moreover, different mixes of determinism and random elements have been utilized at each of these filters. This will become clearer as the discussion becomes more specific.

An attrition model of potential readers was developed utilizing parameter estimates from a newspaper readership study.[5] This study of newspaper readership in a small community suggested the following attrition pattern. All respondents in this study were subscribers to a twice-weekly paper. On the day of sampling (interview), approximately three of four (78 percent) had actually seen the most recent issue of the newspaper. Approximately 50 percent had seen the article, which was the feature article above the masthead on page one. Finally, approximately one-fourth of the respondents actually read the article. While the original study quantified the knowledge scores of those who read the article and were able to recall specific content, no such attempt was made in this simulation. These three filters (see Figure 8) serve as "cutting" points in which the potential audience is reduced to most probable receivers of the communication based on the saliency of the issue, content of the message, and the attitudinal positions of individual respondents.

As stated previously, the general model was developed from field data that suggested that the filter points or process stages of the model would be the three stages shown. In addition to suggesting the three-stage model, the field data provided the parameter settings for reducing the sample at each stage of the model. These actual percentages—78, 49, and 27—were changed to the standard quartile ranks of 75, 50, and 25 percent, respectively, in the model. It must be emphasized that these stages and the percentage attrition at each filter are devoid of the variable (content) used to reduce the sample at each filter. Therefore, the general level attrition model can be used for any social phenomenon, but the percentages that emit from each filter and the variables used to bring about this reduction must be sensitive to, and developed for, each content area examined.

Random Elements in the Model

The first filter in the model was originally based on a completely random selection. This takes into account various reasons for not being exposed to the newspaper article in question on that particular day. A person may not see the paper because he is too busy, out of town, the newsboy throws it in the bushes and he is unable to find the paper, etc. These diverse possibilities are viewed as random in this model. Obviously, there are many other reasons why an individual may not be exposed to an accustomed form of media on a given day, but these various reasons have been included under the random selection by a random number generator in Filter 1 of this model.

Filter 2 selects those individuals who received the paper and further reduces the sample size to include only those who recall seeing the article. Regardless of the positioning of the article in the newspaper, some people fail to read all sections of the paper and, in fact, may limit their reading to specific sections of the paper.[6] This led to an assignment of a random portion of the probability score for each individual passing into Filter 2 (having seen the article). Up to 50 percent randomness was assigned in the scoring of individuals at this filter. This means that some individuals with higher scores could have had their score increased, while some with lower scores did have their scores increased by random assignment. With regard to those in the latter case, some persons included in the group were assumed to have seen the article.

Filter 3 increases the amount of determinism but is not completely deterministic. The primary concern is saliency of the content and whether one chooses to make the article relevant to action after he has become cognizant of it. Those not continuing on in the simulation are assumed to have cognitively rejected the article. In these instances, the content of the article may not have been deemed sufficiently important, or they may already have been aware of the information in the article. Many kinds of cognitive rejection can be enumerated, but this simulation has utilized only the dichotomous possibility of reading or not reading the article after they have become aware of it. This continuance of the process on reading the article has been set at a minimum of 75 percent determinism and up to 25 percent randomness. Again, it has been assumed that this is not a completely determined act and that chance factors continue to be operative at this stage of the process.

Components Used in Designating Probabilities

The general level model is presented in Figure 8 as an attrition model of (1) individual recipients of a single communication (article) (2) in a single channel (newspaper) (3) on a specific day. Moreover, it was shown that being exposed to a communications message has some random designation in this model. It is assumed that in this model it is possible for an individual to read a particular article as a fortuitous event. In this model, the degree of determination increases as one moves toward cognitive acceptance of and reading of the article. Hence, the end result of this model is an audience known to have received a message and, further, to have read and understood it. From this cohort, 163 individuals were interviewed in depth over an extended period of time. The sample was drawn from a relatively small community previously used in the Iowa Civil Defense studies.[7]

In an attempt to use data currently collected and available, variables were selected which were closely related to those suggested in the literature as relevant. That is, knowledge about a content area is related to the probability that an individual will seek additional information about that area. Hence, the theoretical proposition that an individual will seek additional information in a content area does not explicitly present the operational measure of knowledge. The variables included in the simulation were theoretically grounded, but the operational measure and the variable utilized to represent the theoretical concepts were selected by the researchers. The relationship of the variables, the operational measures, and the validity and reliability of the measurement techniques are the responsibility of the researcher.

A series of predictive variables were selected to assign probabilities to the variables used in the second and third filters in the model. These variables generally deal with facets of saliency of the issue, knowledge about the general issue area, and attitudinal data indicative of a deterministic-fatalistic orientation. In addition, whether or not an individual has performed an overt act in the generalized communication area was included as a saliency variable. Since education was viewed as an important variable in the past, it has been utilized as a determining variable in this simulation. These demographic variables (actual data collected in the above-mentioned study) were used to examine the characteristics of the population remaining after the simulation was completed. In this respect, those remaining in the simulation served as a test of "goodness of fit" of the model since in the original study it was possible to identify those who were aware of the message. If the model was better than a randomly drawn sample, this would be reflected in the number who were aware of the message through newspaper readership appearing on the lists of simulated message readers in greater than predicted numbers.

The six basic variables used in reducing the number of individuals at the second and third filter (behavior) were:

1. knowledge of the content area
2. saliency of the issue relative to perception of threat
3. fatalism
4. information sources
5. education
6. prior behavior in the content area of the message

Each of these six variables was assigned a relationship with the dependent variable (readership), with the nature of the relationship derived from theory, i.e., whether it was a linear or curvilinear relationship. Actual scores for each individual on each variable were attuned to the actual scale values of respondents in the original field data collection. Each of the six variables ranged from 0 to unity (1.0). The formulas used to transfer actual scale scores to the standard scores (0 – 1.0) are shown with the figure for each of the six variables. A discussion of each of the variables follows. The probability for each variable is the standard score for each.

Knowledge

Knowledge in this study was assigned a straight linear probability. As measured knowledge increased, the probability of exposure to the message increased. This was a straightforward extension which did not take into account the fact that the message could have been novel datum for some individuals. This was partially considered, however, in the random element included at each of the filters. (See Figure 9.) The actual range of measured knowledge scores was from 0 to 8, which was also the possible range.

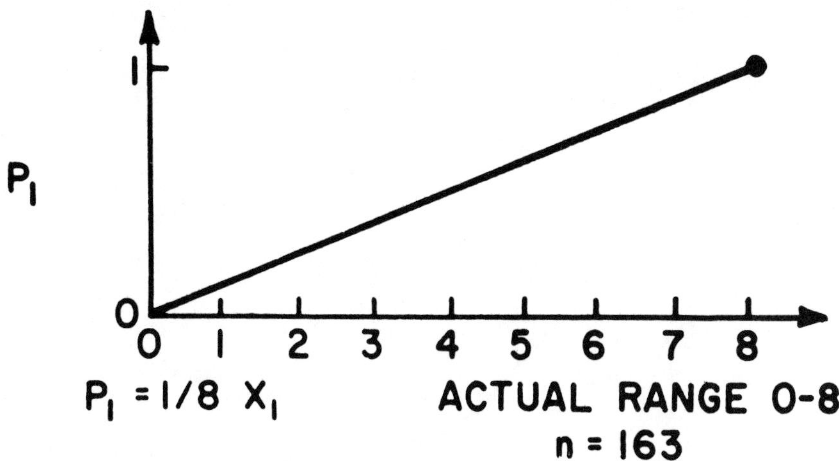

FIGURE 9 X_1 = Technical Knowledge

Saliency Variables

Two variables were selected specifically for probability of saliency, although saliency transcends many variables not specifically labeled as such. Communications models deal with saliency in many facets. The two saliency variables utilized in this simulation were "perception of threat" and the "possibility of protection from nuclear weapons." Both were assigned curvilinear probabilities, though each assumed quite different curves as shown in Figures 10 and 11. "Perception of threat" was assigned probability on the theoretical consideration of an approach-avoidance gradient. The logic involved in Figure 10 indicated that an individual would move toward increased probability of communication exposure as threat

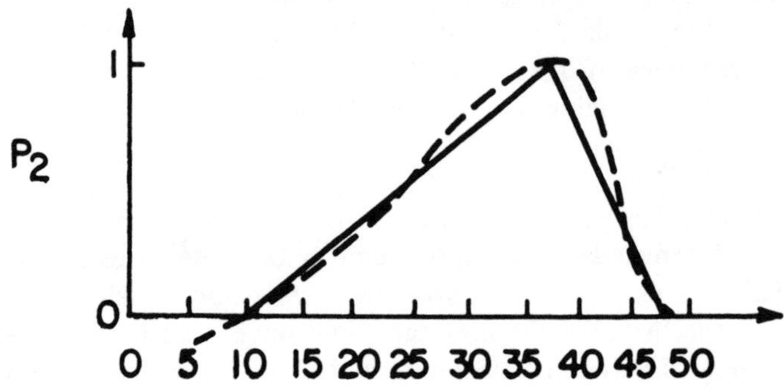

$$P_2 = \frac{X}{26} - \frac{6}{13}$$

$$P_2 = \frac{-X}{8} + \frac{23}{4}$$

Actual Range 12-46
n = 163

FIGURE 10 X_2 = Perception of Threat for X [12, 37]
for X [38, 46]

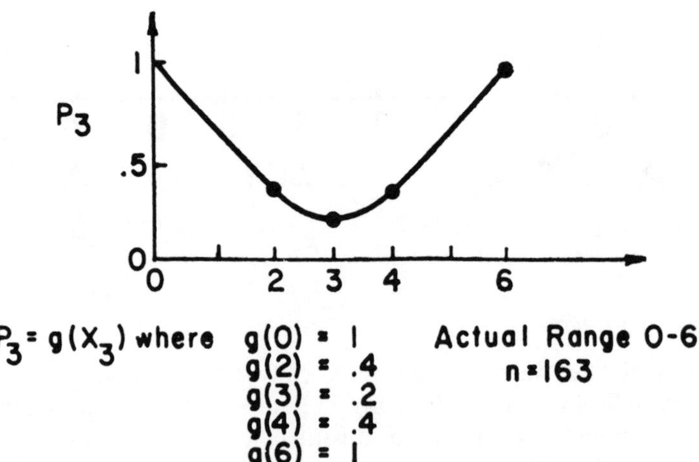

FIGURE 11 X_3 = Possibility of Protection

increased, but beyond a given point the probability would decrease as perceived threat increased. This moves to a point where avoidance behavior becomes manifest and the individual cognitively rejects communications messages related to the topic.[8] A myriad of classical studies have demonstrated this behavior. While the Lane-Sears study is not exhaustive of all such studies, it is representative of the theoretical principle under consideration.

The actual scores indicating perception of threat on a nine-item modified Likert scale ranged from 12 to 46. Two equations were necessary for probability assignment on this variable. (These equations are presented in Figure 10.) "Possibility of protection" in this study dealt with a determinism-fatalism continuum, with higher probabilities assigned to the extreme positions. The extreme position incumbents were often well informed about the activities of the incumbents at the opposite extreme. That is, individuals who held extreme attitude positions were much more likely to receive messages about an issue area than those with less extreme attitude positions. This may be termed *apathy* for the masses or a generalized disinterest in most issues. The range of this variable on a modified five-position Thurston scale was 0 – 6, the same as the possible range for the variable.

This curve is shown in Figure 11. The probability of exposure increases as one moves toward a perception that one can protect himself from the effects of nuclear radiation fallout (determinism) or that the threat is so great that whatever is done will be of no consequence (fatalism). Since data were collected in Iowa Civil Defense studies, these positions approximate the pro- and anti-civil defense attitudes.

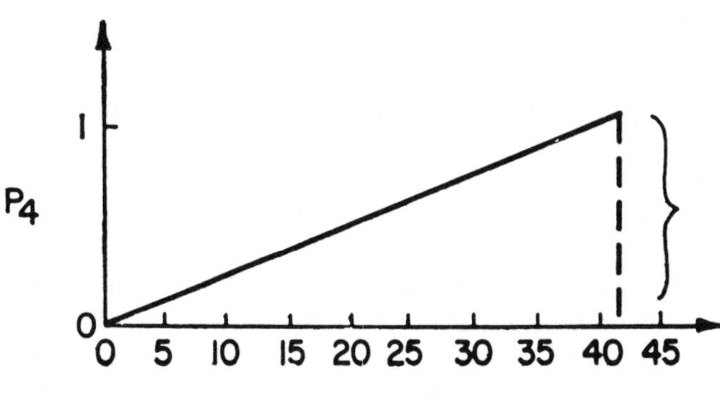

$$P_4 = \frac{1}{41} X_4$$

Actual Range 0-41
n=163

FIGURE 12 X_4 = Competent Information Sources

Competent Information Sources

Competency of sources utilized was represented by a summated score weighted 1 – 6. The probability assignment shown in Figure 12 is a straight linear assignment. As an individual's score increases, his probability of exposure to a message in this content area increases. Actual scores ranged from 0 to 41 while the possible range was from 0 to 61. Theoretically, this relationship demonstrated that information must be thought about and connected to other information, opinions, and values.[9] The more information one has, the more generalizing one is capable of in transferring this knowledge to other circumstances. Hence, the use of competent information sources is indicative of interest and further exposure to additional information about the content area.

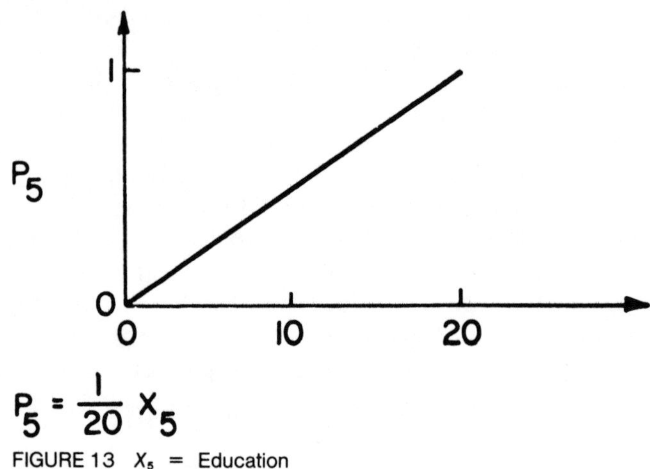

FIGURE 13 X_5 = Education

Education

Education is a discriminating variable, as has been shown in many communications studies. Such studies usually assume the classical "the more the more" hypothesis; that is, the more education, the more exposure.[10] This relationship was examined in this study. Probability of exposure increased with increasing years of complete education as reported. The linear relationship and the range of the education variable is shown in Figure 13. In no way did this demonstrate increased favorability toward the issue, as the result of education, but rather that interest levels and exposure were greater without regard for direction of attitude (favorable-unfavorable).

Adoption of Idea

This variable considered overt action which was taken in the past in the content area of the message. Hence, an individual becoming acquainted with datum for the first time would fit the novel datum situation and be assigned a score of zero. In most cases, information was not novel datum, but was anchored to existing knowledge or experience. It is not unlikely that scores of acceptance of an idea or tangible product can be assigned to most individuals about most situations.

In the reported study, total score indicated the degree of acceptance (actual behavior) of protective measures against radiation fallout. Actual scores ranged from 0 to 7, which was also the possible range (Figure 14). Again it was assumed that an individual who acted in an overt manner had some knowledge, opinions, or attitudes pertaining to the content area in which his behavior fell.[11]

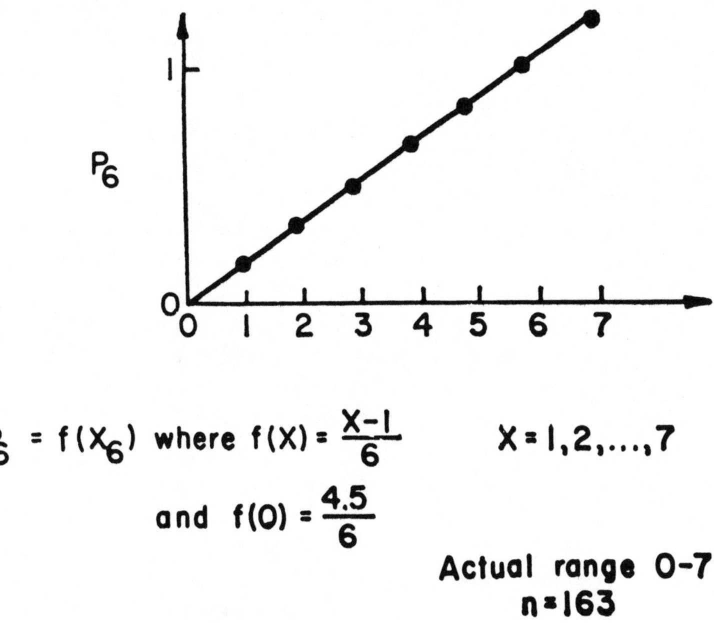

FIGURE 14 X_6 = Adoption

Procedure

Original runs of the simulation were based on completely random selection of individuals at Filter 1. That is, each individual was randomly selected without regard for his actual scale scores or their transformed standard scores (*P*) on the six variables.[12] That was the next step and was accomplished in the following manner.

At Filter 2, each individual was assigned a probability score (*P*) for each of the six variables used in the initial computer run. The range of each of the six scores was from 0 to 1.0 based on the actual scale scores obtained from the field data. Hence, an individual could receive a summated score at Filter

2 ranging from 0 to 6.0. At this point, the first random element enters the scoring in the model. Alpha scores[13] were generated and added (or subtracted) to the summated *P* score derived from the six variables. These alpha (randomly generated) scores were allowed to range ± 0 to 6.0. For example, an individual with a summated *P* score of + 3.0 could pass through Filter 2 with a score ranging from 0 to + 6.0. The 0 would have resulted if a − 3.0 had been generated, and a + 6.0 would have resulted with a + 3.0 assignment. Obviously, these are extreme possibilities and are seldom anticipated in a random assignment from a normally distributed set. It was therefore the summated *P* score that set the range for random generation of an alpha score. Extreme (±) alpha scores cannot exceed the absolute limits of the *P* score; hence, the alpha scores effect the Filter 2 score with up to 50 percent random assignment to the score. In actuality, randomness is somewhat less for most individuals because of the random assignment of normally distributed values whose absolute limits were determined by the summated *P* scores.

After summing the six *P* scores and adding (±) the alpha scores, the individuals were rank-ordered. The 82 (50 percent of original sample) with the highest scores were advanced to the next stage (Filter 3). This step is the second stage of the model shown in Figure 8.

The procedure at Filter 3 was replicated to include another random element, Beta. The random element was reduced at this point by fixing the range of the beta scores at one-half the original summated *P* score. That is, the individual mentioned above with a summated *P* score of + 3.0 was randomly assigned a beta score of ± 0 to 1.5. This reduced the possible weighting of the beta value to one-half of the value of the alpha. Because of random assignment, this may or may not be the case. The last filter (3), analogous to reading the article, contained an additive formula for the reduction to the final forty-one individuals, P 1 . . . 6 + alpha + beta. The scores were rank-ordered, and the forty-one individuals with the highest scores were examined to see if they actually had become aware of the community event through reading the newspaper.

Ranking and evaluation are central to this exercise. By examining the individual as a unit of analysis, one is able to make a discrete decision as to whether his simulated readers actually read the article in question. The intensive data collection mentioned earlier provided this information. When percentage "correct" is used in the results section, the reference is to how well the model and computation fit in terms of reducing the *N* at Filter 3 to those individuals who actually had read the article. This is a quite different unit of analysis and answers different questions than statistics providing single variable relationships or statistics based on group deviations from a line of "best fit."

Results

Data from the community survey were available on whether the individuals in the simulation had actually read about the pending community event in the newspaper. In a series of random samples of forty-one drawn from the *N* of 163, one would expect samples to center around a mean of 44 percent correct because 44 percent of the sample (72 of 163) had actually read something about the pending event in the newspapers. However, not all had read the same article since the information was presented more than once in the newspaper.

The six variables utilized in assigning *P* scores from scale scores all represent concept areas specified as relevant in studies of newspaper readership and communications. The percentage of actual readers advanced through Filter 3 represents a test of the theoretical orientations that specify relationships between education, information seeking, and the like, to newspaper readership. Moreover, the model was tested for predictive ability by an examination of what percentage actual readership had been advanced through Filter 3.

Early runs using the model and parameter estimates developed in the original model produced results only slightly better than those expected due to chance. It is at this point that the flexibility of the simulation technique is brought to bear. Several different possibilities were present to alter the condition of the model and its variables. All possibilities were explored, and the results of alternative model conditions and variable inclusion are presented in Table 8. Further discussion of these alternative runs follows.

The percentage of correct readers predicted was increased principally through two changes in the operating conditions of the basic model. The first of these two increases was brought about by reducing the random element in the model. Making the first filter deterministic based on age, occupation, and income, and allowing Filters 2 and 3 to remain combinations of random and deterministic elements substantially increased the predictive ability of the model. Therefore there was too much randomness included in Filter 1 of the original runs of the model.

The predictive ability of the model was further increased by a combination of two factors: (1) decreasing the random element entered in the model at all three filter points and (2) introducing the additional variables—age, income, and occupation—as determining factors in selecting individuals to be continued on through Filter 3. This determinism based on age, income, and occupation was consistent with generalizations from communications theory. However, the range of occupations and income was reduced in a small community. Age variance was reduced by interviewing only those persons over twenty years of age. For that reason, three variables were not included in the original six factors in the basic model.

While predictive ability had increased substantially over chance (71 percent to 44 percent expected due to chance), considerable error still existed in the 29 percent wrongly predicted as readers of the article.

Table 8
Alternative Models and Percentage Correct Output

MODEL CONDITIONS	FACTORS MANIPULATED	% CORRECT
1st filter random, 2d and 3d combination random and deterministic	6 basic	44
"	6 basic	51
"	6 basic	41
1st filter random, 2d and 3d deterministic	5 (adoption deleted)	56
1st filter random, 2d and 3d deterministic	4 (threat and protection deleted)	71
1st random, 2d and 3d deterministic	6 basic	61
1st filter deterministic based on age, income, education, 2d and 3d random-deterministic	6 basic	63
1st filter deterministic based on age, income, education, 2d and 3d random-deterministic	6 basic	63
3 filters, all deterministic	9 factors, age, income, occupation added	71
3 filters, all deterministic	8 income, occupation added	71
3 filters, all deterministic	8 income, age added	71

All percentages represent the average percentage correct readership predicted on a minimum of three computer runs under identical operating conditions.

SIMULATION OF HUMAN INTERACTION USING NOMINAL DATA: HOMUNCULUS AS A PROGRAM

The work of the Gullahorns points up the possibilities of computer simulation in theory extension and the development of more precise detail in developing flowcharts in the simulation process.

The Gullahorns' HOMUNCULUS simulation was derived from theory using the five propositions presented by George Homans in *Social Behavior; Its Elementary Forms* in 1961. Even though this set of propositions is considered to be very specific, many obstacles had to be overcome in operationalizing it into a computer simulation. The Gullahorns describe this difficulty: "Formulating a theory as a computer model affords one a relatively traceable representation and possibly a more meaningful conceptualization, having increased precision as a result of the clarification concepts the programming process necessitates."[14]

The major point is that a relatively complex but well-specified set of propositions was used to develop a computer simulation of a dyad in social interaction. Furthermore, the lowest possible level of measurement, nominal data, was utilized to develop this simulation. This would seem to indicate that a considerable amount of work is involved in developing a simulation model, even when the lowest possible level of measurement is used. Nonetheless, its development is possible. The first proposition is:

> 1. If in the recent past the occurrence of a particular stimulus-situation has been the occasion on which a man's activity has been rewarded, then the more similar the present stimulus-situation is to the past one, the more likely he is to emit the activity or some similar activity.[15]

This first proposition represents the ability upon stimuli recognition to respond from an experiential background or to adjust response to the perceived similarity of the situation. It is represented graphically in Figures 15 and 16. The difficulties of dealing with even well-specified propositions are recognized by the Gullahorns when they state: "In formalizing this proposition as a computer routine, however, we found that the apparent clarity of the verbal statement actually cloaked certain ambiguities."[16]

In other words, a relatively specific proposition was reduced to nominal responses rated by the + and − symbols in the figures. The original problem stemmed from the fact that both of two co-workers, Ted and George, held the same title but were not equally competent. The nature of the interaction as specified by the Gullahorns was stated as:

> As expected, the more skilled workers received more requests for assistance from their co-workers. While the participants in such consultations benefited, they still incurred costs in their exchange. That is, the agent requesting help was usually rewarded by being able to do a better job; however, he paid the price of implicitly admitting his inferiority to a colleague who by title was supposedly his equal. The consultant, on the other hand, gained prestige; nevertheless, he incurred the cost of time taken from his own work.[17]

Hence, both Ted and George incur costs and rewards for the interaction, but the scanning process depicted in Figure 15 had to be specified at all branch points specified to continue the interaction into Figure 16.

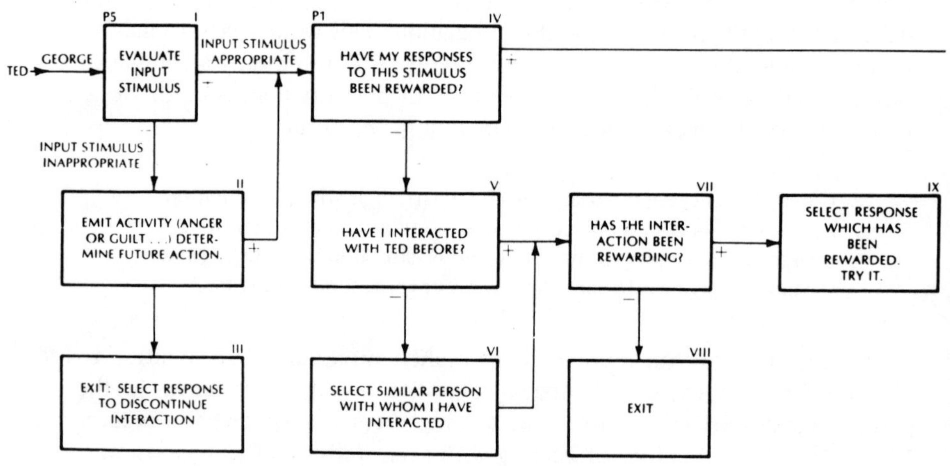

FIGURE 15 HOMUNCULUS Simulation Model

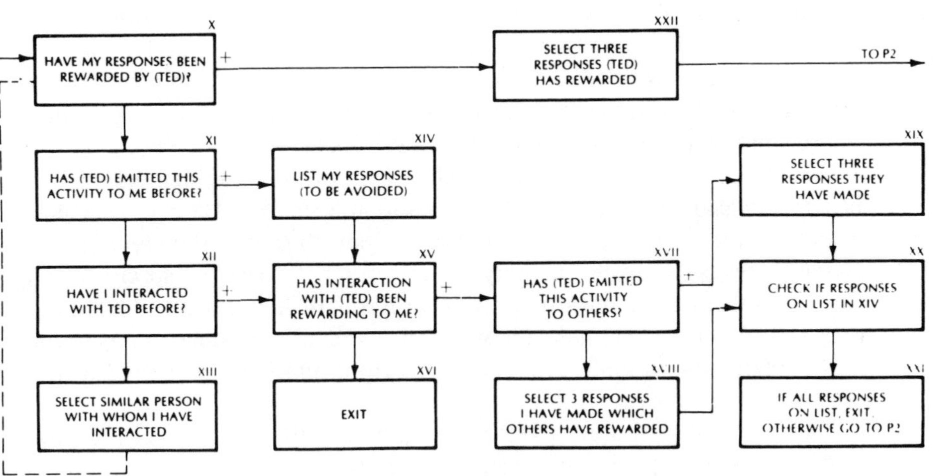

FIGURE 16 HOMUNCULUS Simulation Model (continued)

The next proposition to be considered deals with the reward function of the interaction. Proposition 2 from Homans states: "The more often within a given period of time a man's activity rewards the activity of another, the more often the other will emit the activity."[18]

As can be seen in Figure 16, George evaluated the reward function based on whether he had interacted with Ted before or with another person in a similar situation. Again, it is to be noted that the conditions for exiting each step or box must be specified, based on the response possibilities for George but modified by Ted's previous behavioral response in the same or similar circumstances. Through Figure 16 George is weighing whether he has previously been rewarded, and, if so, what type response from him Ted has rewarded. Moreover, George chose to break off the relationship by exiting and stopping the interaction in both Figures 15 and 16.

In effect, George has begun to consider Proposition 3 in Figure 16, but it becomes crucial in box P3, XXIV. Proposition 3 states: "The more valuable to a man a unit of the activity another gives him, the more often he will emit activity rewarded by the activity of the other."[19] In this specification, George evaluated the reward function in terms of his previous interaction with Ted. After having made this evaluation, the process moves along to the next proposition without possibility for exiting until the next proposition has been considered.

The fourth proposition of Homans' set deals with satiation, or the state of being full, incapable of ingesting or receiving more of a specific unit. Specifically, Proposition 4 states: "The more often a man has in the recent past received a rewarding activity from another, the less valuable any further unit of that activity becomes to him."[20]

At this point, exit becomes possible if George perceives he has had quite enough of Ted and can expect no additional prestige from further interaction with him. However, George can again make additional assessments of alternative responses and continue to the end of the interaction, but if George determines no response is worth his effort, he may exit into box XXVIII and cut off any further interaction. (See Figure 17.)

Homans gives a fifth and final proposition. However, the Gullahorns had dealt with it in box 1 or the initiating set of the process. Homans' Proposition 5 states: "The more to a man's disadvantage the rule of distributive justice fails of realization, the more likely he is to display the emotional behavior we call anger."[21]

This emotion state could result from previous interaction with Ted that has not been rewarded, a decision on George's part that Ted has become a nuisance and that he (George) no longer chooses to assist Ted since they both have the same job description and title. Therefore, the problem as subjected to simulation by the Gullahorns could easily have been viewed as

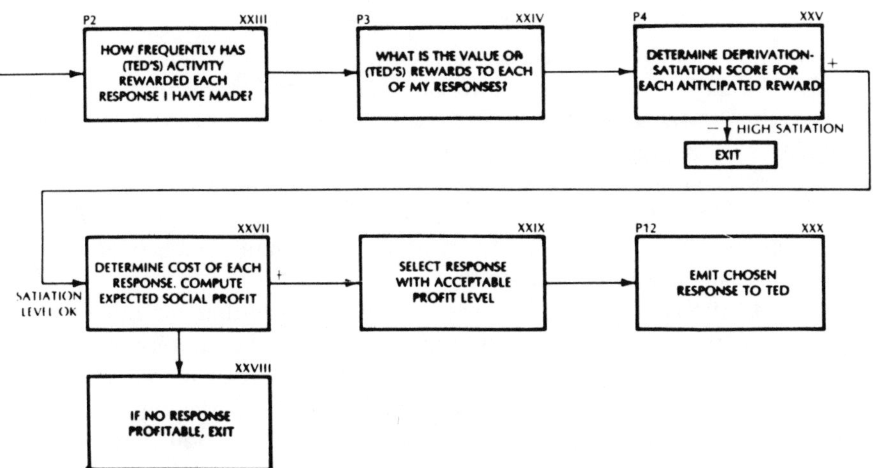

FIGURE 17 HOMUNCULUS Simulation Model (continued)

a decision-making process on the part of George. Either he chooses to consult with Ted or he does not. Even so, the simulation provides additional detail of the decision-making process beyond the mere noting of whether the decision to consult was "yes" or "no."

The point of providing additional detail is of major concern in the social sciences and focuses on basic questions in the discipline. First, is it possible to predict whether George will assist Ted? On some probability basis is it possible to work out an equation giving a probability of a positive outcome of George actually helping Ted? The discipline will be equally (or more) interested in understanding the process whereby an event takes place. In an oversimplification, this could be likened to the problem of prediction versus explanation. It is often possible to predict an outcome with a mathematical equation, but the prediction does little to increase understanding of the process whereby the outcome is achieved.

SUMMARY

The simulation technique holds promise for the social scientist in exercises of this type. It was possible to construct a model from suggested theoretical relationships and to test these predicted readers with empirically collected data. The high-speed capabilities of the computer were used, but more importantly, Dawson's call for examination of an operating model of social process was heeded. Moreover, the model was replicated by manipulating the variables and their interrelationships as well as examining alternative mixes of determinism and stochasticism. This capability, after developing a model of step processes and structures, made it possible to examine problems which cannot be studied with standard statistical techniques.

This kind of research directs attention to the need for specifying relationships between variables. Simple descriptive relationships suffice when one is dealing with aggregates of individuals or with statistics based on pooled estimates of variance. These statements are grossly insufficient when not only the direction but also the intensity of change must be stated. For example, how much should exposure to mass communications be increased with each increment in education?

An added advantage of this type of simulation is that the outcome of multiple variable relationship is sought. Because of the rapidity of calculation, the researcher also maintains a "profile" on each individual in the simulation. The researcher can build and run his model on theoretical grounds before encountering the expense of field verification. Model building from theory prior to data collection is a tenet long advocated in the social sciences.

NOTES

1. Paul F. Lazarsfeld, *Mathematical Thinking in the Social Sciences* (Glencoe, Ill.: Free Press, 1954). Stuart C. Dodd, "Diffusion Is Predictable," *American Sociological Review* 20 (August 1955): 392-401. C. West Churchman, et al., *Introduction to Operations Research* (New York: John Wiley and Sons, 1957).

2. Richard E. Dawson, "Simulation in the Social Sciences," in Harold Guetzkow, ed., *Simulation in Social Science: Readings* (Englewood Cliffs, N.J.: Prentice-Hall, 1962), pp. 1-15.

3. The original model was developed and published by John J. Hartman and James A. Walsh, "Simulation of Newspaper Readership: An Exploration in Computer Analysis of Social Data," *Southwestern Social Science Quarterly* 49, No. 4 (March 1969):840-52.

4. The total N was 163.

5. Donald N. Dillman, "The Effects of Source on Readers of Weekly Newspaper," M.S. thesis, Ames, Iowa State University, 1963.

6. Bernard Berelson, "What 'Missing the Newspaper' Means," in Willbur Schramm, ed., *The Process and Effects of Mass Communications* (Urbana: University of Illinois Press, 1960), pp. 34, 71-73.

7. More detail on the characteristics of the sample is available in George M. Beal, Paul Yarbrough, Gerald Klonglan, and Joe M. Bohlen, "Social Action in Civil Defense," Rural Sociology Report No. 34, Iowa Agricultural and Home Economics Experiment Station, Iowa State University, Ames, Iowa, 1967.

8. Robert E. Lane and David O. Sears, *Public Opinion* (Englewood Cliffs, N.J.: Prentice-Hall, 1974), and Berelson, op. cit., p. 34.

9. Ibid., p. 66.

10. Many such specifications occur in the social sciences where the author specifies that as one variable increases, another variable moves in harmony. In the above case,

the relationship is positive, or as the amount of formal education increases, the probability of exposure to a specific message also increases.

11. Berelson, op. cit., p. 33.

12. The standard scores are referred to as *P* scores in this chapter.

13. An alpha score was a randomly generated score added to the summated *P* score for each individual. That is, limits were set for each individual based on his *P* score for the six variables, i.e., if an *S* had a *P* score of six his alpha score could have been anything from 0 to 12. The zero occurs when a − 6 is randomly generated and the 12 occurs when a + 6 is generated.

14. John T. Gullahorn and Jeanne E. Gullahorn, "Computer Simulation of Human Interaction in Small Groups," *Simulation* (January 1965): 54.

15. Ibid.

16. Ibid.

17. Ibid.

18. Ibid., p. 57.

19. Ibid.

20. Ibid., p. 58.

21. Ibid., p. 61.

16

Evaluation Research

Evaluation research has become increasingly important in the social sciences during the past decade. This recent development appears to have arisen as a response to the practical need for evaluating ongoing social service programs. The evaluative needs of both private and public agencies administering these programs vary, both in complexity and the length of time to be covered by evaluation. For example, there is a need to evaluate such diverse elements as markets, components, cost factors, distribution techniques, material use, techniques of production, or the compatibility of innovation with existing machinery involved in production. Recently, however, evaluative research, both public and private, has been most frequently employed for "people-oriented programs," service agencies, or public-sponsored programs designed to relieve broadly defined social problems or to measure the effectiveness of public expenditures in the public area. Weiss explores the relationship between social action programs and evaluative research:

> Before a study is begun, researchers often call together an advisory committee to help develop the plans, specify the hypothesis or objectives to be studied, decide on design and measures, consider unexpected events and consequences that will affect the research in applied research, purpose for latter use of study reports. . . . it provides the knowledge and insight of a score of the best informed people in the evaluation field what a colleague calls "wise old owls."

Like most advisory committees, the members do not always agree. Their differences arise largely from differing assumptions about why evaluation is undertaken and what use it serves. Once these are clarified, it is possible to consider each expert's advice in terms of its usability for the conditions of a particular evaluation.[1]

Evaluation research is clearly a developing field which provides the behavioral scientist with an opportunity to make his somewhat abstract knowledge and research skills of practical relevance. Equally clear is the lack of agreement on what constitutes the best possible designs in evaluative research and the most appropriate measurement techniques. Although such confusion relates to assumptions regarding the purpose of a given piece of research, it also pertains to research team members being committed to differing disciplines and therefore different assumptions about human behavior. In order to make evaluative research efforts most effective, or at the very least most understandable, the theoretical assumptions and premises underlying them must be made explicit.

Problems of specificity with regard to purpose and theoretical assumptions are not unique in evaluative research; all research projects face these same difficulties. The key word in understanding evaluative research and how it differs from other types of social research is "utility." This is so because the framework of the research is somewhat structured by the evaluative function undertaken and because the individuals who make use of research results are frequently unsophisticated in measuring the reliability or validity of such research. Note also that evaluative research may utilize standard evaluative techniques, but the design of the research and the actual carrying forth of the research often occur in situations that provide few guidelines. Concomitantly, this particular research tradition operates with a particularly thin literature establishing precedence and containing few instances of what could be classified as case studies. Evaluation research at the present could be likened unto exploratory research occurring in a non-academic setting.

In many ways, attempts at design and measurement are simply *attempts* and not examples of complete models. A further complication is the necessity of presenting research results to those uninitiated in interpretation. For such persons, the most important activity is not research, but the service program and the social problem it addresses. For this reason, research is often viewed as a threat to relevant progress and ultimate purpose. Within this framework, research is most often defined as good if it supports the efficacy of the social service or social agency in question, and as hostile or bad if it defines existing programs as ineffective or counterproductive. What is most frequently manifest, therefore, is a conflict between ideology and fact. Research properly done addresses fact with regard to the efficacy of program and is capable of replication. It does not concern itself with the "social worth" of a program in question and does not deal with the ideology that has defined the addressed area as requiring amelioration or systematic service. Perhaps it is because of its neutrality that research is defined as hostile. That there is a line between objectivity and hostility is clear. Research, by both its assumptions and design, serves only to prove that the value of what presently exists is both tautological and, in the final evaluation, useless. The social investigator who designs research to prove the value of a program guarantees the failure of his research and, in many instances, guarantees the waste of social service resources and the most flagrant abuse of the commonweal. Too often, those involved in evaluative research forget Max Weber's words of caution that social science could tell us why we live the way we live or why a particular program is successful or unsuccessful; science as such, however, could not tell us how we should live. Pronouncements on how to live are value judgments and are therefore not the province of sociology or any behavioral science.

Typical of evaluation research efforts that confuse confirmation of social purpose with validity and reliability is a study entitled "Girls at Vocational High."

EVALUATION RESEARCH AND PROGRAM MODIFICATION

"Girls at Vocational High," a study in "social work intervention" done between 1955 and 1960 for the Russell Sage Foundation, involved a New York City girls' vocational school and a professional social work agency. The Youth Consultation Service was a nonsectarian voluntary social agency specializing in services for adolescent girls. It was an innovative organization that specialized in offering services to adolescent girls with manifest problems. The purpose of the program was to identify potential delinquent girls and to use social work skills to intervene and so prevent them from becoming delinquent. The research evaluation of the program was handled by Meyer, Borgotta, and Jones.[2] The objective of the research was twofold: (1) to determine whether potentially problematic subjects could be identified and involved in preventive programs before behavior problems occurred and (2) to evaluate the extent to which social case work was effective in prevention, when applied to subjects so identified and so involved. Lemmert identifies these intentions as being founded on the "tired proposition harbored by the Russell Sage Foundation people since 1920 that deviancy can be prevented if social workers turn their energies and skills to the potential deviant."[3]

The decision as to whether a girl was a potential delinquent was based on a combination of factors, including school records and teachers' opinions generated by the school experience. A pool of potential problem cases was chosen, and from this pool, girls were randomly selected to join either the control or the experimental group. Each group contained approximately two hundred girls. The girls involved in the study were given time off from school for agency appointments, and the agency was obliged to accept all referrals from the experimental group. In fact, the design called for the measurement of both the experimental and the control group after treatment in order to determine the extent of difference, if any, betwen the two groups. Obviously, the question addressed was whether or not treatment had any measurable effect on the behavior.

The youth agency involved offered three different modes of treatment throughout the four-year study:

1. Individual treatment
2. Random assignment to group treatment
3. Treatment on a basis of specified problem

It was decided that successful treatment or intervention was to be defined as the production of appropriate behavior on the part of subjects. The criteria applied therefore included behavior in school and out of school, clinical criteria such as personality and adjustment tests, scores on various inventories, as well as the girls' general attitudes. Sociometric data and judgments of social workers were used as supplementary material. These criteria were used to compare the experimental with the control group and, in some instances, to compare the entire control group with the residual population. The conclusions were as follows:

> The study gave clear answers to questions to which it was addressed. It is possible to identify potentially problematic girls and to involve them in relationships and activities that were designed to prevent the developing problematic behavior. The impact of the preventive effort if any was minor.
>
> Few statistically significant differences between experimental and control cases were found. On the wide range of criteria used to detect impact of the treatment program, the most positive evidence is represented by the small parallel effects found for a number of objects and self report measures. This encourages no dramatic change for this type service program as a major assault on critical school and personal behavior problems of high school girls. The limited demonstration of its effectiveness raises important questions of appropriate goals of service programs as well as issues about the work practice and its evaluation.[4]

The type of research required by this demonstration project was evaluation research, and the findings of that research had great import with regard to the agency's and city's future plans in terms of the treatment of delinquency.

The study itself was fraught with difficulties and was not well received. The study was criticized for its difficulty in defining what was a potential problem girl. The school records used were highly inaccurate, contained contradictory materials, and in general, were fraught with inconsistencies.

In addition to a lack of uniformity, there was no attempt on the part of the researchers to estimate the validity of the references made by teachers about students. Additionally, none of the factors obtained from the records was weighted, and so all elements of the school's records were given equal weight. Perhaps more importantly, the study itself and the program it was evaluating changed several times in the four years of its duration.

Significantly, the study did find that the longer girls stayed in school, the more likely they were to avoid future delinquencies. Hence, it might be true that success in the school situation is indicative of a placid or compliant personality, or the finding itself could be spurious. In any event, 49 percent of the potential problem girls were present at school in their graduate year. This was true for 61 percent of the residual girls.

Throughout the experiment, there was the lack of logical coherence between ascribed goals and means, with investigators not realizing that the case work described could never have attained the goals inherent in the prevention notion. This failing was, of course, that of the Youth Consultation Service since the thrust of research was evaluative and was not meant to structure any element of the treatment program itself. The study can be seriously criticized for omitting data from the final cohort which had completed only two of the three years of high school when the project was completed. Some of the objective evaluative criteria were not applied to this group, nor were clinical criteria. Yet, the group comprised approximately one-third of the total experiment and control groups. This meant that data regarding the 1958 cohort was eliminated from much of the final analysis. Since treatment modes were modified and ostensibly had improved throughout the study, this group would have been subject to sounder treatment methods than previous groups. In addition, many of these young women were said to have been significantly involved in the treatment process. Omitting these cases, therefore, affected results obtained from the evaluation of the treatment.

What is important is not the outcome of the study, but the fact that evaluation research provided the basis for modifying treatment programs as well as allowing decisions to be made as to the effectiveness of treatment programs. In this case, the findings were negative, but the cost savings in dollars in terms of program modification or abandonment must have been enormous.

CHANGING ROLE AND RESPONSIBILITY OF THE RESEARCHER

The research efforts and interests of a discipline are as subject to frequent change as any other segment of society. This was the thesis of Sorokin's book *Fads and Foibles in Society*[5] which demonstrated how interests in sociology change and how interest in a given area tends to generate interest among others. The literature of sociology demonstrates the cyclical nature of research interests. It is not suggested that the discipline wanders aimlessly about reacting to outbreaks of interest in a speculative or a capricious manner. Quite the contrary, there are individuals who devote their entire lives to the development of a single area without regard for what particular perspective currently dominates the field. This is not the case, however, with newcomers to the research discipline who are still in the process of casting about for a theoretical or research framework, nor is it the case with certain persons who by virtue of their wide interests are able to maintain an eclectic approach.

THE GOVERNMENT AND EVALUATION RESEARCH

It is axiomatic that the availability of research money in a given area can quickly generate interest. When such monies come from government agencies, it is frequently found that social action research, agency-oriented research, and, of course, evaluative research frequently reflect dominant cultural themes and relate more to the value structure of the culture than to the interest of the discipline. This trend can best be demonstrated by the proliferation of politically motivated criminal justice research evident since the public and the federal government began to emphasize law and order. This emphasis resulted in the creation of an office whose principal function was to fund programs dealing with crime and law enforcement problems as well as crime prevention measures.

The government-supported social action programs of today are very different from those of the early post-World War II period when no provisions were made for evaluating programs. As a requisite of funding, current programs demand evaluation components in contract proposals. Most of the early Office of Economic Opportunity (OEO) programs had such an evaluation component, although OEO requirements were often unspecific and funds were frequently distributed on a per capita basis. Hence, funds were made available to regions, states, counties, and cities on the basis of population, and not on the merit of proposals submitted for funding or research-defined social needs in a given region. As funds became more difficult to obtain and the early funded programs showed signs of faltering, or simply of reinforcing traditional ineffective mechanisms for dealing with a particular social problem, the research component for programs became more stringent and was required to be submitted with the proposal requesting funding.[6]

In an overview of evaluation policy, Wholey and others connected with the Urban Institute in Washington, D.C., stated:

> . . . although the economy is still of paramount importance, the government has in the past decade given increased attention of national social goals and problems. The reasons are clear—along with our rapid economic growth have come growing social unrest, and the awareness of poverty and affluence. The recent proliferation of federal programs concerned with human resource development and improvements in the quality of life has been in response to our multiplying social ills.[7]

While evaluation as a process has been ongoing for a long time, it has been characteristically a subjective evaluation, and those so engaged have not been fully aware of the impact of their own value set on such evaluations. The Urban Institute points out: ". . . the federal government as a whole, and most federal agencies, have no over all system for objectively evaluating programs and project effectiveness."[8]

Although progress has been made with regard to evaluating social service programs and government-sponsored programs, no system can absolutely evaluate the effectiveness of any program or project. What progress has been made can be said to reflect the funding source's interest in increasing effectiveness through greater accountability.

Of particular importance is the following:

> The Director shall provide for the continuing evaluation of programs under this title (Title II—H.E.W.) including their effectiveness in achieving stated goals, their impact on related programs, and their structure and mechanisms for the delivery of services and including where appropriate comparisons with proper control groups composed of persons who have not participated in such programs.[9]

In the same report, section (B) relates to the evaluation of social programs. It states:

> The Director shall develop and publish standards for evaluation of program effectiveness in achieving the objectives of this title. Such standards shall be considered in deciding whether to renew or supplement financial assistance provided by . . . (Named sections).[10]

Although their phrasing and language leaves much to be desired, the statements above represent a change in philosophy and program for the Department of Health, Education and Welfare in its allocation of funds. The trend is toward the development of guidelines for objective evaluation of operational or newly funded programs. From the researcher's standpoint it is particularly important that avowed purposes include comparative research with the utilization of carefully selected control groups, impact evaluation with regard to the provision of human services, and, above all, effectiveness evaluation which focuses on the extent to which a given program has achieved its stated end. Such definitions and guidelines make clear the researcher's responsibility and serve to change the role of research from reifying preconceived notions to the actual evaluation of the reality of the situation. The evaluation component was made a requisite, and is restated for emphasis:

> . . . including their effectiveness of achieving stated goals, their impact on related programs and structures and mechanisms for the delivery of services and included where appropriate comparisons with proper control groups composed of persons who have not participated in such programs.[11]

The implications for the social scientist are clear. He must be involved in the development of proposals requesting funds where objectives are clearly stated in terms that lend themselves to evaluation. In addition, they are in a position to introduce precision to statements of purpose, terminology, conceptual framework, and, above all, the conditions under which program evaluation will take place. Given this framework, greater specificity will be required than is found in statements such as "Our purpose is to upgrade the level of living of the minority population," which characterize all too many social programs. Such statements and programs cannot be evaluated through research. Returning to the integration example, the control and experimental group format was required with specifications of the research's funding. This requires a cross-sectional design or experimental design as described in detail in Chapter 5. However, other research techniques such as those outlined in the chapter on covert behavior are not precluded. Precision and propinquity are of the utmost importance in utilizing the chosen research design. At no point should methodology be confused with results, or assumptions with intent or, for that matter, fact. Given the trend toward and the increasing importance of evaluative research, social action research with all of its evaluative implications must become a part of ongoing direct programs, and the social scientist must become involved as a consultant in designing entire project proposals or as personnel responsible for fulfilling the contractual obligation of evaluation. The social scientist must therefore develop data collection instruments and research designs, as well as data flow and information systems; test and analyze data for significant differences; and be involved in the writing of research reports. In addition to providing services to the local communities involved, through such programs students have been trained, improving generally the quality of professional services offered throughout city government programs and other administrative bodies.

In short, federal policy is largely responsible for the social scientist's increased interest in evaluation research. At the same time, federal programs have been moving toward increased action programs and direct service programs. Meanwhile, federally sponsored grants for pure research having no action component have been diminishing. It is curious that the implications of such "pure" research are seldom used as the basis for social action programs. Current programs seem to spring from traditionally defined "social welfare concerns" and through modifications derived from evaluation research often reify a point of fact previously pinpointed by "pure research." Nonetheless, traditional government funding sources have been accustomed to dealing in a grant format where the reputation of the demonstrated ability of the researchers and the amount of time to be spent in such research are taken into account in allocating funds. Indeed, it can be said that a list of the recipients of National Science Foundation grants reads like a list of Who's Who in the discipline of sociology. Some would say that this policy is one way to guarantee a research "status quo" in any discipline. Such funding policies must certainly stifle innovation through its support of the old and established rather than the recently trained.

GRANTS AND CONTRACTS

The switch to evaluation sections of action programs has brought about two major changes with regard to competition for granting funds at major agencies. First, the evaluation component requires a specific task to be performed; hence, the funds that become available are in the form of contracts. Such contracts mandate a "fee for services agreement" for a specific task, while the grant format is likely to be less specific in dictating how the proposed objective of the grant is to be met. Therefore, although more money has become available to a larger number of social scientists for evaluative research, the money provided is in a contract format. Thus, the requirements are more stringent, the research design is more specific, and its importance to the general discipline becomes devaluated. In many ways, this change in funding has brought about a deemphasis upon the theoretical growth of the discipline, and many have charged that, as a result, sociology has become atheoretical in its application and less general as a science. Even given this, we must note that a second major change has occurred with regard to funding, having to do with the distribution of resources. Since most counties and some multicounty regional planning agencies were receiving funds, these funds became available to individuals and representatives of agencies who could not have successfully competed for them in the earlier grant market. The student therefore should recognize that politics and political decisions have played a part in the direction and the intensity of research effort in recent years. Despite this, as funds become available to individuals in a more widely dispersed number of cities and counties, results have not always been positive and the general quality of research done in the name of social science has suffered. Many persons feel capable of attempting evaluation projects for which they are ill prepared. This problem is compounded by the fact that over the past decade, many project directors have had little experience with evaluation as a management tool and have feared the possible results of program evaluation, viewing them as personally threatening:

> Program managers may view evaluation of the impact of their national programs as a process from which they have more to lose than to gain, if not as a threat to their own position. One possible conclusion of an objective evaluation study, for example, is that the program manager is not performing his job competently or that the principles underlying a program have proven faulty in whole or in part. In either case, the administrator may prefer to take his chances on ignorance about the worth of the program. There may also be legitimate fears that evaluation might give misinformation or unbalanced views of the worth of programs, either because of the underdeveloped state of evaluation methodology or because unsuitable output measures might be chosen by evaluators removed from program responsibilities.[12]

This potential problem exists in all evaluation research settings whether the evaluation is performed by an independent agent from a nearby university or research institute or is done by the managers of the action program itself. In general, it can be said that despite good intentions, social service programs often fail. Where research pinpoints this failure, it is not research that betrays the purpose of the program, but the service program itself. Research should be defined as the guarantor of improved service. This very basic problem was described by Gouldner and Miller a decade ago in *Applied Sociology: Opportunities and Problems.*[13] The authors distinguish between the role of social engineer and social clinician. The engineer acts in the capacity of a managing consulting contract, and his aims are to determine whether employees are satisfied with working conditions, wages, hours, supervisors, and so on. In this framework the problem is designated by the client. The social scientist acts in the role of social engineer, for he agrees to apply his expertise to the problem designated by the company officials.

The clinician appears to act as a kind of go-between in the settling of a dispute. In their book, Gouldner and Miller cite a dispute over cattle at Hacienda Vicos.[14] It was suggested by the social clinicians that the cattle be branded to eliminate disputes. Branding was accomplished after the wealthier leaders consented to it. Gouldner and Miller sum up the differences between the engineer and the clinician roles as follows:

> Even from this brief account, certain contrasts between the clinical and engineering model already are evident. Most importantly, the clinicians of Hacienda Vicos did not assume as did the engineers and the management consultancy firm that their client's own formulation of their problem could be taken at face value. Instead the clinicians took their client's complaints and self formulations as only one among a

number of "systems" useful in helping them conceive in their own diagnosis of the client's problems. In the employee attitude study, the engineers studied what they were told to: at Hacienda Vicos, the clinicians made their own independent identification of the group's problems.[15]

To this point, evaluation research has been discussed as the application of existing research methods to problems defined as social problems by the culture and supported by components of social action programs. Although this makes possible the wider distribution of research funds and opportunities and tends to make research less elitist, it also tends to delimit the researcher's imagination. He finds his horizon bound by what are generally defined as "social work" or "social welfare" prerequisites and concerns. While some researchers can be innovative and develop new methods and pure research concerns under these limitations, specific tasks still have to be performed to satisfy the contract requirement's characteristic of the "new evaluation research." The major distinction, of course, lies in who specifies the problem to be examined and who acts to evaluate the ameliorative impact of problem solution. Both social engineers and social clinicians can be defined as necessary in the social sciences, and both contribute in their own way.

SPECIFICATION OF EVALUATION PROBLEMS

Evaluation problems are concerned primarily with the analysis of people-oriented or service-oriented programs. In that sense, they differ from theory testing or hypothesis testing research, or research concerned with hypothesis generation, as is the case in most exploratory research. In evaluation research, the basic question for the agency is, "How well do we do what we purport to do?" From a program director's perspective, the thrust of the evaluation research is to measure efficacy and provide the foundations for management decisions with regard to the direction the program in question will take. Second, the evaluation research component satisfies project requirements. In this regard, evaluation should consist of the following basic states:

1. Defining the basic goals of the program.
2. Translating these goals into measurable indicators of goal achievement.
3. Collecting data on the indicators for those who have been exposed to the program.
4. Collecting similar data from those who have not been exposed to the program (control group).
5. Comparing the data on a program participant and controls in terms of goal criteria.[16]

That these stages complement the legal structure underlying social action programs is obvious. Note, however, that stages include the use of a control group comprised of persons who have not participated in the relevant program. Previously cited sources, Wholey and Weiss have pointed out at earlier times that there are several different criteria by which a program can be evaluated other than to measure the perceived effectiveness of the program for participants in the program. Suchman's general discussion of these criteria centers on the following:

1. effort—the criteria of success is the quantity and quality of activity that takes place; it is an assessment of input (work load) without regard to output.
2. effectiveness—this is essentially a performance criteria measuring the results of effort rather than the effort itself; it requires a clear statement of objectives.
3. impact—the criteria on success for the impact component is the degree to which effective performance is adequate to the total amount of need.
4. cost effectiveness—this criteria is concerned with the evaluation of alternative methods and their relative cost with regard to our other criteria of effectiveness; it represents a ratio between effort and impact.
5. process—this is not an inherent part of the evaluation research component but rather an analysis of the process whereby a program produces the result it does; it is a descriptive and diagnostic measure and seeks unanticipated negative and positive side effects.[17]

Thus, evaluation research is rightfully the province of the social science researcher. Although the category of evaluative research appears to be separate and distinct from basic sociological research, the two are of a piece and differ only in terms of the intended use of their results. Even so, many of the variables involved in the research of action-oriented programs are not behavioral variables. For example, cost effectiveness is not a ratio of dollar cost divided by the number of units served. If counseling ten persons costs $100 and the cost is $10 per case, how much would it cost to counsel ten persons in a group session? Would the desired results be achieved in both techniques? Would it be better to choose a slightly higher cost technique because it produces clearly superior results? These are not variables but are management decisions based on research results presented by the evaluation researcher. In this type of research, the researcher's role is to consider his function as that of the technician providing a service to what are essentially political decision-makers who in turn exercise judgments as to the best uses of research findings. The evaluation researcher's role has thus been fulfilled when a research report has been filed. However, Gouldner and Miller were aware of the sometimes less than gentle fate awaiting the typical research report:

Usually the company management invites the consultants to a discussion concerning the implications of these findings. Then, after a decent interval, the report may be quietly interred in the great graveyard of creativity, the filing room. Although widely outlined, this is probably a representative history of the engineering types of applied social research. It is often with such a case in mind that people discuss the "gap" between research and policy making.[18]

The authors' experience in evaluation research also extends into policy research. In general, it parallels the models already presented, but enough differences exist between the two types to present the following observations and an example pinpointing these differences.

SOCIETAL COSTS

Difficulties in assigning societal costs lie in the justification for placing dollar values or figures on events or outcomes. The underlying methods are quite similar to any other area of research using statistical methods. The Department of Transportation (DOT) has assigned dollar costs to types of accident. The figures were derived from several years of accident statistics. While these figures can be challenged (as any set could be), they do bring standardization to all cities, counties, and states reporting accident statistics. DOT uses the following figures for cost per accident calculations of societal cost:

fatal crash	$207,000.00 per person
nonfatal injury	7,300.00 per injury
property damage accident	300.00 per accident[19]

Data summarizing the severity, cost per accident, and occurrence are presented in Table 9. The societal costs were calculated for Wichita-Sedgwick County in 1973. For example, nonfatal injuries accounted for 81 percent of the dollar value of all crashes in the area, but represented far fewer actual crashes than the 81 percent dollar cost factor. Sixteen percent of the societal cost was attributed to fatal crashes, but the number of accidents was actually less than 1 percent. The most accidents were "property damage only involvement" (about 51 percent), but they represented only 3 percent of the total societal costs.

Although these trends were similar to those developed in the 1972 results, there was a decrease in the number of fatalities. In 1972, there were fifty-seven fatalities compared to fifty in 1973. This decrease was not as large as that recorded in the control city (Topeka and Shawnee County), but the decrease is significant when compared to the preceding year.

Here one should note the evaluation research implications and be aware that data were collected for more than one year (1972 and 1973). Hence, the

Table 9
Summary of Costs by Severity Type, Wichita-Sedgwick County, 1973

ITEM	FATALITY	NONFATAL INJURY	PROPERTY DAMAGE ONLY INVOLVEMENT	TOTAL
Average cost per occurrence[1]	$ 200,700	$ 7,300	$ 300	—
Number of occurrences	50	7,000	7,221	14,271
Total cost in dollars	$10,035,000	$51,100,000	$2,166,300	$63,301,300
Percent of total societal cost	16	81	3	100

1. National Highway Transportation Safety Administration figures from Report #H.S. 820, 185, 1972.

analysis was both longitudinal and comparative. This experimental and control group examination fulfills the requirement of the 1967 federal act requiring comparison between groups when appropriate.

The total societal cost based on these figures was considerable—$63 million, or about $257 for each man, woman, and child in the area. The public can relate to such figures and interpret them with regard to the impact on the Wichita area.

Most of the units of analysis which social scientists study cannot be so easily examined. What dollar value can be assigned to damage done a child reared in a derelict home? What is the societal cost of delinquency? What does it cost to fail to learn in school? All are valid questions, and all have societal cost implications. However, a common denominator of evaluation and comparison has not been developed. Human costs on a comparative basis are difficult to assess. Hence, much remains to be done in evaluation research at all levels.

NOTES

1. Carol N. Weiss, *Evaluating Action Programs: Readings in Social Action and Evaluation* (Boston: Allyn and Bacon, 1972), p. 3.

2. Henry J. Meyer, Edgar Borgotta, and Wyatt C. Jones, *Girls in Vocational High* (New York: Russell Sage Foundation, 1956).

3. Edwin M. Lemmert, "Review of Girl's Educational High," *American Sociological Review* 31 (February 1966): 139.

4. Meyer, Borgotta, and Jones, op. cit., p. 3.

5. Piterim Sorokin, *Fads and Foibles in Society* (Chicago: H. Hegnerg Co., 1956).

6. It is not intended here to discuss this subject at length. Experience proves that many early programs, as well as those individually connected with such action programs, were interested more in getting their share of federal funds than in the results obtained by spending these funds.

7. Joseph S. Wholey, et al., ''Federal Evaluation Policy Analyzing the Effects of Public Programs,'' *The Urban Institute*, 2d ed., Washington, D.C., 1972, p. 20.

8. Ibid., p. 22.

9. Ibid., p. 54, Section 223(A).

10. Ibid., Section 223(B).

11. Ibid., p. 54.

12. Ibid., p. 67.

13. Alvin W. Gouldner and S. M. Miller, *Applied Sociology: Opportunities and Problems* (New York, Free Press, 1965).

14. Ibid., pp. 11-15.

15. Ibid.

16. Weiss, op. cit., p. 6. Note that this is only one methodological approach to evaluative research.

17. Edward A. Suchman, *Evaluative Research: Principles and Practices in Public Service and Social Action Programs* (New York: Russell Sage Foundation, 1967), pp. 60-61.

18. Gouldner and Miller, op. cit., p. 11.

19. National Highway Transportation Safety Administration, Report #H.S. 820, 185, 1972.

17

Statistics

Some rudimentary knowledge of statistics is invaluable to the student in understanding and evaluating research readings. In taking a research course, not all students are exposed to statistics. For those who have had such exposure, this chapter provides a mini-review. Since there has been no attempt to condense a statistics course into a single chapter, what follows is a simplistic discussion of statistics and its importance in analysis.

COMMON PROBLEMS

Those who have problems with statistics generally fall into two categories. First, there are those who "fear" anything statistical or mathematical, assuming that such subjects are too difficult and abstract for them to master. Such an attitude can become a self-fulfilling prophecy. Second, there are those who have difficulty in applying statistics. Even researchers with strong mathematical backgrounds have experienced problems in knowing where and when to apply a particular statistic.

At one point or another in the study of methods, one may have read about the controversy as to whether sociology is or is not a science. Without resolving the issue, let us assume for the moment that it is a science. Those who define it as such designate it a special kind of science. It is not an exact science but rather a probabilistic one. As such, it enables a researcher to predict behavior and to make "law-like statements" about human behavior within specific margins of error. Unlike the natural sciences (e.g., chemistry and biology), a probabilistic science does not enable the researcher to make predictions based on certainty of outcomes. Can the differences between the probabilistic and the exact science be attributed to methods? The scientific method may vary with regard to application to units of analysis, but the logic of the method does not change from discipline to discipline. Given that the difference is not in the method, perhaps it relates more to measurement and the subject of measurement. Behavioral observations and the measurement of attitudes cannot be accomplished with the accuracy associated with the measurement of the physical world. They are subject to constant flux and change, and as such defy exact prediction. Furthermore, complications of exact prediction pertain to those very individual differences created by the nature of the socialization process itself. There are, of course, culturally imposed similarities between people in a general sense, but individualization increases with age. In essence, everything that happens to an individual structures his perception of the immediate present. Perception is related to such things as values and impact, which in turn further structure the next frame of perception. Since perception is an ongoing process and involves the constant interplay of the past with the present, what has immediately preceded perception is included as well as the totality of what has gone before, making up the experiential background of the individual. The problem of prediction is obviously enormous. In many ways, absolute theories about behavior are frequently static statements made without consideration for the dynamic process that is human behavior.

PROBABILITY AND ASSUMPTIONS

Consider an experiment designed to ascertain what effects temperature, moisture, and soil content have on the germination of a wheat kernel. The unit of analysis, a kernel of wheat, will behave like a wheat kernel. With proper equipment, it is possible to control temperature, moisture, and soil conditions in a closed laboratory environment. Each kernel can be assumed to be essentially equal to any other if all are of the same variety, come from the same field, and have been handled and stored in the same manner. Can these laboratory conditions be duplicated with human subjects? Obviously, the natural environment of human interaction cannot be duplicated in a laboratory, nor can it be turned into a laboratory. Extraneous factors cannot be controlled, nor can one assume that the environment is the same for all research subjects since each individual perceives his environment through his own "filters." Individual or situational perception can be understood in the following example. If ten cameras were aimed at the same scene under exactly the same conditions and fired at exactly the same moment, the result would be ten exact duplicate reproductions of the same scene. If, however, ten different color filters were placed over each lens under the exact same conditions and the cameras were then fired at exactly the same moment, the result would be ten different pictures derived from a duplicate reality. In the case of the individual, his "filter" is the sum total of his socialization—his total interaction and perception. Within this framework reality is an individual interpretation. Measurement, given such conditions, is difficult at best.

Since behavioral science is anchored in probability, an examination of the basis of probability is in order. All parametric statistical tests used in the analysis of data are based on events studied or analyzed having a probability factor of 0.5. Given this probability factor, a curve may be derived that allows the researcher to predict within known limits the occurrence or nonoccurrence of given events. Consider the expansion of the binomial distribution which follows. At a later point in the chapter the special case of nonparametric statistical analysis is considered.

THE BINOMIAL DISTRIBUTION

Although there will be few, if any, situations where the behavioral scientist will actually solve the binomial distribution, the concepts underlying it are of considerable importance. The traditional method of dealing with probability problems by researchers is to utilize the properties of the normal curve. In fact, almost all parametric statistics involve assumptions about the normal distribution of data.[1] The normal curve approximates the binomial distribution and differs from it in the sense that it approximates probabilities. The binomial distribution gives exact probabilities.

The binomial distribution is symmetrical when the p[2] of the event considered is one in two, 50 percent, i.e., in the case of coin flipping or + and − scoring in schedules or scales. The basic formula for the binomial is:

$$(p + q)^N$$

The characteristics of the statistic are best seen in expansion of the above formula. The equation will be expanded to the 6th power. Put another way, the probability of each of six different possible outcomes occurring will be examined.

$$(P + q)^6 = 1{:}P^6q^0 + \binom{6}{1}p^5 q^1 + \frac{6.5\,p^4}{1.2} q^2 +$$

$$\frac{6.5.4.\,p^3\,q^3}{1.2.3.} + \frac{6.5.4.3.\,p^2\,q^4}{1.2.3.4.} +$$

$$\frac{6.5.4.3.2.\,p^1\,q^5}{1.2.3.4.5.} + \frac{6.5.4.3.2.1.P^0\,q^6}{1.2.3.4.5.6}$$

Note that as the exponent of P goes down, the exponent of q goes up, or q is the residual of P and will vary in proportion to changes in P. The sum of P and q must always equal unity of 1.0.

The prediction of 4-heads in sequence followed by N-r tails requires the following equation:

$$P_r = p^r q^{N-r}$$

This means that the P of any other sequence or ordering of heads (r) in any order will result in (N-r) tails expressed as $q^{(N-r)}$.

To get the P of any given r in any order, it is only necessary to count the number of ways one can get r heads and (N-r) tails. This is expressed in the following formula:

$\binom{N!}{r!}$ – N in this case means number of trials or events while the r is equal to the number of desired events (success), i.e., number of groups of 3 in a given N trial.

Note that:

$$\binom{N!}{r!} = \frac{N!}{r!\,(N-r)!}$$

Recall that where $P = 0.50$, the distribution obtained from 1-N is symmetrical. It is in this characteristic, the symmetrical 0.5 expectation, that the binomial distribution is approximated by the normal curve. In statistical reasoning, probability statements do not allow one to state that an event will absolutely occur. One can estimate the probability of an event occurring or not occurring and estimate probable errors of prediction through the use of the critical region or significance levels. The notion of a critical region is an arbitrary decision based on the cost involved in rejecting a true hypothesis or accepting a false one. (The type I and type II errors are discussed elsewhere.)

All steps in statistical tests involve making assumptions, obtaining a sample distribution, selecting a significance level and critical region (0.05 – 0.01), computing a test statistic, and deciding whether or not to accept a hypothesis.

In order to use probability theory in obtaining a sampling distribution, researchers must make certain assumptions about the population to which they are generalizing, as well as about the procedures used in sampling. These assumptions are of two kinds: (1) those which appear to be certain or probable, and (2) those which are dubious—and sometimes most interesting.

Those assumptions which are accepted as valid often form the model, and those which are to be tested are called the hypothesis. From a statistical point of view, however, all assumptions have equal status.

A sampling distribution can be defined as the relative number of times one can expect a certain outcome in a large number of events. This type of sample, in simple terms, can be thought of as a sample of samples. This is based on randomness in that a sample is random if all cases or groups of cases have had an equal chance of being included in the sample. The model assumptions must be accurate in order that the null hypothesis can be considered the dubious assumption. No statistical procedure can be used to locate faulty assumptions in the model.

It is the distribution of probabilities which tells us how likely an event will occur, given that true assumptions are supported as true. With a small critical region, it is unlikely that one will reject a true assumption, but one is also less likely to reject a false one. The type II error can be reduced as a possibility if we assure ourselves of an appropriate model. As a rule of thumb, the researcher sets up a null hypothesis to attempt to prove himself wrong. If one honestly cannot prove oneself wrong, the affirmation of the consequent is stronger than if an attempt was made to affirm the positive.

There is nothing sacred about confidence levels. However, traditionally, the 0.05 significance level has been used. This means that one can be relatively confident of having obtained true results 95 times in 100 cases. Put another way, it means that one could have obtained these results only 5 times in 100 events due to chance factors. This, in part, is the importance of probability in the social sciences.

In the consideration of significance levels in Chapter 19, two-tailed tests are discussed. Since the two-tailed test does not specify direction, statistical significance can require the affirmation of the hypothesis in either direction. If theory states that there would be a positive relationship between variables, only one side of the normal curve would pertain. In the coin flipping example, if it was said that three of the same sides (heads or tails) would appear in ten flips or trials, one set of probabilities would pertain. The probabilities would be quite different if one had predicted three heads or three tails in a row. The first example, three of either side, would be analogous to the two-tailed test, while the prediction of either three heads or three tails in a row would be analogous to the one-tailed test.

The decision pertaining to the acceptance or rejection of events on the basis of probability involves error. Probability (*P*) by its very definition includes the possibility of error in prediction. As mentioned previously, the size of the designated critical region depends upon the relative cost of type I or type II error. Note also that there is an inverse relationship between type I and type II error.

In the binomial distribution, a type I error is the sum of probabilities in the critical region. At the 0.05 confidence level, 5 times out of 100 a true hypothesis will be rejected. It is the *P* of making a type I error that is called the significance level.

It has been suggested that with a *P* of 1/2, the binomial distribution is symmetrical. Since the two-tailed model is being used, 0.25 will be needed from each end of the distribution to form the 0.50*P*. In the distribution of ten flips of a coin, if it is decided to reject the assumption of an honest coin at the 0.01 level and nine of ten heads or tails appear, the critical region would be obtained in the following manner.

NO. OF HEADS	*P* = 0.50		
0	1/1024	=	0.001 Critical + 1
1	10/1024	=	0.010 Region + 10
2	45/1024	=	0.004
3	120/1024	=	0.117
4	210/1024	=	0.205
5	252/1024	=	0.246
6	210/1024	=	0.205
7	120/1024	=	0.117
8	45/1024	=	0.004
9	10/1024	=	0.010 Critical + 10
10	1/1024	=	0.001 Region + 1

The type II error is difficult to ascertain. Knowing that the relationship between type I and II error is inverse, however, allows one to say that the smaller the critical region the greater the possibility of committing a type II error in one direction or the other.

COUNTING

A number of measures in research consist of nothing more than counting the number of events that occur over a specified time frame. These types of studies are more likely to be observational studies where, for example, one can observe the number of individuals who violate the "don't walk" light at an intersection. Observations may be organized by some classification such as male, female, black or white, young or old (an arbitrary decision), well dressed or dressed in working clothes, or any group of characteristics. Certain kinds of secondary data, such as U.S. Census data, are of this type, and the figures presented are the total number of persons, males, females, number and percentage under fifteen years of age, and the like. These demographic data are devoid of detail other than that which is derived from simple counting.

Figures such as the relative number of men and women in a culture at a given time may have social implications relative to opportunities to marry, the birth and death rates of the country, migration rates, and many other social interaction situations. No matter how sophisticated the collection technique, however, these data are limited in terms of which statistics can be applied to them. In general, only nonparametric statistics can be applied to them. The researcher, in this case the U.S. Bureau of the Census, is only collecting information and relegating it to specific categories. The level of data collected is nominal or at best ordinal. Hence, it does not satisfy the mathematical requirements for use of parametric statistics.

MEASUREMENT

Most examples of counting consist of summing up the number of units with the described attribute—male, old, single, black, and so forth. The count says nothing about the degree of any of these attributes. It gives no indication of the people's attractiveness, their weight, height, or disposition. Each of these qualities can be arranged along a continuum and in terms of degrees of the characteristic. Even this low level of measurement, called an "ordinal measure," allows use of statistics that could not be employed with the simple counting measures termed nominal measurement.

Measurement becomes more precise as it moves from merely counting an item to classifying it as being "more" or "less" than another (from nominal to ordinal scale). The next higher level of measurement is called "interval." It differs from the ordinal scale in that it is possible to specify exactly how much greater or less one thing is from the other. At the interval level, there exists a uniform unit of measure, and it is possible to say that A is larger than B and to express that difference in equal units.

The last measurement level to consider is the "ratio scale." There are few such scales in the social sciences that are not transformed scales. A percentage distribution is a ratio scale. The 10 percentage points difference between 30 and 40 percent are exactly equal to the 10 percentage points between 90 and 100 percent. This cannot be said of the interval scale, such as an IQ score where point differences at various levels of the scale are not equal. It is not known if a 10 point IQ difference between 150 and 160 is equal to a 10 point difference between IQ scores of 70 and 80.

Parametric statistics are generally used with ordinal, interval, and ratio scales of measurement, while nonparametric statistics are normally used with nominal or numbering measurement levels and always with ordinal data.

NONPARAMETRIC STATISTICS

Traditional statistics such as correlation, regression, and analysis of variance are based on normal distribution of the data, unidimensionally, and known intervals. Most of these statistics require at least ordinal levels of measure and normally involve interval or ratio levels of measurement. Nonparametric measures use distribution-free statistics. That is, they are not based on known interval distance, and the measures typically used are of central tendency (the mean) and distribution (standard deviation). In nonparametric analysis, the key concepts include the median (position of probability of $P.5$ ½ in the distribution), the quartile, and the decile.

Examples of nonparametric statistics are chi square (X^2), the difference of proportions tests, Fisher's exact test, Cochran's Q, Contingency C, and many other special purpose statistics.[3] Consider the computation of a X^2 test to illustrate the relative simplicity of computing such statistical tests.

In setting up the problem, assume that there are one hundred students in a class, and it is intended to ascertain if any relationship exists between those who smoke and those who drink alcoholic beverages. Both variables are dichotomous: smoker-nonsmoker, drinker-nondrinker (nominal measure or counting). The problem is constructed in the following way. Individuals are asked to check whether they drink alcohol or smoke tobacco. For each individual there is information on two variables.

	Smokers	Non-smokers
drinkers	A 60° 48.91e	B 13° 24.09e
non-drinkers	C 7° 18.09e	D 20° 8.91e

Classification of Smokers and Drinkers

As can be seen,

73 drink and 27 don't drink
67 smoke and 33 don't smoke
60 both drink and smoke
20 neither drink nor smoke
7 smoke but don't drink
13 drink but don't smoke

How can these data be interpreted? From a single perusal of the data, associations are not immediately apparent. A X^2 test will determine if the distribution frequencies observed differ from what might have been expected based on chance (probabilities). The equation for X^2 is as follows:

$$X^2 = \sum \frac{(fo - fe)^2}{fe}$$

where fo = frequency observed, which is noted in the upper part of the four cells (ABCD), and fe = frequency expected, which is located in the lower right of each cell in the example. To obtain the expected frequency for a cell, multiply the row marginal by the column marginal and divide by the N size (number of cases in the sample). For example, for the smoking drinkers, multiply $73 \times 67 = 4891 \div 100 = 48.91$. Subtract 48.91 from $60 = 11.09^2 \div 48.91 = 122.988 \div 48.91 = 2.51$ for cell A. Now complete the process for the other three cells. Square the difference between these two figures for each cell and divide each by the expected frequency for each cell. The sum (the sign for summation is Σ) of these four cell figures $= X^2$. Refer to a table of X^2 distribution to see if the results are significant. These have been previously computed by other researchers. The computation is as follows:

$$\frac{(60 - 48.91)^2}{48.91} + \frac{(24.09 - 13)^2}{24.09} + \frac{(18.09 - 7)^2}{18.09} + \frac{(20 - 8.91)^2}{8.91} =$$

$X^2 = 2.51 + 5.10 + 6.80 + 13.80 = 28.21$

Note that the differences between the observed and the expected frequencies for each cell are all the same, 11.09, and the expected frequencies sum to the row and column totals, or they equal the same figures as the observed frequencies. Moreover, the calculated X^2 value for each cell is determined by the denominator or division by the expected frequency. Two steps remain: (1) determine the degrees of freedom, which is determined by the formula:

$$df = r - 1 \times k - 1$$

where r = rows and k = columns. Substituting, we get $2 - 1 \times 2 - 1 = 1$ degree of freedom. (2) Refer to the appropriate table in a statistics book to ascertain what values are required for significance of difference at the designated levels.[4] X^2 is required for significance at the following levels with 1 df.

$$\begin{aligned} 0.05 &= 3.84 \\ 0.01 &= 6.63 \\ 0.005 &= 7.88 \end{aligned}$$

Since the computed X^2 is 28.21, the association is significant at greater than the 0.005 level. If phrased differently, one could expect that a X^2 value of 7.88 or larger could occur only 5 times in 1,000 due to chance. Since the example X^2 value is much larger, it can be maintained with some confidence that there is an association between the behavior habits of drinking and smoking tobacco.

The four-cell X^2 is a relatively easy statistic to calculate. It takes feelings about associations and tests them to see if they exist in reality. In addition, it allows researchers to talk about the strength of such relationships. The measure level is counting or the simple notion of instances of behavior.

Nothing is said about how much each respondent drank or smoked, or what they smoked or drank, or when last they had done either. The problem therefore, is a a lower level measurement (nominal) of the relationships of two variables using a nonparametric statistic—the X^2.

PARAMETRIC STATISTICS

Nonparametric statistics differ from parametric statistics in that they require neither a normal distribution of scores or items nor the same level of relevant measurement. Most parametric tests assume equal-appearing intervals and a normal distributed population. Scores on units of data in this sense can be expressed in terms of deviations from a measure of central tendency. The arithemetic mean is the measure of central tendency generally used in parametric statistics, and in the case of the normal curve is equal to the median and the mode. These measures of deviance from the central tendency measure, such as "standard deviation" and "standard error of the mean," are of importance in both describing and analyzing data. In using parametric statistics, the researcher turns from dichotomous data (he-she, old-young) to continuously distributed data. The researcher now measures degrees along a continuum rather than merely sorting items into one pile or another.

Statistics normally considered as parametric include the "Student's *t*" test, correlation, multiple regression, partial correlation, analysis of variance, and factorial analysis.

An example of correlation should suffice to demonstrate the process of computation and the reasoning involved in this higher level of associational reasoning. Consider the following example. (A small sample size will be used in simplifying computation.) The research question asks if there is a relationship between the height of brothers and sisters. Or, is height an inherited characteristics based on family genetics? The statistical test to be computed is a test of association and variance, or what is called a correlation coefficient. Its equation is:

$$r = \frac{\Sigma xy}{\sqrt{(\Sigma x^2)\ (\Sigma y^2)}}$$

where Σxy is defined as the sum of the cross-products, Σx^2 is the sum of the little x squared (raw score $-$ the mean), and Σy^2 is the little y squared (*raw* score $-$ the mean). To repeat, little x and y are defined as $X - \overline{X} = x$ and $Y - \overline{Y} = y$; where $\overline{X}$ is the mean of the X distribution and $\overline{Y}$ is the mean of the Y distribution. In this case, X and $\overline{X}$ represent the brothers' height, and Y and $\overline{Y}$ represent the sisters' height.

Data for eleven pairs of brothers and sisters are presented in Table 10.

Table 10
Stature of Brothers and Sisters in Inches

FAMILY	X	x	x^2	Y	y	y^2	XY
1	71	+2	4	69	−5	25	10
2	68	−1	1	64	0	0	0
3	66	−3	9	65	+1	1	−3
4	67	−2	4	63	−1	1	2
5	70	+1	1	65	+1	1	1
6	71	+2	4	62	−2	4	−4
7	70	+1	1	65	+1	1	1
8	73	+4	16	64	0	0	0
9	72	+3	9	66	+2	4	6
10	65	−4	16	59	−5	25	20
11	66	−3	9	62	−2	4	6
Totals	$X = 759$	26	74	$Y = 704$	20	66	$xy + 39$

$\overline{X} = 69$ $\qquad\qquad \overline{Y} = 64$

$$r = xy / \sqrt{(\Sigma x^2)\ (\Sigma y^2)}$$
$$r = 39/ \sqrt{74 \bullet 66}$$
$$= 39/ \sqrt{4884}$$
$$= 39/69.88$$
$$= +.558$$

As can be seen in Table 10, the little x and little y scores are deviations between the mean and the raw score, or actual measurement in inches for each brother and sister. They are squared to avoid the addition of positive and negative numbers. Recall that in algebra, squaring a number automatically gives it a positive value. For family one, the brother was two inches above the mean for males and his sister was five inches above the mean for females. The other figure required is the sum of the cross-products. This figure is obtained by multiplying the little x by the little y scores, or for family one it is $2 \times 5 = 10$. Note that family three has a -3 and a $+1$ score which when multiplied produce a negative 3, while family four has a -2 and a -1 which when multiplied produce a positive 2. When the process has been completed, the result is the net $xy + 39$, or the numerator of the correlation problem. Next we substitute x^2 with 74 and y^2 with 66 and multiply. The result, 4884, is under the radical ($\sqrt{\ }$), and it is necessary to extract the square root. The square root is 69.89. The problem can now be computed by dividing 39 by 69.89 to produce $r = +0.558$. When consulting a book of tables for the needed r for significance, it is found that the r of 0.576 is needed for significance at the 0.05 significance level. It must therefore be concluded that there is not a significant relationship between the height of brothers and sisters, based on the small sample of eleven pairs examined.

The materials presented are simply examples of one type of nonparametric and parametric statistical tests of strength of association between two variables. Actual research, regardless of the level of the problems addressed, will require more thought and more computation. The logic of analysis and the analysis of significant levels of association between variables remain the same. Clearly, the interpretation and understanding of research reports require not so much the skills involved in the actual manipulation of data, but an understanding of the logic and the levels of analysis that underlie such manipulations.

SUMMARY

One of the principal reasons for studying statistics is that an understanding of statistics allows the practitioner to critically and objectively evaluate his own work as well as the work of others. In addition, a knowledge of statistics provides the student with a skill that finds acceptance in the after-graduation marketplace.

This chapter discusses the role of statistics in understanding the social sciences. It also attempts to create an understanding of the theory and assumptions underlying the use of statistical tests and measures. The scientific method makes constant use of statistically based justifications for deductive techniques, hypothesis testing, generalizing to other populations, sampling, significance levels, and confidence limits. Much of what sociologists and other behavioral scientists do requires an understanding of probability and the various means by which the researcher may declare his findings to be real or the result of random chance. Such evaluation and reasoning require an understanding of statistics.

NOTES

1. Both parametric and nonparametric statistics are discussed later in the chapter.
2. p = probability for brevity.
   q = $1 - P$ the reciprocal of P.
   N = number of trials.
   r = number of successes or number of heads or tails in coin flipping.
3. The expected frequencies have already been placed in the four cells and designated by the *e* following the number.
4. George W. Snedecor, *Statistical Methods*, 5th ed. (Ames: Iowa State University Press, 1956), pp. 28-29.

18

Secondary Data Analysis

Much of the discussion thus far has focused on the logic and process of data collection for specific research projects. Another type of research involves analysis from secondary sources of data.[1] There are many potential sources of secondary data, and in general their number is increasing through the availability of data handling techniques for storage and retrieval. The earlier chapter on demography (Chapter 13) mentions the U.S. Census as a frequent source of secondary data for social scientists. Before examining the sources of such data further, secondary data must be defined and the differences in analysis between secondary and primary data must be considered.

The availability of data retrieval techniques is not the only reason for the increasing use of secondary data for analysis. There are at least two other reasons. First, some researchers simply do not like leaving their office and the known territory of the computer center; others are not temperamentally suited to interviewing or collecting data as observers or field researchers. Recall that in many instances, research is almost an extension of life-style interests and opportunity. However, research which utilizes secondary data can be sophisticated and as valuable as any other type. Certain types of research seem to "fit" certain researchers. While those uniquely suited to observational research may find secondary data research tedious beyond description, for those interested in secondary data analysis quite the reverse may be true.

The second reason for the increasing use of secondary data hinges not on the preference of the researcher, but rather on the subject of that research. With the increasing number of social scientists and social science students and the increase in the number of social programs since 1966, the general public has been approached too frequently and asked to participate in too many surveys. Perhaps it is a measure of our alienation that all too frequently subjects randomly selected and approached in their homes consider participation to be an invasion of their privacy. Interviewing studies are not automatically meeting with the success they achieved a decade or two ago. The social changes of the last two decades, especially higher crime rates, have increased the potential respondent's suspicion.

Apart from these two reasons, secondary data analysis has a rich tradition in the behavioral sciences. The collection of census data has been around in the United States since the oldest sources of written material. The use of census data was more pragmatic in purpose in earlier times than now since the census was taken as a means of (1) assessing and collecting taxes, (2) selecting individuals for conscription into the military service, or (3) calculating the number of individuals within the boundaries of the political or religious unit. Currently, such data find far more extensive use.

SOCIODEMOGRAPHIC ANALYSIS

Collection of the sociodemographic characteristics of respondents has become so widespread in survey research that it is considered a standard part of any survey. Analysis of data with regard to age, sex, education, occupation, race or ethnicity, residence, income, marital status, number of family members, religious preference, and residence mobility is just as frequently given slight attention, if any at all. Although included, such data are seldom related to the main objectives of the survey. If the data are presented in the report, they are often presented as "characteristics of the sample" in the methods section. These sample characteristics are frequently compared with the known parameters of the universe in order to determine how closely they approximate the universe. In this way, generalizations from the sample to the universe may be justified, if deviations between the two are not large. As a result of this minimal analysis of the data collected, in most studies they provide a ready source of data awaiting analysis.

The secondary analysis of sociodemographic data and the basic sources of these published data are presented in Chapter 13. Consider the following two examples of studies resulting from the use of secondary data. The first is *Negroes in Cities* by Karl and Alma Taeuber.[2] While the work is of necessity well documented with tables, maps, and graphs, it goes well beyond the sterile presentation of facts and figures. Indeed, this extension beyond the secondary data is what makes it analysis rather than the simple presentation of statistical facts. For example, the Taeubers focus on patterns of residential segregation but look at segregation in terms of neighborhood change, regional differences in interracial contact, and movement of the Negro population from an essentially rural base in the early part of this century to a principally urban one in the last half of the century.

The Taeubers' examination goes well beyond the basic data in terms of analyses, recommendations, and conclusions. While more than ten years have elapsed since their analysis, the trends examined then have remained essentially unchanged. For example, the central cities continue to become more black, and the suburbs, for the most part, remain white. In concluding, their "Review of Principal Findings," the Taeubers state: "Continuing conflict over residential segregation thus seems inevitable, not only because of Negro dissatisfactions over housing, but because residential segregation is a particularly tenacious barrier to the full participation of Negroes in the general society."[3] Given this example, census data can be used to develop and test hypotheses even about such elusive phenomena as social movements.[4]

THE MASS MEDIA

In addition to official records, the mass media have been used as sources of data for analysis. Studies of phenomena that attracted national attention have been done using regularly published national magazines. In one such study, the magazines were examined over a period of time to ascertain what type of individual was most frequently chosen as the subject of biographical articles. At the turn of the century and during the first decade or two in the 1900s, biographical articles tended to focus on "captains of industry," or those involved in manufacturing, in railroads, the development of companies, empires, and fortunes.

At the turn of the twentieth century, the United States had just defeated a major imperial European power, Spain. The automobile was coming into common use. Neither radio nor television had come into existence, and not all of the territory we now call the United States was so organized. Immigrants poured in during the 1910s, and a strong sense of national pride existed as a young nation flexed its industrial muscles and took its place among the major producing nations of the world.

During the midpart of the century, the articles focused on what sociologists call "expressive" areas and included singers, bandleaders, movie stars, and sports figures. While few noted these general themes in popular literature, they were interpreted to be a social indicator of national interest written in an historical context.[5] If the primary media of today were surveyed, it might be found that the focus has changed from people to issues.

Community power has also used the printed media. Researchers have searched the newspapers to see whose name appears in the newspaper over a specified period of time (usually several months to a year). This method of assessing community status is generally used in conjunction with other techniques measuring community power. Hence, the newspaper has been used as a data source in conjunction with either the "reputational" or "self-report" techniques in community power studies.[6]

Mass-distributed magazines also provide a useful means of examining social movements. The crazes and fads of the 1930s are covered much more extensively in the mass literature than in scientific reports, monographs, and books. The Townsend movement, the Farmer's Holiday movement, the Banker's Holiday, and labor union growth, strikes, and violence were part of this depression decade, and the feminist movement saw its beginnings in the 1920s. All of these topics can be documented in the pages of national magazines and the large city newspapers of the time. This type of literature tends to be less objective than the scientific literature, but this shortcoming is of little consequence when no scientific treatments exist.

Newer forms of media such as television also have had cultural impact. It has become the subject of a great deal of scientific analysis. The amount of violence on television and its effects on the young are currently under study by the scientific community, as well as the Congress.

Many of these media examinations can be classified as content analysis.[7] More recently, work of this type has been done utilizing the computer. In this case, the chief task is to develop codes and tags for the computer to search for words that will determine if themes or content areas exist. The key to this computer analysis is building a code and cross-referencing similar words or themes. The computer will develop only those indicators designated and programmed into the search routine.

A transition type of study is a combination of demography and history. E. A. Wrigley's *Population and History* is an example of this type of research.[8] In examining such topics as historical demography, preindustrial population, social and economic conditions in preindustrial societies, and the relationship of population to the Industrial Revolution, Wrigley had to rely heavily on official records of other nations and historical accounts of the results of famines, mortality, statistical reports, and whatever material might be available.

Much as the Tauebers' research, Wrigley's was able to bring secondary source data together in an interesting and informative manner. His work is full of material explaining cross-cultural differences such as age at first marriage in such widely separated places as Hedmark, Norway, and Ting

Hsien, China. In both areas, the brides of wealthy families tended to be younger than brides from poor sections of the community. Wrigley interpreted the data to indicate that two different social customs were at work. Families attached importance to securing the male line of the family. Therefore, because these wealthy families could pay the "bride price" and wanted to see their lineage secure, they married off their sons in their early teens. As a result, an inverse relationship was established for both males and females between age at marriage and size of family holdings. The larger the holdings, the younger the age of marriage.[9] Analysis of this type serves a positive function in the literature of the behavioral sciences.

The use of secondary data does not promise an easy means of research, nor does it provide an easy source of generalizations about the elusive nature of human behavior. The method is best applied to those problems for which data cannot be obtained in any other way. Although it is limited in terms of the problems to be addressed, it should not be ignored as a legitimate method of social data analysis.

HISTORICAL RECORDS

Not all historical data analysis deals with examination of the sociodemographic characteristics of a population. It has been said that histories need to be considered in "interrogative methods" and that it makes no difference whether the data are of individuals (case histories), of cities, states, or nations. It has also been argued that whether the data have been collected from records or in face-to-face situations, the data functions remain the same and that data should be subjected to test using a thesis or hypothesis in order to bring an orderly analysis to the data. Without question, if historical data are treated as a conglomerate, they remain just that. Lastrucci regards the hypothesis as the "screen" through which data must be passed to be judged relevant or irrelevant to the hypothesis.[10] He concludes that to be of scientific use historical data must (1) contain facts *accessible* to the researcher; (2) must have *pertinency* which can be judged only in terms of the hypothesis; (3) contain reliable facts, or facts capable of substantiation by indirect means and other data; and (4) use only those facts that are verifiable. The verification must come in terms of substantiation with other known facts.[11]

Historical research using secondary data and/or records should attempt more than merely arranging events in chronological order. Such an ordering would be interesting and perhaps useful; research, however, should attempt to relate the four variables of persons, events, times, and places. As such, the researcher then must be viewed within his or her historical context. No individual group, institution, or organization can be viewed as isolated or removed from the sweep of social and historical movements.

For example, a researcher might want to examine major developments in education in terms of the paradigm shown in Table 11.

Table 11
Examples of the Historical Interrelationships Between Men, Movements, and Institutions

MEN	MOVEMENTS	INSTITUTIONS	
		General Type	Name
Ignatius of Loyola	Counter-Reformation	Religious Teaching Order	Society of Jesus, 1534 (Jesuit Society)
Benjamin Franklin	Scientific Movement Education for Life	Academy	Philadelphia Academy, 1751
Daniel Coit Gilman G. Stanley Hall Wm. Rainey Harper	Graduate Study and Research	University Graduate School	Johns Hopkins University, 1876 Clark University, 1887 University of Chicago, 1892
John Dewey	Experimentation Progressive Education	Experimental School	University of Chicago Elementary School, 1896
W.E.B. Dubois Walter White	Racial Integration Public Schools	Persuasion Organization	National Assn. for the Advancement of Colored People, 1909
B. R. Buckingham	Scientific Research in Education	Research Periodical Research Organization	Journal of Ed. Research, 1920 American Educational Research Assn., 1931

Source: John W. Best, *Research in Education*, 2d ed. (Englewood Cliffs, N.J.: Prentice-Hall, 1970), p. 95.

In Table 11, Best presents the individuals involved, the movements they were identified with, the resulting type of institution, and the name and date of the event that occurred in the institution. By reading down the columns of the table, it can be seen that the major movements are in their order of occurrence. The dates and major institutions are identified in the last column. This table represents the bare-bones outline of events that can be developed into a full-blown historical study. Other types of literature would be used to fill in the report with relevant social factors that made these events possible. It would be entirely in order to discuss factors that had prevented these developments prior to that time. As such, they lack supporting data and conditions of interrelationship. Using historical data requires that the researcher recognize that events are written and recorded within the framework of their time. Recording can therefore be selective with regard to the prejudices of the recorder or the peculiarities of the time.

One must ask if a hypothesis can be tested using historical data. Merton's discussions of ex post factum, or after the fact, research would seem to indicate that it is possible within limitations. The data relevant to the test of a particular hypothesis should be available to the researcher. As such, the hypothesis would be tested as a plausible explanation of the data and would differ from that of an "a priori hypothesis" as a test of theory.

In discussing whether historical investigation can be considered research and/or scientific, Best points out the following limitations of the technique:

> 1. Although the purpose of science is prediction, the historian cannot always generalize on the basis of past events. Because past events were often unplanned or didn't develop as planned, because there were so many uncontrolled factors, and because the influence of one or a few individuals was so crucial, the same pattern of factors is never repeated.
> 2. The historian must depend upon the reported observations of others, often witnesses of doubtful competence and sometimes of doubtful objectivity.
> 3. The historian is much like a person trying to complete a complicated jig-saw puzzle with many of the parts missing. On the basis of what is often incomplete evidence, he must fill in the gaps by inferring what has happened.
> 4. History does not operate in a closed system such as may be created in the physical science laboratory. The historian cannot control the conditions of observation nor manipulate the significant variables.[12]

He then attempts to counter these arguments with the following points.

> 1. The historian delimits a problem, formulates hypotheses or raises questions to be answered, gathers and analyzes primary data, tests the hypotheses as consistent or inconsistent with the evidence, and formulates generalizations or conclusions.
> 2. Although the historian may not have witnessed an event or gathered data directly, he may have the testimony of a number of witnesses who have observed the event from different vantage points. It is possible that subsequent events have provided additional information not available to contemporary observers. The historian rigorously subjects the evidence to critical analysis in order to establish its authenticity, truthfulness, and accuracy.

3. In reaching conclusions, the historian employs principles of probability similar to those used by physical scientists.
4. Although it is true that the historian cannot control the variables directly, this limitation also characterizes most behavioral research, particularly nonlaboratory investigations in sociology, social psychology, and economics.[13]

Best's strongest arguments appear to relate not to whether history can approach a scientific classification, but to whether the historical method can be employed in the analysis of secondary data as he suggests. Every hypothesis can be tested within a plausible framework.

As an example, he cites the analysis of a problem dealing with fighting in the Civil War. He advances the following four hypotheses to explain the fall of the Confederacy:[14]

1. The military defeat of the Confederate Army.
2. The dearth of military supplies.
3. The starving condition of the Confederate soldiers and the people.
4. The disintegration of the will to continue the war.

Continuing this discussion and using data from another source, Best states:

Channing produced evidence that seemed to refute the first three hypotheses. More than 200,000 well-equipped soldiers were under arms at the time of the surrender, the effective production of powder and arms provided sufficient military supplies to continue the war, and enough food was available to sustain fighting men and civilians.

Channing concluded that hypothesis 4, the collapse of morale and the will to fight, was substantiated by the excessive number of desertions of enlisted men and officers. Confederate military officials testified that they had intercepted many letters from home urging the soldiers to desert. Although the hypothesis sustained was not specific enough to be particularly helpful, the rejection of the first three did claim to dispose of some commonly-held explanations. This example illustrates a historical study in which hypotheses were explicitly stated.[15]

This treatment of data is essentially the same as that proposed by Merton in this ex post factum research design, that is, the development of a hypothesis as a plausible explanation for the data at hand. In the example of the Confederate collapse, any one of the four hypotheses could be considered a "plausible explanation." By use of data at hand from various sources, the fourth hypothesis, the morale and will to continue the fight, appeared to be the most plausible.

USES OF MULTIPLE SOURCES FOR PROJECTIONS

Most of the data manipulations presented here have dealt with putting the data collected for one purpose to yet another use. Consider the following study wherein secondary data were used to develop a computer simulation of the results of the 1960 and 1964 presidential elections. Ithiel de Sola Pool and associates joined the results of sixty-five surveys spanning the period 1952-1960 to produce a large data base of approximately 130,000 respondents for this time period.[16] They were interested in developing categories and the voting tendencies of these categories based on the following characteristics (these have been called "face-sheet" or sociodemographic data):

1. Region of the United States
2. Socioeconomic status
3. Size of the community of residence
4. Sex
5. Religion
6. Race
7. Political affiliation

These seven factors were combined into social groups to produce multidimensional groupings. For example, one such grouping might be middle -status-rural-Midwestern-white-male-Protestant-Republican: all possible combinations of the seven factors would have produced 3600 such possible groups. This would have been unmanageable and many of the groups would have had small numbers. The combination upper status-Roman Catholic-Southern-rural-black-female-Republican would have been a possibility between 1952 and 1960, but there would not have been many in that combination. As a result, Pool decided to use only 480 multidimensional groupings.

In addition, fifty features were developed and designated as "issue clusters," e.g., civil rights, neo-fascism, New Deal philosophy, and attitude toward Israel. The combinations of issue clusters and multidimensional groupings were used to develop their computer simulation. They then made projections of the percentage of the vote that the Democratic candidate (Kennedy in 1960 and Johnson in 1964) should receive from each state. Based on these projections, campaign strategy was planned. Some states were solidly in the Democratic camp, and others were so inflexibly committed that no variance could occur. In addition, there were those states that could go either way. These were the states wherein the Democrats decided to concentrate their campaign efforts. Both Democrats, Kennedy and Johnson, did win. It is less well known that social scientists, using secondary data, were in part responsible for the campaign strategies in these two elections. Pool and his associates hit the exact percentage of the Democratic vote in some states. Their simulation effort was a landmark in use of these data in a national campaign. With regard to the use of secondary data, it was necessary to use data from a large number of surveys, over an extended period of time, to accomplish this predictive purpose. An undertaking of this magnitude requires staff, money, and facilities beyond the reach of most researchers, but the principle of combining data from a number of surveys and producing results of pragmatic use in decision-making is an important one for social scientists. That Pool and his associates were successful makes the technique even more practical to consider.

SUGGESTIONS FOR SOURCES AND USES OF SECONDARY DATA

Some years ago, Barney G. Glaser said that there were some sociologists for whom secondary data analysis seemed particularly appropriate. For various reasons, including the life-style of the individual, he said that the analysis of secondary data provided one potential technique to solve the independent researcher's needs. He characterized the independent researcher as one who engages in a personal research venture; is not a member of a research team or associated with a center; and wishes to work with his or her own "conception of a scientist's standards." Hence, the researcher remains free to examine problems of his own choosing or to act in the role of the social clinician. Through such independence, the researcher would be free to set his standards, his time frames for working, and where and when he would release and report the data. Most of these positions are not possible within the traditionally funded grant or contract research. Glaser states that the individual is what Merton termed a "lone scholar."[17]

Secondary data are not immediately available for use without cost. There are costs involved in obtaining decks of IBM cards or computer tapes of stored data. In addition, the researcher often has to have access to computer facilities and obtain programming assistance to make data transformations compatible with available facilities. Operating funds are needed to make additional runs, cross-tabulations, and tests of significance.

In *Secondary Analysis of Sample Surveys*,[18] Herbert H. Hyman states:

> Consider, for example, the work of Norval Glenn, whose association with archives resulted in no less than nine published secondary analyses in the years 1966-69. Clearly, the relationship was enduring and fruitful. With various collaborators he produced studies of differences in attitudes and behavior between Negroes and whites, between religious groups, rural and urban groups, regional groups, groups varying in education, occupation and age.[19]

Further:

Contrast Glenn with another investigator whose purposes fell within the same domain but were more narrow and specific. He found "that a national sample contains too few subjects from class and ethnic groups of special interest" to him, and with respect to the patterns he wished to describe for these groups—"the nature of individual attachments to the community and to society and especially the nature of those attachments which the citizen feels impose some obligation on him"—he reports that "the questions they ask did not measure the attitudes in which I was interested."[20]

Whereas one researcher looked and found reasons why the data would not serve, others looked and saw potential.

SUMMARY

The analysis of secondary data is limited only by the researcher's imagination and innovativeness after the data have been located and examined for content. This analysis can focus on the sociodemographic characteristics of the respondents usually found in survey data, or the analysis can extend well beyond the mere recombining of elements already present in tha data. The Tauebers, Wrigley, Best, Pool, and Glenn have all demonstrated what can be done with secondary data. While each has a different emphasis, each has all the same contributed to the discipline.

Many of the classics in early sociology evolved from the use or awareness of secondary data. The works of Max Weber, Frederick Le Play, Florian Znaniecki, and W. I. Thomas, among some of the most notable, have at least in part involved the use of secondary data. As in most other areas, the results of these studies are a tribute to the insights, innovativeness, and perseverance of the individuals who developed significant works from data which others viewed as irrelevant or less than useful. Secondary data analysis can be a fruitful area of research and as such should not be overlooked. The list of data archives given in the glossary should prove helpful.

NOTES

1. Data not collected by the researcher are considered to be secondary data; in contrast, primary data have been collected by the researcher and/or the research team or center to which they are attached.

2. Karl E. Taeuber and Alma F. Taeuber, *Negroes in Cities* (Chicago: Aldine Publishing Co., 1965).

3. Ibid., p. 8.

4. Census data can be considered to be official documents or records, of which

many abound at national, state, and local levels, as well as international census data collected under the auspices of UNESCO.

5. Leo Lowenthal, *Literature, Popular Culture and Society* (Englewood Cliffs, N.J.: Prentice-Hall, 1961), p. 196.

6. The reputational approach makes inquiries of community persons as to who has power or influence in the community, while the self-report technique asks individuals to place themselves within the community power structure.

7. Bernard Berelson, *Content Analysis in Communication Research* (New York: Free Press, 1952).

8. E. A. Wrigley, *Population and History*, (New York: World University Library, McGraw-Hill Book Co., 1969).

9. Ibid., pp. 103-104.

10. Carlo L. Lastrucci, *The Scientific Approach: Basic Principles of the Scientific Method* (Cambridge, Mass.: Schenkman Publishing Co., 1963), p. 165.

11. Ibid.

12. John W. Best, *Research in Education*, 2d ed. (Englewood Cliffs, N.J.: Prentice-Hall), p. 98.

13. Ibid., pp. 98-99.

14. Ibid., p. 101.

15. Ibid.

16. Ithiel de Sola Pool, Robert P. Abelson, and Samuel L. Popkin, *Candidates, Issues and Strategies: A Computer Simulation of the 1960 and 1964 Presidential Elections* (Cambridge, Mass.: MIT Press, 1964).

17. Barney G. Glaser, "Retreading Research Materials: The Use of Secondary Analysis by the Independent Researcher," *American Behavioral Scientist* (June 1963): 11-14.

18. Herbert H. Hyman, *Secondary Analysis of Samplé Surveys: Principles, Procedures and Potentialities* (New York: John Wiley and Sons, 1972), p. 101.

19. Ibid., p. 79.

20. Ibid.

19

Generating and Testing Hypotheses

After data have been collected and subjected to the analysis outlined in the original design, a decision about the hypothesis must be made. Based on the design, the logically drawn hypothesis, the operational measures, and the statistics used, the researcher must ultimately decide to accept or reject the hypothesis. This decision follows logically in the time sequence of the research process. Although it is possible to generate an alternative hypothesis through testing, this process must await the completion of analysis. Ordinarily, the generation of an alternative hypothesis is an additional process entered into when the original hypothesis is not supported. The normal reporting sequence is ordered in the following way: testing the hypothesis, reporting results, drawing any conclusions, and ending with a summary of the report. This sequence is followed whether the researcher has supported the hypothesis, failed to support it, or claimed limited support or even inconclusive results. The conditions under which the hypothesis will be rejected must be considered before the process of developing an alternative hypothesis is considered.[1]

There are a number of ways of bringing an hypothesis to test, but whichever method is chosen, it should be chosen prior to actual testing. To do anything else is to run the risk of being accused of fitting the mode of analysis too closely to the data. This will make the research tautological, or at the very least would compromise the data and results. For this reason, the design of the total project should be developed.

THE HYPOTHESES

Bringing hypotheses to test actually differs very little with regard to the type of design or the type of the hypotheses. Whether the hypothesis has been deduced from theory, is a working one, or is a replication of an existing hypothesis is of little importance in deciding if it should be accepted or rejected. Differences in types of hypotheses pertain more to what can be done with test results. The ability to generalize to other populations or to another universe is more a function of design than of the test used to determine the truth of the hypothesis. Therefore, the total research design is of relevance in interpreting the results, the meaning of those results, and their use.

Before providing examples, perhaps it is best to review the hypotheses in terms of levels of abstraction. The conceptual, analytical, or abstract hypothesis has been described as the general hypothesis. The example given in Chapter 5 and expressed as a general hypothesis was:

General Hypothesis: Role strain will be related to the degree of organizational complexity.

Both role strain and organizational complexity are concepts and as such are abstractions. To test the relationship between these concepts, it is necessary to move to a lower level of abstraction and operationalize them both.[2] It is at this point that the problems of reliability and validity discussed elsewhere are encountered. Whether the operational measure and/or variables are actually measuring what it is claimed they measure is at the base of the hypothesis-testing process. If the measure has no validity, obviously any results obtained would be less than useful. For this reason, it is suggested that all but seasoned researchers use scales or measures with reported validity and reliability coefficients when possible. It is also possible to use two measures of the same variable—one with a coefficient of validity and reliability, and one without. A correlation coefficient between the two would then provide an indirect measure of the validity and reliability of the unevaluated scale. The use of existing scales does not rule out development, modification, and refinement of the measures. Research as a discipline should attempt to be interrelated and cumulative, not an isolated group of studies using different measures, tests, hypotheses, and methods.

Operational Hypothesis

The operational hypothesis, which is the next level of abstraction, should contain the variables to be measured and tested.

Operational Hypothesis: Job-related tension (measured by the JRT Index) will be related to the type of organizational characteristics.[3]

The operational measure, the JRT Index, and organizational characteristics have been brought together to form the operational hypothesis. In this hypothesis, the JRT is defined as measuring role strain, and organizational characteristics are defined as a measure of organizational complexity. The validity of the JRT Index may be questioned, but the clarity of its definition and presentation cannot. In many studies, it may not be possible to ascertain clearly and exactly how the variables were operationally measured. Clarity of specification and thorough documentation of operational definitions should be a part of every research design.

Some researchers have expressed concern about the word choices used in connecting two concepts. They state that the words "associated with" or "related to" should be reserved for those statistical tests measuring covariance. In other words, they would reserve terms such as correlation, regression, partial correlation, and two-way analysis of variance for statistics. Although such a distinction might be appropriate in advanced texts and reference works, there is no constant usage in the literature of the social sciences. In the case of the operational hypothesis presented, there is one continuous variable, the JRT score, and one set of dichotomous variables dealing with organizational characteristics. This can be seen in the four subsidiary hypotheses developed in Chapter 5. They were developed to test General Hypothesis I. The variables and their measures were:

Variable	Measure
SH 1 Ownership	Public-private
SH 2 Size	large-small
SH 3 Educational	teaching-nonteaching
SH 4 Affiliation	denominational-nondenominational

The actual test was done in the following manner. The dichotomy in each of the four subhypotheses was used to divide the 385 nurses into the two groups. The 64 nurses working in public hospitals were assigned to one side, and the 321 nurses in privately owned hospitals to the other. A statistical test of differences between means (or scores on the JRT Index)[3] was run between the two groups. Only the JRT scores were used in actual computation of the test, based on the mean value for each of the two groups divided on the basis of ownership (public versus private). The same dichotomous division into groups was necessary for each of the first four subhypotheses stated in the following manner:

Operational Hypothesis: Nurses in large hospitals will have significantly higher JRT than nurses in small hospitals.

The hypothesis has become more specific in that instead of stating "association or relationship," it states that there will be a significant difference in the criterion variable, JRT, based on hospital size. The hypothesis has taken on a new dimension because it now indicates the direction of the expected difference, stating that the JRT score will be higher (on the average) for nurses working in large hospitals compared to nurses working in small hospitals. Clearly then, formulating the hypothesis has implications for the tests to be used to establish the differences between groups on a particular measure. The tests establish whether the differences are "real" or could have occurred as a result of chance. Furthermore, the hypothesis designates whether the test should be directional and how conservative the test will be. A one-tailed test is a more conservative test in that the statistical coefficient must not only be significant, but also in the specified direction. Therefore, there is more opportunity to be wrong in the one-tailed test than in the two-tailed test.[4] It is also possible to have a significant statistical result and not support the hypothesis because the direction is wrong. An examination of the distribution of the *t* table of significance levels is required for the two-tailed test.[5] For example, it requires a *t* value of 31.821 or larger with 1 degree of freedom for significance at the 0.01 level with the one-tailed test. This same value, 31.821, is required for significance at the 0.02 level for the two-tailed test with 1 degree of freedom.

The null hypothesis should be considered next as the test to which the statistic is applied. Following the development of the operational hypothesis, it is now possible to state the hypothesis under null conditions.

Null Hypothesis

Null Hypothesis: There will be no relationship between JRT and organizational characteristics.

The logic for this test is discussed in Chapter 5. In essence, the null principle is based on finding differences in a comparison (i.e., there will be no difference) rather than confirming the positive (there will be a difference) in all cases. Thus, the null test really says that the score for one group will not differ significantly from that of the second group. In the test of the hospital nurses, JRT, and hospital size, the hypothesis states that the mean score for nurses in large hospitals will be approximately the same as the mean score for nurses in small hospitals. Statistically, the statement would be depicted as $\overline{X}_1 = \overline{X}_2$, where $\overline{X}_1$ is the mean score of the large hospital subsample and $\overline{X}_2$ is the mean score of the small hospital subsample.

The phrase "approximately the same" is used above because the two mean scores do not have to be exactly the same for there to be no difference between groups statistically. The amount of difference required between the two mean scores before the difference becomes significant is a function of the N size.[6] When samples are large, the differences can be very small but statistically significant. For example, a researcher might find differences of four to five points in mean scores between two groups with a sample of thirty and not have statistical significance. On the other hand, with a sample of ten thousand, a difference of 0.1 to 0.2 could be statistically significant.

In testing the null hypothesis in the example, a null hypothesis is required for each of the subhypotheses because the design was set to do a single variable relationship test. Upon computing the required t test, a t value of 0.09 was found which was not significant for size of the hospital. Nurses in large hospitals did not have significantly higher JRT scores than did nurses in small hospitals. There was a difference in the mean scores—38.5 for the large hospital nurses and 36.8 for the small hospital nurse. Although the difference was in the expected direction, it was not statistically significant. Consequently, the null hypothesis was not rejected. In fact, no differences appeared between the two groups of nurses. Since the null hypothesis was not rejected, the general hypothesis may be assessed. Technically, consideration of the operational hypothesis is complete and the general hypothesis may be tested next.[7] In order to consider the general hypothesis, it is necessary to test each of the four subhypotheses and then consider the general hypothesis based on the support or lack of support found for the four subhypotheses.

Have the theoretical underpinnings that originally prompted the test of the relationship outlined been tested? The answer is partly yes, at least inferentially. Theory is never brought to test as a whole. Logically deduced portions are tested on the premise that if the theory is correct, the hypothesis logically drawn from it should also prove correct. When testing a given hypothesis, if it is supported by inference the theory that gave rise to the hypothesis is also supported. The process is similar to the example used in the chapter on sampling. A slice of pie (a sample) provides evidence as to the taste and content of the entire pie. The same process pertains in that the researcher takes a small piece of theory (pie) and subjects it to a test (tasting) and then makes claims relative to support or a lack of support with regard to the hypothesized relationship.

Whatever the results, they pertain to the reasons for originally testing a particular aspect of theory. Theory might be tested for a number of reasons, but whatever the reason or the method of hypothesis testing, the process is essentially the same. Among the reasons to test theory are:

1. To confirm existing theory
2. To challenge an existing theory
3. To extend theory to include new concepts, new social types (samples)[8]
4. To replicate existing theory or studies

1. *Confirmation* studies are essentially of the type previously described involving nurses and role strain. The aim of the project was to measure role strain and relate it to other concepts to which it has been linked. Substantiation of the hypothesis would have supported previous findings and lent additional credence to the theory. Note, however, that nonsubstantiation did not automatically disprove the relevant theory.

2. *The challenge* of existing theory through presentation and test of alternative theory and/or hypothesis is not as widely done as other types of research. The scientific method is one of questioning and ever subjecting present positions to examination. New methods, new theory, and new measurement techniques can allow, and in fact should mandate, the examination of a number of previously unchallenged hypotheses.

3. *New concepts and new populations* covered by an extension of existing theory serve to extend the explanatory power of the theory being tested. When the study of the promotional organization was undertaken, a number of theoretical possibilities existed. Extending any one of them to a test in an unusual voluntary organization would have served to broaden the scope of the theory. It is further generalized if it is found to cover a new situation and the results obtained substantiate a logically drawn hypothesis. The members of the voluntary organization were a new population, so the theory was tested on a new population or a population that had not been previously studied.

4. *Replication studies* add additional support for existing theory or bring a certain aspect of it into question by failure to support (all or part of) previous studies. The replication study can be an excellent option for a student seeking a Master's degree or honors paper topic. The replication can sometimes take the form of reexamining an existing study in a different place or setting, or it can be duplicated with a different sample. In any case, the replication would include the methods, hypotheses, and theory to see if they hold for another setting. The best known replications tend to be those of communities or anthropological in nature.[9]

Consider the following replication. The original study was of rural youth and concerned their occupational and educational aspirations and what they perceived to be the sources of influence on these decisions. The sample was of youth drawn from communities of less than ten thousand population or residents of farms in Iowa. The replication study, using the same questionnaire as the original, drew its sample from a metropolitan community of about two hundred and eighty-five thousand. There were many similarities in responses in the two studies. The objective was to test whether the results obtained in Gross's original studies in the Northeast would be supported in a replication done involving a Midwestern sample. Gross stated that young men in urban settings, particularly from the poor sector of the city, lacked role models in making career decisions.[10] They were therefore limited in their perceived options. The results of the replication were inconclusive in that mixed results were obtained. Some of Gross's findings held in the samples; some did not. For example, Gross stated that parents, peers, counselors, and other adult models serve as sources of influence for youth in their selection of future occupational choices. In general, he suggested that since lower class youth are locked into relatively homogeneous areas, they lack access to a sufficiently broad range of role models. Since the Midwest has been characterized as relatively homogeneous, the researchers wanted to test the relative influence and lack of role model options hypothesis. From the rural Iowa sample of 830 senior males, it was found that the significant difference in the perception of importance of groups in occupational plans was in the perceived importance of school counselors. This finding pertained largely to the college-bound youth. In general, the perceived importance of all groups was relatively low, or between "some" and "little" influence on the scale used in this replication study.

Data which the respondents wrote on the questionnaires indicated that a number of the individuals perceived that no one had exerted any influence on their occupational and educational decisions other than themselves. Neither did the data permit the conclusion that perceived influences from any source would have prompted them to attend any sort of college program. However, it is possible that the perceived influence recognized by the senior males should have been examined in a directional mode. While the replication study indicated some degree of influence, it was not possible to specify the direction of that influence with regard to attending college. For example, some individuals responded that their parents exerted much influence (3 or 4 on the 4-position scale) in their educational plans but that the influence was exerted in the negative direction or against further education at this time. Hence, the data are limited in that the instrument did not specify the direction of influence where influence was indicated.

In summary, the perceived influence of selected individuals on the educational and occupational plans of senior youth was relatively low. In six of the eight statistical examinations, the college-bound youth perceived more influence (hence, higher means) than the noncollege-bound youth. In general, the perceived influence was greater for the educational plans of all youth than for their occupational plans. While the college-bound youth perceived more influence on their plans than the noncollege-bound youth, only five of the eight comparisons were statistically significant. Hence, it was possible to conclude that influence was perceived to be higher on educational plans than on occupational plans.

On the other hand, almost 20 percent of these youths were in a transitional stage of their career. That is, they were immediately going into military service or were undecided about their plans less than six months away.

Although there was some evidence that role models were not overly important to the Iowa youth, it could not be concluded that role models existed, and the occupational choices of the responding youth indicated no lack of range of awareness of occupational choices. Hence, the researchers tentatively concluded that the rural nonmetropolitan youth were able to perceive a wide range of occupational choices through the mass media and other souces, and that the lack of role models from a wide range of occupations was not as important a factor as Gross had perceived among urban lower class youth in the Northeast.[11]

MULTIPLE VARIABLE HYPOTHESIS TESTS

The study of role strain among nurses was chosen to illustrate a number of points. It contained a simple hypothesis and four subhypotheses relating independent variables to the dependent variable role strain. It could be considered a multiple variable (multivariate) study because each of the four independent variables was tested independently of one another. The following discussion begins at this level and moves to more complex techniques of examination.

The nurse study was not difficult to test because the results were the same for all four independent variables. Since there was no significant relationship between variables tested, the decision not to support the general hypothesis specifying expected relationships between role strain and organizational complexity was an easy one. If, however, some of the independent variable-dependent variable tests had been significant, how would the general hypothesis and the underlying theory have been tested? Although this problem was discussed in Chapter 5, perhaps clarification is in order here. "Limited" or "partial" support for the hypothesis could be claimed if three of four independent variables were statistically significant. Some researchers would claim limited support if only one or two of the independent variables were significantly related to the dependent variable. This is a matter of interpretation, and not all would agree with the conclusion. There are no absolute rules to guide the researcher in this area; however, the researcher should be prepared to defend the interpretation presented.

The difficulty in discussion lies in the nature of the null test. The null test is a dichotomy based on the level of significance chosen. It can be said that the relationship was or was not significant based on the 0.05 level of significance, a dichotomous decision. While all relationships have a degree of significance that ranges from 0 to +1.0, the zero occurs when there is complete random variance and no relationship or difference. In actual studies, tests seldom produce 0 coefficients.[12] On the other hand, the +1.0 or −1.0 perfect relationship seldom occurs. When these coefficients are transferred to significance levels, usually by use of a table in the back of a statistics book, it can be seen that most relations are neither 0 nor 1.0, but somewhere between. In short, there is a continuum of significance in terms of probability. The decision to be made is, however, dichotomous (significant or not significant) based on a previously determined cutoff point such as the 0.05 or 0.01 level of significance.[13]

We mean that significance exists between all variable tests in the form of probability of having produced the results not by chance factors alone. For this reason, sample size is relevant in computing the statistic. Those who claim limited support are, in fact, reverting to the concept of the continuum rather than using the traditional either/or choice of statistical significance at the 0.01 or 0.05 level. This same discussion, logic, and reasoning apply to the multivariate techniques discussed in the following section.

Consider what is done in terms of analysis if the development of a questionnaire is based on the dependent-independent variable relationship model. If the researcher attempts to maintain a single dependent variable and approximately fifty independent variables, how would he interpret fifty different statistical tests relative to the acceptance or rejection of the hypotheses? This kind of question must be considered carefully in the development of a research design before data evaluation and analysis have begun.

Multivariate Analysis

Multivariate analysis overcomes the problem of what to do with findings of two significant and two nonsignificant subhypothesis tests. In fact, the problem would not arise since by using a multivariate statistic, all of the variables are examined in concert or all at the same time. How many variables can be tested at once is contingent on the statistic. While most of these tests are parametric statistics, there are multivariate techniques that can be used with nominal data.

Perhaps it would be easiest to grasp the essence of the multiple variable test by continuing to use the example of the four structural or organizational variables tested in relationship to nurses and role strain. First, only the general, operational, and null hypotheses are required because the statistic produces a single coefficient and there is only one null test to examine. Therefore, the four null hypotheses used in the single variable tests are not required. Without becoming entangled in statistics, a regression analysis could be used where the dependent variable (role strain) would be tested against all the designated independent variables. However, regression is a parametric statistic generally requiring ratio or interval data, and a higher level measurement than the nominal or dichotomous measurement used in the four independent variables (size, ownership, training, and denominational affiliation). Fortunately, there is a technique which allows the use of nominal measurement variables in a regression analysis.[14] Ignoring the measurement question for the moment, continuing the logic of bringing the hypothesis to test the regression coefficient takes all four variables into account at the same time. Hence, a significant multiple correlation (*R*) eliminates the problem of limited support for the hypothesis discussed where four null tests exist and all do not have equal value in terms of statistical significance. As a result, the test has been put back into a dichotomy. Either the multiple *R* is significant or it is not. Again the same process of inferentially testing the general hypothesis is undertaken, and the researcher can support or fail to support the theory from which it was drawn.[15]

Multivariate studies have a place in the discipline because few single variable explanations for social facts or phenomena are capable of the kind of explanation demanded by an interactional framework. The single variable study and subsequent tests of significance do not usually take interaction into account. Multiple variable studies usually do, however. The interaction of the variables affects the statistic in most parametric statistics and the resulting estimate of error terms which indicate that not all of the variance has been accounted for. It should be emphasized that interaction here is that of variables and not of persons or groups. Although the technique is not complicated, it is nonetheless more complete and powerful than the analysis of the two variable relationships.

If a researcher wants to go beyond the composite score represented by the multiple *R*, it is possible to hold a single variable constant and control for the effects of the variable in the relationship. It is also possible to hold two, three, or more variables constant at the same time. This gives some indication of what each is contributing to the resulting multiple *R*.[16]

Another technique used to accomplish virtually the same task is called partialing or partial correlation. Using this technique, we can determine if each of the independent variables is significantly related to the existing covariance. Several other techniques, including two-way analysis of variance and some specialized nonparametric tests, are available for multivariate analysis. Since most of these statistical techniques require a good deal of sophistication in statistics, the researcher with limited statistical skills should use them with caution.

HYPOTHESIS-GENERATING STUDIES

If all research in sociology depended upon researchers having to deduce a hypothesis from theory, the discipline would soon become tautological. That is, only supporting types of data would be generated by the methods available. Hypotheses evolve from the statement of the problem to be researched and from the relevant theoretical underpinning. The research design is then structured to bring relevant data to test these hypotheses. Obviously, data are brought into focus by the design needs. However, social psychology teaches that individuals who are looking for something will probably find it. For example, a bigot is more likely to accept, without question, negative statements and findings about particular minorities than a person with a more humane or cosmopolitan point of view. Witness how those who are phobic about communism point to the "communist conspiracy" to criticize every social reform movement. In short, stereotypes and prejudices seem to generate reification rather than research.

The same principle applies in research. A project tightly designed for only one purpose and biased in favor of one set of findings is not likely to reject current theories or to generate a new theory to test. Merton was aware of this idea when he discussed serendipity or unanticipated findings. A case was presented by Barber and Fox under the unusual title of "The Case of the Floppy-Eared Rabbits: An Instance of Serendipity Gained and Serendipity Lost."[17] They describe an example from experiments on rabbits rather than a case in the social sciences.

The case of the floppy-eared rabbits involved the injection of laboratory rabbits with a drug which made their ears wilt or become floppy. Two different medical researchers experimenting with rabbits and the same drug had occasion to record this occurrence. One researcher pursued what might be causing the rabbits to experience the floppy-eared syndrome. He explained that the nature of his examination caused him to explore all of the expected possibilities. (In this sense, this is what is meant when it is said that research design structures what data and what focuses are screened as important.) He was looking for tissue change. He had not thought of the possibility of cartilage change. Since his focus was on tissue and cartilage was believed to be a quiet inactive tissue, he had no occasion to think of cartilage until all the possible tests on tissue had been exhausted. Because of pressing needs, he stopped his research and moved on to other "more productive" work.

Some years later, the researcher again encountered the phenomenon in the course of his teaching duties, but this time he solved the dilemma. The solution came as a result of a change in methods. This time he developed a comparative design, giving some rabbits no treatment and others the injection. In this manner, he "discovered" that the change was in the cartilage matrix and that the cartilage change resulted in the floppiness. Barber and Fox describe this experience as a case of serendipity gained.

Parallel circumstances resulted in "serendipity lost." The second medical researcher also noted the floppy ears of the injected rabbits. Curious about this penomenon, he ran some tests on cross-sections of the rabbit ears. Since the focus of his experiment was not on this unanticipated condition, he continued with his original problem and purpose. While he, too, was concerned about this strange syndrome, he did not pursue it. As a result, Barber and Fox called his case one of "serendipity lost."

The lesson lies in the persistence of one researcher upon finding a phenomenon for which he has no explanatory theory or hypothesis. This is not to recommend an endless pursuit of futility; rather, it is to stress the importance of the researcher noting the regular occurrence of an event and seeking an explanation for it. In the case of the rabbits, understanding the original problem was related to observing the regularity of a given occurrence tied to the original problem. Persistence was rewarded in this case. A problem cannot always be properly tested with a single group; sample, sample size, and total design are dependent upon the nature of the problem to be addressed. In the rabbit example, the design and problem precluded finding the solution in first discovery since it did not suggest as relevant the focus needed for the final solution.

Researchers sometimes generate hypotheses about themselves and their work. Gideon Sjoberg developed certain tentative hypotheses about social scientists' involvement in a project entitled Camelot. This was an ill-famed and much discussed project of governmental involvement with a number of prestigious social scientists. Sjoberg's statements on the tentative hypotheses were:

> First, American social scientists (including sociologists) have been socialized, both as citizens and scholars, to an almost unquestioning acceptance of authority and power wielded by their own nation-state system and consequently, the administrative controls of the national government. (Nationalism is perhaps the most pervasive, yet the least explored, of the influences that shape the research carried out by American social scientists in other nations). Second, the increasing stress in social science upon achieving professional (as opposed to scientific) status serves to rationalize the acceptance of administrative controls emanating from the national level. The professional organizations of social scientists in fact encourage their members maintain a position of "respectability" in the eyes of the broader society. One means of achieving this image is to forge links with the major institutional systems in the society, notably those that exert administrative controls over citizen and scientist alike.[18]

The generated hypotheses were: American social scientists allow nationalism (and ethnocentrism) to shape research carried out in other nations, and emerging professionalism and the desire for respectability lead social scientists to accept administrative controls emanating from the national level. Much has happened since Sjoberg proposed these hypotheses in 1968, but the position of the social scientist remains essentially the same. Perhaps the Sjoberg hypotheses would be even more true today because of the relative lack of research money available, apart from that distributed by the major funding agencies of the government.

While most of the discussion in this section appears to pertain more to the statistical hypothesis-testing framework, such is not the case. It is also mandated that the observers or participant observers assess the validity and reliability of their data against the structure that prompted the original research topic and design. For the purposes of this work, it was a matter of finding examples of alternative hypotheses, or of finding reports or articles wherein the researcher reported the process of generating hypotheses or developing alternative hypotheses in the post-field work phase of study.

The primary objective of some observational studies is the development of hypotheses; other studies are well structured and have specific hypotheses to test. The principal factor is whether the observer has the problem well delineated and is engaged in looking for evidence to bring a hypothesis to test. On the other hand, the researcher may not even have the problem sufficiently specified to know what to look for. In this case, some contend that this type of data recording may, in fact, be less biased than the prespecified problem in that the observer is not actively looking for any specific kind of data. Becker makes the following comment on this subject:

> The evidential value of items in these field notes will vary accordingly, the basis of consideration being the likelihood of discovering negative cases of the proposition he eventually used the material to establish. The best evidence may be that gathered in the most unthinking fashion, when the observer has simply recorded the item although it has no place in the system of concepts and hypotheses he is working at the time, for there might be less bias produced by the wish to substantiate or repudiate a particular idea.[19]

Becker further pursues the idea that some observational or field studies test hypotheses and others are designed to generate them:

> In the post field work stage of analysis, the observer carries on the model building operation more systematically. He considers the character of his conclusions and decides on the kind of evidence that might cause their rejection, deriving further tests by deducing further logical consequences and ascertaining whether or not the data support the deductions. He considers reasonable alternative hypotheses and whether or not the evidence refutes them.[20]

The participant observers or direct observers are no less scientists than those who use statistical techniques in presenting tests and proofs based on their data. The participant observers' task is perhaps more difficult, but the quality of their work depends equally upon their adhering to the canons of the scientific method. They, too, engage in generating and testing hypotheses: by use of the null principle of searching for negative cases and reporting results within model building and relationship frameworks.[21]

NEGATIVE RESULTS

Despite careful development of a research design and execution of all stages of the process, frequently the results do not substantiate the hypotheses or support the theory underpinning them.[22] This fact may not be apparent to the new or casual reader of the literature of any discipline because negative results studies are seldom, if ever, published. For many of the same reasons forwarded as hypotheses by Sjoberg in discussing Project Camelot, social scientists generally do not discuss or publish lack of substantiation studies. Although they claim scientific objectivity and affective neutrality, many social scientists view negative results studies as a kind of failure. This is a paradox and leads to a needless loss of information which might have helped or at least prevented others from attempting the same study.

Much can be learned from the negative results generated by a study. When results substantiate expected or hypothesized findings, one is less likely to go beyond the initial test. When nonsupport occurs, a number of areas should be checked, namely:

1. Sample
2. Measurement
3. Statistics
4. Hypotheses

1. *The sample* should be checked to determine whether the responses are distributed normally. The dependent variable can be plotted with a couple of independent variables to see what kind of distribution and range are present in the results. It may be possible that the theory being tested covers the range of social strata which would suggest the need for a random sample. A random sample of college students would not be a random sample of all strata; because of compressed or reduced variability, the hypothesis has not been tested under satisfactory conditions. Of course, this should be considered prior to drawing the sample. Unfortunately, this is not always done. Checking the sample is one way of examining the design possibilities for nonsubstantiation in the study.

2. *Measurement* lacking reliability and validity can lead to negative results in studies. In this case, additional work on the instrument may be warranted, even if the scale has established validity and reliability coefficients. Some statistical techniques are available to bring about these tests. It may be that a test of the "known groups" technique would help in this situation, but again, the question of time and cost factors must be considered. How much time, money, and effort can be expended based on the possibility of limited returns?

3. *The statistics* should be checked to see if appropriate statistics have been used. Again, this area should have been checked prior to data collection, but at times, additional data analysis will turn up results that the original test failed to reveal. All of the statistics discussed are based on the assumption of linearity, and, at times, data are found to have curvilinear relationships. It is also advisable to be certain that the design has included a sufficient number of cases to justify the statistic utilized. There are correction factors for small samples and for X^2 (chi square) statistics when certain assumptions are not met.

4. *Hypotheses* examinations should reexamine the concepts and the linking terms to see that the tested hypothesis has been logically deduced or is empirically grounded. Furthermore, the tests of the null hypotheses should be reexamined to make certain that the results have been properly interpreted. Confusion frequently occurs in conclusions drawn when the null is accepted and the general hypothesis rejected, or vice versa. Both the formulation of the hypotheses and the process by which they are brought to test are areas to examine.

If all four of these areas are thoroughly examined and each is determined to be operationally sound, it is possible that the suggested relationship of variables or behavioral explanations expected is not correct.

Recall that one does not invalidate, change, or discard a theory based on a single study. Theory is never fully brought to test. Inferentially, parts of theory are brought to test and are supported, or not supported. Sometimes a flaw in the design, measurement, sample, or conclusions is spotted quickly by someone less involved with the work than the researcher. Occasionally, the originator of a given design is so close to the work that even glaring errors seem correct.

SUMMARY

This chapter discusses the process of testing by patterns. Whether the study is a survey or a participant observation, a decision must be made ultimately as to whether the hypotheses (if any) have been supported by the research effort. There are a number of reasons to engage in hypothesis testing, but the testing process is essentially separate from the type of design or data collection technique. The hypothesis is a logical derivative of theory, and inferentially, it tests the underlying theory. If the theory is true and the hypothesis logically drawn, then the hypothesis should be substantiated.

In addition, the foregoing discussion is based on the logical deductive process wherein hypotheses can be deduced from existing theory. There are legitimate reasons why studies are undertaken as hypothesis-generating studies rather than hypothesis-testing studies. This is more likely to occur in observational studies than in attitudinal surveys or statistically oriented studies. However, one is a logical extension of the other, rather than a conflict between two types of studies.

The statistical test of hypotheses, with multivariable relationships, is examined here, as are the conditions under which the hypotheses would be declared to have support, limited support, or no support at all. With regard to the use of negative results, it is suggested that a negative result in a study is not in and of itself a failure. It is what is done with the results that ultimately determines whether the study must be judged a failure. Most studies stop short of full and complete examination, including development of the alternative hypothesis. The press of time, money, and other projects often prevents the researcher from returning to previously used data.

NOTES

1. The alternative hypothesis is derived from data collected to test another explanation (hypothesis) of a given relationship. It is therefore an ex post factum explanation and must be tested by new data. If a researcher attempts to support the alternative hypothesis with the data from which it was derived, his reasoning is tautological.

2. This point is debatable in that operational variables also are usually abstractions, and although we talk of them as if they exist in the "real world," in actuality they do so only by definition. In all probability, it would be better to discuss operational variables as being less broad in scope, or more specific, rather than a lower level of abstraction. Many of our operational variables do not exist in reality or "out there" in the sense that we can taste, touch, hear, see, or smell them. This concept of indirect reading of another measure should not prove difficult to grasp. The gasoline gauge on one's auto is an indirect reading of the level of fullness of the gasoline tank. The gauge approximates the amount of gasoline left in the tank. It does not "read out" in the same sense that the gallons and dollar amount "read out" on the gasoline pump at the service station. Both the gauge and pump are indirect readings, but the pump is the more accurate of the two.

3. The difference of means test ("Student's *t*") is discussed in Chapter 17 and once again in Chapter 12 notes.

4. One-tailed versus two-tailed tests are based on whether direction has been specified in the hypothesis.

5. Hubert M. Blalock, Jr., *Social Statistics*, 2d ed. (New York: McGraw-Hill Book Co., 1972), p. 559.

6. *N* is defined as the number of people in a sample.

7. This is the case unless there are a number of subhypotheses, as is the case in our example. In the case of multiple subhypotheses, it is necessary to deal with each of the subhypotheses in turn, finally moving to the general hypothesis based on the subhypotheses results.

8. I.e., if JRT has been established to exist in white-collar and professional occupations, does it also exist in blue-collar jobs? Since it has been tested in free-enterprise nations, does it exist in socialist or communist states?

9. Art Gallaher, *Plainville Fifteen Years Later* (New York: Columbia University Press, 1961).

10. Neal Gross, unpublished research findings presented to the HEW Strategic Intelligence Unit on Education, Iowa State University, Ames, Iowa, 1966.

11. The last statement could be considered to be the generation of an alternative hypothesis.

12. The discussion centers on type I and type II errors. We may want to be relatively confident 95 times in 100 tests; or to gamble a bit more and choose the 0.10 or the 0.15 level of significance. Hence, some null tests we would accept, but you would reject.

13. There are exceptions to this statement in both parametric and nonparametric statistics. Some measures render only positive scores, while others never approach 1.0 at all. This reasoning, however, pertains to most commonly used measures of association.

14. I. A. Goodman, "A Modified Multiple Regression Approach to the Analysis of Dichotomous Variables," *American Sociological Review* 37 (February 1972): 28-46.

15. It is not suggested that the researcher develop an erroneous set of assumptions and then develop them into a research strategy.

16. The interested student should consult Blalock, op. cit., which is a representative general statistics text.

17. Bernard Barber and Renee C. Fox, "The Case of the Floppy-Eared Rabbits: An Instance of Serendipity Gained and Serendipity Lost," *American Journal of Sociology* 54 (1958): 128-36.

18. Gideon Sjoberg, *Ethics, Politics and Social Research* (Cambridge, Mass.: Schenkman Publishing Co., 1968), pp. 124-43.

19. Howard S. Becker, "Problems of Inference and Proof in Participant Observation," in Dennis P. Forcese and Stephen Ricker, eds., *Stages of Social Research: Contemporary Perspectives* (Englewood Cliffs, N.J.: Prentice-Hall, 1970), p. 214.

20. Ibid.

21. For a description of observational research that both tests and generates hypotheses, see Chapter 14.

22. Negative results studies are defined as those in which the hypotheses have not been supported in most instances. We would have trouble classifying a study testing seven hypotheses with four substantiated and three rejected or three supported and four rejected.

20

Reporting Research Results

Research is not ordinarily a private activity; results are reported for the benefit of others. Most results, however, are not published in national or regional journals relevant to a discipline but rather are reported in a thesis or dissertation or as part of a grant or contract. When research studies have been funded by national or regional agencies,[1] such reports are usually mandatory. Many universities and colleges have funds which provide limited amounts of money to researchers on their campus for selected projects. Even this form of funding usually requires a final research report. In short, funding sources almost invariably require reports of findings and provide guidelines to be followed in preparing these reports.

Whatever the source of funds, the first consideration in reporting research is to consider the audience for whom the report is being prepared. An excellent piece of research presented poorly in terms of format and logical structure or filled with typing errors, misspelled words, punctuation faults, and inconsistent usage of terms is seriously compromised.

GRANTS AND CONTRACTS

A distinction should be made between grants and contracts as sources of funding. Individuals receive grants because they have relevant or researchable, innovative ideas, and because their qualifications and achievements offer some assurance that their project will be productive. A grant tends to be less structured and can often be termed exploratory in design. It can be both developmental and exploratory in this sense. While this explanation oversimplifies the grant process, it does point up the essential differences between grants and contracts. When research funds "dry up" or become more difficult to obtain, an increase can frequently be seen in the contract form of funding wherein the researcher must write a proposal specifying what will be done in the project and precisely how much it will cost. Such contracts usually contain clauses specifying when reports are due to the funding agency, what must be contained in the report (often quarterly), and in some instances, that the contract may be terminated for nonsatisfactory progress on the project.

In recent years, much social science research funding has gone from the grant award to the contract obligation. This shift would appear to mandate a change in orientation in the sense that scholarship, creativity, and innovativeness frequently resist a time schedule and quarterly and annual reports may prove anathema. If there is a danger in the current predominance of contracts over grants, it is that scientists may become slaves to funding. The funding source may in turn tend to structure and direct research rather than encourage innovation. The researcher thus becomes a bureaucrat concerned with "reports" rather than creativity and scientific relevance.

THE RESEARCH REPORT

What sections should be included in the research report? The following format can be used in cases where a funding agency does not provide a format. It can also serve as an appropriate framework within which to present a Master's thesis or, with some modification, a Ph.D. dissertation.

PROPOSED RESEARCH REPORT OUTLINE

I. Introduction
    - Statement of the Problem
    - Relevance of the Research
    - Statement of Hypotheses

II. Literature Review of Theoretical Orientation
    - (Statement of Hypotheses) Optional

III. Methods
    - Sample
    - Data Collection
    - Measurement
    - Statistics
    - Hypotheses Testing

IV. Results

V. Summary and Conclusions

VI. Bibliography

VII. Appendix

Although this format is clearly not the only one possible, it is one that has proven very useful and capable of both stylistic and content modification.

Introduction

The introduction should be exactly that: it should introduce the reader to the problem and contain a problem statement that can be recognized by the reader. In the introduction of Liebow's *Tally's Corner*, a number of pages must be sifted through to find such a statement, but Hunter's *Community Power Structure* has a rather precise problem statement. Generally, it is best to present a specific, clear, and concise problem statement. In this way the statement of the problem, any subsidiary problems, as well as any limitations in the project can be addressed. For example, one may not be fully aware of all literature related to a problem and therefore not realize that a measurement scale exists to test the concepts to be examined. If a scale has to be developed, the study will be limited because at least one of the measurement scales will lack a measure of reliability and/or validity. The establishment of these scales may be included, however, as part of the proposal (a pilot study to test the scale).

Some researchers propose that hypotheses be presented in this section. The placement of the hypothesis in a report is a stylistic choice, and, in fact, there are three or more equally defensible places to present them. An alternate placement of an hypothesis—after a complete review of relevant literature—theoretically links it to existent research and tradition in the discipline.

Any terms used in an unusual manner or those requiring special definitions should be presented in a section entitled "Definition of Terms." Not all studies will require this section. Its inclusion depends upon the intended audience and word usage. Abbreviations used in the study may be included in this section but if they are extensive, they can be presented in footnotes or in a special subsection. When extensive use is made of cumbersome names, it is a good practice to use abbreviations. Consider studying the National Organization of Federated Meat Packers, Incorporated (NOFMPI); this near sentence-length name could become tiresome if used in its entirety throughout a report.

The importance and relevance of the study can be discussed as a concluding portion of this first major section of the report. An outline of the report may be presented as the last part of this introduction, but it is optional.

Literature Review of Theoretical Orientation

In many ways, a thorough literature review should anticipate a formal statement of a theoretical orientation. This section should include a discussion of concepts and the relationship between concepts. It can be handled under either a section on literature review or a section on theoretical orientation, but inclusion of the theory being used, relevant variables, and justification for inclusion of concepts and their relationship is mandatory.

There are two distinct schools of thought as to what constitutes a review of literature. Some advocate what is termed an exhaustive review in which the researcher includes all literature relating to the problem. This kind of review frequently takes the form of an historical presentation of the development of the theory, concepts, measurements, field studies, conflicting results, and so forth. A review of this scope also provides a developmental framework and highlights the relationship of the current problem to the discipline. Literature reviews of this type are often found in traditional Ph.D. dissertations or as part of a research proposal to a funding agency. Such reviews give the researcher the opportunity to demonstrate thorough knowledge of the area to be researched, and they also highlight what omissions of significant research have been made.

A less thorough review of the literature may be adequate. The extent of review may well be limited by time or library resources. This limited review should focus directly on the concepts and the relationships between concepts, measurement techniques, and relevant sociodemographic characteristics and their relationship to the problem, but it does not historically trace the development of theory or relevant concepts.

Either type of review should state how the problem is derived from supporting theory; how the problem will be tested and how it will be amended; how it will substantiate existing concepts or relationships between concepts or unusual measurement or operational techniques; and any additional information relevant to the problem being studied. The review should apprise the reader of what should be known to understand and evaluate the work in question. At this point in the process, the researcher must decide where to state the hypothesis. Some researchers prefer to present their hypotheses and subhypotheses in the introductory section following their statement of problem. Most, however, prefer to present the conceptual or general hypotheses at the end of the literature review section. This preference reflects a general feeling that the hypotheses should logically flow from the theoretical underpinnings, as well as the notion that the concepts discussed in the literature review should (at least in part) be included in the hypotheses to be tested in the project.

Methods

The methods section should include the delineation of areas based on the type of study being done. Not all of the following list of discussion areas may appear in any given study, but all should be discussed before being discarded:

A. Sample
B. Data collection
C. Measurement
D. Statistics
E. Hypotheses testing

A. Most studies should include a description of the sample. What type of sample has been selected? What is the sample size? What is the relationship of the sample to the population? As discussed in Chapter 10, the interviewers in the example were to choose the respondent in the field by following a carefully devised technique. Interviewers were told to make three attempts to interview the individual initially selected. These three attempts were not to be made on the same day, but were to be spread over the two- to three-week period the interviewers were to spend in the field. If they were unable to obtain an interview after three attempts, they were provided a list of alternates from which to pick replacements. The process was the same as for the original interview; however, reports were to include how many or what percentage of the sample was made up of the alternate selections. They were also to report the percentage of the sample that responded. It was simple enough to state, "we obtained 93 of the 100 possible interviews for a response rate of 93 percent."

B. The manner in which the data were collected and the type of data collected should be part of the complete research report. For example, one can say: "The data represent personal observations over a three-year period, questionnaire responses from selected respondents, and records obtained from the municipal court of common pleas." In this way, the reader knows that data have been collected using a number of techniques and in the section presenting results would expect to be told which data were being discussed—the observational data, interviewer-collected data, or secondary records data. The use of scales within a questionnaire should be noted in this section.

Multimethod, multitrait studies are often designed to attempt validity checks on scales or on the quality of data collected by each method. When such techniques are used, they should be reported in the data collection section of the report.

The length and technical detail presented in this section are a function of the nature of the study. If the study is relatively straightforward using standard procedures, less needs to be reported. If the report is a methodological one, significantly more detail and description should be presented. In all cases, however, this section should contain sufficient detail to allow for replication by another researcher.

C. In the measurement section, the variables should be reported in terms of measurement. If attitudes toward the law have been measured, the scale used should be designated and the direction of its measure defined. For example, a Likert scoring format[2] should be defined so that score magnitude indicates either positive or negative attitude. One might report that individual scale scores ranged from 26 to 130 based on a five-position response mode for a twenty-six item scale and that the higher the total score, the more positive the respondent's orientation toward the law. Since what has been described is a continuous variable, it is amenable to the use of parametric statistics, given appropriate sampling procedures.

Operational measures should be presented and discussed at this point if they pertain. Again, the information presented should be sufficient to allow for exact replication. The researcher must explicitly document, discuss, and explain the logic underlying measurement and operational decisions.

D. Not all studies use inferential statistics for analytic purpose. However, even statements made about the percentage distribution of given samples having certain characteristics are statistical statements. Whatever statistical tests or reporting measures are used in data analysis or hypothesis testing, they should be identified and their use justified. It may be possible to justify minimal statistical analysis with a simple statement: "Since nominal data were collected, the chi square (X^2) test was deemed appropriate for data analysis." (A short description of chi square is presented in Chapter 17.)

When extensive statistical analysis has been used to develop a scale (such as item total correlations or split half techniques of reliability) or when multivariate analysis such as regression, path analysis, or partial correlations have been presented, a thorough discussion is in order. Again, the prospective audience should be taken into account. At no point, however, should consideration of the proposed audience compromise the accuracy or the completeness of a research report. Practical evaluation of funding and audience, or even utility, cannot be allowed to prostitute the research effort.

E. If hypotheses are to be tested, the basis on which they are supported or rejected should be discussed. The statistical significance level to be used in accepting or rejecting the hypothesis should also be presented. For example, a statement that all results reported as statistically significant will be significant at the 0.05 level or below will assist the reader in interpreting the power of reported results.

It is important to be consistent in the use of any technique in testing hypotheses. If a hypothesis is to be tested that has five independent variables related to the dependent variable and mixed results are obtained, this must be reported.

For example:

GH Role strain will be related to sociodemographic variables.

Subhypotheses

SH 1 Role strain will be related to income.
SH 2 Role strain will be related to educational attainment.
SH 3 Role strain will be related to occupational status.

SH 4 Role strain will be related to financial status.
SH 5 Role strain will be related to indebtedness.

If the first three hypotheses are significantly related and the last two are not, problems exist in deciding whether to accept or reject the general hypotheses. Would three of five significant relationships justify support? Could such findings be interpreted as limited support? No support? Although such decisions are open to question, a discussion of the limited support found based on the three significant relationships is not overly ambitious. Likewise, it would be appropriate to seriously consider the finding of two insignificant relationships, but in neither case could it be concluded that the general hypotheses had been supported. To claim limited support for the hypotheses, use of the term *limited* is in order so that confusion in interpretation can be avoided.[3]

Results

The results section of a report should follow the structure presented earlier in the report. If the study in question was designed to test hypotheses, the results presented should follow the hypotheses in order of presentation. This pertains whether they have been accepted or rejected. Presenting findings out of order to emphasize those that significantly support hypotheses will confuse issues rather than strengthen the research report. Findings should be presented in an order dictated by the sequence of the tests or logic, or by occurrence in the questionnaire if single questions are being analyzed and discussed.

Several options are usually available to the researcher. A recent statewide survey of youth drinking-driving patterns focused on attitudes toward alcohol use, knowledge of the effects of alcohol, and attitudes toward enforcement, treatment, and rehabilitation of problem drinkers. While many possible presentation options were available, considering the project's purposes and audience, the format shown in Table 12 was adopted.

Since the report was written for a general audience, no statistics other than percentages were presented. In addition, there were two major variables as constants for all tables presented in the report; the first was residence, or the Wichita youth sample, compared to all other respondents from the state. Second, using a definition proposed by one of the departments of the government, each residence sample was divided by alcohol use. Those youths who had drunk alcohol within the last month prior to the survey were classified as alcohol-involved. Those youths who had nothing to drink within the last month and those who had never consumed alcohol were classified as nonalcohol-involved. The point was not that Kansas high school students prefer beer to other beverages, but that this was a structure within which to present the results from all questions in the survey based on

Table 12
Drink Preference by Sample Group
and Alcohol Involvement

	WICHITA				KANSAS			
	Alcohol Involved		Nonalcohol Involved		Alcohol Involved		Nonalcohol Involved	
Preference	*No.*	*Pct.*	*No.*	*Pct.*	*No.*	*Pct.*	*No.*	*Pct.*
Beer	175	62	46	20	461	68	96	24
Wine	38	14	39	16	61	9	39	10
Liquor	42	15	19	8	58	9	25	6
Anything	18	6	4	2	77	11	10	2
Don't drink	1	0	124	52	7	1	233	58
Multiple response	8	3	4	2	13	2	2	0
Total	282	100	236	100	677	100	405	100
	54%		46%		63%		37%	

residence and the "alcohol-involved" classification. Research design and relevant operationalized definitions provide a logical format within which to report data-based results. If the example study had been subjected to extensive statistical analysis, the "alcohol-involvement" classification would have been the dependent variable. The dependent variable can and often should be used as the constant variable in each table presenting data.

There is a lack of agreement on exactly what should be presented in the results section. Some researchers believe that the data should be presented with no comments or conclusions about results. Others feel that it is appropriate to include discussion of existent relationships, and whether or not previous findings and theory were supported. If present findings contradict previous findings, discussion should focus on the way in which current data differ from previous studies. Both methods are satisfactory. In a formal thesis or report, options are reduced; thus, flexibility exists even in technical report writing.

It is a commonly held view that the uninterpreted presentation of data can be sterile and can present difficulty of interpretation for the reader unfamiliar with the area being considered. In addition, total data arrays are difficult to remember. Data should be presented in a manner consistent with the entire report. Unticipated findings should be reported separately in a section labeled "Additional Findings."

Summary and Conclusions

The summary and conclusions section of a report is occasionally divided into two independent sections. In a lengthy report this is a good practice, but most research reports do not require this separation. This section should be an abstracted overview of the project and should generally state the problem, the major concepts, theoretical underpinning, hypotheses, methods, and findings. Findings should be highlighted in sufficient detail, but, obviously, should not be presented completely. A summary should provide a general understanding of the study, the manner in which it was conducted, and an idea of the major findings.

Conclusions should be drawn and reported from the study. They should be logical extensions of the data and should be warranted in light of the data collected for the project. A sample summary is presented from the study of alcohol and youth mentioned earlier. Reading this short summary of about one thousand words should enable one to decide if the study is worth reading.

Summary of Alcohol and Youth Study

In order to obtain information regarding the drinking/driving attitudes, behavior, and concerns of youth, a statewide survey was conducted. Respondents for the survey consisted of a proportional random sample of youth in the state based on the relative population density of the eleven designated multicounty regions of Kansas.

The analysis of the data consisted of a comparison of responses of youth from Wichita and youth from rural Kansas. Each sample group was further subdivided into alcohol-involved and nonalcohol-involved groups for within- and between-sample comparisons. Designation of alcohol-involved status was based on the students' self-reported indication of consumption of alcohol within the thirty days preceding participation in the survey.

The results of the survey were presented in categories of survey questions designated as Socio-Demographic Characteristics, Driving Record and Status, Drinking Behavior, Drinking-Driving, Social Activities and Opinions, and Support for and Knowledge of Alcohol Countermeasures.

The Wichita and Kansas samples of respondents obtained were quite similar in terms of the characteristics of sex, age, family income, racial background, and class standing. A greater proportion of the Kansas sample was alcohol-involved compared to the Wichita sample (63 percent to 54 percent). The notable finding for both samples was the high percentage of alcohol-involved respondents compared to the theoretical percentage legally able to purchase alcohol in the state. Only about 13 percent of each sample was old enough to legally purchase alcohol (eighteen years for 3.2 percent alcohol beer); yet, 45 percent of the Wichita sample and 52 percent of the Kansas sample below eighteen years of age were alcohol-involved by definition. Alcohol involvement tended to increase with grade level in both samples and with increasing family income. This last-named trend evened out at about the $15,000 annual income category for the Kansas sample.

Compared to the Wichita sample, a greater percentage of the Kansas sample held a valid driver's license/permit, owned their own auto, and had received three or more moving traffic citations. The same trend existed for the alcohol-involved in each sample. Thus, a greater percentage of the rural Kansas youth and the alcohol-involved youth in each sample drank alcohol, were legally able to operate an auto, owned their own auto, and received a greater number of traffic tickets.

The drinking patterns of the alcohol-involved respondents in both samples were similar in that beer was the preferred alcoholic beverage and alcohol was typically consumed on one day each week. Whereas a greater percentage of the Wichita alcohol-involved group drank one to two drinks on an average drinking day, a greater percentage of the Kansas sample drank three or more drinks. Another distinction between these two groups was that 24 percent of the Kansas alcohol-involved group did most of their drinking while driving around, compared to about 10 percent of the Wichita group. A relatively large proportion of each sample's alcohol-involved group also preferred to drink at parties, which presumably also involved automobile transportation. Thus, compared to the Wichita sample, the rural Kansas sample may be characterized by more youth who were able to drive an auto, owned their own auto, received more traffic tickets, more of whom drank alcohol and also drank greater amounts when they did drink, and more of whom preferred to drink most often while driving around.

The self-reported drinking and driving behavior of youth was consistent with the above findings. Unfortunately, most respondents felt that alcohol consumption either had no effect on their driving or, at most, made their driving ability "a little worse." Only the alcohol-involved respondents felt that their driving ability was improved after consuming alcohol. More of the Kansas alcohol-involved sample reported driving after drinking and driving when drunk more often than their Wichita counterparts.

The great majority of all respondents considered the chances of involvement in an auto accident when driving after drinking to be "high" or "very high," and their greatest concern was the consequence of possible injury to others. Although these feelings were shared by nearly all respondents, they were held by a greater percentage of the nonalcohol-involved than alcohol-involved respondents.

Almost all respondents also indicated that driving while intoxicated was the greatest single cause of most fatal traffic crashes, but they also shared a very limited understanding of the relationship between blood alcohol concentration levels and the legal definition of intoxication for drunk driving. In addition, there was either considerable uncertainty about the definition of social drinkers and problem drinkers, or mixed feelings, since social drinkers and problem drinkers were cited as the major cause of alcohol-related traffic crashes in relatively even proportions.

General knowledge and attitudes about alcohol were quite similar for both samples, although the alcohol-involved groups and the Kansas sample tended to be a bit more knowledgeable overall. The great majority of all respondents considered alcohol a drug and understood the synergistic effect of alcohol and other drugs, including prescribed medication. However, significantly more respondents in the Wichita sample than the Kansas sample used other drugs (29 percent compared to 4 percent). Drug use ranged from light to heavy. Comparison of the alcohol-involved in each sample showed that use of other drugs was about three times more frequent for the alcohol-involved compared to the nonalcohol-involved in the Wichita sample and four times more frequent in the Kansas sample. Thus, use of drugs, other than alcohol, was more common for alcohol-involved respondents in each sample, but area of residence was the most distinguishing factor overall.

There was little difference between samples for reported attitudes about social life and opinion formation. All respondents preferred to go to parties with a date or friends than to go alone. A greater percentage of nonalcohol-involved respondents considered themselves loners and showed a greater tendency to depend on parents in forming opinions, whereas alcohol-involved students tended to depend on multiple sources.

Wichita respondents were generally more aware of, and favorably disposed toward, alternative countermeasures to control the drunk-driver problem. More significant was the greater level of support for alcohol countermeasures among the nonalcohol-involved than alcohol-involved students.

Since no statistics were used in the report, no conclusions were drawn. Statistics were computed and the conclusions presented in other studies (reports), in other report formats, i.e., papers, journal articles, and monographs.

Bibliography

The bibliography is related to the literature review presented in the report. That is, the limited review would tend to have fewer sources listed, and the extensive review would tend to have a large bibliography. There are exceptions to including only the references cited in the report. When the report has been prepared for some audiences, it may be appropriate to list suggestions for further reading (as is done in this text). This inclusion is for the benefit of the readers and is most frequently found in reports for non-technical or lay public audiences. If guidelines pertaining to the report are provided, they should be consulted before the bibliography is prepared. There are variations in style and form. Generally, the last name of the author or the last name of the first author is presented first, and the bibliography is developed in alphabetical order. Some bibliographies move through all authors in this fashion, and others make distinctions between type of literature. For example, major sections would be Books; Journal

Articles and Periodicals; Publications of Government, Learned Societies, and Other Organizations; and Unpublished Materials (e.g., papers read at meetings, correspondence, theses, and dissertations).

Appendix

The appendix serves the function of an "other" category in the questionnaire. It is useful because it provides a residual for overflow from the report. Typical inclusions are a copy of the questionnaire, tables that are too bulky or too marginally related to the analysis to be included in the main report, computer processing input formats, maps locating sample areas, statistical formulas, and extensive discussion of either methods or results that require additional treatment for interested individuals. Not everyone would be equally interested in any one of these appendix items, but they are important to the individual who might want to replicate a given study.

There are many reasons for including an appendix or appendices to a report. The appendix should be considered a special part of a report that includes elements which are essential to a study, (though not mandated for inclusion by design or logic) and which nonetheless enrich the report by their inclusion in this special form.

DATA PRESENTATION FORMATS

In presenting research results, some techniques are more appropriate than others. The necessity of gearing the presentation of research results specifically to the intended audience has been discussed earlier. Those who work with statistics and research will have no difficulty with the statement "the zero order correlation between the dependent variable (job-related tension) and the independent variable (years formal education) was +0.56 significant at the 0.01 level." A more general audience, however, would have difficulty understanding the meaning of such a statement. The following generalizations are meant not to absolutely structure the report, but rather to aid in developing a report that communicates:

1. Keep the report as simple, straightforward, and uncomplicated as possible.
2. When presenting tables to support written material, summarize the major points or unusual points in the table. *Do not present every figure in the table in the written discussion.*
3. Make tables, graphs, and figures free standing and capable of being understood without written explanations.
4. Make table footnotes meaningful to help clarify the table (examples presented in the following material).

5. When possible, provide visual aids to facilitate understanding the data. (Some examples are presented in the following material.)
6. It is better to overdocument than to underdocument.

Tables

Tables should clearly tell the reader what is being presented. Table 13 is an illustration of a table that (1) is simple, (2) summarizes major points, and (3) is free standing and self-explanatory.

Table 13
Sex of Respondents by Sample Groups and Alcohol Involvement

	WICHITA				KANSAS			
Sex	Alcohol Involved		Nonalcohol Involved		Alcohol Involved		Nonalcohol Involved	
	No.	*Pct.*	*No.*	*Pct.*	*No.*	*Pct.*	*No.*	*Pct*
Male	149	53	78	33	344	52	157	40
Female	134	47	157	67	314	48	235	60
Total	283	100	235	100	658	100	392	100
	55%		45%		63%		37%	

Note: The data presented indicate no difference in the percentage of males and females classified as alcohol-involved for the Wichita versus Kansas comparisons. The 53 percent male Wichita sample is matched by the 52 percent Kansas sample. On the other hand, sex differences are striking among the nonalcohol-involved. Only 33 percent of the nonalcohol-involved respondents in Wichita were male and 40 percent of the nonalcohol-involved Kansas sample were male. Although a significantly greater percentage of females constitute the nonalcohol group within each sample, the difference between males and females within the Wichita sample is greater than for the Kansas sample.

The title of the table should contain all relevant identifying information. In Table 13, the title makes it clear that data are presented on sex, different samples (Wichita-Kansas), and alcohol involvement status. Moreover, the "stems" (male-female) and "heads" (No. and Pct.) identify column and row variable presentations.

Tables can become complex, and sometimes the complexity is justified. In general, a table is only as good as its ability to communicate. If complexity interferes with communication, then more than one table may be required.

Footnotes

Footnotes can help clarify a table to the audience when they provide additional information or explain discrepant information. Examples are:

1. The N size is reduced in the table and represents data for all who responded to the question.
2. The "other" category represents other than the listed responses, nonresponse, or refusals to answer the question.
3. Column and row totals do not add to 100 percent because of a rounding error.
4. Significance level information on statistics can be made more useful to the reader by providing additional information. For example:

   Standard notation:
   $\chi^2 = 1.48$ not significant at 0.05 level with 2 degrees of freedom.

   Improved notation:
   $\chi^2 = 1.48$ not significant at 0.05 level with
   2 degrees of freedom
   $\chi^2 = 5.99$ needed for significance at the 0.05
   level with 2 degrees of freedom

In the standard notation, few people would know what χ^2 value is required for significance at the 0.05 level with 2 degrees of freedom. The improved notation quickly allows the reader to determine if the statistic presented approached significance. Few readers will consult a statistics book to understand levels of significance. An explanatory footnote can clarify the issue.[4]

Visual Aids

Bar graphs and population pyramids are presented in Chapter 13. Two additional plotting techniques are of particular value in presenting data, especially scale-item data to those who are not statistically knowledgeable. The first was used by Lionberger in presenting the mean and the range of responses for the total sample and for each of nine subgroups contained in his sample. The responses represent scores on an 11-point Likert-type response format, with a score-rank 11 representing total agreement and a score-rank 1 representing total disagreement with each statement. The two graphs also represent first responses of individual perception on each item in the Q-sort technique ("real sort"). The second technique represents what respondents would like the situation to be. This is what is termed an "ideal sort." In the table, the reader can see at once the perceived actual mean response and range for each group, as well as the mean of the ideal sort. The technique can be used for pre-post (T_1 and T_2) scores, or for a comparative or cross-sectional design for samples from two different universes.

For clarification, one of Lionberger's items is presented here. The accompanying discussion and visual aids (Figure 18) should help:

The Extension Service is concerned with the improvement of* both *country and city life.

A second item in the Q-sort dealt with the broader extension orientation namely that the extension service is concerned with the improvement of country and city life. All groups except legislators and farm organization officials rated this item in the actual sort in about the same position as the previous item. The farm organization officials did not agree among themselves. Agribusiness executives and legislators strongly agreed that the College was dedicated to improving both city and country life. Farm organization leaders were generally neutral, which is somewhat contrary with their favorable "help everybody" vote on the previous item.

The only groups not at least moderately agreed that the Extension Service should be dedicated to improving life in city and country were farm organization officials and farm commodity representatives, who tended to be neutral. On the "help everybody" statement, they had tended to agree that extension efforts should be directed to both the rural and urban segments of the state. Agribusiness executives agreed most strongly that this should be the case. Although legislators and farm commodity representatives thought it desirable to maintain a broad extension orientation, their ratings indicated a belief that these efforts had moved a little further than the ideal. Farm comodity representatives also indicated a somewhat less "help everybody" orientation as an ideal than they thought existed. However, for most groups, the ideal rating deviated little from the perceived actual.

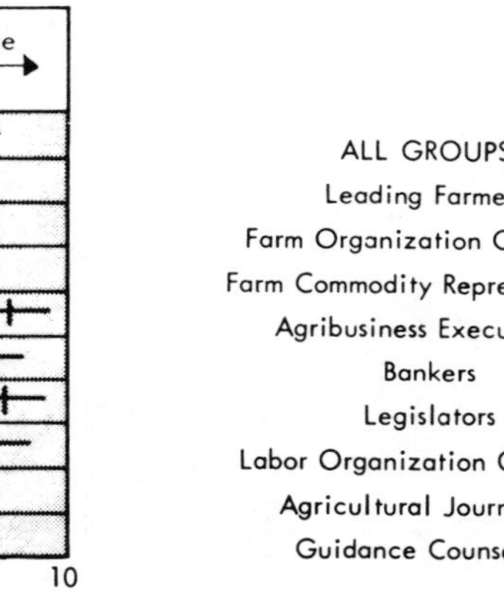

FIGURE 18 Extract from Herbert F. Lionberger, "Images of the College of Agriculture," Agricultural Experimental Station B822 May 1964 Columbia Missouri pp. 24-25

This presentation can be modified to include the actual mean and the mean plots for different subsamples in any report. Table 14 reports survey data for each question in the instrument based on Likert-type scoring. The scale was a seven-point scale ranging from Disagree (1) through Neutral to Agree (7) on items in a police-community relations survey.

Table 14
Use of Helicopters by the Police
in My Neighborhood Is Disturbing

		DISAGREE			NEUTRAL			AGREE
Response Group	Mean	1	2	3	4	5	6	7
1. Model Cities residents – pre	4.18				X			
2. Model Cities residents – post	4.38				X			
3. Non-Model Cities respondents	3.21			X				
4. Wichita Police Department	2.91		X					

Each of these visual aids helps us to see the total picture of the differences in the subgroup, or sample, responses. Avoid the use of overly complex tables. Generally, simple tables communicate more readily than complex ones.

Style, Language, and Form

A number of manuals have been prepared to assist in the preparation of theses, reports, and formal technical papers. A representative list of these is presented in the chapter bibliography.

As a rule, research reports should be consistent in terms of word choice and tense, and should not contain personal pronouns such as I or we. While it is difficult to avoid such pronouns, minimizing them will increase clarity. The report should flow in time sequence, with the introduction and design logically presented before research operations, data collection, analysis, and interpretation. The entire report will read more clearly if the entire report is phrased in the past tense. Graphs and tables may be reported in the present tense but only with regard to the immediate presentation. The researcher should be consistent and should avoid mixing tenses unless it is appropriate, i.e., the data were collected (past) and are representative (present) of the group in question. Whatever the nature of the presentation, it is only as good as its ability to communicate.

SUMMARY

Reporting research results is an important part of the complete research study. In order to communicate effectively, the report should contain sufficient detail to allow evaluation by the reader. Reports that are poorly organized and full of mechanical errors frequently result in misunderstanding or outright dismissal. In addition, the format and the language of the report should be chosen with the audience in mind.

As a general rule, overpresentation is preferable to underpresentation of detail and documentation. At the very least, a report should contain a complete description of sample size and type, how the data were collected, how concepts were operationally defined and measured, as well as what techniques of analysis were applied. Free standing visuals and tables should be presented if they aid in the reader's understanding of the report.

The standard reference form should be used on technical reports and formal writing. The complete report requires no explanation beyond what is written.

NOTES

1. Such agencies are the Departments of Health, Education and Welfare, Commerce (Census Bureau), Agriculture, Transportation, and Defense, and such philanthropic agencies as the Russell Sage Foundation, Ford Foundation, and Danforth Foundation.

2. See the description of the Likert scale on pp. 123-24.

3. Dennis Kelso and John J. Hartman, "A Comparison of Wichita Youth and Kansas Youth Regarding Drinking/Driving Knowledge, Attitudes and Behavior," Alcohol Safety Action Report, Fin-Sec-2-7, Department of Transportation, 1975.

4. The same logic and reasoning apply to footnotes in the written material. Formal quotations require formal footnotes; several acceptable forms are available in the works suggested in the bibliography for this chapter. Explanatory footnotes, such as this one, help to emphasize, or clear up a point in the text that might interrupt the flow of the presentation.

21

Ethical Considerations

Throughout this work, ethical considerations have been raised without dealing with them as such. The integrity of data has been addressed and stressed, as well as the awareness of the intrusion of research into the lives of others. In fact, promises of full disclosure of data or anonymity of respondents are all statements of ethical considerations in the research process. Inappropriate disclosures or violations of preresearch agreements can result in minor inconvenience, or even tragedy. Recently, two persons whose covert lives were publicly disclosed in activities that were tangentially related to research tragically committed suicide. Harm was not intended in the disclosure. Harm, however, was the result. Unintended consequences can occur in any research framework. Therefore, care must be taken to insure the integrity of those researched and the research itself.

There are strict, well-defined regulations regarding the use of human subjects in research. For example, agencies funded by federal money must file a statement regarding the use of human subjects. The law requires that these statements extend to all research formats involving human subjects interviewing individuals. Recently, public reaction focused on black male subjects in a southern state who contracted a progressively degenerating venereal disease. When they became involved in the research project in question, they were not told they had the disease nor were they treated for it. Observations were made of the progressive states of debilitation resulting from the disease. This project was conducted under the auspices of the government and in the name of science.[1] Such blatant disregard for the use of human subjects cannot and should not be tolerated.

The use of human subjects for medical experiments occurs frequently in our culture. Experiments have ranged from simple diet tests done over time to measure the impact of diet on metabolism to experiments that place the life of the subject in jeopardy. It is a comment on our culture's values that these human guinea pigs are drawn from categories of people manifestly peripheral to the mainstream of American life—prisoners, the indigent, the infirmed, and the aged. Since the relative position of people in each category affects the nature of the decision to cooperate or not with a research project, the very nature of choice in the research situation should be examined. For example, in a large eastern city the county jail is the scene of a large number of medical experiments involving varying degrees of physical risk. Typical of these are "burn tests" as inmates call them. They are in reality toxicity tests which result in scarring and, in the case of blacks, gross discoloration of the "burned" area. The tests are popular and competition to get "on" one is fierce since they pay well. Tests are virtually the only source of income for inmates aside from their daily earnings of 15 cents from the state. Additional funds are needed to pay for necessities in the prison and to provide a start after release.

During World War II, prisoners were used to test drugs developed to combat yellow fever and malaria. Prisoners were first infected with the diseases and then treated. Several persons died. Since they were told of the risks involved, what could prompt them to take such risks with little or no reward to be earned? Given the gravity of the research and its national importance, the implication was made that cooperation would be noted at parole hearings, and that early release was not out of the question. Was their cooperation voluntary? Did they really have a free choice? The answer is clearly no. The very fact that they were offered such a choice is indication that as prisoners they were defined as being somewhat less than human.

The nature of choice and cooperation in such experiments must be carefully considered. When students are used in an experiment or study, is their cooperation freely given or is it coerced? The decision is the researcher's, but he or she must be aware of its quality and its ethical implications.

In another context, the use of disguised research techniques is widespread in medical, sociological, and social psychological studies. For example, observations of individuals from behind a one-way mirror is an unobtrusive measurement technique commonly used in the laboratory setting. Not making subjects aware that they are being observed is justified on the basis that to make known the intent and purpose of the research would falsify behavior observed and preclude the possibility of doing the research. That such research has an effect on those observed is discussed in Whyte's *Street Corner Society*. This effect is so well known that it is referred to as the Hawthorne effect in the social sciences. It is defined as the subject's awareness of his participation in the research, which modifies his behavior to the extent that an atypical rather than a typical situation is observed. Many studies make use of deception in the conduct of laboratory experiments. For example, there are studies that focus on the process of leadership formation and employ dupes who attempt to sway individuals from one position to another.[2] Is the potential result worth the cost of deceiving the human subjects? Could the data be obtained in any other way? Will the experiment expose the subject to undue psychological stress? Will the experience lower the subject's self-esteem or sense of self-worth? Will it be embarrassing to the extent that it will affect the subject's behavior after its conclusion? If the answers are yes, it can be argued that more care should be taken in planning the study.

Let us return to the consideration of the willingness of the subject to engage in the research project. When deception is a requisite to obtain data, the choice not to cooperate is no longer available to the subject. In such cases, if the project were explained to the individual, the possibility of his being used as a subject would be eliminated. Deceiving the subject or cloaking the researcher's intent is a cost that must be weighed. A balance must be struck between the right to "know" and the "need" to advance scientific knowledge.

Although covert research has its place, it multiplies the possibilities of abuse. The research on lesbianism reported earlier was done with no deception practiced. Regardless of the openness with which a project is approached, however, certain kinds of research excite controversy. For example, a study recently undertaken at a major state university attracted considerable press coverage as well as exciting reaction from the general public. Its design met reasonable expectations of openness and full disclosure, and guaranteed its subjects anonymity. The project centered on the impact of smoking marijuana on sexual arousal when viewing pornographic material, both printed and visual (movies or television projections). Although the volunteers understood what would be required of them, the project was canceled as a result of the pressure of forces outside the university. An organized group which worked against the project charged that the money allocated for the project could be better spent elsewhere and that the state university should not be in the business of encouraging students to smoke pot or to view pornography. The major factor in the canceling of the project, however, was the state's refusal to allow them to have the necessary amount of marijuana.

This particular research effort raises some fundamental questions. What are the researcher's obligations to those people who support the institutions that in turn suggest research? Does a reliance on public funds imply that research must be limited by the prejudice and ignorance of an untrained, uneducated public? Who is to define the thrust of scientific research if not the scientist? In the not so distant past, public interference in a research project would have been defined as a violation of academic freedom. Today such interference may frighten some already oversensitive university administrators as they go to the legislature seeking funds to meet the ever-increasing costs of higher education. Making research the servant of public opinion may make university administrators and legislators more comfortable, but it prostitutes the very nature of scientific inquiry.

The same problems pertain to the observer or the participant observer of research. Commenting on participant observation, some leading sociologists have concluded that the use of disguises compromises both those who wear them and the people for whom they are being worn.[3] Most maintain that extreme care must be exercised in these undertakings because they have relevance for the discipline as a whole and for those subjects involved. Erickson concludes that the practice is unethical, and that there is a difference between personal morality and professional ethics. In citing some studies which employ unethical practices, he states:

> In recent years, a handful of studies have been reported in the literature based on the work of observers who deliberately misrepresented their identity in order to enter an otherwise inaccessible social situation. Some of these studies have already provoked a good deal of comment among them, for instance, the case of the anthropologist who posed as a mental patient by complaining of symptoms he did not feel, the sociologists who joined a gathering of religious mystics by professing convictions they did not share, the Air Force officer who borrowed a new name, a new birth date, a new personal history, a new set of mannerisms and even a new physical appearance in order to impersonate an enlisted man, and the group of graduate students who ventured into a meeting of Alcoholics Annonymous wearing the clothes of men from other social classes than their own and the facial expressions of men suffering from an unfortunate disability.[4]

While Erickson obviously does not approve of covert research involving misrepresentation or guile, his criticism extends to the consequences for the discipline, the research subjects, sociological colleagues, students, and the data generated by the mode of research. He notes that in the studies mentioned in the above quote, all but one of the observers were graduate students. He disapproved the use of graduate students in this type of research because as students they were not ready to perform as fully trained sociologists and because they were forced to make decisions that posed some discomfort for them. The dilemma was deepened by the fact that the professional staff had them make such decisions when they (the students) were "likely to be academically, economically, and even psychologically dependent upon those elders who ask them to choose."[5]

Erickson makes an additional point: "Julius Roth has reminded us that all social research is disguised in one respect or another and the range of ethical questions which bear on the issue must be visualized as falling on a continuum."[6]

There are ethical questions in all types of research, not all of which relate to the well-being of the subjects. For example, what should a researcher do when he discovers events that would not have come to his attention had he not been engaged in the research task? Student as well as professional interviewers frequently become perplexed by their observations. They often return from assignments to report poverty, squalor, filth, disease, incest, and child abuse, conditions that they have come into contact with as a result of choosing a random sample and interviewing persons where they live. Obviously, the interviewers are concerned with the plight of others but can do nothing to correct the conditions they have seen. In one study, an interviewer reported to her supervisor that she had observed a badly beaten child in the home in which she had completed an interview. She wanted to turn the case over to the local authorities so that corrective action could be taken. The situation posed a dilemma; in seeking the cooperation of a respondent and promising anonymity, had the interviewer lost the right or the responsibility to report legal violations to the authorities? Did the battered child in question deserve protection? The interviewer's presence in the home was contingent on a single role; did the interviewer have the right or the mandate to play another? Did good intentions justify actions in reporting a parent believed to have been involved in child abuse? Recall the example of the public exposure of two people whose identities were defined as deviant. The reporter's good intentions ended in tragedy. The situation cited posed a dilemma for both the researchers and the interviewer. It was resolved by the interviewer discreetly calling back to see if there was anything the parent (respondent) needed in the way of referrals to appropriate facilities. Fortunately, the community had a Community Information Referral and Information Services (CIRIS) which was able to handle the situation. Theoretically, however, the following question remains: what would the best action have been? What is the researcher's responsibility if in the course of researching covert behavior he becomes aware of a crime that has been committed? An even greater problem is what should be done if an interviewer becomes aware that a crime will be committed and reporting it would not only violate confidence and promises, but would also destroy the research. Such questions are not easily resolved. Researchers do not enjoy a privileged position in the eyes of the law and may well be vulnerable to prosecution.

Ethics in research are arrayed along a continuum, and it is impossible to make specific rules that pertain in all circumstances. Neither can one give such a list to another to follow; hence, no such list has been attempted.

Ethical questions must be considered and weighed in all types of research, even in secondary data analysis.

ETHICS WITH REGARD TO THE INTEGRITY OF THE RESEARCH ACT

The term *affective-neutrality* has been used to specify those conditions whereby the researcher does not become emotionally involved in conclusions derived from data, the way in which data are collected, or the subjects of the research act itself. Although the literature abounds with discussions as to whether or not sociology is a science and as such "value free," the selection of problems and the theory underlying the approach to the study of that problem (theoretical underpinning) have some biases built into them. The best that can be hoped for is an awareness of these implicit biases and direct efforts to minimize them. Goode and Hatt discuss the necessity for honesty and state that the basic value in science is that "it is better to know than not to know."[7] There is value in seeking knowledge for its own sake, but that value is enhanced by sharing:

> This value, the seeking after knowledge, does not apply to the scientist alone, however, and carried with it, therefore, is the further injunction to disseminate knowledge. Since knowledge is believed to be better than ignorance for ordinary people as well as for scientists, the findings of science must be made public. They are not to be closely guarded secrets, but essentially unpatentable and unsalable, a part of the public domain, freely given.[8]

Individuals engage in research for audiences other than themselves. Therefore, the integrity of the research act must be preserved for those audiences not trained in the rigors of science and therefore not as discerning as the scientist. For this reason, a scientist does not structure a research design in such a way that it validates a preconceived position. Research design is independent of results, as is data collection. This is so despite the fact that data collection methods limit and structure the tools used for data analysis. Data are interpreted in a manner consistent with acceptable practice. One does not select portions of the data substantiating desired results and thereby avoid contradictory findings. Not only would that be unscientific, but it would also be downright dishonest. It should be noted, albeit sadly, that not all scientists are guided by ethics and that research findings will not always be used for ethical purposes. The importance of research ethics becomes inculcated in the student as he proceeds in his professional training and identifies increasingly with the scientific orientation. When the data do not substantiate a hypothesized relationship, the scientist must be prepared to follow the data and to let the results fall where they may.

If one follows the principle of sound research design, his ethical responsibilities will have been discharged. Perhaps the most important consideration is to avoid tautology—that is, creating a design that includes elements in it that guarantee a particular outcome. Another important area is the complete disclosure of the reasoning behind choices in the research process. All too frequently researchers are less than candid about why they choose a particular group to sample. It would be refreshing to read a report that stated a particular group was sampled because it was convenient, in addition to other reasons.

In the research process, as many steps as possible should be completed before collecting data. This provides the least number of opportunities to deviate from the original design. When changes are made, they should be reported and the reasons explicated; full disclosure is necessary if the study in question is to be capable of replication.

In executing a design, the researcher should obtain the best possible test of the data and report the results based on that test. If alternative analyses have resulted in significant findings, they should be reported as such. Frequently, findings or insights derived from data are serendipitous, and it is not discrediting to report them as occurring in this way.

FINDINGS—THE ETHICS OF USE

Given a sound research design, an appropriate sampling procedure, and a thoroughgoing, completely defensible interpretation of data, what does the researcher do with unpopular or potentially dangerous findings? Hypothetically, consider the following: a researcher investigates the relationship between school achievement, IQ, race, and delinquent acts. The design is well thought out, and tests comparing the sample with the known universe indicate that the sample is truly representative. The data analysis is most pristine, and in order to minimize the possibility of error, the differences between research groups are to be evaluated at the 0.01 confidence level. The findings indicate that differences between black and white racial groups on all variables are statistically significant. Blacks have lower IQs and lower grades in school, and commit a disproportionate number of delinquent acts. What then is the hypothetical researcher to do? Do such findings raise any ethical questions? Is some research by its very nature prone to controversial interpretations? Are some findings, regardless of scientific merit, best left unreported? Should the reporting of scientific findings depend on the extent to which they concur with popular sentiment and social or political philosophy? Indeed, is the researcher responsible for the use to which others put his findings? These questions are easily raised but are exceedingly difficult to lay to rest.

In the case of the hypothetical researcher above, his findings could well be used to justify two diametrically opposed social programs. On the one hand, given the validity of the findings in question, differences between black and white groups in the sample on IQ scales could be interpreted to be the result of gross cultural differences between black and white students. This in turn could be used as a way of questioning the universal standardization of the IQ scale. Given the validity of the IQ scale, however, differences between those two groups could be interpreted to be indicative of the cultural deprivation of blacks in this society. If underachievement in school and poor test performance and delinquency are related to cultural deprivation, then this research could be used to justify programs geared to ameliorate the blacks' cultural deprivation in this society.

On the other hand, given the validity of the IQ scale and real differences between black and white groups, it is possible to interpret the findings as reflecting biologically based differences in learning abilities. These interpretations would seem to be reinforced by differences in social performance and the commission of delinquent acts in the same direction. Rather than lending support to the creation of social programs in the best liberal tradition, the study would seem to recommend a racist interpretation of social problems and solutions.

In the case of both interpretations, the findings were accepted as real. Interpretations differed in the example as a function of both social and political philosophy. Is the research responsible for either interpretation? The researcher can at least offer his own interpretation of findings couched in the conceptualization of the society of which the relevant sample was a part. In this regard, the researcher discharges basic ethical responsibilities. If findings run contrary to popular sentiment, they can be tested through replication or questioned through a careful examination of the entire research process. Research is not the slave of current moral and social interpretations. Ethics are therefore a function of honest design and interpretation.

Without doubt, certain research subjects are more controversial than others. Even so, findings must see the light of day if the frontiers of social science are to be advanced. That this is an ideal cannot be denied. The scientific world is frequently as hostile to findings that attack moral, social, or political sacred cows as the general public. Recently, a well-known eastern university refused to allow a controversial scientist to present his research and perspective to its student body. He was denied a forum not because of his methodology but because he had presented findings which contradicted both the ideology and popular sentiment of the decade. This was a deplorable situation. The university, after all, should be a forum for the discussion and evaluation of all points of view. All too frequently, the extremist wants to hear only those opinions that correspond to his preferences. Freedom of expression must include all extremes or it becomes simply freedom to agree. Who is to judge the long-term impact of science or fact? The discovery of atomic energy resulted in its misuse during World War II, with attendant tragedy; yet, in the long run it may be the answer to man's energy problem. All findings have both positive and negative impact potential and no researcher can be expected to read the future.

SUMMARY

The right to know and investigate does not include the right to injure someone in the research process. Even well-intentioned efforts to investigate, or, through research, to ameliorate the human condition must be carefully weighed in light of possible negative outcomes.

NOTES

1. Stories reporting the study were carried widely in newspapers all over the country in late 1975.
2. Informed individuals working in conjunction with the goals of the researcher and/or the research project.
3. Kai T. Erickson, "A Comment on Disguised Observation in Sociology," *Social Problems* 14 (Spring 1967): 366-73.
4. Ibid., p. 367.
5. Ibid., p. 369.
6. Ibid., p. 372.
7. William J. Goode and Paul K. Hatt, *Methods in Social Research* (New York: McGraw-Hill Book Co., 1952), p. 21.
8. Ibid.

Glossary

Acquiesce: This term refers to the tendency to say "yes" or to act passively. Sometimes the tendency is referred to as "yea saying."

Alternate Hypothesis: An hypothesis is a testable statement of relationships between phenomena. As such, it can be considered to be a plausible statement or explanation of the relationship. An alternate hypothesis is an additional statement of plausible explanation. The original hypothesis tested may not be the only possible statement of relationship.

Analytical Design: The term usually means separating into parts or subunits for analysis or examination of the parts. Studies examining and contrasting various subunits can be called an analytical design.

Anonymity: When used in methods as "a promise of anonymity," the term means the individual will not be identified in the research reports. The respondent is promised that information provided will be analyzed with all other responses, and only group statistics or "pooled data" will be presented. Anonymity is one of two disclosures that must be made when a project has been funded by a governmental agency that subscribes to HEW guidelines concerning the rights of human subjects.

Apparent Symbol: In dramaturgy, an actor must establish identity and in so doing assembles a set of apparent symbols to carry from social interaction to social interaction. These symbols may vary from individual to individual but usually consist of some or all of the following: hairdo, length of hair, beard, condition and presentation of self, clothing, accessories such as purses, shoes, backpacks, and bags.

Appearance: Appearance establishes the identification of the participants, and these identities are communicated by symbols such as gestures, grooming, clothing, location, and props. Personal appearances set the scene for encounter, and these appearances may arouse challenges or be accepted (validated). In either case, the character has been established at least in part.

Appendix: An appendix is placed at the back of a book or report to augment the main text. Material that is supportive of contextual material or of such minute detail that it might detract from the text would be placed in an appendix. When properly used, the appendix can add an important dimension to the main body of the work.

Applied Research: This type of research attempts to ascertain the "best" techniques to bring about social change, implement policy, or ascertain possible alternative solutions to pragmatic problems. In contrast, basic research has no such orientation or concern about how or whether the results are utilized.

Assumption: An assumption is a set of statements about relationships between units of analysis. There can be fundamental assumptions of a theory and as such they provide the basis upon which the theory is based. A fundamental assumption of functionalist behavior is that "persons' actions are goal oriented and rational." Accepting this assumption along with others structures research development.

Assumptive Base: This term designates the assumptions from which theory, axioms, or theorems are derived. It can be said that the assumptive base of most social science research is that of a rational man or that behavior is rational given certain conditions of behavioral alternatives.

Attrition Model: An attrition model is one in which units are exited as the process model moves through time. If the model starts with one hundred subjects or units techniques are devised to eliminate or drop part of them out of the model. The rules and technique for exiting units must be part of the model, and these decisions must be made before completing the model. In the above example of one hundred subjects, the model may move through a process of eliminating all but twenty-five, or any number of remaining subjects.

Audience Attributes: In symbolic interaction, the audience must be taken into account in that the audience is both observer and participant in social interaction. The attributes or characteristics of the audience exist as they are perceived. These characteristics affect actors in the sense that they are perceived as the interactive scene unfolds, identities are validated, roles are established, and communications shown in the material creation of both meaning and action.

Basic Research: The systematic study and results of research without regard for or concern with any utilitarian purpose is called basic research. Its purpose is to expand the discipline through theoretical, methodological, or conceptual development. While there may be a tendency to separate basic and applied research, in fact some basic research becomes the basis for later applied research efforts.

Bias: Bias refers to lack of objectivity or to prejudicial behavior. In science bias is the tendency to attempt to bring about desired rather than actual outcomes.

Binomial Distribution: The binomial distribution gives the probabilities of successful outcomes within a specified number of trials. For example, the basic formula is $fx = (p + Q)^N$, where x is the number of observations of a particular event in N trials. For example, what would be the probability of obtaining only one head in four coin tosses? Using the above equation with the given information, we have

1 head $= p$
4 tosses $= N$ of 4
$Q = 1 - p$

Hence, the probability of one head in one toss is 0.5. If q also equals 0.5 we can now solve for probability:

$$4\,(0.5)^1\,(0.5)^3 = 4\,(0.5)\,(0.125) = 0.25$$

or the probability of obtaining only one head in four tosses is 0.25. As N size increases, the expansion approaches a normal distribution curve.

Bivariate Distribution: This term is usually reserved for an either/or classification such as male-female or yes-no. This is also called a dichotomy.

Block Sample (or *cluster sampling*): This sample is one in which large units are selected, and then data are collected from all smaller units within the larger segment. For example, a researcher may select city blocks as the sample and then collect data from all household units within a block.

Canned Program: The canned program is an existing program with prescribed routines to be followed in the computation of statistics and the computer analysis of data. Such programs have been run and contain no errors if the prescriptions are followed. The advantage of these programs is that most persons can follow the routine procedures to obtain the desired results. This ability can be learned very quickly, whereas it takes some time to become a competent computer programmer.

Captive Sample: A term used in the same manner as captive audience only applied to a sample. Often college students are used in research, and while the professor in charge may state that participation in the project is voluntary, the class of students would actually constitute a captive sample.

Card Assist: This term indicates a card handed to questionnaire respondents to structure their responses into desired classes. For example, it may be desirable to obtain age in five-year cohorts rather than actual age; hence, respondents would be asked to indicate which of the five-year cohorts represents the age of the respondent. Cards are often used for income, education, region, and other sociodemographic variables.

Case Study: This is a unit or study as a whole wherein the group, clique, or organization tends to be examined in depth and as a unit instead of as isolated parts. Some researchers have contended that case study investigators can focus on data not available to the statistician. That is, the investigators can concentrate on an intensive, detailed, and free-flowing collection of data on interactions or traits that are perceived to be relevant and important to the study.

Case Study Technique: This technique refers more to the unit of analysis than to the data collection technique. For example, an individual group, or large formal organization might be the unit of analysis, but data collection techniques would probably vary with the unit of analysis. The common thread is that each of the above-mentioned units would be studied as a whole, not as a number of units.

Cell: The term *cell* describes a time period and/or a data collection or sample in a research design. It is a designated word for ease of use in discussing the various combinations of data collection-variable measure in a design. Each cell must be mutually exclusive.

Census: A count of the population of a political unit. In the United States the census is taken every ten years in years ending in zero. These counts have been continuous since 1790.

Character: A character is a person with a distinctive organization and personal characteristics such as appearance, mannerisms, habits, traits, motives, and social statuses. The character is one of the major concepts of the dramaturgy model.

Check-off Responses: Structured questions with possible answers to be "checked" by the respondent are called check-off responses. The same principle can be applied to the interviewer-administered questionnaire, but in general use generally means the respondents are actually marking their own responses in a group setting or are replying to a mailed questionnaire.

Clarity: This term is used in questionnaire construction to indicate unambiguous meaning.

Classical (Experimental) Design: This design is used with a control group and an experimental group, and of necessity requires a time dimension (data collected during at least two points in time). In addition, an intervention or manipulation is made on the experimental group between time one (pre) and time two (post), with the expectation that this manipulation will result in observable differences between the control and experimental group at time two on the post-test.

Clinical or Diagnostic Interview: The purpose of some interviews is to collect information to be used in making a diagnosis and prescription for treatment based on the information collected. In research, this type of interview is not usually undertaken, but at times one may use these data in secondary data analysis. The technique is normally used by social workers, psychologists, and medical doctors.

Clinician Role: The role of social scientist as clinician is spelled out by Alvin Gouldner as one in which the researcher observes the social setting and makes the diagnosis of the problem based on these observations. The role is one relatively free of intervention or imposition of self-diagnosed problems specified by participants in the system.

Closed or Structured Question: This term indicates questions that respondents usually check in self-administered questionnaires. Instead of writing a response, the respondent merely checks one already presented or has the option of checking the "other" category explaining what is meant.

Closing the Interview: After obtaining the data needed for the project, the interviewer must terminate the process. At times it is difficult to end an interview because some respondents want to talk or ask the interviewer a number of questions about the research project. As firmly and politely as possible, the interviewer must get on to the next interview, but should remember that the respondent has assisted the interviewer and often feels a right to ask questions in return.

Cluster Sample: This sampling type is used to minimize cost and geographical spread in sampling. Often a county will be randomly selected in a state, and respondents are sought in a single county rather than from all over the state. The technique is also used in a city to minimize cost and travel costs in data collection.

Code Book: A code books is built to identify the location of data in the data cards used for analysis. Some form of identification is necessary in most projects because it is easy to forget the ordering and placement of data on cards, especially when it takes multiple cards for each respondent. Time spent in trying to identify data cards without a code would have been much better spent in preparing a code book for the project.

Cohort: A cohort is a group sharing the same characteristics of classification. Females fifteen to nineteen years of age can be called a cohort, but the female cohort could refer to all females in the population. The researcher should be sure of the cohort definition when using cohort data.

Column: In data cards as in table building, reading, or analysis, the vertical placement of figures is called a column.

Comparative Designs: Comparative designs are those in which one sample is usually tested (compared) against one or more other samples to see if differences exist based on the criterion measure. For example, a comparative study could be: Is there a difference in completion of tasks requiring finger dexterity based on sex? In other words, are females better at tasks requiring finger dexterity than males?

Concept: A concept is an analytical abstraction used to develop, test, and analyze theory. One must examine a term in context to ascertain whether it is a variable or a concept. For example, social class might be either a concept or a variable, depending upon how it is used. Concepts are the basic building blocks of a theory. They, along with connecting terms, form propositions. In turn, linked propositions are logically related and interrelated to form an explanatory mode called a theory.

Confidence Limits: Confidence limits are statistics specifying the confidence placed on the true results falling within specified limits. For example, mu (universe mean) falls within limits specified for a predetermined confidence limit (95 percent confidence limits). Hence, it can be said that the researcher is 95 percent confident that in repeating a sample, mu would fall within the confidence limits 95 percent of the time.

Confirmation of Social Purpose: Research involved in attempting to justify or demonstrate that a social program is bringing about social good can be called confirmation of social purpose. Research of this type purposely initiated violates all canons of science and brings into question the research ethics of anyone willfully participating in these activities. The concept is sound if the evaluative research is undertaken without an attempt to substantiate a preconceived or desired favorable position.

Continuous Variable: A variable with intervals that continue within designated limits is called a continuous variable. Percentage ranging in value from 0 to 100 is an example; an interview response ranging in response values from 1 to 5 is another. The following response mode is often used: Strongly Agree, 5; Agree, 4; Undecided, 3; Disagree, 2; Strongly Disagree, 1.

Contract: A contract in social research is contrasted to the traditional grant format of receipt of research money. In a contract, the researcher must specify exactly what is to be done, in which manner, to whom, at what cost, and in what time framework. A contract is well specified and usually can be terminated for lack of performance.

Control Group: The control group is generally used in an experimental design to be tested against the experimental group. The experimental group receives some treatment, but the control group does not. After both the pre- and post-tests, the differences (if any) between the two groups are tested. If difference has occurred, it is assumed to have resulted from the treatment on the experimental group.

Conversationalizing: In questionnaire construction, this term means written leads into a new section of material or an indication that a new dimension is being considered. It may be used in self-administered questionnaires, or it may be read by an interviewer to insure consistent use by different interviewers.

Corollary: A corollary is defined as that which accompanies or goes along with something else. Max Weber saw Protestantism and capitalism as corollaries in his classic work on the subject. It is also used in a formal sense to mean that which is deduced from existing theorems; hence, no additional proof is needed.

Covert Behavior: Covert behavior is defined as behavior which is not exhibited in the public arena. Individuals can form subcultures and engage in the behavior in a collective setting, but only in the presence of subculture members; hence, the behavior remains covert when judged from the norms of the larger society. For the most part, covert behavior is a private affair because of the possibilities of stigmatization by members of the larger culture base. Homosexual behavior or satanic rituals can be considered examples of covert behavior.

Covert Research: This term can have two meanings: (1) research into areas of covert behavior and (2) disguised or covert research. Research undertaken without the knowledge or approval of those being researched can be called covert research. Almost of necessity observation or participant observation is required in this type of research. It does have a legitimate place in social research, but it raises questions of ethics.

Criterion Variable: This term designates the measurement variable employed in statistical analysis. In some cases, this will be the same as the dependent variable, but it need not be. The criterion variable can be any variable in a survey that is being used in a statistical test. It is the variable being examined as the measure under evaluation.

Critical Region: The critical region is the area in which study results will be rejected as having been capable of occurring by chance. That is the area of the statistical test under the ordinate of the normal distribution. The concept is more fully demonstrated with regard to tests for supporting or rejecting hypotheses. As the region or area increases, it is more probable that the hypotheses will be rejected.

Cross-Sectional Model: The cross-sectional model is one of data collection and analysis based on data collected from two or more samples at a single time period. Hence, the model is principally comparative between the samples drawn.

Cross-Tabulation: When analyzing data, selected variables, including the dependent variable, are often run against all other variables. For example, sex, race, occupation, and social class may be used to cross-tabulate all other variables or questions contained in the questionnaire.

Crude Rate: In population studies, the crude rate is calculated on all persons in the population and is then standardized by multiplying the ratio by 1,000. For example, the number of events (births, deaths, marriages, divorces, and so forth) is divided by the total population and then multiplied by 1,000. If there were 50 births in a total population of 300 persons, the crude rate would be 166 births per 1,000 persons.

Curvilinear Relationship: In statistical terms a curvilinear is opposed to a linear relationship. When two variables operate in a linear relationship, both are moving in the same direction or each is moving in an opposite direction to the other. The line is straight from one point to another. In a curvilinear relationship, one line may be straight while the other is curving or arching from one point to another. It is also possible that both lines are curving between points.

Data: These constitute the set of phenomena also referred to as a product or listing of responses collected as the basis of examination in the research design. Many types of data are distinguished in measurement classifications.

Data Bound: This term indicates that the results obtained from a particular study may be (probably are) relevant to that study alone. This usually occurs because of sampling problems, and the researcher is then reluctant to generalize to other populations. Uncertainty or limited sample (such as only those who have experienced a specific event) often causes researchers to state carefully that their results may be limited and that generalization beyond their sample is not warranted.

Data Card: A data card is a standardized card used in computer analysis. The data are transferred from the questionnaire or other sources to such cards by a keypuncher. The cards are then used in the data analysis. Data cards contain eighty columns and twelve rows.

Data Collection Interview: For convenience, this term has been used to differentiate the collection of data from those interviews with other purposes. The clinical interview has purposes other than the mere collection of data, while the data collection interview does not.

Data Statement Pad: A data statement pad is a business type form, usually prepared in a tablet form, that contains eighty columns. These forms are used when the researcher does not want a keypuncher to take the data directly from the questionnaires. All of the data that can be placed in the eighty columns for twenty-five respondents can be placed on a single data statement sheet. These sheets eliminate keypunchers handling questionnaires, turning pages, or interpreting data responses.

Debugged: This term means that computer routine has been run and has been found free of errors. This can occur in the original run in which no errors were found or after a number of problems have been eliminated from a complex program.

Definition of the Situation: This phrase is used to recognize that each individual interprets each situation or encounter in a unique way in terms of previous background, experience, and cultural values. This is the imposition of a value set upon the perception of an individual. It has been said to be relevant in most, if not all, social processes.

Definition of Terms: When terms are specialized or too technical for a lay reader, it is good practice to have a definition of terms section in an early chapter. In addition, if there is contradictory usage of terms, it is best to indicate which definition is being followed in the work presented. Any attempt to clarify and better communicate with an intended audience is good practice.

Degrees of Freedom: In interpreting some parametric statistics, it is necessary to ascertain how many degrees of freedom are operating in their computation. It has to do with the unrestricted and random sampling process involved in the computation, and the table value of ascertaining the coefficient value required for statistical significance. As degrees of freedom rise, a smaller coefficient is required for significance.

Demographic Characteristics: These characteristics are often called face sheet data and include such items as age, sex, race, religion, education, marital status, occupation, place of residence, voting behavior, and organizational memberships.

Demographic Research Sources:

I. National Survey Archives

Data Archives and Research Centers

1. Bureau of Applied Social Research, Columbia University, New York City
2. National Opinion Research Center (NORC), University of Chicago, Chicago, Illinois
3. Roper Public Opinion Research Center, Williams College, Williamstown, Massachusetts
4. Inter-University Consortium for Political Research, University of Michigan, Ann Arbor, Michigan
5. Laboratory for Political Research, Social Science Data Archives, University of Iowa, Iowa City, Iowa
6. Lou Harris Political Data Center, University of North Carolina, Chapel Hill, North Carolina
7. UCLA Political Behavior Archives, University of California, Los Angeles, California

II. Educational

8. The Department of Health, Education and Welfare has a numer of designated centers, each focusing on a special area relating to education. Write the Secretary, HEW, inquiring into the location and area of emphasis for each of the ERIC centers (federal centers also known as Educational Research Information Centers).

III. Medical Archives—Relating to Social Science Interests

9. Columbia University School of Public Health and Administrative Medicine Research Archives, New York City.
10. Governmental Sources
    Tapes for recent census data are available from the Department of Commerce, Bureau of the Census, Washington, D.C., for the decennial census. Data for the five-year agriculture census are available through the Department of Agriculture, Human Resources Division, Washington, D.C.

Several other more specialized data archives are available. Generally, however, it is best first to consult local and state sources of data. For a very thorough listing of data sources, see Pauline Bart and Linda Frankel, *The Student Sociologist's Handbook*, (Cambridge, Mass.: Schenkman Publishing Co., 1972), pp. 101-83, Chs. 5 and 6.

Density Rate: This rate measures the distribution of a population on a per square mile basis in the United States. The total number of persons in a county is divided by the number of square miles to produce the density figure for the county.

Dependent Variable: This variable can be "explained" through its relationship with other variables called independent variables. For example, an attempt may be made to explain social cohesion (dependent) by the type and goal orientation (independent) of the group.

Depth Interview: The interview that flows with the responses of the respondent designed for a special purpose is called the depth interview. Interviews of this type usually precede the structured, closed question type. The purpose is to allow the respondent freedom in developing the topic of consideration. The interviewer should remain as neutral as possible and at the same time keep the interview flowing; hence, the respondent rather than the interviewer structures the responses.

Deterministic Relationship: Deterministic implies that a relationship is known and is capable of being specified. That is, the relationship is caused or is a causal relationship. The term is used in both the verbal sense (as group size increases, group solidarity decreases), or in a logical and/or mathematical sense (if A then B, or where values are substituted for A and B).

Disguised Role: The disguised role is that of researcher as participant observer, but to avoid confusion not all participant observation requires a disguised role. Obviously, a researcher can be a participant observer only in the groups he belongs to or in those into which he can gain acceptance over time. Some covert research requires disguised roles for a single observation of covert behavior that would not be accessible to the researcher if he were not disguised. Disguised in this sense merely means assuming a role that is not his regular role. Examples of the disguised role are the individual attending and participating in a Pentecostal church service to observe the services, or assuming the role of an alcoholic to attend a meeting for alcoholics. It is probable that neither group would allow an interested observer to sit in and observe their meetings.

Documentation: This term refers to the process of substantiating a statement or position by footnoting or documenting its source. The process reinforces the credibility of the author's statement or position by reference to other authorities in the field.

Dramaturgy: The dramaturgical approach is an offshoot of symbolic interaction. It views interaction from a heuristic stance as an ongoing or unfolding of behavior setting between actors. The dramaturgist views the individual as a character, a performer whose activities create the self or character for an audience. The success or failure of the actor is reflected in the audience accepting or failing to accept the character.

Ecological Variable: The density rate is an ecological variable. Others include Park and Burgess's concepts of invasion, succession, segregation, and others that relate to how persons are distributed and interact with their physical characteristics.

Editing: Editing in data analysis does not have the same meaning as English, journalism, or book editing. It means examining a questionnaire to see that responses are properly checked, that missing data are properly coded, and that open-ended question responses have been assigned a number corresponding to a code (if a code has been made from these responses). In general, editing means a complete examination of and coding by circling or marking the proper code on the questionnaire. The edited questionnaires are then used to transfer data to the data statement sheets.

Efficacy: The term means having the power to produce the desired results. In this context it means, is the design effective in producing the necessary data, tests, and results to bring the program to test? It does not mean to produce desired results in the sense of a favorable evaluation if such is not warranted.

Engineer Role: In describing the role of the clinician, Gouldner also outlines the role of the social engineer. This role he describes much as the technician with services for sale or the funding agency describes the problem as they see it or as they want it researched. The social engineer then applies expertise to examination of the problem as others view it. This role definition more closely approximates the current state of contract research funding.

Equation: This term indicates an equality between two elements; hence, an equation will indicate that integers, functions, and outcomes on one side of the = are the equivalent of or equal to those on the other side. For example, $q = 1 - p$ or q is the residual of $1 - p$.

Expected Frequency: In computing chi square, the difference between the observed or actually counted value of each cell and the expected frequency is needed. A formula obtains that defines the expected number of cases for each cell based on the distribution observed. This difference is squared and divided by the expected frequency to obtain the magnitude of deviation for each cell of the chi square.

Experimental Group: The experimental group as opposed to the control group does have some treatment, manipulation, or intervention between the pre- and post-tests. For example, data are collected in the pre-test from both groups, the "treatment" is applied to the experimental group, not the control, and then data are collected in the post-test. Any differences are said to result from the treatment and should be reflected in change scores in the experimental group.

Experimental Model: The experimental model consists of four cells with the headings at the top, pre and post, and at the side, experimental and control groups. The cells are mutually exclusive, and the model attempts to exert at least a minimal degree of control over the data. Most other models exert little or no control in the analysis.

Exploratory Study: An exploratory study is one in which an attempt is made to develop new techniques, new variables, new relationships, new scales, or new data collection techniques. It is a valid technique when not used as an excuse for not engaging in other types of studies. The emphasis is on obtaining information about an unknown.

Exponent: The number placed above and to the right of any number of symbol is called the exponent. For example, 2^2 has a number 2, and the exponent means to multiply the number by itself or $2 \times 2 = 4$. At times, the exponent will be expressed as raised to the 3rd or *N*th power, i.e., 2^4 means $2 \times 2 \times 2 \times 2$.

Face: Face is defined as a positive social value presented by actors and reinforced by others in the interactional process. It is an image of self delineated by approval of social attributes and is confirmed by audience evidence conveyed in social encounters. Face becomes translated into such things as poise, control of physical and psychological space and fixing the boundaries of behavior. For example, "a person might have become embarrassed, but he didn't lose face."

Face Validity: This term means no validity checks have been made on the scale or measurement device other than the researcher's claim that it measures what it purports to measure.

Fee for Services: The term means an agreed-upon fee is paid for the completion of the specified services. Such an exchange occurs for a haircut, but it can just as well apply to social research of the contract variety.

Field: In computer data analysis, field indicates the number of columns used to record the data in a data statement sheet. For example, 02 would require a field of two columns, while 50000 would require a field of five to record the data. We have suggested standardized or the same number of columns in each field as an easier data format for most studies. Obviously there are exceptions.

Field Research: Field research is often called field work, but when properly used, either term means to observe human interaction in its natural setting. At times, interviewing is referred to as field research, but that is not the meaning intended in this book.

Field Study: In the field study, human behavior is observed and studied in the natural setting. Hence, the focus of these studies is behavioral, and they tend to consist of observation techniques, with systematic recording geared to maintain the integrity of what is observed.

Forecast: A population forecast is based on a person's knowledge and estimate of the population of an area. It is not mathematical in the sense of a projection that extends past trends into the future, but rather is based on the expertise of an individual. A forecast can be as accurate or more accurate than a projection, but the technique probably should be considered an art rather than a technique based on science.

Fortuitous Relationship: A fortuitous relationship is one that occurs by chance and involves no known deterministic factors.

Free Standing: As used in research, this term means that a question, table, or section stands without need for explanation. All tables should be free standing and should not require explanation to help the reader understand what is being presented or what format has been used.

Functionalist: This term describes one who focuses on research of behavior that contributes to or detracts from social-cultural phenomena related to these systems. A functionalist specifies behavior to be functional (contributing to) or disfunctional to (contrary to) the goals of a specified system. The system properties are implicit in functional analysis.

Funded Research: When research is funded wholly or in part, some restrictions or obligations may be placed on part of it. Quarterly or annual reports on progress may be required, and it may be specified that any resulting publications bear a specified statement that the research was funded by the agency, but that the agency does not endorse or accept responsibility for the findings.

General Hypothesis: A general hypothesis is an abstract or conceptual level statement of relationship to be tested. For the most part, an hypothesis at this level would be derived from theory, and the test would inferentially test the theory. An example would be: Group solidarity is inversely related to group size.

Generalization: Samples are selected to eliminate the necessity of measuring or assessing a total population. Hence, the whole scientific process is based on transferring the findings from the sample to the larger population. This process of generalizing from the sample to the population from which it was drawn or to other similar populations is a key element of the scientific process.

Goodness of fit: Goodness of fit in a statistical sense refers to the closeness of fit, or how well an equation of a correlation or regression approximates the line of least squares, that is, the line that, when drawn through all plotted paired coordinates, represents the least deviance from all observations. The line and technique are referred to as the least squares method. In a verbal or nonmathematical sense, the term is used to mean how well the data fit the model used in the study.

Grant: A grant is usually awarded to researchers or institutions only after careful evaluation of the grant proposals submitted. Award is often based on previous research in the area as well as on the "track record" or prestige of the researcher. The principal element is that funds of a specified amount are provided in the nature of the clinician role, but the general area of examination has been specified. Hence, there is more freedom in a grant than in a contract, and there is usually no promise of results other than a "writeup" or final report.

Group Data (Pooled): These data are pooled or summed data collected from individuals. They are often summarized and presented as representaive of the group as a whole. Examples are averages, means, ranges, and deviations.

Group Setting: Data are often collected from a large number in a group setting. Each respondent is asked to complete his own questionnaire. A highly structured or check-off type questionnaire is generally used when several respondents can be assembled at the same place. It is much less expensive than the individually administered interview, but it lacks many advantages of the individual interviewer technique.

Halo Effect: The halo effect represents the tendency to rate something favorably rather than unfavorably. For example, some respondents do not wish to give negative evaluations or responses.

Hard Methods: A term of convenience rather than reality referring to quantitative techniques, usually involving the use of statistics. Such methods are hard in contrast to nonqualitative methods.

Hawthorne Effect: An effect recognized as the research effecting the normal functioning of those being observed, i.e., a group or individual behavior being modified due to the awareness that they are the subject of research.

Heuristic: Something that is used for heuristic purposes encourages further analysis, study, experimentation, or discovery. It may or may not be capable of proof, but it does serve as a catalyst in developing further interest and research into an area.

Hypothesis: A hypothesis is a statement of relationships between two concepts or variables. The type of hypothesis depends on intended use and level of abstraction (general, operational, or null). The hypothesis is generally used as a predictive statement of a relationship to be tested. For the most part, hypotheses are derived from theory and serve as tools to inferentially test that theory. A simple hypothesis would be: Group solidarity is inversely related to group size.

Identity: As used in social psychology, this term means an individual's awareness or consciousness or definition of self. In dramaturgy, the term established the "what" and "where" of a person in social terms. Identity expressed in one's actions indicates situation and announces placement in the situation.

Identity Documents: Identity documents are the apparent symbols of those characteristics (hairdo, makeup, clothing, and the like) that allow the audience to validate the identity presented by the character.

Independent Variable: This variable is used in an attempt to explain the dependent variable. A causal relationship is implied in that the independent variables are assumed to determine variance in the dependent variable, but these variables are not usually subjected to a test for causality.

Individual Data: These data are collected from the individual. They may become group data by adding together a number of individuals, but a number of statistical techniques require that individual scores be used to derive the collective measure or coefficient. Correlations, analysis of variance, and *t* tests are examples.

Informal Power Structure: Power that is exercised from behind the scenes is referred to as an informal power structure. For example, are the elected officials of a city commission the real power, or are those who have influence or authority over these individuals able to influence outcomes of the city commission? Many real power brokers prefer to operate at the informal rather than the formal level.

Instrument: "Instrument" is a generic term encompassing several terms used in referring to data collection devices in the social sciences. Opinionnaire, questionnaire, schedule, and scale all fall within the meaning of instrument as used in sociology.

Interval Scales: These scales provide data of the highest level of measurement with the assumption that the distance between units is known. For example, the distance between 1 and 2 is known, and is the same as the distance between 2 and 3.

Intervening Variable: This variable occurs between the dependent and independent variable. In the social sciences, such variables are seldom recognized or included in research designs because of the difficulty of dealing with them with contemporary measurement techniques. An example of a study situation might be an examination of the variable relationship of group morale (dependent) and productivity (independent) with foreman leadership style (intervening) between the dependent and independent variables.

Interview: In an interview, a respondent provides information to an interviewer who records the information. There are several types of interviews, providing various types of information to the interviewer.

Intrasubjective Testability: This technique is used to determine whether objective or disinterested parties agree on what is being examined. For example, if a concept is developed and described, could five such observers agree with the development and description? If so, a claim of intrasubjective testability can be made for that event.

Jury Opinion: This term indicates that a jury panel has been used to assess the validity of a measurement device. The process is essentially the same as intrasubjective testability or as the use of experts to render independent judgments about items in scale construction.

Known Groups: The known groups method of establishing validity is to administer an instrument to a group known to possess the dimension measured by the scale. If the scale is valid, the known group should score higher (have more of) on the dimension measured than would a random sample of respondents. It is one of several ways to establish validity. One drawback is that some groups may be unwilling to participate in such an exercise.

Lead-in Questions: Questions considered to be "throw-away" questions or those used to set up a following question are often called lead-in questions. It serves much the same function as conversationalizing, but in a single question.

Life-style: This term refers to the living patterns, attitudes, values, and options important to an individual as a result of internalization of norms. One can choose to live a suburban life-style with a home, yard, patio, community organized activities, and facilities, or one may choose to live in a commune, a homosexual subculture, or a downtown highrise. All styles have certain value orientations, living arrangements, activities of preference, and so forth.

Likert Format: A Likert format of response is often used when no scale or additive items have been developed. Attitudinal items are usually structured with the following possible responses: a Strongly Agree (SA), Agree (A), Undecided (U), Disagree (D), and Strongly Disagree (SD). The use of this response format does not imply that a scale has been developed, nor does it rule out the possibility of scalagram analysis after the data have been collected. The response format does not imply that the items constitute a scale.

Line: In each encounter, individuals act out what has been defined as a line. The line is defined as a pattern of verbal and nonverbal acts by which actors express their views of the situation and their evaluation of themselves and the participants involved.

Literature Review: Before starting a research effort, the extent of knowledge should be examined. The presentation of relevant research in a paper, article, thesis, or document is often referred to as the review of literature section. Selected literature should be related to the problem and research at hand unless the paper is a "state of the art" paper inclusive of all known research in the problem area. The review should be short, relevant, and as inclusive as space or time permit.

Longitudinal Model: The longitudinal model is one based on the same group over an extended time period. Hence, data are collected, and at a later time, at least one year, preferably five or more, data are again collected from the same group. Few longitudinal studies are undertaken because it is not possible to control extraneous influence and because it is usually costly and time consuming to find the same group members and reinterview them five or more years later.

Management Decision: A decision made by central management or administration can affect evaluation in that it can facilitate or make it impossible to engage in evaluative research. If an outside agency such as the federal government orders the evaluation to be performed on a city agency receiving federal funds, difficulties can easily arise.

Mean: The mean value of a distribution of values is its average. It is called the arithmetic mean. The mean is obtained by adding all scores and dividing by the number of scores. The obtained value is graphically shown as $\overline{X}$.

Meaning: Any social encounter must be interpreted and put into context by the participants. Meaning is based on experience or generalizations from other sources to establish appropriate modes of interaction in a given setting. Hence, role, expectations, evaluation of role performance, face, line, character, front and so forth are established and are given structure by the assignment of meaning by an actor in any situation.

Measurement: This term refers to the process of assigning values or classifications to data. Measurement may consist of observing and recording the number of times something occurs, or it may consist of a scale score. It is used in both observational studies and attitudinal surveys.

Milieu: Milieu means essentially the same thing as environment, but in a social sense. The physical environment includes space, air, bodies, and buildings, while the social milieu would be analogous to life-style in many ways. Milieu includes values, orientations, beliefs, behavior, and culture for a group or individual. When the social and the physical are combined, they are referred to as the sociophysical environment.

Mixed Model: A mixed model has elements of both determination and chance or stochastic factors. It is not a completely deterministic model, but one that attempts to incorporate elements of probability along with the deterministic relationships.

Model: A model serves as a pattern or guide for use in bringing order to statements of relationships between elements within the pattern. Models may be as simple as a verbal statement of relationships, or they may be extremely complex statements, graphic presentations, and extended statements of relationships and designated conditions of action.

Morbidity: Morbidity rates are those of illness or disease and are often expressed in terms of the number of cases per 10,000 or per 100,000.

Mortality: Mortality rates are death rates usually expressed as the number of deaths per 1,000 persons.

Multimethod, Multitrait: Multimethod, multitrait studies are combinations of various research designs and data collection techniques which are used to establish the validity and/or reliability of the research. It is not uncommon to use other data collection techniques in an observation study. Denzin has discussed these techniques as triangulation, or the attempt to establish certain points by viewing the situation from different vantage points in much the same manner as a surveyor establishes points on property. The multitrait combination stems from logical constellations of traits, attitudes, beliefs, and behavior in an examination of logical consistency. A researcher should be accomplished before starting a multimethod, multitrait study.

Multivariate Analysis: Many studies consist of single variable relationships, and many of the statistics are of the type amenable to relationships between two variables or differences between two groups based on one variable. Some statistical techniques allow examination of a number of variables at the same time. These techniques include multiple regression, factorial analysis, and two-way analysis of variance. Since most relationships in the social sciences are complex and not of a simple single-cause nature, multiple variate analysis techniques are needed, but they are not for the beginning researcher.

N Size: N size refers to the sample size. The term is commonly used to indicate the number of subjects or units of analysis in the sample.

Neutrality: In interviewing, the interviewer must remain as neutral as possible. Nothing should be done or said that prompts the respondent to give biased or socially desirable responses. If specifically asked a question calling for an opinion, the interviewer should defer the answer until the conclusion of the interview.

Nominal Data: These data are examined at the simplest level of classification and are measured at the lowest possible level, with no qualitative measurement of the variable involved. The literature abounds with this level of measurement, such as black-white, high-low, male-female, and yes-no.

Nonparametric Statistics: This generic term is applied to a number of statistical tests not based on the assumption of normal distribution of the sample. Chi square, difference of proportions, and the McNemar test are all examples of nonparametric statistics.

Nonprobability Sample: This sample is also called accidental, purposive, or any name indicating that a random-type sample has not been used. The nonprobability sample is used when the parameters of the universe are not known or when individual units cannot be numbered and then drawn by some random process.

Nonrandom Sample: The nonrandom or purposive sample is a special use sample consisting of individuals available for interview who possess qualities uniquely required by the research question to be addressed. The obvious disadvantage in such samples has to do with a lack of knowledge about the total population from which the sample has been drawn: hence, generalization is limited, if not eliminated. The nonrandom sample should be used with caution by those inexperienced in research.

Note-Taking: An interviewer needs to develop a system of note-taking during an interview to indicate when a probe has been made, and when a respondent hesitates or asks a question prior to responding. In addition, upon the conclusion of an interview it is good practice to make notes if any unusual circumstances occurred during the interview. It is all too easy to put off making notes until the end of the day and then fail to do so or fail to remember some pertinent details.

Novel Datum: Novel datum refers to data that are new or unfamiliar to the researcher. Hence, the meaning of the term is "strange" or "having no precedent in the experience of the researcher or the discipline."

Null Hypothesis: A null hypothesis is based on the mathematical principle of exclusion by an exception. The hypothesis (usually symbolized H_0) is one of no difference or no relationship between variables or group measures. It is the hypothesis implicitly tested by statistical tests. An example could be: there is no difference in job-related tension based on organizational complexity.

Observed Frequency: Actual counts or the number of units classified by each category are called observed frequencies in chi square tests. A number of statistical tests use observed frequencies in computation, but the term is most closely associated with the chi square test.

One- and Two-Tailed Tests: These terms refer to decisions in interpreting statistical test results. It is sometimes possible to specify direction in formulating hypotheses, and in this case, a one-tailed test should be used. When it is not possible to specify the direction of relationship examined, the two-tailed test should be employed. These tests are often used with the "student's *t*" test when direction is stated.

Open-Ended Instruments: These instruments consist of open-ended questions, and they require careful consideration in both constructing the questions and interpreting data obtained in this manner. Open-ended questions must be coded, or the sample size must be kept small in order to interpret these data. Under either format, using data collected from open-ended questions can be a time-consuming task.

Open-Ended Questions: Open-ended questions have no precoded responses to be checked in self-administered or interviewer-asked questions. These questions require the respondent to formulate his response and to set it down in his own words.

Operational Hypothesis: An operational hypothesis can be considered to be an intermediate-level hypothesis between the general hypothesis (conceptual) and the null hypothesis. It is an hypothesis that includes the operational variable measures in the statement. For example, organizational stress (job-related tension scores) will be higher in more complex organizations (those with over two hundred members versus those with fewer than two hundred members).

Operational Variable: In the hierarchy of abstractness associated with real-world versus abstract concepts, the operational variable falls into the empirical or real-world classification. The concept "social class" can be an abstraction at the concept level, and it is still essentially abstract when specified as a variable. When it becomes operationalized, the designated measure must be specified. For example, by operationalizing social class by use of Warner's Index of Status Characteristics, the declaration can be made that income, occupation, education, home, and neighborhood are to be used to measure social class. The process of attaching modes of measurement to concepts results in an operational variable.

Opinionnaire: An opinionnaire is a survey of opinions. The term is generally used in a nonscientific context; the preferred term is questionnaire.

Ordinal Data: Ordinal data are quantified and compared in a "more than" or "less than" manner. This measurement implies no exactness of differences between intervals and does not have a zero point. For example, attitudes about race relations may be quantified and scored, but the one scored 44 cannot be assumed to be twice that scored 22; it is merely greater than the second score of 22.

Orientation: An individual's orientation structures meaning for the situation. It defines the limits of things relevant and inclusive within the selected orientation. While structural variables such as a group size, status role, rank, and similar concepts would be inclusive within the structural functional orientation as framework, these same concepts would be marginal and described in other terms in symbolic interaction as orientation. For example, group size might be translated to audience; status role to character or identity; face to front; and rank to apparent symbols, significant symbols, and audience validation of identity. The difference would be in the interactionist view of the unfolding patterns of interaction versus the functionalist's evaluation of the positive contribution to the behavior.

Overt Research: In contrast to covert research, overt research means that the subjects included in the research project are aware that research is underway and that they are potential subjects. It does not designate whether the research is observational or attitudinal, both of which can be overt.

Parameter: A parameter typically represents the limit of a universe or population. A parameter represents a line for the universe and is used much as a statistic is used to denote a characteristic or limit of a sample.

Parametric Statistics: This term is generically used to indicate a group of statistics based on an assumption of normality underlying the population from which the sample was drawn. As a rule, parametric statistics also require at least ordinal measure for computation.

Parsimony: The principle of parsimony is one of simplicity. If three concepts are sufficient, let them suffice. The fewer units (concepts, hypotheses, axioms, theorems, and so forth) used, the better.

Participant Observation: In this data collection technique, the researcher is involved in two roles in the same situation—first as a researcher and second as a group member of the interaction being observed. As a result of this method, some data recording techniques are lost to the researcher. For example, one usually cannot use a tape recorder, take notes immediately, or structure the nature of the interaction without distorting the research.

Per Capita Basis: In computing a number of indices, the total population of a political and/or geographical unit is used. For example, redistribution of tax money on a per capita basis is based on the number of individuals in a state, county, city, or township.

Permutation: A permutation is an ordered set of things which may be arranged in a sequence or series, but usually exhausts all possible combinations of units in the set. For example, with a set of 0, 1, 2, the possible permutations are 0, 1, 2, 0.1, 1.0, 1.2, 2.0, 2.1, 012, 021, 102, 120, 201, 210. This would exhaust all possible combinations of any three units.

Personal Front: By personal front is meant the identity one assumes in role playing. This term is borrowed from the theater, and refers to one's stage presence and awareness of the unfolding scenario. It describes the process of self-awareness and the psychological preparation to "perform" in interaction.

Personalization: Personalization is an attempt to develop some degree of rapport between the questionnaire and the respondent by written comments, instructions, or explanations between sections of the questionnaire. It clarifies the questionnaire for the respondent and improves the quality of the data collected by the use of questionnaires.

Pilot Study: A pilot study or exploratory study is usually undertaken as a prelude to a later study. Such studies are done to develop scales and data collection techniques, establish relevant populations, or any number of reasons. A pilot study may be undertaken when literature on the subject is sketchy or conflicting.

Policy Decision: The management decision differs from the policy decision in representing alternative choices directed toward a specified goal. A policy decision would involve changing entirely or at least modifying the goal. When policy decisions are based on questionable or faulty evaluation research, they can be no better than the assumptions and research upon which they rest. This is all the more reason for quality evaluation research.

Polls: Polls are commonly used in data collection, but are probably best known through their use in contemporary elections. In many instances, poll respondents receive a telephone call asking them to indicate their preference for a candidate, whether they were watching television, and, if so, which channel, and similar information. Results are usually tabulated in percentages, and results are made available immediately because few questions are asked, the opinions are sought for a specific reason, and time lags or delays may make the information obsolete.

Population Pyramid: A population pyramid is a graphic presentation of a population structure, a county, city, state, or nation. The pyramids are usually based on five-year cohorts separated by sex.

Post Factum Research: This research is undertaken "after the fact" or after data are collected. Hence, the technique is usually employed when records, archives, or data are available to test or to use in developing a plausible hypothesis explaining the data relationship.

Postulate: A postulate is a principle accepted because it seems self-evident or because it has been substantiated so often in research that it is no longer questioned. It can be used interchangeably with axiom or as one of a number of hypotheses formally deduced through a deductive process.

Pragmatic Research: This research is similar to applied research or research designed to ameliorate some social problem or circumstance.

Pre-test or Pilot Interview: Before collecting data with an untested instrument, the researcher should test the questions in a number of trial interviews. In this setting, the primary focus is a check of the questionnaire, not the data collected. The respondent should be asked why he hesitated or failed to provide the requested data. The emphasis in the pre-test is on testing the instrument and modifying it where necessary.

Primary Data: Data collected from the source first-hand are called primary data. These data can be collected by observation, questionnaire, and so on, and are distinguished from secondary data, which are data gathered by someone other than the researcher.

Probabilistic Science: The social sciences are often referred to as probabilistic science in the sense that they are not deterministic. When a book is dropped from the table, the law of gravity pertains and the book falls to the floor. Seldom, if ever, can such deterministic predictions be made with human subjects or groups. By using statistical techniques, the behavioral scientist can predict human behavior with varying degrees of accuracy.

Probability: As used in this book, probability is a formal mathematical statement of the chance of an event occurring. For example, in one toss of a coin, both heads and tails have a 50 percent probability of turning up. This is based on ratio of ½ or 0.5 probability. The probable odds (probability) of any event occurring can be calculated if the total number of possible outcomes and the universe size is known.

Probe: A probe occurs when an interviewer asks a respondent an additional question or in some manner encourages the respondent to provide further information on an open-ended question. When the first response is incomplete or a lack of response occurs, the interviewer has set routines to obtain further information. The number of probes is usually specified before the interviewer begins interviewing for the project. Various techniques are used indicating a probe has been made; one of the most common techniques is the use of a slash (/) with following information.

Projection: A population projection is an extension into the future of the most recent demographic variables of births, deaths, and migration. The resulting figures indicate what the population will be if the recent past continues into the near future. Severe changes in birth, death, or migration rates can distort projection figures because of the assumptions used.

Proposition: A proposition is a statement of concept relationship that to be meaningful must be capable of being brought to test with experience as the basis of the test. A proposition makes no theoretical contribution without empirical meaning. Whether a statement is a proposition or an hypothesis is a matter of contextual use and individual choice rather than a difference in essence or abstraction.

Purposive Sample: A purposive sample is a sample selected for a specific purpose, usually based on an event that has already occurred. For example, one might sample persons with unique expertise or characteristics in order to examine a particular related question or behavior. Random sampling would not be appropriate under such circumstances.

Quasi-Experimental Model: This model is an approximation of the experimental model. It is an attempt to inject some degree of control and to bring a dimension beyond the cross-sectional or the test-retest method of establishing validity.

Quasi-Longitudinal Model: This model attempts to overcome the time-cost factors of the longitudinal model. The longitudinal model is expensive, and at times it is impossible to relocate a sample drawn years before. One must be aware of generational differences in using this model. For example, marital satisfaction scores of college females in 1950 can be compared with those of college females in 1976, but there is the question of whether the experiences and attitudes of the two generations are really comparable.

Questionnaire: Opinionnaire, questionnaire, instrument, schedule, and, at times, scale are interchangeable terms. While each has a slightly different meaning, for standard usage the terms *questionnaire* and *scale* are preferred when instruments are used to collect data. The term *opinionnaire* may or may not indicate that data have been obtained via paper-pencil (they could have been obtained via a telephone response); instrument has a scientific usage that may not be warranted in the social sciences; scale tends to have a precise meaning of measurement; and schedule has an indeterminate meaning. Hence, the terms *questionnaire* and *scale* should be used when appropriate.

Random Elements: Elements of a model or relationship that are not deterministic or probabilistic and appear to be chance are called random. That is, there appears to be no discernible pattern other than chance operating in the relationship. A table of random numbers has no pattern; a random element in a model allows for and incorporates chance factors into the model.

Random Error: As a concept, random error is used in at least two contexts. First, it is used in a statistical sense meaning that error occurs throughout the statistical arrays without apparent pattern. One can do little about random errors of this type. It is much easier to adjust or overcome systematic errors. A second use is in data responses or in data handling and analysis. Have all respondents read and interpreted the question in the same manner? Have data editors been consistent within and between their own assessments and assignments of open-ended question answer codes? Both represent examples of possible insertion of random error in data analysis, in addition to the regular use in the statistical meaning.

Random Sample: A random sample is a process whereby all units drawn into the sample have an equal chance of being selected. A random sample can best be used when the researcher believes the phenomenon to be studied is randomly distributed throughout the universe. An example is numbering all units and then drawing a portion (sample) of the units to be included in the sample.

Random Selection: This term refers to the process of random or chance selection of units. It differs from a random sample in that random selection can be made within strata (stratified samples) or blocks. Hence, random selection is a technique of selecting units, not a sample per se.

Rapport: To establish rapport is to establish a relationship sufficient to achieve desired ends. In interviewing, the goal is to establish sufficient rapport to obtain the data sought in the interview.

Ratio Scale: A ratio scale is a form of measurement based on the degree of the characteristic being measured at present. The scale is based on intervals between points on the scale. This basis makes it possible to compose scores in terms of ratios. Examples of ratio scales include weight determined by pounds or ounces, time, degrees in angles, and the like. All such scales have an absolute zero. Few scales in the social sciences meet this standard.

Refined Rates: Refined rates are more specific rates of demographic data. Where crude rates are based on the total population, a refined rate would be intended for a limited or relevant population. An example is an age-specific death rate for females ten to fourteen years of age.

Relationships: Relationships are states of association between concepts or variables which may express intensity, direction, or both. One concept may be said to be inversely related (direction) to another, while another statement may specify that one group has more of a quality than another group (intensity). Hence, several types of relationships can be expressed.

Reliability: Reliability means that the scale being used measures essentially the same dimension each time it is administered. For example, test-retest reliability means that there will be a high positive correlation between the respondent's first score (test) and his second score (retest) when the same scale is used to interview the same individuals with a time lapse between the two administrations of the scale.

Replication: Replication means to reproduce a study in another setting. It would be expected that the same methodological procedures used in the original study would be followed in the replication—that is, the same sampling technique, the same instrument, the same analysis procedures, but a different sample and obviously a later time period. It is through replication that science expands and develops.

Representativeness: This term indicates whether a sample is appropriate (representative) in terms of being characteristic of the population or universe from which it was drawn. It has implications for whether the results obtained from the sample can be generalized to the population. If the sample is not representative, generalizations cannot be made to other populations.

Research: In a general sense, research can be defined as the careful study or search for information relating to a specific question or problem. More specifically, research refers to careful and systematic examination, exprimentation (or manipulation), or collection of data to test theory or to add to a body of knowledge. The first part of the definition represents the pilot or exploratory study, and the second the experimental design.

Research Design: The research design generally refers to the total research process, including (1) the statement of the problem or question to be addressed; (2) the technique of obtaining necessary data; and (3) the method of data analysis and reporting. Each segment can be isolated and evaluated, but in reality all three steps overlap and must be developed as a total process.

Residual Migration Method: This method of computing migration is a crude rate. It uses a base-year population (e.g., 1970) and adds all births between the time period to 1980, subtracts the deaths between 1970 and 1980, and arrives at what the 1980 expected population should be. When the 1980 census counts become available, the actual count is examined. The actual difference between the 1970 and 1980 figures would be assumed to have resulted from migration if the geographical area were the same (no annexation).

Respondent Feedback: Respondent feedback is needed in the development of questions and questionnaires. In a pre-test situation, respondents should be asked the questions and then asked *about* the questions. For example, "Why did you hesitate to answer the question?" "Is it too personal?" "Don't you understand the question?" In such interviews, the feedback is more important than the actual responses obtained.

Response Rate: The response rate is the percentage of the total possible interviews or data desired obtained. For example, if there are one hundred possible responses and seventy-four persons respond, the response rate is 74 percent.

Rights of Human Subjects: Most universities, research centers, consulting firms, and individuals engaged in research with human subjects have ethical standards and/or issue formal statements on the rights of respondents. The two major considerations in such research are a promise of anonymity and full disclosure. Full disclosure deals with making the subjects fully aware of what is being done in the research project. It rules out masked or hidden agenda research as inappropriate.

Role: In symbolic interaction, the part to be played is termed a role or playing at a role. It is self-definitional and reflexive in that the actor must convincingly play the role with regard to both self and audience. As in most uses of the term, position, action, and expected behavior must be taken into account.

Role Playing: Role playing, or assuming roles with an awareness of taking on another role, is central to some therapeutic treatments. It is also central to symbolic interaction and role theory as an awareness that individuals can take on characteristics they wish to portray.

Row: As used in data analysis, a row refers to the vertical location (row) on a data analysis card, data presentation, or table. A data card usually has twelve rows and eighty columns. The top two rows are alphanumeric (letters of the alphabet formed by combination row-column punches). These rows cannot be used in numerical analysis. The remaining row values usually begin with 0 and end with 9.

Rural Definition: The census definition of rural population includes all open country farms and small communities of less than 2,500 persons.

Sample: A sample is a small number of units drawn from the total population under investigation on the assumption that if the procedure is carefully applied, the smaller group (sample) will be representative of or a microcosm of the population or universe. There are several types of random or nonprobability samples.

Sampling: This term describes the process of drawing units into the sample or indicates that a small number or portion of the whole has been selected for use in a study. Sampling can be of either the probability or nonprobability type.

Sampling Error: Sampling error represents the difference between estimates of sample measures and universe measures. It represents error that cannot be attributed to measurement devices, question bias, interviewer bias, or analysis errors in recording and handling data.

Scale: A scale may contain any number of items, but the major feature is that items individually or collectively form a continuum of possible responses ranging from most to least positive on the dimension being measured. A scale is assumed to be unidimensional, with higher scores usually indicating more of the dimension being measured.

Scale Score: The result obtained from subject responses to a scale is called a scale score. It is an actual score which a respondent gives to a scale directly or indirectly.

Scanning Process: A scanning process refers to an examination by computer process. It can range from the familiar machine-sorted tests commonly used on campus to a full-blown research project utilizing an appropriate format. An electrograph or soft pencil is required for marking the response in order for the machine to grade and score each test. Since scanning processes are now possible in a number of new areas, it would be wise to check the computing facilities available for use.

Scene: The scene defines the place or region wherein action is taking place. It is where the performing character's self is composed along with other members of the cast. Along with the other actors, props, and identity documents, the scene is formed of both a front and a backstage area. The front area or that seen by others is only one part inasmuch as the total scene also has the backstage regions where other actors are involved in the process.

Scientific Laws: Laws are statements of the occurrence of events in science. Often they take the form of if—then, specifying conditions under which the sequence of events will occur. "If I drop a book, then it will fall to a solid base" is an example of a statement of the law of gravity on earth. It does not apply in space. While the social sciences strive for lawlike statements, in actuality few such statements exist.

Secondary Data: Data already collected and usually first reported or assembled by other than the researcher are known as secondary data. An example would be church records or the census data collected by the Department of Commerce. In most instances, these data represent characteristics of the unit being reported rather than measures of behavior.

Secondary Data Analysis: Additional analysis of data frequently occurs after the hypothesis has been tested. This process is variously termed secondary data analysis, sublevel analysis, and additional analysis. An additional use of the term is to identify data already collected and reported elsewhere. An example of secondary data analysis would be the analysis of church records or census data.

Self and Situation: The self must always be interpreted within a framework of awareness of self and a nonself or others. The self, then, is the actor cast against other actors in the unfolding drama, and together with the other props necessary for the scene to be set are referred to as the self and situation. Together, they constitute the major elements of interaction within the meaning defined by the actors and props.

Self-Report: Material provided by individuals is sometimes called self-report material. It may or may not constitute responses to a questionnaire. Individuals may be asked to keep a log of how much time they spend watching television and which programs they watch. Such material can be called self-report material.

Series Questions: These questions (also sometimes called follow-up questions) are contingency questions that follow or are contingent on the previous question. Quite often they are used in conjunction with trap or screen questions whereby respondents are moved from the general to the specific and exit when they are no longer able to answer the next question.

Set: Set is used to indicate the tendency to respond to questions based on an existing position (set) of the respondent. For example, a respondent may be biased toward an issue and respond to all questions based on this biased position. Set in a respondent can be avoided by careful placement and wording of questions.

Setting: The setting represents the collection of props, scenes, actors, and interaction necessary for the drama to continue. The setting may or may not have been manipulated by the actors to portray specific symbolic meanings. If candlelight, soft music, and certain beverages convey a specific meaning, a setting or backdrop has been achieved, but it must be remembered that interaction is ongoing whether or not the self has had a hand in developing the setting for the interaction.

Sex Ratio: The sex ratio is expressed as the number of males per 100 females. It is calculated by dividing the number of females into the number of males in an area and multiplying the result by 100 to standardize it.

Significant Relationship: This term is properly used only when a statistically significant relationship has been established by a statistical test. An a priori level of significance must be established prior to the calculation of the tests. Usually the 5 percent or the 0.05 level is designated as the level to be used to establish significance. When the statement is made that variable A is significantly related to variable B at the 0.05 level, it means that a test has been run and results of this magnitude could be obtained because of chance (an error) only five times in one hundred examinations. Any statistical significance level can be established to designate significance, but the 0.05 and 0.01 levels are most frequently used.

Significant Symbol: To the symbolic interactionist, a significant symbol is one that is understood by both the initiator and the receiver. Hence, it is a communication process that must be shared by the overlap of experience of the actors.

Simulation: As used in this work, simulation is the development and use of models for the study of the dynamics of existing or hypothesized systems. The definition here is limited to computer simulation and does not include role-playing situations said to simulate an experience.

Skip Question: The skip question is designed to direct the questionnaire respondent to the next relevant question. The rationale is that the respondent need not read and check "not applicable," or leave blank questions that do not apply to them. An example is: "If 'no' to question 8 go to question 12 next."

SMSA: An SMSA, a Standard Metropolitan Statistical Area, is defined as one or more central cities of 50,000 or more, the remainder of the county in which the city is set, plus any additional designated counties that are socially and economically dependent on the central city. The Bureau of the Census designates whether an area is an SMSA.

Social Change: This term applies to changes in social relationships over a time period. It is used to describe any change in the state of social structure and organization. However, it has not been limited to social relationships as some use the term to include culture change.

Social Interaction: The term as used in sociology means individual actors are involved in reciprocal actions. These actions are understood and induce the response of other members involved in the interaction.

Social Meaning: Social meaning is the shared agreement of the transfer from symbol to perception and understanding. It is the created social reality based on norms evolved and diffused to the significant population. It is reality as viewed, accepted, and repeated by the actors in the social system.

Social Worth: The concept of social worth is used at the verbal level without too much difficulty. When attempts are made to quantify the term or to put dollars or priority rankings to it, however, arguments ensue. Questions about the United States' technological ability to put a person on the moon but inability to eradicate poverty are questions involving the concept of social worth. It is personalistic and normative as a concept.

Socially Desirable Responses: Some respondents are concerned about how their responses will be interpreted. As a result, they sometimes respond as they think it best rather than report their true feelings or actual remembrance of events. The situation is one of attempting to manipulate the question responses to put the respondent in the most socially acceptable position.

Societal Costs: Societal costs are somewhat similar to social worth, but in some areas individuals, corporations, law, or governmental agencies have assigned actual dollar values to specific events. The actual social cost of an undereducated person may never be known. The same can be said for most social areas, but the example cited in this book did put a dollar value of approximately $200,000 on a traffic fatality. While societal costs can be calculated in some areas, they are best considered as arbitrary approximations used to standardize areas for comparative purposes.

Sociodemographic Characteristics: This term describes the social and demographic characteristics of a group or sample. These characteristics usually include sex, race, age, marital status, educational attainment, occupation, income, place of residence, parenthood, and religion.

Sociometry: This technique is used in small group settings to ascertain attraction and rejection between members in a group setting. It can be extremely useful in determining the leadership potential of the group or in selecting those who choose to work or associate with one another.

Soft Methods: This term specifies qualitative data collection and analysis techniques, usually observation and/or participant observation.

Sponsor Group: In survey research or community studies involving a survey, the assistance of a prestigious group often facilitates the research effort. Such assistance can range from actually interviewing to merely supporting the project by allowing use of the group's name. For some research efforts, obtaining the sponsor group can often mean the difference between success and failure.

SPSS: This abbreviation for the Statistical Package for Social Scientists refers to a manual of procedures to use canned programs. The SPSS is one of the canned program packages available to most students in the social sciences, but before setting up codes and preparing for data analysis with any program format, it is always best to check with the computing center.

Stage Props: Stage props are visible and tangible assists which are integrated into the social interaction setting. Obviously, they must be significant symbols to effectively and collectively become the setting or source wherein the drama is played.

Staging Performances: Again using the theatrical simile, the actor involved in role playing engages in staging performances. The degree of staged or managed performance is contingent on the importance of the role to be played. Hence, degrees of staging range all the way from the near totally orchestrated performance to mere walking into minor performances without thought or preparation of staging.

Standardization: In statistics and mathematics, this term indicates that two or more units have been made comparable. At times this is no more than a ratio or percentage figure, and at other times it is represented by standard deviations and other statistics. Birth and death rates are standardized scores that allow comparison of rates in a large city or state with those in a smaller one.

Stigma: Use of this term in the social sciences implies "spoiled identity," or negative acceptance by the larger group or society. One may be stigmatized for homosexual acts, cowardice, mental illness, skin color, ethnic background, or any contrived reason. The stigma usually represents a response to stereotypical notions that set the individual apart from the group. Hence, it is easier to engage in assigning stigmatized responses to visible cues such as skin color, eye shape, or some physical characteristic.

Stigmatized Behavior: Any behavior not approved by the larger culture can be stigmatized behavior, but relatively few behavioral areas actually are stigmatized. Of all possible behaviors, the most notable areas of stigmatization are those of sexual expression (prostitution, homosexuality, child molestation, rape, etc.), mental health problems, and some forms of criminality.

Stochastic: A term meaning chance or random probability of occurrence. It is usually used in models or mathematical expressions when variables cannot be assumed to have a deterministic relativity. Variables in such instances can be said to have a chance, random, or stochastic relationship to other variables.

Stratified Sample: This sample is a form of probability sample in which the researcher wishes to assure respondents from each of the known strata of the universe. An example may be a cross-sectional research problem requiring male versus female examples. Each sex would be sampled randomly to assure representations of each category.

Structured Instruments: Structured instruments or questionnaires are closed ended or have predetermined check responses. The interviewer sometimes hands the respondent a card and asks him to choose the appropriate response. These card assists aid the interviewer to elicit responses in the desired format and with a minimum of discussion or explanation.

Subculture: This term describes a unit smaller than the culture as a whole. It can be a group based on ethnicity such as the Polish in Chicago, or on similarity of interests and life-styles such as professional musicians, or on a variable such as age. Examples are the youth or the rising awareness and cooperation of the aged and retired.

Subject: A subject is an individual who provides data to the researcher without regard to type of research design or data collection technique.

Survey: A survey is a systematic collection of data by the use of individual interviews or questionnaire (mailed or administered). The technique tends to focus on perceptual and attitudinal data since behavior is not observed but is recalled by the respondent.

Systematic Error: Systematic error occurs when the error is induced and reoccurs on a regular basis. It is somewhat similar to a constant in that each time the circumstances occur, the error is again induced in the same manner. While error in measurement is to be avoided, it is often possible to find and eliminate systematic error, which is usually not the case with random error.

Systematic Sample: A systematic sample can be drawn when a list is available. It consists of randomly selecting the first respondent and then selecting each specified individual. For example, one may decide to draw a 10 percent sample. After selecting the first individual, each tenth name on the list is selected for inclusion in the sample. Any sampling percentage can be used in the same manner.

Tautology: A tautology is a statement of circular reasoning, or needless repetition of a word, thought, or idea. Where possible, the practice is to be avoided, but scientific preciseness should not be sacrificed to avoid repetition.

Taxonomy: A taxonomy is a classification technique based on relationships between the units being classified. It moves beyond mere classification so that the relationship among classes can be described. An example is Parson's work on social action in which he suggests behavior has four major classes or characteristics: (1) it is goal oriented, (2) it occurs in situations, (3) it is normatively regulated, and (4) it requires some expenditure of energy.

Theatrical Posture: A theatrical posture is taken by those in social science who use the terms of symbolic interaction and dramaturgy. Of course, the assumptions underlying these positions are also included when this orientation is selected to guide the development of one's research. The theatrical posture would include assumptions about behavior in natural settings. Concepts such as role, front, setting, symbols, and identity documents are relevant to the development of the research.

Theoretical Orientation: This loosely defined area of theoretical concern is specified by the resarcher. Individuals frequently engage in research without close examination of theory or a logically deduced problem specification. It is not uncommon to see references to a theoretical orientation (translated as stance) rather than a test of theory in the general sense.

Theory: Theory is a set of interrelated propositions used to explain or predict a correlated set of social phenomena. (A number of definitions of theory exist, but this definition is most suitable for our purposes.) Theories may range from large-scale, grand ones to a narrow set about limited social relationships. They deal with abstractions or concepts at the analytical level and may be tested only inferentially by operationally defining variables and submitting them to a real-world situation. Theory relating concepts to propositions and propositions to a logically related set is how the term is used in this book.

Trap or Screen: The trap is used when the researcher does not want to eliminate a respondent because he may be unaware of some technical program name or specific information. Is it more important to ask a respondent if he has heard of the ASAP (the Alcohol Safety Action Program) or an alcohol program dealing with the problems of drinking drivers? At times, the acronym will be of most importance; at other times, awareness of and information about the program will be of more interest than the technical name of the program. Using two or three questions of this type may precede a skip question.

Treatment: Treatment is used interchangeably with intervention in the classical experimental design, and occurs between the pre- and post-tests for the experimental group. Generally, it is difficult, if not impossible, to set up the experimental design in field research or observation because of the need for controls to minimize extraneous influence.

Triangulation: A process of examining the validity of measurement from a number of perspectives is called triangulation. It can consist of interviewing group members about the accuracy of observations previously made on the group, or it may be some combination of survey data, observation, descriptive data, document or secondary data analysis, and statistical analysis. The logic of the process is that multimethods are more likely to reveal more facets of empirical reality than any single method.

Type I and Type II Errors: Type I and type II errors deal with supporting or failing to support an hypothesis. A type I error consists of rejecting a true hypothesis as unsupported, while a type II error involves supporting an hypothesis that should be rejected as false or unsupported. Both deal with statistical tests, but there can be a number of causes for type I and type II errors.

Unit of Analysis: The unit of analysis is the basic unit under study. In some instances, it may be individual attributes or characteristics, while in others, the focus may be on larger units such as a group or social system. It may be behavioral or perceptual (attitudinal).

Universe: A universe is the unit from which the sample is drawn and the unit to which the results of the research will be generalized. The term is generic, and the researcher may apply it to any definable group. For example, the students at a college could be called a universe and a sample drawn could be drawn from this universe. On the other hand, all college students in America could be called a universe, and a sample could be drawn from this larger universe.

Urban Population: The census definition of urban population includes all persons residing in communities of 2,500 persons or more.

Utilitarian Program: A utilitarian program is defined as one with pragmatic payoffs. An almost universal program in cities providing at least one hot meal per day to the elderly is an example of a utilitarian program; a survey of the attitudes of a Model Cities area toward the police may or may not be a utilitarian program.

Validity: The concept of validity deals with whether the measurement device is actually measuring what is purported. When no measure of validity has been made, the scale can be said to have face validity. It is valid only because the researcher has stated that it measures a dimension. There are a number of statistical tests to establish validity coefficients for scales.

Variable: Generally, variable is the term assigned to a phenomenon measured on a continuum—for example, social class or religiosity. It is to be noted, however, that the term is used to refer to dichotomous measures such as sex (female-male) or race (white-nonwhite).

Verstehen Sociology: Associated with the sociologist Max Weber, Verstehen sociology is an introspective view and understanding of sociology based on awareness and empathy for a particular role or role set. It is characterized by taking the role of the other, but it implies more in that some understanding and awareness of the other's role definition would be a prerequisite.

Visual Aids: Any data presentation format—table, chart, graph, or population pyramid—that aids in the reader's understanding of the presented material is a visual aid.

Weighted Factors: In most social situations, including research, a number of factors are involved. Are all factors of equal importance? Often it is difficult to know, but treating all factors or variables as equal is a weighting of sorts. It says that all are of the same weight. If there is reason to believe variables should have differential weights, there are techniques to assign different weights to each factor. Multivariate analysis such as multiple regression or partial correlation often involves factor weighting.

Weighting: Weighting is a process designed to equalize or allow elements of the sample to account for equal influence. Weighting can be applied to individual units or subunits as a weighted average. The attempt is made to minimize distortion resulting from unequal distribution of characteristics of the sample.

Working Hypothesis: A working hypothesis, like a general hypothesis, should contain two concepts and a statement of relationship. Unlike the general hypothesis, it has no theoretical base or home. It is made to be modified (if necessary) as data are collected and analyzed. It does guide, structure, and limit research in the same sense as a general hypothesis does.

Bibliography

CHAPTER 1

Blalock, Hubert, M., Jr. *An Introduction to Social Research.* Englewood Cliffs, N.J.: Prentice-Hall, 1970.

Braybrooke, David. *Philosophical Problems of the Social Sciences.* New York: Macmillan Co., 1965.

Hoult, Thomas Ford. *Dictionary of Modern Sociology.* Totowa, N.J.: Littlefield, Adams, and Co., 1969.

Inkeles, Alex. *What Is Sociology?* Englewood Cliffs, N.J.: Prentice-Hall, 1964.

Labovitz, Sanford, and Robert Hagedorn. *Introduction to Social Research.* New York: McGraw-Hill Book Co., 1971.

Lazarsfeld, Paul F. "Problems in Methodology." In Robert K. Merton, et al. (eds.), *Sociology Today.* New York: Basic Books, 1959.

______, A. K. Pasanella, and Morris Rosenberg, eds. *Continuities in the Language of Social Research.* New York: Free Press, 1972.

Merton, Robert K. *Social Theory and Social Structure*, revised. New York: Free Press, 1972.

Wallace, Wallace L. *Logic of Science in Sociology*, Chicago: Aldine-Atherton, 1971.

CHAPTER 2

Blumer, Herbert. *Symbolic Interactionism: Perspective in Method.* Englewood Cliffs, N.J.: Prentice-Hall, 1969.

Denzin, Norman K. *The Research Act: A Theoretical Introduction to Sociological Methods.* Chicago: Aldine Publishing Co., 1970.

Goffman, Erving. *Presentation of Self in Everyday Life.* New York: Doubleday and Co., 1959.

______. *Stigma.* Englewood Cliffs, N.J.: Prentice-Hall, 1963.

______. *Behavior in Public Places.* New York: Free Press, 1963.

______. *Strategic Interaction.* Philadelphia: University of Pennsylvania Press, 1969.

Jacobs, Jerry (ed.). *Penance: Field Studies and Self Disclosure.* Palo Alto, Calif.: National Press Books, 1974.

Mead, George Herbert. *Mind, Self and Society.* Chicago: University of Chicago Press, 1934.

Morris, Jerome G., and Bernard W. Moltzer. *Symbolic Interaction.* 2d ed. Boston: Allyn and Bacon, 1972.

CHAPTER 3

Bredmeier, Henry C., and Richard M. Stephenson. *The Analysis of Social Systems.* New York:Rinehart and Winston Publishing Co. 1963.

Buckley, Walter. *Sociology and Modern Systems Theory.* Englewood Cliffs, N.J.: Prentice-Hall, 1967.

______ (ed.) *Modern Systems Research for the Behavioral Scientist.* Chicago: Aldine Press, 1968.

Merton, Robert K. *Social Theory and Social Structure*, revised. New York: Free Press, 1967.

Parsons, Talcott, Edward Shils, Kaspar D. Naegele, and Jesse R. Pitts. *Theories of Society: Foundations of Modern Sociological Theory.* Vol. 1. Glencoe, Ill.: Free Press, 1961.

______. *Theories of Society: Foundations of Modern Sociological Theory.* Vol. 2. Glencoe, Ill.: Free Press, 1961.

CHAPTER 4

Batten, Thelma F. *Reasoning and Research: A Guide for Social Science Methods.* Boston: Little, Brown and Co., 1971.

Di Renzo, Gordon J. (ed.). *Concepts, Theory and Explanation in the Behavioral Sciences.* New York: Random House, 1966.

Franklin, Billy J., and Harold W. Osborne (eds.). *Research Methods: Issues and Insight.* Belmont, Calif.: Wadsworth Publishing Co., 1971.

Helmstadter, G. D. *Research Concepts in Human Behavior Education, Psychology, Sociology.* New York: Appleton-Century-Crofts, 1970.

Hunter, Floyd. *Community Power Structure, A Study of Decision Makers.* Garden City, N.J.: Anchor Books, Doubleday and Co., 1963.

Land, Kenneth C., and Seymour Spilerman (eds.). *Social Indicator Models.* New York: Russell Sage Foundation, 1975.

Leedy, Paul D. *Practical Research: Planning and Design.* New York: Macmillan Co., 1974.

Merton, Robert K., Leonard Broom, and Leonard S. Cottrell, Jr. (eds.). *Sociology Today: Problems and Prospects.* New York: Basic Books, 1959.

Selltiz, Claire, et al. *Research Methods in Social Relations.* 3d ed. New York: Holt, Rinehart and Winston, 1976.

Smart, Vivian. *The Science of Religion and Sociology of Knowledge: Some Methodological Questions.* Princeton, N.J.: Princeton University Press, 1973.

Smigel, Erwin O. *Handbook of the Study of Social Problems.* Chicago: Rand McNally., Chicago, 1971.

CHAPTER 5

Babbie, Earl R. *The Practice of Social Research.* Belmont, Calif.: Wadsworth Publishing Co., 1973.

Batten, Thelma F. *Reasoning and Research: A Guide for Social Science Methods.* Boston: Little, Brown and Co., 1971.

Diesing, Paul. *Patterns of Discovery in the Social Sciences*, Chicago: Aldine-Altherton, 1971.

Di Renzo, Gordon J. (ed.). *Concepts, Theory and Explanation in the Behavioral Sciences.* New York: Random House, 1966.

Forcese, Dennis P., and Stephen Richer. *Social Research Methods.* Englewood Cliffs, N.J.: Prentice-Hall, 1973.

Helmstadter, G. C. *Research Concepts in Human Behavior: Education, Psychology, Sociology.* New York: Appleton-Century-Crofts, 1970.
Labovitz, Sanford, and Robert Hagedorn. *Introduction to Social Research.* New York: McGraw-Hill Book Co., 1971.
Lastrucci, Carlo L. *The Scientific Approach: Basic Principles of the Scientific Method.* Cambridge, Mass.: Schenkman Publishing Co., 1963.
Miller, Delbert C. *Handbook of Research Design and Social Measurement.* 3d ed. New York: David McKay Co., 1977.
Stephens, William N. *Hypotheses and Evidence.* New York: Thomas Y. Crowell Co., 1968.
Stogdill, Ralph M. (ed.). *The Process of Model-Building in the Behavioral Sciences.* Columbus, Ohio: Ohio State University Press, 1970.
Zetterberg, Hans L. *On Theory and Verification in Sociology.* 3d ed. Totowa, N.J.: Bedminster Press, 1965.

CHAPTER 6

Barker, Bernard, John J. Lally, Julia Loughlin Makarushka, and Daniel Sullivan. *Research on Human Subjects: Problems of Social Control in Medical Experimentation.* New York: Russell Sage Foundation, 1973.
Best, John W. *Research in Education.* 2d ed. Englewood Cliffs, N.J.: Prentice-Hall, 1970.
Edwards, Allen L. *Experimental Design in Psychological Research.* 3d ed. New York: Holt, Rinehart and Winston, 1968.
Goode, William J., and Paul K. Hatt. *Methods in Social Research.* New York: McGraw-Hill Book Co., 1952.
Labovitz, Sanford, and Robert Hagedorn. *Introduction to Social Research.* New York: McGraw-Hill Book Co., 1971.
Lastrucci, Carlo L. *The Scientific Approach: Basic Principles of the Scientific Method.* Cambridge, Mass.: Schenkman Publishing Co., revised 1967.
Leedy, Paul D. *Practical Research: Planning and Design.* New York: Macmillan Co., 1974.
Miller, Delbert C. *Handbook of Research Design and Social Measurement.* New York: 3d ed. David McKay Co., 1977.
Selltiz, Claire, et al. *Research Methods in Social Relations.* 3d ed. New York: Holt, Reinehart and Winston, 1976.
Simon, Herbert A. *Human Problem Solving.* Englewood Cliffs, N.J.: Prentice-Hall, 1972.
Sjoberg, Gideon, and Roger Nett. *A Methodology for Social Research.* New York: Harper and Row, 1968.
Warwick, Donald P., and Samuel Osherson. *Comparative Research Methods.* Englewood Cliffs, N.J.: Prentice-Hall, 1973.

CHAPTER 7

Babbie, Earl R. *Survey Research Methods.* Belmont, Calif.: Wadsworth Publishing Co., 1973.
Campbell, Donald, and Julian Stanley. *Experimental and Quasi-Experimental Designs for Research.* Chicago: Rand McNally, 1963.
Festinger, Leon, and Daniel Katz. *Research Methods in the Behavioral Sciences.* New York: Dryden Press, 1953.
John, Rex. *Discovering Sociology: Studies in Sociological Theory and Methods.* Boston: Routledge and Kegan Publishing Co., 1973.
Liebow, Elliot. *Tally's Corner.* Boston: Little, Brown and Co., 1967.

Lofland, John. *Analyzing Social Settings.* Belmont, Calif.: Wadsworth Publishing Co., 1971.

McCall, George, and J. L. Simmons (eds.). *Issues in Participant Observation: A Text and Reader.* Reading, Mass.: Addison-Wesley, 1969.

Mey, Harold. *Field-Theory: A Study of Its Application in the Social Sciences.* New York: St. Martin's Press, 1972.

Wylie, Ruth C. *The Self-Concept: A Review of Methodological Considerations and Measuring Instruments.* Vol. 1, Lincoln, Nebr.: University of Nebraska Press, 1974.

CHAPTER 8

Bonjean, Charles M., Richard J. Hill, and S. Dale McLemore, *Sociological Measurement: An Inventory of Scales and Indices.* San Francisco: Chandler Publishing Co., 1967.

Gillespie, John V., and Betty A. Nesvold (eds.). *Macro-Quantitative Analysis Conflict, Development and Democratization.* Vol. 1 of Sage Readers in Cross-National Research. Beverly Hills, Calif.: Sage Publications, 1971.

Hage, Jerald. *Techniques and Problems of Theory Construction in Sociology.* New York: John Wiley and Sons, 1972.

Leedy, Paul D. *Practical Research: Planning and Design.* New York: Macmillan Co., New York, 1974.

McDaniel, Clyde O. *Research Methodology: Some Issues in Social Science Research.* Dubuque, Iowa: Kendall/Hunt, 1974.

Miller, Delbert C. *Handbook of Research Design and Social Measurement.* 3d ed. New York: David McKay Co., 1977.

Mokken, R. J. *A Theory and Procedure of Scale Analysis.* Paris: The Hague, 1971.

Shaw, Marvin E., and Jack M. Wright. *Scales for the Measurement of Attitudes.* New York: McGraw-Hill Book Co., 1967.

Shepard, Roger N., A. Kimball Romney, and Sata Beth Verlove (eds.). *Multidimensional Scaling: Theory and Applications in the Behavioral Sciences.* Vol. 7. New York: Seminar Press, 1972.

Summers, Gene F. *Attitude Measurement.* Chicago: Rand McNally, 1970.

CHAPTER 9

Babbie, Earl R. *The Practice of Social Research.* Belmont, Calif.: Wadsworth Publishing Co., 1973.

Batten, Thelma F. *Reasoning and Research: A Guide for Social Science Methods.* Boston: Little, Brown, and Co., 1971.

Blackman, Sheldon, and Kenneth M. Goldstein. *An Introduction to Data Management in the Behavioral and Social Sciences.* New York: John Wiley and Sons, 1971.

Cole, Stephen. *The Sociological Method.* Chicago: Markham Publishing Co., 1972.

Forcese, Dennis P., and Stephen Richer. *Social Research Methods.* Englewood Cliffs, N.J.: Prentice-Hall, 1973.

Hannan, Michael T. *Problems of Aggregation and Disaggregation in Sociological Research, Working Papers in Methodology.* No. 4, Institute for Research in Social Science. Chapel Hill: University of North Carolina Press, 1970.

Helmstadter, G. C. *Research Concepts in Human Behavior: Education, Psychology, Sociology.* New York: Appleton-Century-Crofts, 1970.

Labovitz, Sanford, and Robert Hagedorn, *Introduction to Social Research.* New York: McGraw-Hill Book Co., 1971.

Seen, Peter R. *Social Science and Its Methods.* Boston: Holbrook Press, 1971.

CHAPTER 10

Cochran, William G., et al., "Principles of Sampling." *Journal of the American Statistical Association* 49 (March 1954): 13-35.

Hansen, Morris H., et al. *Sample Survey Methods and Theory, Volume 1, Methods and Applications.* New York: John Wiley and Sons, 1953.

Hyman, Herbert H. *Survey Design and Analysis.* Glencoe, Ill.: Free Press, 1955.

Kish, Leslie. *Survey Sampling.* New York: John Wiley and Sons, 1965.

Som, Ranjan K. *A Manual of Sampling Techniques.* New York: Heineman Educational Books, distributed in U.S. by Crane, Russak, and Co., 1973.

CHAPTER 11

Becker, Howard. "Interviewing Medical Students." *American Journal of Sociology* 62 (September 1956): 199-201.

Chambliss, William. *Box Man.* New York: Harper and Row, 1972.

Convers, Jean M. and Howard Schuman. *Conversations at Random: Survey Research as Interviews.* New York: John Wiley and Sons, 1974.

Garrett, Annette. *Interviewing: Its Principles and Methods.* New York: Family Service Association of America, 1942.

Glazer, Myron. *The Research Adventure: Promise and Problem of Field Work.* New York: Random House, 1972.

Polansky, Norman. *Ego, Psychology and Communication: Theory for the Interview.* New York: Atherton Press, 1972.

Richardson, Stephen A., et al. *Interviewing: Its Forms and Functions.* New York: Basic Books, 1965.

Rosenthal, Robert, and Ralph L. Rosnow. *The Volunteer Subject.* New York: John Wiley and Sons, 1975.

CHAPTER 12

Babbie, Earl R. *Survey Research Methods.* Belmont, Calif.: Wadsworth Publishing Co., 1973.

Baumel, C. Phillip, Daryl J. Hobbs, and Ronald C. Powers. *The Community Survey, Its Use in Development Action Programs.* Ames: Iowa State University, 1964.

Best, John W. *Research in Education.* Revised edition. Englewood Cliffs, N.J.: Prentice-Hall, 1970.

Glock, Charles Y. (ed.). *Survey Research in the Social Sciences.* New York: Russell Sage Foundation, 1967.

Hyman, Herbert H. *Survey Design and Analysis.* Glencoe, Ill.: Free Press, 1955.

Moser, C. A. *Survey Methods in Social Investigation.* London: William Heinemann Co., 1958.

Simon, Julian L. *Basic Research Methods in Social Science.* New York: Random House, 1969.

CHAPTER 13

Books

Bogue, Donald J. *Principles of Demography.* New York: John Wiley and Sons, 1968.

Davis, Kingsley. *World Urbanization, 1950-1970: Volume I: Basic Data for Cities, Counties and Regions.* Berkeley, Calif.: University of California, Population Monograph Series, No. 4, 1969.

______. *World Urbanization, 1950–1970: Volume II: Analysis of Trends, Relationships and Development.* Berkeley, Calif.: University of California, Population Monograph Series, No. 9, 1972.

Keyfitz, Nathan. *Introduction to the Mathematics of Population*, revised. Reading, Mass.: Addison-Wesley Publishing Co., 1977.

Peterson, William. *Population*, 3d ed. London: Macmillan Co., Collier-Macmillan Limited, 1975.

Government Material

County and City Data Book, Washington, D.C.: U.S. Bureau of the Census, U.S. Government Printing Office.

Statistical Abstracts of the United States. Washington, D.C.: U.S. Government Printing Office.

U.S. Bureau of the Census. *Census of Population and Housing: 1970 Census Tracts.* Final Report, PHC (1)—(relevant city), SMSA. Washington, D.C.: U.S. Government Printing Office.

U.S. Bureau of the Census Materials, especially 1970, *General Population Characteristics*, Final Report, PC (1) — B United States Summary. Washington, D.C.: U.S. Government Printing Office, 1972.

United Nations Demographic Yearbook, New York, 1975.

CHAPTER 14

Denzin, Norman K. *The Research Act: A Theoretical Introduction to Sociological Methods.* Chicago: Aldine Publishing Co., 1970.

Douglas, Jack C. *Research on Deviance.* New York: Random House, 1972.

Durphy, Dexter C. *The Primary Group: A Handbook for Analysis and Field Research.* New York: Appleton-Century-Crofts Educational Division, 1972.

Filstead, William J. (ed.). *Qualitative Methodology: Firsthand Involvement with the Social World.* Chicago: Markham Publishing Co., 1970.

Johnson, John M. *Doing Field Research.* New York: Free Press, 1975.

McCaffrey, Joseph. *The Homosexual Dialectic.* Englewood Cliffs, N.J.: Prentice-Hall, 1972.

McCall, George and J. L. Simmons. *Issues in Participant Observation: A Text and Reader.* Reading, Mass.: Addison-Wesley Co., 1969.

Polsky, Ned. *Hustlers, Beats and Others.* New York: Aldine Publishing Co., 1967.

Schatzman, Leonard, and Anselm L. Strauss. *Field Research: Strategies for a Natural Sociology.* Englewood Cliffs, N.J.: Prentice-Hall, 1973.

Speier, Matthew. *How to Observe Face-to-Face Communication: A Sociological Introduction.* Pacific Palisades: Goodyear Publishing Co., 1973.

Vallier, Ivan (ed.). *Comparative Methods in Sociology: Essays on Trends and Application.* Berkeley: University of California Press, 1971.

Whyte, William Foote. *Street Corner Society.* Chicago: University of Chicago Press, 1955.

CHAPTER 15

Collins, Lyndhurst (ed.). *The Use of Models in the Social Sciences.* Boulder, Col.: Westview Press, 1975.

Dawson, Richard E. "Simulation in the Social Sciences." In Harold Guetzkow, ed. *Simulation in Social Science Readings.* Englewood Cliffs, N.J.: Prentice-Hall, 1962.

Dutton, John M., and William H. Starbuck. *Computer Simulation of Human Behavior.* New York: John Wiley and Sons, 1971.

Farano, Thomas S. *Mathematical Sociology: An Introduction to Fundamentals.* New York: John Wiley and Sons, 1972.

Greenberger, Martin (ed.). *Computers, Communications, and the Public Interest.* Baltimore: Johns Hopkins Press, 1971.

Loehlin, John C., *Computer Models of Personality.* New York: Random House, 1968.

Raser, John R. *Simulation and Society: An Exploration of Scientific Gaming.* Boston: Allyn and Bacon, 1969.

Shaffer, William R. *Computer Simulations of Voting Behavior.* New York: Oxford University Press, 1972.

Singleton, Robert R., and William F. Tyndall. *Games and Programs: Mathematics for Modeling.* San Francisco: W. H. Freeman, 1974.

CHAPTER 16

Caro, Francis G. (ed.). *Readings in Evaluation Research.* New York: Russell Sage Foundation, 1971.

Fellin, Phillip, Tony Tripodi, and Henry J. Meyer (eds.). *Exemplars of Social Research.* Itasca, Ill.: F. E. Peacock Publishers, 1969.

Gouldner, Alvin, and S. M. Miller. *Applied Sociology.* New York: Free Press, 1965.

Lake, Dale G., Matthew B. Miles, and Ralph B. Earle, Jr. *Measuring Human Behavior: Tools for the Assessment of Social Functioning.* New York: Teachers College Press, Columbia University, 1973.

Rossi, Peter H., and Walter Williams (eds.). *Evaluating Social Programs, Theory, Practice and Research.* New York: Swenson Press, 1972.

Suchman, Edward A. *Evaluative Research: Principles and Practice in Public Service and Social Action Programs.* New York: Russell Sage Foundation, 1967.

Tripodi, Tony, Phillip Fellin, and Irwin Epstein. *Social Program Evaluation Guideline for Health, Education and Welfare Administration.* Itasca, Ill.: F. E. Peacock Publishers, 1971.

Tripodi, Tony, Phillip Fellin, and Henry J. Meyer. *The Assessment of Social Research: Guidelines for Use of Research in Social Work and Social Science.* Itasca, Ill.: F. E. Peacock Publishers, 1971.

Weiss, Carol H. *Evaluating Action Programs: Readings in Social Action and Evaluation.* Boston: Allyn and Bacon, 1972.

Wholey, Joseph S., et al. *Federal Evaluation Policy.* Washington, D.C.: The Urban Institute, 1970.

CHAPTER 17

Anderson, Teodore R., and Morris Zelditch, Jr. *A Basic Course in Statistics with Sociological Applications.* 2d ed. New York: Holt, Rinehart and Winston, 1968.

Blalock, Hubert M., Jr. *Social Statistics.* 2d ed. New York: McGraw-Hill Book Co., 1972.

Campbell, Stephen K. *Flaws and Fallacies in Statistical Thinking.* Englewood Cliffs, N.J.: Prentice-Hall, 1974.

Hauser, Philip M. *Social Statistics in Use.* New York: Russell Sage Foundation, 1975.

Hollander, Myles, and Douglas A. Wolfe. *Nonparametric Statistical Methods.* New York: John Wiley and Sons, 1973.

Leonard, Wilbert Marcellus II. *Basic Social Statistics.* St. Paul, Minn.: West Publishing Co., 1976.

Levine, Jack. *Elementary Statistics in Social Research.* New York: Harper and Row, 1973.

Marascuilo, Leonard A. *Statistical Methods for Behavioral Science Research.* New York: McGraw-Hill Book Co., 1971.

Morrison, Denton E., and Ramon E. Henekel (eds.). *The Significance Test Controversy: A Reader.* Chicago: Aldine Publishing Co., 1970.

Siegel, Sidney. *Nonparametric Statistics for the Behavioral Sciences.* New York: McGraw-Hill Book Co., 1956.

Steger, Joseph A. (ed.). *Readings in Statistics for the Behavioral Scientists.* New York: Holt, Rinehart and Winston, 1971.

Tanur, Judith M., Frederick Mosteller, William H. Kruskal, Richard F. Ling, Richard S. Peters, and Gerald R. Rising. *Statistics: A Guide to the Unknown.* San Francisco: Holden-Day, 1972.

CHAPTER 18

Bart, Pauline, and Linda Frankel. *The Student Sociologist's Handbook.* Cambridge, Mass.: Schenkman Publishing Co., 1972.

Best, John W. *Research in Education.* 2d ed. Englewood Cliffs, N.J.: Prentice-Hall, 1970.

Englehart, Max D. *Methods of Educational Research.* Chicago: Rand McNally, 1972.

Glaser, Barney G. "Retreading Research Materials: The Use of Secondary Analysis by the Independent Researcher." *American Behavioral Scientist* (June 1963): 11-14.

Hyman, Herbert H. *Secondary Analysis of Sample Surveys: Principles, Procedures and Potentialities.* New York: John Wiley and Sons, 1972.

Lastrucci, Carlo L. *The Scientific Approach: Basic Principles of the Scientific Method.* Cambridge, Mass.: Schenkman Publishing Co., 1963.

Nachmias, David, and Chava Nachmias. *Research Methods in the Social Sciences.* New York: St. Martin's Press, 1976.

Sanders, William B. (ed.). *The Sociologist As Detective: An Introduction to Research Methods,* New York: Praeger Publishers, 1974.

Tuma, Elias A. *Economic History and the Social Sciences: Problems of Methodology.* Berkeley and Los Angeles: University of California Press, 1971.

Wrigley, E. A. (ed.). *Nineteenth Century Society: Essays in the Use of Quantitative Methods for the Study of Social Data.* New York: Cambridge University Press, 1972.

CHAPTER 19

Armer, Michael, and Allen D. Grimshaw (eds.). *Comparative Social Research: Methodological Problems and Strategies.* New York: John Wiley and Sons, 1973.

Bartholomew, D. J., and E. E. Bassett. *Let's Look at the Figures: The Quantitative Approach to Human Affairs.* Harmondsworth, Middlesex, England: Penguin Books, 1971.

Costner, Herbert. *Sociological Methodology.* San Francisco: Jossey-Bass Publishing Co., 1975.

Denzin, Norman K. *The Research Act: A Theoretical Introduction to Sociological Methods.* Chicago: Aldine Publishing Co., 1970.

Goode, William J., and Paul K. Hatt. *Methods in Social Research.* New York: McGraw-Hill Book Co., 1952.

Greer, Scott. *The Logic of Social Inquiry.* Chicago: Aldine Publishing Co., 1969.

Sjoberg, Gideon, and Roger Nett. *A Methodology for Social Research.* New York: Harper and Row, 1968.

Stephens, William N. *Hypotheses and Evidence.* New York: Thomas Y. Crowell Co., 1968.

Wallace, Walter L. *The Logic of Science in Sociology.* Chicago: Aldine-Atherton, 1971.

Young, Pauline V. *Scientific Social Surveys and Research.* 4th ed. Englewood Cliffs, N.J.: Prentice-Hall, 1966.

Zetterberg, Hans. *On Theory and Verification in Sociology.* 3d ed. Totowa, N.J.: Bedminster Press, 1965.

CHAPTER 20

Bart, Pauline, and Linda Frankel. *The Student Sociologist's Handbook*. Cambridge, Mass.: Schenkman Publishing Co., 1972.

Batten, Thelma F. *Reasoning and Research: A Guide for Social Science Methods*. Boston: Little, Brown and Co., 1971.

Berke, Jacqueline. *Twenty Questions for the Writer: A Rhetoric with Readings*. 2d ed. New York: Harcourt Brace Jovanovich, 1976.

Bernstein, Theodore. *The Careful Writer*. New York: Atheneum, 1965.

Campbell, William G. *Form and Style in Thesis Writing*. 3d ed. Boston: Houghton Mifflin Co., 1969.

Strunk, William, and E. B. White. *The Elements of Style*. 2d ed. New York: Macmillan Co., 1972.

CHAPTER 21

Babbie, Earl R. *The Practice of Social Research*. Belmont, Calif.: Wadsworth Publishing Co., 1975. Appendix B.

Berger, Peter L. *Invitation to Sociology: A Humanistic Perspective*. Garden City, N.Y.: Anchor Books, Doubleday & Co., Inc., 1963.

Blumenthal, Albert. *Moral Responsibility: Mankind's Greatest Need*. Santa Ana, Calif.: Bayling Press, 1975.

Index

Style, in scientific writing, 339

ABOUT THE AUTHORS

John J. Hartman is Professor of Sociology at Wichita State University, Wichita, Kansas. His articles have appeared in such journals as *Rural Sociology*, *Southwestern Social Science Quarterly*, and *Midland Schools.*

Jack H. Hedblom is Associate Professor/Associate Chairmen, Department of Criminal Justice, University of Baltimore. He is the author of more than twenty-five articles and conference papers on the subjects of lesbianism and penology, and his books include *Hang by the Neck* (with Negley K. Teeters, 1967), and *Lesbianism: The Other Side of the Coin* (forthcoming).